ST ANDREWS ST
IN PHILOSOPHY AND PL

Founding and General Editor:
John Haldane, University of St Andrews

Practical Philosophy: Ethics, Society and Culture
by John Haldane

Sensibility and Sense: Aesthetic Transformation of the World
by Arnold Berleant

Understanding Teaching and Learning:
Classic Texts on Education
edited by T. Brian Mooney and Mark Nowacki

Truth and Faith in Ethics
edited by Hayden Ramsay

From Plato to Wittgenstein: Essays by G.E.M. Anscombe
edited by Mary Geach and Luke Gormally

Natural Law, Economics, and the Common Good:
Perspectives from Natural Law
edited by Samual Gregg and Harold James

The Philosophy of Punishment
by Anthony Ellis

Social Radicalism and Liberal Education
by Lindsay Paterson

Logic, Truth and Meaning: Writings by G.E.M. Anscombe
edited by Mary Geach and Luke Gormally

The Moral Philosophy of Elizabeth Anscombe
edited by Luke Gormally, David Albert Jones and Roger
Teichmann

Art, Morality and Human Nature: Writings by Richard W. Beardsmore
edited by John Haldane and Ieuan Lloyd

Ethics, Politics and Religion: Essays by Michael Dummett
edited by John Haldane

Art, Morality
and Human Nature

Writings by Richard W. Beardsmore

Edited by
John Haldane and Ieuan Lloyd

St Andrews
Studies in
Philosophy and
Public Affairs

imprint-academic.com

Published in the UK by Imprint Academic
PO Box 200, Exeter EX5 5YX, UK

Distributed in the USA by
Ingram Book Company,
One Ingram Blvd., La Vergne, TN 37086, USA

ISBN 9781845409401 paperback
ISBN 9781845409418 cloth

A CIP catalogue record for this book is available from the
British Library and US Library of Congress

Cover Photograph:
St Salvator's Quadrangle, St Andrews by Peter Adamson
from the University of St Andrews collection

For Pam and Anna

Contents

John Haldane and Ieuan Lloyd

Introduction

I

Part 1 of the present book, entitled 'Art and Morality', first appeared in 1971 as a short monograph published by Macmillan in a series under the editorship of W.D. Hudson entitled *New Studies in Practical Philosophy*. In acknowledging this origin, it is also appropriate to quote the general characterization of that series as described by Hudson himself:

> The point of view of this series is that of contemporary analytical philosophy. Each study will deal with an aspect of moral philosophy. Particular attention will be paid to the logic of moral discourse, and the practical problems of morality. The relationship between morality and other 'universes of discourse', such as art and science, will also be explored.

Although the series in which Richard Beardsmore's text is now reprinted, namely *St Andrews Studies in Philosophy and Public Affairs*, was conceived without reference to Hudson's prior venture, some thirty years after the latter's beginning and short duration, there are significant similarities between the rationales for the two series: broadly, to engage philosophically in an analytical manner with issues of value and practice.

But while the general, though not universal, approach of the present series is also that of 'contemporary analytical philosophy' it is worth noting a degree of difference in what that expression might connote so far as moral philosophy is concerned then and now.[1] At the time of its original appearance *Art and Morality* was

---

[1]   In 1999 a bi-annual journal was launched with the title *Studies in Practical Philosophy*. Its aim was 'to make evident the ethical and political force of Continental thought as it bears on current social problems'. It ceased publication in 2005.

the third of four books in *New Studies* with two more announced
as in preparation (and subsequently published). Of these initial six
books four were collections of essays by R.M. Hare, the then
White's Professor of Moral Philosophy at Oxford. Hare's concern
for the practical, or action-guiding, aspect of philosophy dated
back to the mid 1950s and the choice of his work for inclusion in
New Studies in Practical Philosophy makes sense on that account.

As an academic philosopher, however, Richard Hare was
better known to fellow-professionals for his metaethical views; for
while at the level of normative or practical ethics he believed that
philosophy could contribute to problems in everyday life, at the
level of the analysis of the status of moral claims he held that they
were not statements apt to be either true or false, but expressions
of commitment. To say that a practice or policy is good is not to
evaluate it for what it is in itself, but to recommend it as of a kind
that one would choose given one's fundamental normative
commitments and thereby prescribe for others. Hare saw no contradiction or tension between denying truth to value judgements
and prescriptions while nonetheless claiming that the latter could
be reasonable or unreasonable because he located the place of
reason not in discerning truth but in maintaining consistency.

In the period when Hudson was editing *New Studies* views like
Hare's were generally more widely favoured than versions of
moral cognitivism and objectivism but there was growing support
for the idea associated with writers such as Elizabeth Anscombe,
Philippa Foot, Peter Geach and Geoffrey Warnock that judgements of goodness and of badness, and thereby of rightness and of
wrongness of policy and action, are answerable to objective standards deriving from human needs, that is, requirements the satisfaction of which contributes to or constitutes human flourishing.
Hudson discussed these differing views in a survey book of his
own: *Modern Moral Philosophy* (London: Macmillan, 1970). While
giving fair coverage to the disputing parties, there and in a later
book, *A Century of Moral Philosophy* (Cambridge: Lutterworth,
1983), Hudson gives judgement in favour of Hare's position. In the
latter he writes, 'In my opinion it is the most clearly stated and
comprehensively argued of contemporary ethical theories' (p.
126).

By then, however, the tide had turned and a variety of broadly
objectivist views had become fashionable as positions like Hare's
seemed to fail to account adequately for the place of moral experience, of moral reasoning, and of the idea of the human good.

Different emphases on these different aspects was then taken to support moral realism, moral rationalism and moral naturalism, respectively.

This brings us a decade beyond the period of *New Studies* (which seems to have lasted for only a couple of years), but it is relevant to mention the change in climate to locate the environment in which Beardsmore's *Art and Morality* was first published and to place his own distinctive philosophical views about the nature of morality. So far as concerns the opposition between Hare's 'prescriptivism' and the 'descriptivism' of his objectivist opponents Beardsmore does not address this explicitly. Indeed, he has little to say directly about the 'status' of moral judgements as that was the subject of metaethical debates. What he does address (principally in section 3, 'Autonomism') is the character and subject of moral thinking in relation to other kinds of thought: the aesthetic, and the purposive or prudential. Here he does touch indirectly on the positions of Hare and of the neo-Aristotelians, in the former case by name, in the latter by way of invoking a surrogate criticism by J.L. Stocks of earlier versions of neo-Aristotelianism. His claim is that both Hare and the prudentialists misunderstand the nature of moral considerations and the way in which they feature in someone's thought and life more broadly, and therefore they misunderstand the way in which moral considerations contrast, but may also overlap with aesthetic and artistic ones.

Beardsmore's criticisms are self-contained within *Art and Morality* and fully expressed in its pages. One also gets a sense of them, and of how they were perceived by W.D. Hudson in the following editorial foreword to the original publication:

> In this monograph Mr Beardsmore first identifies and criticises two views of the relationship between art and morality, which he identifies respectively as moralism and autonomism. Moralism is, crudely stated, the belief that the point of art is to teach morality; autonomism, the belief that art has nothing whatever to do with morality. Both points of view are, according to the author of this study, mistaken in their desire to give a simple account of the relationship between art and morality. To consider this relationship, he thinks, is not to consider one question but a collection of problems which are of central importance for both ethics and aesthetics. With a wealth of illustration, Mr Beardsmore brings out what he takes these problems, and their solutions, to be. In the last part of his study he develops his view that art can give men an

understanding which makes their moral judgements more sensitive and intelligent.

One will get a deeper sense of his outlook so far as the character of morality itself is concerned, however, by knowing something of a book he published two years previously entitled *Moral Reasoning* (London: Routledge & Kegan Paul, 1969). In this his criticisms of Hare and of Foot are explicit and sustained (though his sympathy is more with the latter than the former) and again the main focus of his concern is what he regards as the misidentification of the place and character of moral thinking in the life of human agents. In brief, he argues that Hare does not really allow for the existence of genuine rational moral disagreement, while Foot restricts the scope for this by presuming that disagreement occurs only within the context of agreement as to what count as reasons in support of one view or another. Put another way Hare is insufficiently cognitivist and Foot is too restrictedly such.

With this is also revealed a philosophical methodology that owes much to Wittgenstein as that came to Beardsmore initially through his teachers and then his colleagues at the University of Wales, principally Rush Rhees, Peter Winch, Dewi Phillips and Howard Mounce, where he was both an undergraduate and a graduate student, and later a lecturer. One can get a sense of both the line of criticism (of Hare and Foot) and the debt to Wittgenstein in the following extract from the 'Conclusion':

> The fact that philosophers misdescribe things with which they are perfectly familiar ... does not imply any severe lack of comprehension on their part. The mistakes and confusions in their accounts arise because their understanding has been distorted by the models which they have adopted. The result is a systematic lapse into nonsense which can be arrested only by a wholesale rejection of these models. And it is here that the maxim, 'Don't think, but look' [Wittgenstein, *Philosophical Investigations*, 66, p. 31e] becomes important. For in order to escape from the false theories, we have to stop assuming that moral reasons *must* be of a certain sort, and look to see how they actually *are* used by moral agents. This does not involve a superficial or uncritical approach to philosophy (as some writers have thought). It does imply taking seriously what men regard as a justification.
>
>   I have suggested ... that when we do this, there are two important things that we notice. The first is the diversity in what people count as a moral reason. Thus the question 'Why did X do wrong?' asked of a Catholic, may elicit the answer 'X took his own life', but this is not a reason which, for example a Japanese

Samurai might accept. Again the Samurai might justify his condemnation of someone's actions in a way which would be quite
unacceptable to the Catholic.

The second point is that, despite this diversity, not anything
can count as a moral reason. Neither the Catholic nor the Samurai
is at liberty to bring forward whatever considerations he chooses
in defence of his views. What can and what cannot count as a
reason is determined by the communities to which they belong.

...[A]ny account of morality which emphasizes either of these
aspects to the exclusion of the other cannot claim to give an intelligible account of the nature of moral reasoning. (*Moral Reasoning*,
pp. 136–7)

Beardsmore published *Moral Reasoning* when he was 25, and *Art
and Morality* when he was 27. The former was a development of
his MA thesis and testifies to precocious sophistication and
insight. He was not unaware that the idea that the status of a
consideration as 'a reason' is determined by reference to a social
group, and more specifically a tradition of rationality (an idea
analogous to that developed later by MacIntyre) would prompt
charges of relativism (as have also been brought against
MacIntyre's view), but while he thought that too simple a
response he recognized that more needed to be said.

II

Art and Morality is part of that larger story, as are the articles contained in Parts 2 and 3 of this present collection.[2] In the two
decades since then, analytical philosophers have written a fair
amount on the themes of art and morality, with a flurry of publications at the end of the 1990s into the 2000s on the debate
between 'autonomism' and 'moralism'. Prominent contributors
have included Noel Carroll, Gregorie Currie, Berys Gaut, Matthew
Keiran, Jerold Levinson, Colin McGinn, David Novitz, Martha
Nussbaum, Richard Posner and Kendall Walton. Several of these
writers use the term of 'autonomism' but seemingly unaware that
it was introduced into philosophical aesthetics by Beardsmore in
Art and Morality.

---

[2]   For an examination and defence of Beardsmore's account of morality and
moral thought see John Whittaker, 'R.W. Beardsmore: Understanding Moral
Judgement' in John Edelman (ed.) *Sense and Reality: Essays out of Swansea*
(Heusenstamm: Ontos Verlag, 2009). There is also a brief tribute to him by R.A.
Sharpe in the *British Journal of Aesthetics*, October 1977.

In what is the most sustained treatment of the subject, however, viz. *Art, Emotion and Ethics* (Oxford: Oxford University Press,
2007) Berys Gaut explicitly draws on aspects of Beardsmore's
views in developing his own position. He writes:

> Drawing on Beardsmore's suggestion [that it is the *way* that a work
> conveys its ethical or other insights that makes them of relevance],
> what I have proposed, then, is that the criterion of aesthetic
> relevance, in the sense of when ethical qualities of works of art
> tend to be aesthetic values of works, is when artistic means (an
> artistic mode of expression) are employed to convey these ethical
> qualities. (p. 88)

Gaut also observes that recent interest in the subject of how art
and ethics are related, and disagreement regarding it, is but a
resumption of what he terms 'The Long Debate' begun by Socrates
in Plato's *Republic*. Beardsmore's writings assembled in this
volume are significant contributions to that debate and arguably
formed one of the main beginning points of its revival in analytical
philosophy.

At the time of his death he was working on two projects. One
concerned the British idealist philosopher R.G. Collingwood who,
like Beardsmore, combined interests in the social foundations of
morality and the nature and practice of art. The other was his
contribution to a book on animals and humans to have been co-
authored with Catherine Osborne (Rowett). His untimely death
ended these projects in too undeveloped a form to allow for publication, though Catherine Osborne was able to publish a fine book
of her own on the latter theme: *Dumb Beasts and Dead Philosophers:
Humanity and the Humane in Ancient Philosophy and Literature*
(Oxford: Oxford University Press, 2007) which bears the dedication 'To the memory of Dick Beardsmore'.

A common and justifiable criticism of some contemporary
philosophy is that it has become too technical and occupies a
space far removed from the life of the ordinary person who is
curious about the important questions that life throws up. As is
evident from his writings, this criticism could not be laid at the
door of Dick Beardsmore. He was a man of many parts, both
theoretical and practical. His interests were wide, and he was
blessed with a good deal of common sense and humanity.

Dick Beardsmore was born in 1944 and attended Purley
Country Grammar School, Surrey. Later, he graduated in philosophy from what was then University College Cardiff, in 1965,

where he also obtained his M.A. His graduate dissertation was subsequently published as *Moral Reasoning* in 1969, and regarded as one of the most incisive critiques of the then prevailing trends in contemporary ethics. Aesthetics was Dick's other major research field. His book *Art and Morality*, published three years later and included here, is still considered an important work on the topic. Following a one-year post at St David's College, Lampeter, he was appointed to a lectureship at University College of North Wales Bangor in 1968 where he remained for nineteen years, proving himself there as both teacher and administrator. At the closure of the Bangor department in 1987, he moved to Swansea, where he worked until his sudden death in 1997.

Dick was appointed as head of department during a difficult period, typically putting commitment to his duties before his own advancement. During this time, he became absorbed in writing a monograph on Collingwood's *Principles of Art*, and was also preparing a second edition of *Art and Morality*.

While aesthetics and ethics occupied much of his time in teaching, writing and reviewing, his interests in philosophy were wide. At the time of his death, for example, he was close to completing a book on philosophy and animals, with particular reference to Darwin's *Origin of Species*.

But Dick was able to apply himself to wholly unfamiliar subjects, too. At one point in his career, for instance, he was asked to teach Business Ethics, quickly familiarized himself with the main ideas of the subject, and ran a course that would soon enthuse even the most sceptical and hard-headed budding financiers. In addition to all this, Dick served on the Council of the Royal Institute of Philosophy, was a Visiting Professor at the University of Mississippi, 'Ole Miss' in Oxford, MS, and, on several occasions, at the University of Texas, Dallas.

The Swansea department had a long history of teaching Wittgenstein, but Dick Beardsmore remained his own man. While he thought and wrote in the Wittgensteinian tradition, he never felt constrained by it and freely expressed his criticisms of it. Dick was a first-class teacher, conveying his enthusiasm for philosophy with an ability to express the most difficult problems in a straightforward way. His door was always open to students, even though other colleagues urged him to close it and put his own interests first.

As one of his former research students, Hugh Knott, recalls:

> Dick's qualities as a teacher were legendary. He had a special
> ability in seminars both to prompt discussion and then to question
> the assumptions underlying one's contributions—an ability that
> was also evident in meetings with visiting speakers. I often
> remember leaving his seminars with my mind buzzing with his
> probing questioning.

Not surprisingly, his courses in philosophy were always popular.
As a teacher, he was never condescending, however slow or sceptical the responses to his questions. With the inexperienced, he
would be gentle and patient. His teaching was always rich with
examples taken from all walks of life, choosing them from the
backgrounds of his listeners.

In discussion with peers, he could be a formidable opponent,
especially when he met with anything stupid or pompous. On one
occasion, he pointed out to a postmodernist that he had contradicted himself in his paper. The speaker's defence was that there
was nothing wrong with that. Dick's response was, 'In that case,
sod off!'. Others might have launched into the nature of contradictions with much less effect.

Dick Beardsmore's world was not confined to philosophy. He
was an accomplished watercolourist, preferring ignored subjects
such as derelict buildings. Music was an important part of his life.
He had a deep appreciation of jazz, rock-and-roll, blue grass and
country music and not only played such instruments as the
mandolin, banjo and guitar, but also made them himself. He was
at his most relaxed stripping and restoring old cars.

If there was one quality that stood out among his many
qualities, it was his generosity. It was pure and spontaneous.
There are many stories of repairing the failing cars of friends and
neighbours, giving lifts at unearthly hours, and even providing
accommodation for students who had no digs. He had the virtue
of never taking himself too seriously, and was amused when he
saw others taking themselves in this way in academic life. Dick's
courage, integrity and respect for truth never wavered.

The material gathered in the present volume is drawn mostly
from previous publications but these are widely distributed and
hitherto often inaccessible, so gathering it both helps to make it
available and provides a supplement and development of the
themes of *Moral Reasoning* and of *Art and Morality*. In addition,
some previously unpublished later material is included. In each
case permission to use material here has been sought either from
Dick Beardsmore's widow Pamela or from the editors or

publishers. Acknowledgements indicating place of original publication are given below. We are grateful to Christopher Tomaszewski for assistance in the preparation of part of the text and to Graham Horswell for producing the published version.

Acknowledgements

Art and Morality (London: Macmillan, 1971).

'Learning from a Novel' in G.N.A. Vesey (ed.) *Philosophy and the Arts* (London: MacMillan, 1972) pp. 23–46.

'Two Trends in Contemporary Aesthetics', *British Journal of Aesthetics*, 13 (4) 1973, pp. 346–66.

'The Limits of Imagination', *British Journal of Aesthetics*, 20 (2) 1980, pp. 99–114.

'Literary Examples and Philosophical Confusion' in A. Phillips Griffiths (ed.) *Philosophy and Literature* (Cambridge: Cambridge University Press, 1981) pp. 59–73.

'The Censorship of Works of Art' in P. Lamarque (ed.) *Philosophy and Fiction: Essays in Literary Aesthetics* (Aberdeen: Aberdeen University Press, 1983) pp. 93–107.

'Wittgenstein on Tolstoy's *What is Art?*', *Philosophical Investigations*, 14 (3) 1991, pp. 187–204.

'Art and Family Resemblances', *Philosophical Investigations*, 18 (3) 1995, pp. 199–215.

'Consequences and Moral Worth', *Analysis*, 29 (6) 1969, pp. 177–86.

'Atheism and Morality' in D.Z. Phillips (ed.) *Religion and Morality* (London: Macmillan, 1996) pp. 235–49.

'How not to think critically' (previously unpublished).

'Moral Realism' (previously unpublished).

'Autobiography and the Brain', *British Journal of Aesthetics*, 29 (3) 1989, pp. 261–9.

'Teaching Children to Read Stories' (previously unpublished).

'"If a Lion Could Talk…"' in K.S. Johannessen and T. Nordenstam (eds.) *Wittgenstein and the Philosophy of Culture* (Vienna: Verlag HPT, 1996) pp. 41–59.

Part 1

Art and Morality

To Anna

Preface

I should like to express my gratitude to Mr H.O. Mounce of University College, Swansea, and to my colleague, Mr M.D. Cohen, both of whom read this essay in manuscript and suggested many improvements, and to my wife, Pamela, who read the proofs.

R.W.B.
University College of North Wales,
Bangor
August 1971

Introduction

For if it be, as I affirm, that no learning is so good as that which teacheth and moveth to virtue, and that none can both teach and move thereto so much as Poetry, then is the conclusion manifest that ink and paper cannot be to a more profitable purpose employed.[1]
Sir Philip Sidney

No artist has ethical sympathies.
All art is quite useless.[2]
Oscar Wilde

People sometimes ask what point there is in art, or whether it has a point. Often, of course, these are not genuine questions but rather expressions of an extreme scepticism about the value of poetry, of sculpture or of drama. The questioner has never understood these things, or perhaps can no longer imagine what he once saw in them. And he explains his blindness by maintaining that there is nothing to see, and that those who claim to see something are themselves blind. For others, however, the questions are not simply rhetorical, but stem from perplexity about the nature of art, or about what it is for some activity to be worthwhile. They are questions which philosophers try to answer.

It is with questions and answers of this sort that this essay is concerned, and though the above quotations were chosen in order to depict in an especially acute form the sort of controversy which I have in mind, they are, I think, fairly representative of two quite different conceptions of the significance of art, or more precisely of the relationship between art and morality. What is perhaps

---

[1]   'An Apology for Poetry', in E.D. Jones (ed.) *English Critical Essays, 16th–18th Centuries*, The World's Classics (Oxford, Oxford University Press, 1922) p. 32.
[2]   *The Picture of Dorian Gray*, Penguin Modern Classics (Harmondsworth, 1969) pp. 5–6.

misleading in my presentation of these opposing viewpoints is that by opening with a statement of the conclusions which Wilde and Sidney reached, by ignoring the questions and doubts which gave rise to these conclusions, I may have begun by making the debate between them appear unintelligible. One can easily imagine someone unfamiliar with the sorts of arguments and counter-arguments which characterise philosophy being bewildered by such a disagreement. 'How', they may ask, 'can one account for such radical disagreements between men who were themselves artists, or even, for that matter, between anyone familiar with the sorts of things which artists actually do? Why does one man speak of the purpose of art, the other deny that it *has* any purpose? Why does one insist that poetry is a source of moral teaching, the other deny any connection between art and morality?'

This is one possible reaction. But it is not the only one. For there are those who will fail to find such disagreements surprising. Like Katya in Chekhov's *Dreary Story*, they may see them as further evidence of the futility of attempts to discuss art in abstract terms:

> I don't like talk about art. ... If someone philosophises about art, it shows that they do not understand it.

But though neither of these reactions is unusual, even among professional philosophers, they are nevertheless themselves confused. And they are confused because they locate philosophical disagreement solely in misunderstanding, in a lack of insight into art. The implication is that the philosopher is simply a man who fails to see what others, artists perhaps, see clearly, and its obvious corollary is that if philosophers never discussed art then confusion would be unlikely to arise. Yet though there undoubtedly are confusions and misunderstandings in the dispute between Sidney and Wilde, there is also understanding and a concern for art. Both, in different ways, are concerned to defend the activities of the poet or the novelist against the sort of sceptical attack which I said may be expressed in the words, 'What point is there in art?'

For Sidney, as for Tolstoi in *What is Art?*, the attack comes from those who see art as an idle or pointless pursuit. For the most part, so the argument runs, it is something with which no man need concern himself, pleasant or amusing perhaps, but at best a luxury of little or no importance for the life of a society:

And yet I must say that ... I have just cause to make a pitiful defence of poor Poetry, which from almost the highest estimation of learning is fallen to be the laughing-stock of children.[3]

Sidney might have mentioned other related criticisms. For scepticism about the value of art does not spring only from the idea that it is frivolous, but also from those who condemn it as a source of mistaken beliefs, or who fear it as a threat to the moral code. All of these attitudes share a common characteristic in that all condemn art from a moral viewpoint. Sidney's reply to these criticisms is to reject the sceptic's conclusion while retaining the presuppositions on which it rests. He does not deny that the appropriate standards by which to judge a work of art are moral ones, but simply insists that the sceptic's judgement is faulty. Far from its being the case that art is morally indifferent or even antagonistic to moral values, Sidney believes that its 'final end is to lead and draw us to as high a perfection as our degenerate souls ... can be capable of'.[4] In saying this he is making a statement about the nature of poetry. Poetry is *essentially* an activity directed towards a moral good. It aims at man's moral perfection. And great poetry is simply what attains this end.

For Wilde, and for those writers who share the somewhat diverse cluster of views once (though no longer) defended under the slogan 'Art for Art's sake' — and which I shall henceforth refer to collectively as 'autonomism' — the problem is rather different. For though he also is concerned to combat any view which would condemn art from a moral standpoint, this is not because, like Sidney, he believes that a justification in moral terms can be given, but because he regards any attempt to provide such a justification as mistaken from the start. Artistic activities cannot be explained as means to *any* non-artistic end. And either to praise the artist for his moral influence, or to condemn him for his lack of it, is to miss the point. Thus when Dorian Gray in Wilde's novel rebukes Lord Henry Wotton for having corrupted him by lending him a book, Lord Henry replies in terms characteristic of Wilde's position:

'My dear boy, you are really beginning to moralize. You will soon be going about like the converted, and the revivalist, warning people against all the sins of which you have grown tired. ... As for being poisoned by a book, there is no such thing as that. Art

---

3   'An Apology for Poetry', p. 2.
4   Ibid., p. 11.

has no influence upon action. It annihilates the desire to act. It is superbly sterile.'[5]

Like his creator, Lord Henry is inclined to run together factual and conceptual issues. His assertion that 'art has no influence upon action' (like Wilde's dictum that 'no artist has ethical sympathies') may be taken either as an empirical statement of unrestricted generality, or as expressing the conceptual claim that it is not in virtue of its moral influence that we regard something as a work of art. Of course, this is a fairly straightforward sort of confusion and one which has been noted by many philosophers. But there are confusions which cannot be dealt with so easily. For example, I think that the claim that art cannot be reduced to a vehicle for the propagation of moral ideals has often been confused with the rather different claim that there is *no* relationship whatsoever between art and morality, or even between art and life in general. This latter view is implied in the above passage by the remark that art is 'superbly sterile'. It is explicit in Wilde's essay 'The Critic as Artist', where we are told that:

> The first condition of creation is that the critic should be able to recognise that the sphere of Art and the sphere of Ethics are absolutely distinct and separate.[6]

Wilde's view is not unique among philosophers. On the contrary, his remarks bear witness to a deep-seated philosophical prejudice according to which any rejection of the sceptic's demand for a moral justification of art must involve a total isolation of artistic and moral activities. But though I have said, and shall later try to show, that this is a confusion, it is not a *stupid* confusion. It is one which could be made only by someone who possessed a deep understanding of certain aspects of art.

The claim that neither of these positions, neither Sidney's emphasis on the moral influence of art, nor Wilde's emphasis on the independence of the two, is simply the result of confusion, but rests also on an understanding of art, will not, I hope, be taken as implying that there are no important differences between them. Certainly this was not my intention, and if I were to say that the

---

5   *Picture of Dorian Gray*, p. 241.
6   'The Critic as Artist', in *The Complete Works of Oscar Wilde* (London: Collins, 1966) p. 1048.

battle between the 'moralist' and the 'autonomist' is not one which need be fought, this would not be because I think that the issues between them are unreal, but because I think that in many ways the disagreement is secondary to their main concerns.

But though neither view is simply philistine (as, for example, Katya's remarks would suggest), it is nevertheless the case that both Sidney and Wilde are led into error. And they are led into error by their desire to give a *simple* account of the relationship between art and morality. This comes out more plainly in Wilde's epigrammatic remarks, but it is true also of Sidney's essay. Consequently, my purpose in this essay will not be to offer yet another answer to the question 'What is the connection between art and morality?', but rather to show that these and other writers fall into confusion because there is no *one* question which they are attempting to answer. On the contrary, for a writer to consider the relationship between art and morality is for him to concern himself with a collection of problems of central importance for both ethics and aesthetics. In many cases the most which he can hope to do in one book is to bring about a clearer understanding of the issues involved in these problems. On the other hand, it seems to me that in such clarification a philosopher may go far towards combating the sort of scepticism which I mentioned at the beginning of this chapter.

2

Moralism

In the introduction to this essay, I mentioned how doubts about the importance of art, and the attempt to combat such doubts, may lead a man to a moralist view, lead him to locate the importance of art in some moral purpose which it serves. Tolstoi, who himself produced perhaps one of the most comprehensive statements of such a view, clearly felt the force of such doubts, and in an early article he brings out perfectly how they may arise even for a young child:

> 'Lëv Nikoláevitch,' said Fédka to me. ... 'Why does one learn singing? I often think, why really does one ...?' ... His question surprised none of us.
> 'And what is drawing for? And why write well?' said I, not knowing at all how to explain to him what art is for.
> 'What is drawing for?' repeated he thoughtfully. He was really asking, What is art for? And I neither dared nor could explain.
> 'What is drawing for?' said Sëmka. 'Why, you draw anything, and can then make it from the drawing.'
> 'No, that is designing,' said Fédka. 'But why draw figures?'[1]

The schoolboy Fédka's question is philosophical. Noticing the way in which we often explain the importance of something by pointing to the purpose which it serves, he is nevertheless unable to discover any purpose for certain activities which he regards as of the first importance. Because art is one such activity, Fédka asks 'What is the purpose of art?' Tolstoi's reply to his pupil amounts to a rejection of the question:

---

[1] 'Schoolboys and Art', in *What is Art?*, The World's Classics (Oxford, Oxford University Press, 1930) pp. 5–6.

> And we began to speak of the fact that not everything exists for
> use but that there is also beauty, and that Art is beauty; and we
> understood one another.[2]

Tolstoi concludes that in this discussion 'we said all that can be
said about utility, and plastic and moral beauty'.[3] But when,
nearly thirty years later, he came to write *What is Art?*, he could no
longer see things from his earlier viewpoint. The claim that art
was to be equated with beauty seemed now to involve a trivialisation, a trivialisation which he found enshrined in most philosophical definitions of art:

> The inaccuracy of all these definitions arises from the fact that in
> them all ... the object considered is the pleasure art may give, and
> not the purpose it may serve in the life of man and of humanity.[4]

Fédka's request to be told the purpose of art no longer could be
rejected by Tolstoi. It now seemed to him imperative that the
hardships, sacrifices and abuses which men were willing to undergo for their art be justified by a demonstration that this art was a
necessary part of the life of a society. What is meant by 'necessary'
here is shown in a passage where Tolstoi is discussing similar
abuses involved in other sorts of activity:

> I have seen [he tells us] one workman abuse another for not
> supporting the weight piled upon him when goods were being
> unloaded, or at hay-stacking, the village Elder scold a peasant for
> not making the rick right, and the man submitted in silence. And
> however unpleasant it was to witness the scene, the unpleasant-
> ness was lessened by the consciousness that the business in hand
> was necessary and important and that the fault for which the Elder
> scolded the labourer was one which might spoil a necessary
> undertaking.[5]

A 'necessary undertaking' is clearly one which serves a purpose.
And though art cannot be explained in the way in which the
activities of Tolstoi's workmen can, as a means of providing food
or clothing or houses, it will no longer do to say that 'not everything exists for use'. For Tolstoi now equates the value of art with
its use as a means to some end; and if this end is not the physical

---

2   Ibid., p. 6.
3   *What is Art?*, p. 120.
4   Ibid.
5   Ibid., p. 78.

welfare of a society, then it must lie in the society's moral welfare. The purpose of art, he tells us, is a moral purpose. The aim of the true artist is to transmit the 'religious perception of his age', that is, to transmit those feelings which constitute the meaning of life for his audience, and his success or failure in this enterprise determines the success or failure of his art. True, Tolstoi admits that in a very wide sense *any* successful attempt to express feelings, regardless of their moral worth, may be called art. But he holds that in saying that a man is an artist in this sense only, we are at the same time admitting that his work has no significance. For its significance can lie only in its use as a means of moral instruction.

By locating the significance of art in the purpose which it serves, Tolstoi is able to establish an intimate relationship between artistic and moral excellence, for where an object or an activity has a purpose, the primary criterion by which we evaluate it will be its capacity to further that purpose. An axe can be a good axe only in so far as it is adapted to its purpose of chopping wood. Its utility as a hammer is irrelevant to this. For Tolstoi, good art is what successfully transmits morally good feelings. It may fail either by transmitting, successfully or unsuccessfully, the wrong feelings, or by failing to transmit the right ones.

Tolstoi's account then, like Sidney's, removes many of the difficulties involved in explaining the relationship between art and morality. It enables him to combat the scepticism which sees in literature and music only a form of amusement, by providing a simple model of how these things may have a bearing on our lives. In this way it does some justice to the idea that there is something important to be found in novels and symphonies, that they have something to tell us. Despite this, it involves an attitude towards art which many philosophers have wished to reject. One reason why this is so is, I think, brought to light by one of Tolstoi's own comparisons. As we have seen, in expressing the demand for a justification of art, Tolstoi draws an analogy between the way in which non-artistic activities may be shown to have an importance which outweighs the hardships they involve, and the way in which art may be shown to be worthwhile. The demands made upon a man during the course of his work may, we are told, be justified by indicating some end to which they are means.

Now it might be said that, by placing the significance of a man's work in what it brings, rather than what it is, Tolstoi is at the same time admitting that what it is—hay-stacking, unloading goods, cutting grass—is of no importance. All that matters is what it brings, food or houses perhaps. This may be brought out by contrasting such an attitude with that portrayed in the following passage:

> Johnson glances at the report and reads 'fanaticism. Schemes for the amalgamation have therefore — '. At the sight of the capital S (S is his favourite capital), he smiles, takes up his pen, and having completed the word 'fanaticism', wipes the nib, dips it carefully in the ink, tries the point on a piece of clean foolscap, squares his elbows, puts out his tongue, and begins the fine upstroke. His ambition is always to make a perfect S in one sweeping movement. He frequently practises S's alone for half an hour on end. He looks at the result now and smiles with delight. It is beautiful. The thickening of the stroke as it turns over the small loop makes a sensation. He feels it like a jump of joy inside him. But the grand sweep, the smooth, powerful broadening of the lower stroke is almost too rich to be borne. He gives a hop in his chair, coming down hard on his bottom, laughs, puts his head on one side, and licks his lips as if he is tasting a good thing.[6]

The Negro clerk Johnson is not concerned with his writing for any purpose which it may serve, but for what there is in it. Certainly what Johnson finds in writing the letter S is not what we find in art, but there are points of contact. What Cary shows us in this passage is what Tolstoi had recognised in his conversation with Fédka, namely that a man's sense of the importance of an activity does not always show itself in his seeking to use that activity to further his ends. It may have a quite different significance, a significance which is conceivable only where this activity does not draw its value from something else to which it is a means. Many philosophers would say that in this respect what applies to writing the letter S applies also to writing a novel or composing a symphony. They would maintain that any view which sees the importance of these activities only in their suitability to further moral aims cannot be regarded as a serious attempt to explain this importance. Rather it involves the unasserted assumption that art itself has no value but is simply one aspect of something whose value is not in question, namely morality. While such a view does go some way to explaining how we can learn from art, it might be

---

6   Joyce Cary, *Mister Johnson*, Penguin Modern Classics (Harmondsworth, 1962) pp. 24–5.

said to do so only by degrading it to the level of an educational contrivance.

But such an account of the relationship between art and morality need not be thought of only as a disservice to art. It may also be criticised for involving confusions about morality. Such a criticism is particularly applicable to a writer like Tolstoi who claims to judge art from the standpoint of the 'religious perception' of his age, that is to say, by reference to some moral position held by *all* men. By doing so, Tolstoi opens himself to the sort of criticism which John Anderson directed against the system of censorship which led to the suppression of Joyce's *Ulysses* 'in the name of morality'. Anderson says:

> In professing to speak 'in the name of morality', the supporters of the ban on *Ulysses* assume that their conception of morality is one which all must accept. Their position would obviously be weakened if they admitted that they were speaking in the name of *a* morality, if they had to uphold what we may call the morality of protection against the morality of freedom.[7]

Anderson goes on:

> Whatever the detailed differences may be, the first point to be made is just that there are different moralities, opposing sets of rules of human behaviour. This is because there are different ways of life, different 'movements', each with its own rules of procedure for its members.[8]

It is clear that in resting the evaluation of art upon whether or not it evokes 'the Christian feeling of love to one's fellow-man'[9] (which, we are told, *is* the religious perception of Tolstoi's age), Tolstoi is guilty of ignoring just those differences which Anderson emphasises. And like Joyce's censors, he is at the same time excluding the possibility of any significant artistic criticism of his own moral position.

If I do not develop these two lines of argument at this stage, it is not because I do not regard them as having considerable justification, but because in the context of this essay it is more important to notice a far more radical criticism which may be brought

---

[7]   'Art and Morality', *Australasian Journal of Philosophy and Psychology*, 19 (3) 1941, p. 280.

[8]   Ibid.

[9]   Tolstoi, *What is Art?*, p. 272.

against purposive accounts of art, a criticism which is not restricted by the particular form which the account may take. For what I wish to argue is that there are crucial differences between justification in the sphere of art and the justification of purposive activity. By attempting to merge these sorts of justification, writers like Tolstoi are in danger of obscuring the type of importance which an artist attaches to his work, and the importance of the considerations in terms of which that work may be judged.

Let us take as an example of purely purposive activity, the sort of case which has already been mentioned in connection with Tolstoi, namely that of a man who is concerned with a task only for its result. One example might be that of a clerk who, unlike Johnson, takes no particular pleasure in writing, but who writes simply in order, say, to duplicate a report. Two points may be made about such a man.

(i) In so far as our clerk is at all efficient at his job, he will be careful to avoid any activity which does not contribute to his purpose. Where, for example, Johnson is concerned with the precise proportions of each letter he writes, this man will consider such aspects only to the extent that they contribute to the legibility of the copy. On the other hand, however efficient he is, however much the thought of his future purpose governs his present activity, his writing will nevertheless possess characteristics which, though irrelevant, he will be unable or unwilling to exclude. For example, though the ink which he uses is necessarily of a certain colour, it is unlikely that its colour will be relevant to his purposes. Or again, he will use one type of paper where several alternatives would have done as well. Neither the colour of the ink nor the type of paper employed can be justified by reference to the purpose in question. Nor, of course, do they need to be so long as we are thinking purely in purposive terms, since neither involves any unnecessary expenditure of time or energy.

It is worth noting that the point I am making, though it may at first sight seem a merely contingent matter, is in fact conceptual. Certainly the extent to which aspects of a purposive activity or a functional object are irrelevant to its purpose will depend on the extent to which a detailed specification of the purpose or function in question can be given. If, for example, a craftsman needs a screwdriver only for various unspecified jobs in his home, then it may well be quite irrelevant what sort of handle the screwdriver possesses. If he needs a screwdriver for the more specific task of installing electrical equipment, then he may demand one with an insulated handle. But even where the screwdriver is, as we say, 'completely functional' (like those which receive the Design Centre seal of approval), so that every characteristic is justified by reference to its purpose, it is nevertheless always possible that changing circumstances, a change in the characteristics of screws perhaps, will give rise to irrelevancies of the sort which we have noted. Indeed, the only way in which we can conceive of these irrelevancies as being *necessarily* excluded, the only case in which we can be certain that every feature of a given object or activity will always be relevant to its purpose, will be where the purpose is identical with the means of attaining it. It is clear that such a case can be described with less risk of confusion by saying that there the means-end distinction would be no longer applicable. We should be no longer speaking in purposive terms.

A purposive attitude towards an activity, then, justifies aspects of that activity only in so far as they conduce to a given end. And it does so by excluding certain of these aspects as irrelevant. In this it differs fundamentally from an artistic attitude. Paradoxically enough, an example from Tolstoi's *What is Art?* illustrates this point perfectly:

> Once when correcting a pupil's study, [the painter] Bryulov just touched it in a few places and the poor dead study immediately became animated. 'Why you only touched it a *wee* bit and it is quite another thing', said one of the pupils. 'Art begins where the *wee* bit begins', replied Bryulov.[10]

Discussing this example, Tolstoi suggests that it is in the attention to just such details that art consists. With a work of art it is 'impossible to extract one line, one scene, one figure or one bar ... without infringing the significance of the whole work'.[11] He goes on:

> No instruction can make a dancer catch just the time of the music, or a singer or a fiddler take exactly the infinitely minute centre of his note, or a sketcher draw of all possible lines the only right one, or a poet find the only right arrangement of the only suitable words.[12]

---

[10]   Tolstoi, *What is Art?*, p. 199.

[11]   Ibid., p. 205.

[12]   Ibid., p. 201.

The precision which Tolstoi is discussing here is not the precision with which a man may construct means to ends, though Tolstoi is not always clear about this. As we have seen, justification in terms of results always involves the recognition that certain features of an object or activity cannot be so justified, without a corresponding admission that this is a fault in its construction or performance. By contrast, the admission that *any* aspect of a work of art has no part to play in its development is always an artistic criticism.[13] Consider, for example, the changes in critical appreciation of Shakespeare's work brought about by the recognition that the 'low-life' scenes in plays like *Measure for Measure* and *A Midsummer Night's Dream* are not merely 'comic relief', insignificant digressions from the main issues with which Shakespeare deals, but have a role to play in the development of the main themes. Or again consider Dickens's difficulty in excluding irrelevant humorous episodes from his novels, and his comparative success in *Dombey and Son*, a success which Chesterton suggests 'marks his final resolution ... to be a serious constructor of fiction in the serious sense'.[14] Chesterton's comparison of *Dombey and Son* with *Martin Chuzzlewit*, one of the books written prior to this 'resolution', is illuminating. The episodes in the latter are, he tells us, only 'isolated sketches', often irrelevant to the development of the story:

> Even Todgers's boarding house is only a place where Mr Pecksniff can be delightfully hypocritical. It is not a place which throws any

---

[13] A confusion is possible here. For someone may object that, for example, the pattern which the words of, say, Donne's 'Forbidding Mourning' make on the printed page is irrelevant to an appreciation of the poem, though this is not regarded as a fault in its composition. The answer to this objection would be that the printed words are not a part of the poem in this sense. It would still be the same poem if heard at a poetry reading. And though there are poems where this is not so, where, that is, the visual impression made by the arrangement of words *is* relevant, and where we lose something if the poem is recited (for example, Dylan Thomas's 'Vision and Prayer'), in this case the printed words *do* form a part of the poem, and any irrelevancy in their presentation may be regarded as a fault. A similar distinction between what does and what does not form a part of a functional object would of course be impossible. No one could maintain without absurdity that the wooden handle was not a part of a screwdriver simply on the grounds that the material from which it was fashioned is normally irrelevant to the instrument's purpose.

[14] G.K. Chesterton, 'Dombey and Son', in *Appreciations and Criticisms of the Works of Charles Dickens* (London: J.M. Dent, 1911) p. 120.

new light on Mr Pecksniff's hypocrisy. But the case is different with that more subtle hypocrite in *Dombey and Son* — I mean Major Bagstock. Dickens does mean it as a deliberate light on Mr Dombey's character that he basks with a fatuous calm in the blazing sun of Major Bagstock's tropical and offensive flattery. Here then is the essence of the change. He not only wishes to write a novel; this he did as early as *Nicholas Nickleby*. He wishes to have as little in the novel that does not really assist it as a novel as possible. ... The change made Dickens a greater novelist.[15]

The change to which Chesterton refers is marked by an intolerance of irrelevancies, by a concern that every aspect of his novels should contribute to the work as a whole.[16] In a letter to the writer Sergeyenko, Tolstoi once said, 'No detail must be neglected in art, for a button undone may explain a whole side of a person's character. ... It is absolutely essential to mention that button.' To this he added the caution that 'attention must not be diverted from important things to focus on accessories and trivia'. What I am suggesting is that from the standpoint of the purposive account offered in *What is Art ?*, Tolstoi could not have explained the force of this caution.

(ii) Let us now turn to a second, and in many ways more important, distinction between purposive and artistic activity. I have mentioned that where a man is concerned simply with bringing about a certain result, producing a duplicate copy of a report, for instance, there will be always aspects of this activity which are irrelevant to his envisaged purpose. That this is so follows, as we have seen, from the nature of purposive activity, from the distinction between means and end which it involves. But it also follows from this distinction between means and end, from the lack of identity between what a man does and what he hopes to achieve by it, that the actual means adopted are merely one of a number of alternatives. We see this if we contrast such a man with the Negro clerk Johnson, who writes for the enjoyment which it

---

[15]   Ibid., pp. 120–1.

[16]   It is worth noting that when a more recent critic wishes to reject Chesterton's estimate of *Martin Chuzzlewit*, it is just this concern which he finds in the novel: 'Scarcely a page goes by which does not in some way further the central course of development' (Steven Marcus, *Dickens: From Pickwick to Dombey* (New York: Basic Books, 1965) p. 214). Though Marcus differs from Chesterton in his evaluation of the book, he takes it for granted that any unexplained irrelevancy would count against a favourable evaluation.

gives him. Cary tells us that in writing Johnson finds a pleasure which he does not find in, for instance, using a typewriter. You might say that for Johnson writing is not one of a set of alternative activities, all of which will do equally well. It is precisely *this* activity which he enjoys. With the clerk who is concerned only with duplicating a report, it is different. For though as a matter of fact there may be no better (even no *other*) way of bringing about this result, that this is so is always a merely contingent matter. It is always conceivable that more efficient ways of duplicating reports should become available to him, and in this case he would be acting inconsistently if he failed to adopt them. Though the purchase of a duplicating machine need make no difference to the pleasure which Johnson takes in writing, it could not fail to alter the attitude of the other clerk to his task.

I mentioned earlier that one of the virtues of the moralist thesis is that it makes at least some attempt to explain how it is that art can tell us something, how it can make a difference to our ideas of morality. Unfortunately, it explains these things in terms of the means-end relationship. The moralist holds that a work of art, a novel or a painting, is an instrument for transmitting some set of moral beliefs. And in doing so, he introduces a radical confusion about *the way in which* a work of art tells us something, that is, about what 'saying' or 'telling' means here, a confusion which blurs precisely the distinction which I have just drawn.

In order to bring this out, let us consider the difference between a work of literary art and a treatise, say between a sociological or historical account of life in prison, like W.A. Elkin's *The English Penal System*,[17] and the sort of artistic treatment which we find in Dostoevsky's *Notes from the House of the Dead*. If we were to ask what it is for the former to tell us something, how *The English Penal System* can make a difference to our lives, it does not seem that a purposive account need be particularly misleading. The author has certain information about life in prisons, statistics, illustrations of general points, and so on, and her intention is that others should share this information. As with other purposive activities like duplicating a report or stacking hay, a distinction can be drawn between means and end, between the author's purpose of bringing certain facts to her readers' attention and the means which she employs to do so. What this amounts to in the

---

[17]   *The English Penal System* (Harmondsworth: Penguin Books, 1957).

case I am discussing will be a distinction between what the author says and the way in which she says it. And, as we have seen, the possibility of such a distinction entails the possibility of alternative, yet equally appropriate, means. Where the author uses a list of statistics, a graph or a series of case histories might have served as well. Even where she has, as a matter of fact, selected the best way for her present purpose, it is clear that the significance of what she tells us does not depend on the way in which it is told. A treatise may be hopelessly written, but nevertheless give information of the utmost importance.

If we now ask what distinguishes *The House of the Dead* from Elkin's book there is an obvious temptation to describe the difference as a difference of expression. In one sense this can scarcely be wrong. But it is misleading. For example, it cannot be taken to mean that Dostoevsky uses different sorts of words or different sorts of sentence-construction from Elkin. The difference in expression is not the sort of superficial difference in style which schoolteachers sometimes describe to small children in order to distinguish poetry from prose. Nor is it the sort of difference which we notice when we compare writers like Faulkner and Hemingway. Indeed, it is noticeable that in these senses *The House of the Dead* does not differ very greatly from a treatise. Remarking upon Dostoevsky's use of a journalistic tone in the novel, Konstantin Mochulsky comments that:

> the author presents himself in the role of a navigator who has opened up a new world and objectively describes the geography, people, manners and customs.[18]

He goes on to suggest that 'the matter-of-fact and annalistic quality of the style heightens the illusion of documentation'.[19] In consequence, if one wishes to maintain that the difference is a difference in expression, one must recognise that it cannot be elucidated simply in terms of the sort of superficial characteristics which I have mentioned. If there is a difference in the way in which Dostoevsky and Elkin express themselves, it is not a difference in the words or tone which they employ, but a difference in

---

[18]   *Dostoevsky: His Life and Work* (Princeton: Princeton University Press, 1967) p. 185.
[19]   Ibid.

the importance of these features for an understanding of their writings.

In *The House of the Dead*, unlike in a treatise, the way in which Dostoevsky expresses himself, the way in which he uses words and the particular words which he uses, indeed *every* detail of the work, has a part to play in what he says. This is true even of what I have said in a superficial sense does *not* distinguish a work of art from a treatise, namely the author's use of a journalistic tone. Discussing the bathhouse scene in the book, Mochulsky says:

> As a real chef d'oeuvre of the descriptive art there stands the portrayal of the bathhouse, 'simply Dantean' in Turgenev's expression. The studied dryness of tone, the calm sketching of details intensify the impression.[20]

What Dostoevsky tells us here about the life of men in captivity, the impression which we receive from the passage, is not independent of the way in which he writes. The choice of words, the 'studied dryness of tone', are not to be regarded as means by which the author communicates some message only contingently related to them. Rather it is Dostoevsky's ability to select just the *right* word and just the *right* tone, which allows him to tell us anything at all. It follows that any talk of alternative means by which the same end might have been achieved is quite out of place here. Though Dostoevsky might have written *The House of the Dead* in a different way, what he tells us would also have been different.

A work of literature like *The House of the Dead* plays a part in the life of a society which is quite unlike that which a treatise plays. This difference comes out in many ways. It can be seen, for instance, in the way in which people treat literature. A history teacher may be discussing prison reform. He wishes his students to understand certain aspects of prison life and suggests that they read *The Report of the Commissioners of Prisons 1948–9*. If this is unobtainable, he may say 'Oh well, read the report for 1950–1, that will do just as well', or 'The report for 1950–1 brings out the same points, though it is not as well written'. Or perhaps his students read the 1948–9 report but are unable to understand certain passages. Here the teacher may express the point in different words, offer a paraphrase. In the first case he suggests substitutes

---

20   Ibid., pp. 187–8.

for the book as a whole, in the second he offers substitutes for certain parts of the book.

There are no substitutes in this sense either for *The House of the Dead* or for any part of it. We may think that reading this work will bring someone to understand certain things about the life of men in captivity, but if it is unobtainable we shall not say 'Oh, read *Little Dorrit*, it will do just as well', or 'Though Dickens does not write as well as Dostoevsky, he tells you much the same things'. Nor shall we attempt to offer a paraphrase if someone fails to understand part of either work. Understanding a novel, coming to see what it has to tell you, involves a concern with the book itself in a way that understanding a treatise does not. It is a matter of seeing the force of the particular words used, not a matter of being offered different words.

Similar remarks apply to the sort of problems which face an author in writing a novel. Of course, problems may arise in the course of any activity, purposive or non-purposive. But the nature of the problems will be different. The writer who wishes to communicate certain information, or the clerk producing a duplicate report, may face difficulties in his work. Perhaps the writer finds that the information he possesses is of too great complexity to be indicated by a series of examples as he had intended. Or the clerk may find that his writing is not sufficiently legible for the purpose he has in mind. When such problems appear, they may be solved by adopting alternative means. The writer makes use of graphs, the clerk a typewriter. The discovery of such alternatives, the discovery that certain methods will not work while others will, or that different methods are equally efficient, is an important part of any purposive activity.

With a work of literature there may be problems, but they can no longer be seen as attempts to find alternative means of communicating some message external to the work. Difficulties in the development of a character, or a plot, difficulties in finding the right word or in a writer's style, can be understood only if they are seen as involved in the attempt to get *this* particular book right. It would be no solution to suggest that the author write another book or introduce a different character.

Nor would it make sense to suppose that different ways of developing some aspect of a novel might be equally satisfactory; or rather, if it means anything to say this, then it is a criticism of the novel. When Tolstoi was writing *Resurrection*, he is said to have played a game of patience in order to decide how the story should end, that is, whether Nekhludov should or should not marry Maslova, both of which seemed possibilities. What this story, if true, shows is not that Tolstoi was here presented with two alternative yet equally justified ways of ending the novel, but rather that its end is an artistic failure. Because it would not affect the novel's significance whether its main characters ultimately married or not, neither their marriage nor their parting could be justified by reference to the theme of the novel; neither played any part in the development of the work. In a purposive activity two alternatives may be equally justified. In *Resurrection* the alternatives were, from an artistic viewpoint, equally unjustified.[21]

It may be thought that in emphasising the difference between purposive and artistic activity, I have tended to obscure certain aspects of the former. For the distinctions which I have drawn centre around the type of care and attention to detail which characterises artistic endeavour. I have suggested that for the artist with words, unlike the man whose use of language is primarily purposive, all irrelevancies must be excluded, and I have also suggested that there is an incompatibility between the claim that an artist's use of a word is justified and the suggestion that some other word would have served equally well. This may have given the impression that I wish somehow to deny the care which may show in a craftsman's choice of words, and imply that only in art is there any concern to 'get things right'.

This would be a confusion. For nothing that I have said involves the claim that artistic and purposive uses of language are exclusive. J.L. Stocks expresses this point well in 'The Limits of Purpose'. Discussing the use of words for practical purposes, he says:

---

[21] A qualification is necessary here. For it might be a writer's intention (though it was not, of course, Tolstoi's) to show that, given the circumstances described in the story, more than one outcome is possible. The writer might, for example, wish to attack certain ideas about predestination. And in this case it might be said that both of two alternative endings were equally justified. (This would be a way of saying that the author had been successful.) Nevertheless, it is, I think, clear that such a case will be of its very nature an exception, and that there will be, moreover, considerable differences between it and the sorts of standard cases of purposive activity which I have mentioned, though I do not have the space to discuss them here.

> Of course, there is no purely practical man; every man is some-
> thing of an artist, but in any pressing emergency, in which some-
> thing has to be said at once, we are all flung back to the purely
> purposive level.[22]

Moreover, even on this 'purely purposive level' there will normally be found a concern to discover those words which are best
adapted to serve one's purpose. The writer Harrison's remark
about the beggars of his day illustrates how such a concern may
show itself in an undeniably purposive use of language:

> How artificially they beg, what forcible speech, and how they
> select and choose out words of vehemence, whereby they do in
> manner conjure or adjure the goer-by to pity their cases.[23]

The concern for language which Harrison's beggars displayed, the
care shown in their selection of words, could be understood only
by someone who recognised the purpose of what they were
saying, that of obtaining alms. The artist, on the other hand, does
not concern himself with writing or composing because of some
end, moral or otherwise, to which these activities are means. And
though both the beggar and the artist are concerned with finding
the right word, in the former case 'the right word' can be identified as what conduces to the agent's ends. It means something
rather different for the artist.

   At this point one suggestion is likely to be made which I regard
as fundamentally misconceived. For there is a temptation to say
that since an artist does not write for the sake of morality or of
science or of politics, it must then be the case that he writes for the
sake of art; or that since he is not concerned with art as a means to
some end, he must be concerned with art for its own sake. What is
wrong with this suggestion is the implication that where a man
does not choose to involve himself in some activity for the sake of
an external end or purpose, he does so for the sake of the activity
itself. For it is clear that this involves a determination to retain the
terminology of means and ends central to purposive action, even
where it has been shown to be inappropriate.

---

[22] 'The Limits of Purpose', in *Morality and Purpose* (London: Routledge and
Kegan Paul, 1969) edited with an introduction by D.Z. Phillips, p. 25.
[23] *The Description of Britain*, quoted in Boris Ford, *The Pelican Guide to English
Literature*, vol. II: *The Age of Shakespeare* (Harmondsworth: Penguin, 1969) p. 71.

In the present context, this terminology is not merely inappropriate, but leads to positive confusion. What I mean is that it makes *all* cases of artistic creation too like those rather exceptional cases where a man does write or paint for the sake of, not indeed an extra-artistic end, but for the sake of an end which is defined by reference to the activity in question. If one says that an artist writes for the sake of art, one is likely to be understood as meaning that he writes in order to preserve the standards and values of art, or perhaps that he writes in order to further his own artistic development. But though it is true that these ends possess a more intimate relationship to art than those of, say, morality or science, though they can be understood only by someone already familiar with the sorts of things which artists say and do, they are, *for precisely that reason,* worthless in any account of artistic activity itself. To say that a man works for the sake of preserving art, presupposes the existence of practices which are not concerned simply with their own preservation. Again, to say that a man is concerned with his development as an artist, makes sense only if he is already engaged in activities which he is concerned to develop.

In any case it is clear that a man painting a portrait or writing a novel has normally no such concern. He paints simply to get the portrait right, writes simply to get the novel right. And though, of course, a great painting or a great novel does contribute to the development of painting or literature and indeed of the artist himself, the care which goes into it, the importance which he attaches to it, cannot be explained in purposive terms. The artist cannot be said to paint for the sake of anything, even for the sake of art, any more than the man who enjoys conversation can be said to talk for the sake of talking.

3

Autonomism

My intention in the previous chapter was to bring out certain difficulties in moralist accounts of art, and more generally in any
attempt to explain art as a means to an external end. Aesthetic
criticism, I have suggested, cannot be reduced to moral, political
or religious criticism.

It is essential, however, to distinguish this position from
another to which it bears a superficial resemblance, and which I
earlier dubbed 'autonomism'. For though the autonomist is also
opposed to reductionism in aesthetics; though, like myself, he
maintains that aesthetic and moral criticism must be sharply
distinguished; this claim is associated not with any clear-cut
account of the relationship between art and morality, but rather
with a complex of largely confused reactions to the moralist
position. In the present chapter I want to consider two such confusions, both of which are to be found in the writings of Oscar
Wilde.

I

The first is to be seen at work in the quotation with which I
opened this essay, Wilde's assertion that 'no artist has ethical
sympathies'. For it is, I think, clear that this assertion is open to at
least two radically different interpretations. According to the first
interpretation, Wilde is simply registering a protest against the
moralist's conflation of moral and aesthetic viewpoints. In opposition to writers like Tolstoi, he is claiming that in so far as a man
has the didactic aims of the social reformer or the propagandist,
then he is not an artist. On the other hand, the remark might
naturally be taken as implying a rather more extreme thesis. For it
suggests an incompatibility between art and morality, suggests
that a decision to concern oneself with art necessarily involves a
decision to dissociate oneself from moral concerns. Thus, when

Gilbert in Wilde's dialogue 'The Critic as Artist' says 'Even a colour-sense is more important, in the development of the individual, than a sense of right and wrong',[1] he is, for Wilde, expressing the essence of the artistic viewpoint, a viewpoint which is characterised by an elevation of artistic values above those of morality.

It would be wrong to suggest that the above confusion has gone unnoticed. Writing in 1909, the Shakespearean critic A.C. Bradley remarked that 'the offensive consequences often drawn from the formula "Art for Art" will be found to attach not to the doctrine that Art is an end in itself, but to the doctrine that Art is the whole or supreme end of human life'.[2] This latter doctrine Bradley dismissed as absurd, and the absurdity has seemed sufficiently obvious to more recent writers (generally without their explaining precisely wherein the absurdity rests). R.M. Hare, for instance, in a discussion of the relationship between aesthetic and moral considerations, suggests that there is an important sense of the word 'moral' in which moral principles *cannot* be overridden by aesthetic principles. He goes on:

> This characteristic of theirs is connected with the fact that moral principles are, in a way that needs elucidation, superior to or more authoritative than any other kind of principle.[3]

Now to claim that moral considerations are authoritative is (as Hare later indicates) to rule out the possibility of certain sorts of decision. Indeed, this is a feature of the acceptance of any form of authority. If, for example, a soldier admits that his sergeant has authority over him, then he cannot at the same time raise the question whether or not to obey the latter. Again, if I accept someone's statements as authoritative in some sphere, perhaps a golf coach's comments on my game, or what an electrician tells me about the wiring in my house, then I shall no longer need to submit his statements to my own judgement, shall not need to consider reasons for or against what he says.[4] In the same way, to say that moral considerations have authority over aesthetic

---

[1] 'The Critic as Artist', in *Complete Works of Oscar Wilde*, p. 1058.

[2] 'Poetry for Poetry's Sake', in *Oxford Lectures on Poetry* (London: Macmillan, 1909) p. 5.

[3] *Freedom and Reason* (Oxford: Clarendon Press, 1963) p. 169.

[4] Though, of course, such considerations may have a part to play among my reasons for accepting the man as an authority in the first place.

considerations is to say that where they conflict, one does not need to decide which should prevail. One does not need to consider reasons for or against doing what is morally right.

On the other hand, those who (like Wilde) deny or question the authority of moral considerations, insist upon the possibility of such a decision, insist that a man must decide whether to give precedence to moral or aesthetic considerations in his life. A passage from Edward Bullough's book *Aesthetics* makes this quite explicit. 'Ought we', he asks, 'to consider the ethical or the aesthetic the superior attitude? Which of them is ultimately the better?'[5]

The way in which Bullough discusses this question, as if it were a matter of 'inclination and ideals',[6] leads him, like many others, to speak as if a man's answer to it will depend upon the sort of man he is and what he wants; in so far as the agent is concerned with moral values, he will tend to adopt a moral viewpoint; if, on the other hand, his ideals are aesthetic ones, then an aesthetic viewpoint will be more appropriate. Moreover, though he fails to mention it, it is clear that for Bullough the agent may intelligibly give different answers to the question on different occasions. For his inclinations may change. At one time he may be concerned with moral, at another with aesthetic goods. Consequently, at one time he will accept a moral viewpoint, at another an aesthetic viewpoint. Such changes will not be a mark of inconsistency. For on the sort of account in question, the only demands of consistency are that the agent should adopt the appropriate attitude to bring him what he wants, the attitude which is in line with his 'personal views and wishes'.[7]

Now it seems to me that in its account of the role of morality in a man's life, the view which I have just outlined is mistaken, and mistaken not in detail but in principle. On the other hand, I suggest that the account is largely correct in so far as it is intended to apply to art. That is to say, in so far as a man's concern with art brings in no moral considerations, he may well think in the way Bullough indicates. For a man *chooses* to concern himself with art

---

5   *Aesthetics: Lectures and Essays*, ed. Elizabeth M. Wilkinson (London: Bowes and Bowes, 1957) p. 81.
6   Ibid.
7   Ibid.

or to ignore it, and which he does depends largely upon who he is and what he wants.

When a man *does* choose to engage in artistic activities, then he opens himself to certain criticisms, criticisms concerning his capabilities as an artist or the depth of his understanding of literature perhaps. If he regards such criticism as justified, then normally it will influence his conduct in certain ways. But it is important to emphasise that such influence *is* conditional upon the agent's having chosen to participate in these activities of creation or judgement. And this is a choice which may be reversed. Told that he lacks artistic skill or critical ability, the man may reply 'Yes, but I'm doing my best to improve', but he may also reply 'I know, but I can live with it. I don't care about art that much.' In this case, given that they do not doubt the man's sincerity, his friends and teachers will have no choice but to accept this answer as final. Criticism will no longer cut any ice with such a man. For the force of any criticisms they may make is contingent upon his choosing to care about art. And this man has chosen to be a philistine. Though others may regard him as fickle, they cannot convict him of irrationality. For by rejecting the whole form of activity in question, he has also rejected the standards of right and wrong which it embodies.

By contrast, to speak in a similar way of morality, to speak as if men *chose* to engage in the moral life of their society, would be simply a bad parody of moral concern. In *Pudd'nhead Wilson*, Mark Twain indulges in such parody in order to portray a certain type of moral corruption. A Negro servant, Roxana, has been accused of stealing money from her master. But on this occasion she is not guilty. She had, Twain tells us,

> been saved in the nick of time by a revival in the coloured Methodist Church, a fortnight before, at which time and place she 'got religion'. The very next day after that gracious experience, while her change of style was fresh upon her and she was vain of her purified condition, her master left a couple of dollars lying unprotected on his desk, and she happened upon that temptation when she was polishing around with a dust-rag. She looked at the money awhile with a steadily rising resentment, then she burst out with—'Dad blame that revival, I wish'd it had 'a' be'n put off 'til tomorrow'.[8]

---

8   Mark Twain, *Pudd'nhead Wilson* (New York: Zodiac Press, 1955) p. 46.

Twain's subsequent discussion makes the corruption quite explicit. Roxana, he tells us,

> made this sacrifice as a matter of religious etiquette; as a thing necessary just now, but by no means to be wrested into a precedent; no, a week or two would limber up her piety, then she would be rational again, and the next two dollars that got left out in the cold would find a comforter.[9]

Like the writer we have been considering, Edward Bullough, Roxana thinks of morality as something with which one can choose to involve oneself depending on what one wants.[10] At the time in question she wanted the pleasures of piety (a feeling of self-righteousness, a 'change of style') and so was forced to concern herself with moral issues. Unfortunately, her simultaneous desire for her master's money led to a conflict. And though the desire for the pleasures of virtue proved stronger *at that time*, Roxana still hankered after the money and could therefore wish to be freed of the former desire, so that she might enjoy to the full the satisfaction of the latter.

But it is clear that Twain is right to refer to Roxana's attitude as a matter of 'etiquette', as a pretence of moral concern. In expressing a wish that her conversion could have been 'put off 'til tomorrow', Roxana talks as though the possibility of applying moral judgements to one's own or others' actions were conditional upon one's being *willing* to take part in moral reasoning. As though the fact that a man did not care about morality at a certain time prevented others (or himself, should he become converted) from condemning his actions or his feeling remorse for them. If this were so, then one *might* intelligibly wish that one should no longer feel remorse, so that one might enjoy to the full the pleasures of wrongdoing. Kierkegaard, however, remarks of such an idea:

> So wonderful a power is remorse, so sincere is its friendship, that to escape it entirely is the most terrible thing of all.[11]

---

9   Ibid.
10   It should be noted that Bullough's tendency to talk of the moral 'attitude', as if morality were something one adopted (as I may adopt a certain attitude towards my father or my boss), has an important part to play in the deception.
11   S. Kierkegaard, *Purity of Heart*, trans. Douglas Steere (London: Fontana Books, 1966) p. 35.

Kierkegaard is here making a conceptual statement, a statement about the role of the concept of remorse in morality. His point is that if one has a concern for the good, if one cares about doing what is right, then one cannot at the same time wish to be freed from this concern. In this morality is quite unlike any other form of activity, unlike artistic or scientific activity, for instance. For there is no contradiction in a man's wishing to be freed from his preoccupation with art or with scientific issues. He may feel, for example, that he cares *too* much about these things, and so he may say, 'How I wish that I could be free of this compulsion to paint' or 'Perhaps I should be happier if I did not care so much about my research, and could devote some of my time to other things'. The fact that the man wishes he cared less does not lead us to say that he does not care; often, in fact, quite the reverse. On the other hand, Roxana's wish that she had not been converted shows that the conversion was a sham. In wishing that she had no concern for the good, she shows that she *has* no such concern. For, as Kierkegaard's remarks indicate, a real concern would lead her to condemn precisely such a wish.

It is only in morality that such condemnation is possible. For it is only in morality that we judge not *in terms of*, but *upon* the ends which a man has, upon his desires and, in particular, upon his willingness or unwillingness to engage in certain activities. If a man says that he does not care about being a good artist, or a good scientist, then there is nothing more to be said. On the other hand, if he says that he does not want to be a good person, then we can still make a *moral* judgement. 'Well, you *ought* to want to', we say.

It should be noticed that in saying this, I am not overlooking the possibility that a man who claims not to care about art (or science or politics) will meet with a similar objection, 'Well, you ought to care'. But the possibility of such a response proves rather than disproves my claim that it is only within morality that we pronounce upon a man's willingness to engage in certain activities. The paradox of this remark disappears if one recognises that the judgement in question is a judgement made from within morality, a judgement about the moral significance of art. It would be simply a confusion to suppose that the 'ought' which it involves could be explained in artistic or scientific terms (like the 'ought' in, for example, 'If you want to paint like da Vinci, you ought to learn something about anatomy'). And while it is of course important to recognise that, for example, questions of artistic integrity or an artist's dedication to his work may, and often do, conflict with and even override questions of sexual morality, of responsibility to one's family, of honesty, and so on, it is also important to notice that in such cases the former have a force which can only be described as moral.[12] It follows from this that, while the question 'Ought one to bother with art?' is a real question, the question 'Ought one to bother with morality?' is not.[13]

What I am saying here needs to be distinguished from a super-ficially similar view proposed by Stuart Hampshire in a well-known article.[14] For Hampshire too argues that whereas one may choose either to engage in or ignore artistic activity, with morality no such choice is possible:

> Throughout any day in one's life, and from the moment of waking, one is confronted with situations which demand action. Even to omit to do anything positive, and to remain passive, is to adopt a policy.[15]

Hampshire concludes that 'action in response to any moral prob-lem is not gratuitous; it is imposed; that there should be some response is absolutely necessary',[16] but his reasons for this conclu-sion are importantly different from my own. The difference becomes apparent if one considers a point which Hampshire

---

[12] It is his failure to recognise this which leads Orwell, for instance, to insist that there is no incompatibility in denouncing Dali as a 'dirty little scoundrel' whilst emphasising his artistic ability and dedication to his work ('Benefit of Clergy', in *Decline of the English Murder* (Harmondsworth: Penguin Books, 1965) p. 25), on the grounds that the former is a *moral* judgement, while the latter statements involve purely artistic considerations. Elsewhere, however, Orwell shows what is wrong with his own distinction when he condemns Mark Twain, and condemns him in unmistakably *moral* terms, for sacrificing his artistic integrity ('failure to write the books he ought to have written') from a fear that they would have 'wrecked his reputation and reduced his income to reasonable proportions' ('Mark Twain—The Licensed Jester', in *Collected Essays, Journalism and Letters of George Orwell*, vol. 11 (London: Harcourt Brace, 1968) p. 328). Here Orwell clearly implies that lack of artistic integrity may have a *moral* importance.

[13] The necessity for this paragraph was pointed out to me by Mr H.O. Mounce.

[14] 'Logic and Appreciation', in *Aesthetics and Language*, ed. W. Elton (Oxford: Blackwell, 1959) pp. 161–9.

[15] Ibid., p. 162.

[16] Ibid., p. 163.

neglects, namely that the problems of morality are set by morality itself. An example from J.L. Stocks brings this out well:

> Suppose one rejects a possible way of making money on moral grounds. This will not mean that one gives up the purpose of making money where one decently can; it will not mean that any error has been made in the calculation on which the expectation of profit was based; it will not mean that one has thought of a better way of making money. Let us suppose the purpose firm, the calculation correct, and the prospect of gain more assured and more brilliant by far than any discoverable alternative. I suppose that it will be agreed that it may still be rejected on moral grounds. … To the merely practical or purposive man, say a partner … your rejection will seem like madness, something wholly irrational. … The moral contribution seems to be a mere negation. At a certain point, without rhyme or reason, it makes a man see a barrier he cannot pass; he can only say that he does not consider himself free to improve the situation in just that way.[17]

For the man of whom Stocks speaks, it is morality which creates his problem. It is because he feels scruples about certain actions that he faces the difficulties he does. For his partner who feels no such scruples, no problem exists. *He* will simply act in the manner most likely to secure him the greatest gains. Nevertheless, it does not follow that the latter stands outside morality in this respect, as if by ignoring moral questions he thereby rendered himself immune from moral criticism. For, as I have said, the fact that he ignores moral issues is itself grounds for moral condemnation. If he doesn't see the problem, someone might respond, then so much the worse for him.

It is in this sense that moral problems are unavoidable. By contrast, Hampshire speaks as though the problems of morality were unavoidable in the sense that *anyone* will *see* them as problems, as though the problems were set *for* rather than *by* morality. This goes with his idea of morality as 'a general method of solving problems of conduct',[18] as a technique for enabling men to overcome obstacles to the attainment of their ends. Moral problems are 'practical problems', answers to them consist of 'practical advice', and such advice must 'involve some reference to the whole economy of human needs and purposes'.[19] For Hampshire it is the

---

17 'The Limits of Purpose', p. 28.
18 Hampshire, 'Logic and Appreciation', p. 163.
19 Ibid., p. 169.

necessity of satisfying basic human needs and of balancing one man's needs against another's which gives rise to morality in the first place.

But far from being equivalent to my position, it is clear that most of Hampshire's account is ruled out by what I have said. For if morality *were* a technique for attaining certain predetermined ends, then the applicability of moral considerations to an agent's conduct would be contingent upon his possessing those ends. And by refusing to acknowledge the importance of the needs and purposes in question, he would thereby place himself outside moral criticism. Morality would be of no interest to such a man. However, if, as I suggested, morality involves a standpoint from within which we can judge a man's willingness or unwillingness to take part in *any* activity, such a view must be simply confused. If morality is of no interest to a man, then that man stands open to moral condemnation. The possibility of such condemnation proves false Hampshire's conception of morality. It also proves false the autonomist's claim that one may choose between the demands of art and those of morality. For the question of the relative importance of these demands is one which could be raised only from within the standpoint of morality. And from within this standpoint, the question answers itself.

II

The position which I have been discussing in the first part of this chapter, and which I have called 'autonomism', is one type of reaction to moralism. What I have suggested is that it is a confused reaction. For, in his desire to reject the claim that art is a *part* of morality, the autonomist is led also to reject the rather more moderate claim that artistic activity (like any other form of activity) may be subject to moral criticism. In this way, he is tempted to distort the role which moral considerations play in men's lives.

There is, however, another, and in many ways more extreme form of autonomism, which is also to be found in the writings of Oscar Wilde, but which, unlike the first, involves confusions not about morality but about art. It is this position which I now wish to consider.

In his essay, 'The Decay of Lying', one of Oscar Wilde's aims was to attack what he took to be moralist confusions in the work of particular critics and writers. He wished to show how the attempt by an author to employ his creative abilities in the service of moral ends, or the critical demand for such a characteristic in the work of artists, could lead to the corruption of art. But behind this fairly specific aim lay a rather more general thesis. That this is so becomes apparent on p. 976. Wilde says:

> As long as a thing is useful or necessary to us, or affects us in any way, either for pain or for pleasure, or appeals strongly to our sympathies, or is a vital part of the environment in which we live, it is outside the proper sphere of art. For to art's subject-matter we should be more or less indifferent.

Implicit in this passage, as in much of Wilde's writing, is a general philosophical position. Roughly, Wilde's assumption is that since any attempt to represent art as a means to moral ends (or indeed any other ends) rests upon confusion and, in its practical application, leads to a corruption of art, it must follow that similar confusion (and a similar capacity for corruption) is to be found in any view which sees a relationship between art and morality, or even between art and human concerns in general. 'Life', he tells us, 'is the solvent that breaks up art, the enemy that lays waste her house.'[20]

Stated thus baldly, the argument may seem rather primitive. And Wilde was not, of course, a professional philosopher. Nevertheless, it would, I think, be cavalier simply to brush aside his remarks, for though they do not display the rigorous thought desirable in philosophy, they do raise issues of considerable philosophical interest. Nor are similar arguments unknown in philosophical circles. They will be familiar, for instance, to anyone who has given even a cursory examination to the writings of G.E. Moore on ethics. I am thinking in particular of the last chapter of *Principia Ethica* where Moore turns to the question what things are good as ends. In order to decide this, he tells us, 'it is necessary to consider what things are such that if they existed by themselves in absolute isolation, we should yet judge their existence to be good'.[21] The chief aim of Moore's 'method of isolation' is, of course, to exclude from the discussion those things such as financial wealth or surgical operations, which are good only as means. And Moore's suggestion is that 'if we isolate such things,

---

[20]   *Complete Works*, ibid.
[21]   G.E. Moore, *Principia Ethica* (Cambridge: Cambridge University Press, 1960) p. 187.

which are means to good, and suppose a world in which they, and nothing but they, existed, their intrinsic worthlessness becomes apparent'.[22] For to remove any reference to the end is to render the means worthless. A man's fortune may be important to him in our present world, but it would be of little value in a world where there was nothing to buy. Nor should we need surgeons in a world without illness.

Though Moore sometimes talks as though the 'method of Isolation' were simply an imaginative device for distinguishing good means from good ends, his discussion makes it plain that he intends it as a *criterion* of intrinsic goodness and not merely as one test (among others) of what can be shown independently to be good as an end. For not only does he never suggest any alternative method of establishing intrinsic goodness, but it is clear that he does not even consider the possibility of any intrinsic goods apart from those discovered by the method of isolation. On the contrary, we are told that if we employ this method to decide what is valuable,

> the answer ... appears to be so obvious, that it runs the risk of seeming to be a platitude. By far the most valuable things we know *or can imagine*,[23] are certain states of consciousness which may be roughly described as the pleasures of human intercourse and the enjoyment of beautiful objects.[24]

Nor, he goes on, 'does it appear probable that anyone will think that anything else has *nearly* so great a value'.

Moore, then, assumes that whatever is good, not as a means but as an end, will be something whose value can be understood in complete isolation from everything else. And this, of course, is simply a more general version of the assumption which I have said characterises Wilde's writings. For Wilde assumes that if literature cannot be understood as a means to something external to itself, then it must be intelligible in complete isolation from the rest of our lives. Nevertheless, the assumption, as it appears in the writings of both Wilde and Moore, is a false one, and I think that this can be shown by a consideration of the first of Moore's intrinsic goods, that is, what he calls 'the pleasures of human intercourse' or 'personal affections'.

---

22   Ibid.
23   My italics.
24   Ibid., p. 189.

If someone were to try to explain why personal affections, the love of his wife, or the pleasure he gets from the company of his friends perhaps, were important to him, we should not expect him to point to any purpose which love or friendship serves. This, I take it, is Moore's point in denying that personal affections are good as means to ends, and it is a point which is well brought out in Kierkegaard's *Purity of Heart*. Love, Kierkegaard tells us, is incompatible with double-mindedness. It is incompatible with seeing the object of one's love as a means to an end: 'If a man love a girl for her money', he asks rhetorically, 'who will call him a lover? He does not love the girl, but the money. He is not a lover, but a money seeker.'[25]

Kierkegaard's point is not restricted either to the particular end which he mentions, nor to the particular relationship he is discussing. Whatever end a man proposed as the purpose of his love, similar remarks would apply. We should not say that he cared for the girl, only for the end. And the same might be said of any relationship which involves the notion of concern for an individual. What both Kierkegaard and Moore see is that caring for someone is incompatible with making use of them to further one's aims.

On the other hand, if we try to apply Moore's method of isolation here, if we try to imagine a world in which nothing exists apart from some man's love for his wife, or his relationship to his friends, then though Moore is perhaps right to say that personal affections do not fail the test, this is only because they are debarred by their very nature from taking it. Love and friendship are not unsuccessful candidates, only because they are not candidates at all. For it makes no sense to speak of such relationships in abstraction from all the circumstances which make them what they are.

Of course, I recognise that love and friendship may mean different things to different people. For though marriages are often founded on trust, and friendships on conversation, a man may still love an untrustworthy wife and friends may not feel the need to talk much. And similar remarks might be made about all the other things which often characterise these relationships: loyalty, shared interests, sexual attraction, and so on. But if you said that none of these things was necessary, you would mean that

---

[25] *Purity of Heart*, p. 62.

there is no one of them which is essential, nothing which alone makes it love or friendship, and not that they might all be absent. For though it is true that we may refer to their relationship as love, even though certain features are lacking, even though he no longer trusts her much perhaps, it is also true that as we describe more and more such aspects of their life together disappearing ('He's not as loyal as some men', 'They no longer have anything to say to one another'), we are necessarily approaching the case where it would be proper to say that they no longer love one another.

Yet none of these things which together make it a friendship or a love-affair (as opposed to, say, a business relationship) makes much sense unless there is something in people's lives apart from *this* relationship. We could not speak of trust between a man and his wife unless it were at least conceivable that there should be something which could put their love to the test, a long separation or another woman, for example (otherwise what is it that she trusts him to do?). Again, if he is loyal to her, then this is something which also shows itself when they are not together, in the way he works to support her, or in his remaining true to her memory when she is gone. And, of course, there can be conversation between them only if they have something to say to one another, if their lives are *not* bounded by the relationship they have, so that each can bring something *to* this relationship from the rest of his or her life. Otherwise, his conversations with her would be like his talking to himself.

My point, then, is that if one man can be friends with another, or if a man can love a woman, this is possible only because they stand in relations to these people and to others which are not those of love or friendship. There could be no personal affections unless people were born into and grew up in families, married, bore children, worked to support others, and stood towards one another in relations of trust, loyalty and obedience. Even to imagine one of these factors absent is to imagine a situation where our concepts of love and friendship have undergone a fundamental revision. To imagine one where *none* of the factors could have any part to play in people's lives is to imagine a situation where there is no love and no friendship.

Yet it is precisely such a state of affairs which Moore invites us to imagine when he introduces his method of isolation. And in rejecting this invitation, I am rejecting Moore's general argument in chap. v of *Principia Ethica*. Moore was wrong to suggest that what is valued as an end can be equated with what is valuable in isolation from everything else. He was wrong because at least one case, his own example of personal affections, provides a conclusive counter-example to such an equation. While personal affections are not valued as means to ends, it is simply a confusion to suppose that they could have any significance in complete isolation from the rest of human life.

If we now turn to the second of Moore's intrinsic goods, 'the appreciation of what is beautiful in art or nature', it is, I hope, clear that similar remarks apply. Nor am I singling Moore out for criticism, for, as we saw earlier, Moore's arguments here are identical with those of Wilde. Both assume that since aesthetic goods cannot be construed as means to ends, they must therefore be intelligible in isolation from the rest of life. What I have tried to show is that in so far as this assumption rests upon a general equation between 'What is good as an end' and 'What is good in isolation', it is a false assumption.

Clearly much remains to be said here, and some of it I hope to say later. But rather than developing my present line of criticism at this point, I should like instead to relate what I have said so far to certain issues discussed earlier. In particular, I want to indicate a similarity between moralism and autonomism in a way which will bring out the precise nature of the autonomist's confusion.

As we saw in the previous chapter, the moralist assumes that if art is to say anything, if it is to tell us anything about life, then the relationship in question must be explicable in purposive terms. Grasping the significance of, for example, a novel or a play must be a matter of appreciating how it conduces to some end. My main criticism of this purposive account of the meaning of a work of art was that it introduces a distinction between what an artist says and the way in which he says it (the means which he employs), a distinction which, I suggested, is not merely unnecessary, but indeed falsifies the nature of artistic activity. Now it seems to me that when we turn to the autonomist's account, though we find many important differences, we find also just the same conception of meaning, and just the same misleading distinction.

This claim is not contradicted, but on the contrary borne out by the autonomist's rejection of moralist conclusions. For what we have here is the familiar case (familiar in philosophy at least) of one mistaken account being rejected, while its basic presuppositions are retained to play havoc with subsequent accounts. Thus the autonomist holds that to regard a work of art as a means to some end is to divert attention from the qualities of the work itself. But since he remains wedded to the moralist's assumption that the only way in which a work of art *could* have significance would be by its functioning as a means to an end, since he cannot conceive of any account of meaning *other than* a purposive one, he concludes that art can tell us nothing about life, that its significance is divorced from human concerns, or even that it is simply a confusion to speak of significance in this context. Such an assumption is quite clearly presupposed by Whistler's claim that if a work of art has something to tell us, then 'it becomes merely a means of perpetrating something further, and its mission is made a secondary one, even as a means is second to its end'.[26] But it is an assumption which survives in contemporary philosophy. Whistler's words are, for instance, echoed in Professor Saw's claim that 'If I use language, i.e. marks or sounds with meaning, I am presenting the marks or sounds not for you to look at or listen to, but to "look through" at the meaning'.[27] And, like Whistler, Professor Saw draws from this the obvious conclusion that no plausible account of the meaning of a work of art can be given. Any such account, she tells us, 'suffers from the defect that if we are to "read the signs", what is there is there not for its own sake and for the sake of its sensible properties, but for its meaning'.[28]

Both of the above claims rest upon a conception of meaning which, though it may diverge in details from that espoused by moralists like Sidney or Tolstoi, is in principle no different. Like the moralist accounts to which they are opposed, they involve a distinction between what a work of art says and the way in which it says it, between what the artist has to tell us and the particular words or phrases which he selects. That this is so is apparent from the contrast which both Whistler and Professor Saw draw between reading something 'for its own sake' and reading it 'for the sake of its meaning'. It is also implicit in the latter's equation of 'grasping the meaning' of a work of art, and 'reading the signs'. For the function of a sign is to draw attention or point to something else. If I ask a passenger in my car the meaning of a road-sign with which

[26] J.M. Whistler, 'The Ten-O-Clock Lecture', in *The Gentle Art of Making Enemies* (New York: John W. Covell, 1890) p. 147.
[27] R. Saw, 'Art and the Language of the Emotions', *Proceedings of the Aristotelian Society*, sup. vol. 36, 1962, p. 239.
[28] Ibid., p. 235.

I am unfamiliar, then to answer my question he must mention
something *other than* the sign itself, say a T-junction or children
crossing the road. Generally there would be no point in asking me
to look at the sign more closely.

But whatever precise form it takes, the account of meaning in
question is a limited one, and it is limited because it ignores precisely the points which I emphasised in the previous chapter. A
work of art is not a means by which some independently identifiable message is communicated, it is not a sign or even a
collection of signs which indicate some independently identifiable
state of affairs. And though what a critic tells me about *King Lear*
or *Vanity Fair* may bring me to a deeper understanding of these
works, it will not do so by explaining what Shakespeare or
Thackeray wrote in different terms, as the passenger's remark
'Look out for schoolchildren' explains the road-sign by drawing
attention to the danger ahead in an alternative manner. Unlike the
road-sign or the passenger's remark, the writings of critics do not
draw our attention away from the novel or the play to something
else which is its meaning. If they did, then Professor Saw would
be right to protest, 'Either you attend to Shakespeare's words or
you attend to his meaning, but not both'. But the distinction is a
false one. For if the critic's explanation of what Shakespeare tells
us is to help at all, then it will do so by concentrating our attention
on the particular words which he uses, and by bringing out the
force of these words; not by leading us to regard them as superfluous once their message has been explained. To see that Whistler
and Professor Saw neglect these points is to see the limitations in a
conception of meaning which, though tempting, is hopelessly
inapplicable to art or literature. Since this conception of meaning
is one shared by both autonomists and moralists, in rejecting it I
am rejecting the assumptions on which both accounts rest, the
assumptions which make it plausible to regard them as exhaustive
alternatives.

4

Art and Society

In the previous chapter I suggested that the autonomist's confusion of the notions 'good as an end' and 'good in isolation' is shared also by his moralist opponents; and both in this chapter and in Chapter I, I tried to show that such a conflation rests on confusion. Unfortunately, it might be argued that what I have said, though true, nevertheless leaves untouched the autonomist's main contentions. 'It has been argued', someone might say, 'that since works of art cannot be understood as means to any end, they must be intelligible in isolation from everything else. You have criticised this argument, but you have yet to show that its *conclusion* is false. Though you have shown *one* defence of autonomism to be unsatisfactory, you have not shown that the same is true of *any* defence which might be offered.'

Such an objection would, of course, be justified, and since it is crucial to the argument of this monograph that the conclusions of both moralist and autonomist, as well as the arguments adduced in favour of those conclusions, are mistaken, it is an objection which must now be considered. In the present chapter I shall therefore turn to consider the question: Can any work of art be understood in independence of the life of the society within which it is produced, and in particular of the traditions, both artistic and non-artistic, of that society?

I

It might be thought that it is at least superfluous to ask whether a work of art can be understood in independence of *artistic* traditions. For it seems evident that no one could appreciate, for example, *The Rape of the Lock* without some understanding of the heroic couplet form, without some grasp of the conventions within which Pope worked. Nor do I think that many writers have wished explicitly to deny this (though Whistler's reference to the artist as a 'monument of isolation'[1] is sometimes taken to involve such a denial). Rather, I suggest that the denial has been *implicit*, that philosophers have ignored the role of standards and conventions in artistic understanding because of *other* views which they have held.

A case in point would be the views of those who have made the notions of likes and dislikes central in explaining artistic appreciation, at least in so far as liking is conceived on the analogy of having a 'sweet tooth' or a taste for tobacco. Of course, the bald denial that art appreciation is a matter of likes and dislikes is not particularly illuminating, for likes and dislikes are a mixed bunch, and it is not always out of place to speak of liking a work of art. It may, for example, be significant that Dryden preferred Chaucer to Ovid, in a way that it is not significant that a four-year-old prefers Enid Blyton to both. But where a man's likes do have significance for us, it is because they show understanding, because the man can defend them by an appeal to standards which others share. If he is a better judge than I, I may learn from his views, learn for instance to like a book which I used to dismiss, or come to see that my dislike of a school of painting is just a prejudice. This will not be merely a matter of my seeking what before I had shunned, but will involve a change in my comprehension of art and in the standards which I invoke there. And in this respect the preferences of critics are quite different from a taste for ice-cream or tobacco. For in the latter case there is no question of learning or understanding. No one can *teach* me to prefer tobacco to ice-cream; not because there is no one better qualified to judge than I, but because in this context there is no such thing as judgement. Even here my preferences may change, of course. It may be that I have never really tried tobacco seriously, perhaps because of a puritanical upbringing, and when I do, I find that I like it more than I thought. Or I may become accustomed to the taste. But the change in my likes does not show that I understand anything which I had missed, does not show that I have come to a deeper comprehension of what is involved in some tradition, for instance. And if I were to come once again to prefer ice-cream, no one would say that I had forgotten what I had learned. Such a way of speaking is appropriate only where a man's *views* have changed, and his like (or dislike) of tobacco is not a view which he holds. On the

---

[1]   Whistler, 'The Ten-O-Clock Lecture', p. 155.

contrary, liking tobacco is compatible with holding any view about it whatsoever.

Writers who have tried to reduce aesthetic appreciation to a matter of taste have this much in common with more recent views which try to explain the notion of art in terms of an aesthetic attitude which men may adopt towards *any* object, that both involve a denial of the role of understanding in aesthetic appreciation. Often of course the latter account is introduced in order to explain the unity of art without having recourse to some property common and peculiar to all works of art (significant form, for example). But it has the disadvantage that, by minimising the differences between our attitudes towards works of art and towards natural objects, it tends also to minimise the importance of the traditions and conventions which have a role in the former, though not in the latter. An extreme example of this tendency is to be found in J.O. Urmson's contribution to the symposium 'What Makes a Situation Aesthetic?' In a paper whose alleged intention is 'to make explicit what it is that distinguishes aesthetic thrills, satisfactions, toleration, disgust, etc., from thrills, satisfactions, etc., that would properly be called intellectual, economic, etc.', Urmson says:

> No doubt many of our most intense aesthetic satisfactions are derived from plays, musical works, pictures, and other works of art. But to me it seems obvious that we also derive aesthetic satisfaction from artefacts that are not primarily works of art, from scenery, from natural objects, and even from formal logic.[2]

In its implication that the enjoyment of natural objects differs from that of works of art only in intensity, this passage brings to mind L.A. Reid's claim that 'the difference between the appreciation of a wild rose and of Bach's complete Goldberg variations is just one of degree'.[3] And Urmson's subsequent remarks do nothing to destroy the comparison. He suggests, for example, that a philosophical analysis of what is involved in the appreciation of flowers is likely to be more illuminating than an examination of what people find in plays like *Hamlet*, since 'it is obviously very difficult to get straight our grounds for appreciating anything so complex'.[4]

---

[2]   J.O. Urmson, 'What Makes a Situation Aesthetic?', *Proceedings of the Aristotelian Society*, suppl. vol. 31, 1957, p. 76.

[3]   L.A. Reid, *A Study in Aesthetics* (London: Allen & Unwin, 1931) p. 43.

[4]   Urmson, op cit., p. 87.

But Urmson's remarks, like those of Reid, are confusing; for by concentrating attention upon the beauty of a rose or an orchid one is ignoring precisely what is important in the appreciation of *Hamlet* or the Goldberg variations, namely a grasp of the traditions within which Shakespeare or Bach worked. There are no traditions surrounding the appreciation of flowers. People may look at roses and say 'Beautiful!', but in doing so they do not apply standards, as an antique dealer does when he says the same of a fine piece of Staffordshire pottery, or as a chess player may when faced with a particularly clever move from his opponent. An appreciation of the chess move depends on an understanding of the rules and standards which make it what it is. Without these it would not be a chess move at all, but simply the arbitrary redistribution of pieces of elaborately carved wood on a chequered board. It is the set of conventions governing the aims of the players and the permissible use of the chess pieces which make it possible for the move to have the significance which it does. Without these I could not marvel at its brilliance, nor wonder what to make of it.

In the same way, the difference between knowing what to make of a picture or a play and failing to see anything in it, is also connected with a grasp of traditions and conventions. It was, for instance, precisely the lack of such a grasp which led Tolstoi in a famous passage of *What is Art?* totally to misconstrue the significance of an opera he describes. It was, he tells us,

> one of the most ordinary of operas for people who are accustomed to them, but also one of the most gigantic absurdities that could possibly be devised. An Indian king wants to marry; they bring him a bride; he disguises himself as a minstrel; the bride falls in love with the minstrel and is in despair, but afterwards discovers that the minstrel is the king, and every one is highly delighted. That there never were or could be such Indians, and that they were not only unlike Indians, but that what they were doing was unlike anything on earth except other operas, was beyond all manner of doubt; that people do not converse in such a way as recitative, and do not place themselves at fixed distances, in a quartet, waving their arms to express their emotions; that nowhere except in theatres do people walk about in such a manner, in pairs, with tinfoil halberds and in slippers; that no one ever gets angry in such

a way ... and that no one on earth can be moved by such performances—all this is beyond the possibility of doubt.[5]

It is worth asking why Tolstoi's description *does* reduce what he
saw and heard to a 'gigantic absurdity'. And in this respect perhaps the most important thing to notice is his insistence that what
he saw and heard was unlike anything 'except other operas' or
that 'nowhere except in theatres' did people act in such a manner.
For given what I have said about the importance of, for example,
theatrical and operatic traditions in aesthetic appreciation, this is
precisely what one would expect. *Of course* the proceedings in a
theatre could not have the importance which they do elsewhere,
any more than the movements of pieces in a chess game could
have the significance which they do outside this context. To complain that it is only in a theatre that 'people converse in such a way
as recitative' is as absurd as complaining that only in a chess-game
do people try to checkmate one another. For just as it is only given
the traditions of chess that checkmating is even conceivable, so it
is only given certain operatic and theatrical traditions that recitative can have the significance which it does.

By ignoring these traditions, Tolstoi makes the proceedings on
stage appear arbitrary; for the viewpoint which he adopts
necessarily prevents distinctions being drawn—distinctions, that
is, between what is relevant to an appreciation of opera, and what
is irrelevant. It is, for example, irrelevant that the Indians should
carry *tinfoil* halberds (as opposed to steel or silver ones, I suppose),
just as it would be irrelevant to remark upon the colour of their
eyes or what they ate for breakfast. But it is not irrelevant that they
converse in recitative. For there are conventions in terms of which
the latter, though not the former, can be given sense. By divorcing
what he sees from these conventions, Tolstoi makes the one
appear as pointless as the other. Similar sophistry is at work in
Tolstoi's reference elsewhere to the ballet as 'simply a lewd performance' in which 'half-naked women make voluptuous movements twisting themselves into various sensual wreathings'.[6] His
misunderstanding of ballet differs from his misunderstanding of
opera only in that it does not lead him to dismiss what he sees as
unintelligible. But because he cannot (or will not) understand the
conventions surrounding what he sees, he is led to view the

---

5   *What is Art?*, p. 77.
6   Ibid., p. 79.

dancers' movements as if they were part of a quite different context, as a variety of striptease in fact.

The sort of lack of understanding which I am discussing here is impossible with matters of taste. It is impossible, for example, in the case which Urmson mentions, the delight which people take in flowers. Or rather it is possible only in rather special cases. For flowers *may* mean things. The girl's delight in the roses she receives stems at least in part from a knowledge of what they mean; just as the lilies on a child's grave are not merely pretty. And here, of course, someone (someone from another society, perhaps) may fail to understand. But normally there is nothing like this. Normally I do not have to worry what to make of a flower. I may not like it but it does not lack sense.

But while it is important to recognise the role of tradition in art, this is not enough to show what is wrong with the autonomist's thesis. For though, as I mentioned earlier, some philosophers have ignored (and some still do ignore) this factor, the writers with whom I am chiefly concerned and whom I have called autonomists wish to defend a rather different thesis. They maintain, not that individual works of art have no relation to artistic traditions, but rather that the traditions themselves stand in no relation to anything else.

Now it should be clear that this conception of artistic culture as distinct and isolated from the rest of our lives remains unaffected by what I have said so far. For the question which it raises is not whether a particular work of art can be explained except in terms of artistic traditions and the standards and conventions which they embody, but rather whether an account of art in terms of conventions and standards is sufficient here; whether, that is, art can be explained in complete independence of religion, politics and, in particular for the purposes of this monograph, morality.

An example may bring out what is involved here. Earlier in this chapter I drew an analogy between understanding a move in chess and understanding an opera, both of which I contrasted with finding a rose attractive. As we saw, the distinction centres around the role played by standards in the former though not in the latter. What may, however, lead to confusion is that with the chess move these standards are all that there is. When I understand them, then I understand the game completely.

One reason why this is so is that the moves in a game of chess (or indeed in *any* game) are not related to the rest of our lives, but only to one another. What I mean is that they do not have any bearing on anything outside the game of chess, nor do they depend for their significance on anything outside. The participants do not bring anything to the game, nor do they show us anything. Certainly, a good player may show expertise, even brilliance, in replying to his opponent's moves, or in initiating new moves, and in this sense we may say that he brings something to the game. Nevertheless, the skill which he displays is defined by reference to the game. It is an ability to choose one move from a limited set of possibilities, possibilities limited by the point of chess and by the rules governing the use of chess pieces. And however brilliant his choices they never tell me anything except perhaps new ways of defeating opponents.

True, it may be said that there are some relationships between the game of chess and other practices. The game was developed from ideas about military strategy, for example. And I suppose it is conceivable that subsequently it should have had some influence on these ideas, though I doubt it. Again, the disciplined thought which it involves might be felt to be a valuable training for other activities. Nevertheless, the connections I am discussing are purely contingent ones. It would still be the same game even if it were discovered to have been invented by people who had never fought wars, and no change in military ideas or indeed in any other aspects of our lives need bring about a change in the way in which it is played. A mating-move might have the same significance whatever the world and the people in it were like.

What this suggests is that the question with which this chapter is concerned can be represented as one of how far my earlier analogy between chess and art holds. All that I have suggested so far is that it holds in the minimal sense that both involve standards and traditions. In both the individual is to some extent bound by what others do and what others have done before him. Unless this were so you could have neither the game of chess nor any form of artistic activity. The autonomist whom we have been considering, however, wishes to push the analogy still further. For he wishes to say that just as chess stands in no relationship to the rest of our lives (or at most a merely contingent relationship), so art and literature are divorced from non-artistic activities. What I want to show is that this leads him into confusion.

II

In part v of *Anna Karenina*, Vronsky, bored with his life in voluntary exile from his native Russia, turns to painting in order to pass the time. Tolstoi's comment upon Vronsky's hobby, however, brings out the superficiality of his interest:

> He had a taste for art and a gift for imitating, which he imagined to be the real thing, so after wavering for a while as to whether to choose the religious, historic, *genre* or realistic school, he began to paint. He understood all schools of painting and could find inspiration in any of them, but he did not know that it was possible not to understand a single one and yet find inspiration within one's own soul. ... Thus he accomplished what he set out to do very rapidly and produced something resembling the particular school he was trying to imitate.[7]

Now in one sense it is indisputable that Vronsky understands art. This means that he has some considerable acquaintance with artistic standards, unlike, for example, Anna, who admits that she is 'no judge of art' and whose remarks about it generally amount to mere statements of likes and dislikes. On the other hand, it is clear from the above passage that Tolstoi sees something lacking in Vronsky's understanding, something which *cannot* be explained in terms of artistic standards. He did not know, Tolstoi says, that it was possible to find inspiration in his own soul.

This failing on Vronsky's part can be seen in his lack of inventiveness, his unoriginality. 'He had a gift for imitating', we are told, but he draws no inspiration from 'nature and life'. Because of this, Vronsky has nothing to contribute to the artistic traditions within which he paints. His work is simply parasitic upon them. This comes out clearly when Tolstoi is discussing the difference between Vronsky's portrait of Anna and a similar portrait by the artist Mihailov. Mihailov brings something *to* his work. It has something to say:

> By the fifth sitting the portrait struck everybody, especially Vronsky, by its accurate likeness as well as its particular beauty. It was strange how Mihailov could have discovered that peculiar beauty. 'One must know her and love her as I have done to understand that sweet spiritual expression of hers', Vronsky thought, though it was only through this portrait that he himself had

---

7   *Anna Karenina* (London: J.M. Dent: Everyman's Library, 1939) vol. II 29.

discovered it. But the expression was so true that it seemed to him and others that they had always known it.[8]

But Vronsky, because of his attitudes towards art, cannot see the force of this difference between his work and Mihailov's. He attributes it merely to the latter's superior technique, that is, to an adeptness in working within certain traditions, a mere 'mechanical ability'.[9]

I said above that Vronsky's own work is parasitic. What I mean by this may become clearer if one considers some remarks which D.H. Lawrence once made in an essay on John Galsworthy. Lawrence says:

> The Forsytes are all parasites and Mr Galsworthy set out, in a really magnificent attempt, to let us see it. They are parasites upon the thought, the feelings, the whole body of life of really living individuals who have gone before them and who exist alongside with them. All they can do, having no individual life of their own, is out of fear to rake together property, and to feed upon the life that has been given by living men to mankind. They have no life, and so they live for ever in perpetual fear of death, accumulating property to ward off death. They can keep up a convention, but they cannot carry on a tradition. There is a tremendous difference between the two things. To carry on a tradition you must add something to the tradition.[10]

Vronsky is a parasite in the sense that the Forsytes are. He can keep up certain conventions, but he cannot, in Lawrence's words, 'carry on a tradition' (in his case, an artistic tradition). The difference between these things cannot be explained simply in terms of a knowledge of the standards involved in any form of activity. Rather, it is a distinction between simply knowing the standards, which Vronsky does, and being able to extend or enrich them, which Vronsky cannot do. The whole of his inspiration comes from what others have done; he cannot find inspiration in his own life.

Now it is clear that the philosophers with whom I am concerned cannot admit the distinction which Lawrence draws, nor that which is implied by Tolstoi's portrait of Vronsky. For

---

8   Ibid., p. 40.
9   Ibid., p. 37.
10 'John Galsworthy', in *D.H. Lawrence: Selected Literary Criticism*, ed. Anthony Beal (London: Heinemann, 1955) p. 123.

according to them it means nothing to speak of a man's bringing to art anything from his own life. We see perhaps the most extreme statement of this view in the writings of Clive Bell. Bell was, of course, chiefly concerned to attack the widespread misconception of art as essentially representational. He wished, that is, to oppose a purposive account, in particular an account in which the artist's purpose is held to be that of producing a likeness. To Bell, this view seemed fundamentally mistaken. 'The representative element in a work of art', he tells us, 'may or may not be harmful; it is always irrelevant.' What is interesting is that Bell continues with an almost classic statement of the argument which I criticised in the previous chapter:

> To appreciate a work of art we need bring nothing with us from life, no knowledge of its ideas and affairs, no familiarity with its emotions. Art transports us from the world of man's activity to a world of aesthetic exaltation. For a moment we are shut off from human interests; our anticipations and memories are arrested; we are lifted above the stream of life. The pure mathematician, rapt in his studies, knows a state of mind which I take to be similar if not identical. ... Both he and the artist inhabit a world with an intense and peculiar significance of its own; that significance is unrelated to the significance of life.[11]

Part of what Bell means when he speaks of art as having 'an intense and peculiar significance of its own' is that it does not require explanation in terms of any external standards. It is to Bell's credit that (unlike Tolstoi) he recognised the confusion in supposing that art can be explained as one aspect or one variety of the other activities in which human beings engage. Where Bell himself goes seriously astray is in supposing that it follows from this recognition that the significance of art is *unrelated* to these other activities. And his confusion here leads him to miss much of the significance of his own comparison between art and mathematics.

If one said that pure mathematics was distinct from the rest of human activity, that it had an 'intense and peculiar significance of its own', one thing which one might have in mind would be a distinction between the truths of mathematics and their application in other fields. A glazier may use mathematics in replacing windows and an engineer in building bridges. If the window is

---

11   *Art* (London: Arrow Books, 1961) pp. 36–7.

three foot square and glass costs 20p a square foot, then the glazier will charge his customers £1.80 for materials. And the engineer uses similar, though more complicated, calculations in deciding how many girders are required to support the bridge. Nevertheless, Bell's pure mathematician is not concerned with the cost of glass nor with the properties of steel girders. The proposition $3^2 \times 4 = 36$ is not an empirical proposition; it could not be disproved by the discovery that glass shrinks when fitted into a window frame, for example, though in this case the glazier would charge his customer more. Nor do we need to make experiments in steel-girder construction to decide whether the builder's calculations are correct or not. In *this* sense the truths of mathematics are independent of their application outside mathematical contexts.

But in another sense they are not, and Bell's claims are misleading. On p. 133 of *Remarks on the Foundations of Mathematics*, Wittgenstein says:

> I want to say: it is essential to mathematics that its signs are also employed *in mufti*. It is their use outside mathematics, in other words the meaning of the signs, that makes the sign-game mathematics. Just as it is not a logical conclusion if I change one configuration into another (say one arrangement of chairs into another).[12]

Wittgenstein's point is that the significance of the inferences and proofs which we find in mathematics (indeed, what makes them *inferences* or *proofs* in the first place) cannot lie simply in their role *within* mathematics. Of course, mathematical propositions cannot be regarded as a *part* of any other activity (as, for example, a technique for attaining practical ends, or as a species of empirical proposition). An explanation of why one mathematical calculation is correct and another incorrect will not involve any reference to the cost of glass or to the properties of steel girders, but only to the rules of mathematics. Nevertheless, in order to explain the point of such calculations, in order to see how they can prove anything or show us anything, one must look at the ways in which they are used elsewhere, in buying and selling, in engineering, in measuring distances, and so on. There may be no contradiction in imagining a society where they would have no such use, a society

---

12   *Remarks on the Foundations of Mathematics*, eds. G. von Wright, Georg Henrik; trans. R. Rhees & G.E.M. Anscombe (Oxford: Blackwell, 1956).

where people never charge more for one item than they do for two, perhaps. (I suppose shopkeepers might make their customers pay for the first purchase and ignore the others, or put up signs saying 'As much as you can carry for 25p'.) But I think that the members of this society would want a very different way of doing mathematics from us, and that among them our sorts of calculations could be nothing more than a game. And if one emphasises only the rules and conventions which are a part of the discipline, if one ignores the way in which it enters into our lives, one will not see why mathematics is any more than this, even in our society. While mathematics and engineering or the institution of buying and selling may be said to be distinct, if this means that they cannot be regarded as all parts of the same activity, they are not distinct in the sense of being totally isolated.

Bell nowhere indicates that he recognises this distinction, and in view of his analogy between art and mathematics this is unfortunate, for I think that a similar distinction can be made with respect to art. Certainly the standards by which we judge an artist's work are not those of morality or science, any more than the standards of the mathematician are those of the glazier or the engineer. When an artist writes a poem or paints a portrait, his problems—I mean the sort of problems which bring his work to a halt, or make him wonder whether he can write *anything* worth while—are not moral problems or political problems. Nor are discoveries in art, discoveries about the means of attaining some extra-artistic end. On the other hand, just as the propositions of mathematics are not isolated from activities like measuring, buying and selling, building and counting, so the poet's work, and the problems and discoveries which are a part of it, will not be isolated from other aspects of his life and the life of his society. If it were, if these different aspects of his life had no bearing on one another, then writing a poem would not differ from playing a game. And there are *no* problems or discoveries of the sort I have mentioned in a game, difficulties which have to be overcome before I can even begin playing.

But the different activities in which a man engages could have no bearings on one another unless it were the same language which he used in each of them. An artist can bring into his work something from the life he leads only because the language of art is used also outside art. This is clear in the case of literature or poetry, but it is also, I think, true of musical phrases or what a man draws on canvas. In his paper, 'Art and Philosophy', Rush Rhees says:

> A piece of music is written in musical phrases or in music, as a poem is written in language and in poetry. Wittgenstein said in conversation once that Schubert's *Wiegenlied* is clearly deeper than Brahms' *Wiegenlied*, but that it can be deeper only in the whole of our musical language. He would have included in musical language not only the works of recognised composers, but also Volkslieder and the way people sing and play. If anything these are more fundamental, since they give the idiom in which the formal compositions are written, making it possible for the themes of these compositions to have the meaning they do. Not that any of these themes need be taken from the songs people sing. But they are themes which belong to that language and have meaning in that language.[13]

The fact that the language which is used in poetry or in music is the same language that is used elsewhere, in one's job or in talking to one's children, runs counter to the autonomist's claim that art is isolated from the rest of life. When Clive Bell suggests that 'To understand art, we need bring nothing from life', what he ignores is that in order to understand, for example, a poem, one thing which I must bring from life is an understanding of the language in which it is written. This may seem a trivial point, and one may feel that no one could have failed to recognise it. In a way I think that it is obvious (though the significance of what is obvious is not always apparent in philosophy). But to suppose, at least in this context, that it is trivial implies a trivial conception of language and understanding.

For when I say that in order to understand a poem, one must understand the language in which it is written, I do not mean simply that one must be able to give synonyms for the words which appear in it, or that one must know the rules for the correct use of the expressions it contains. If a teacher asks a pupil whether he understands a poem written in a foreign language, then he may mean just this. And he may be satisfied if the pupil can give a literal translation, even though it shows no grasp of what made the original a great poem. Nor will the pupil understand this either unless he does have some knowledge of the vocabulary and

---

13 'Art and Philosophy', in *Without Answers* (London: Routledge & Kegan Pail, 1969) pp. 136–7.

the rules of grammar. But if this is all that he has, he will never show any sense of the force of the words or lines in the poem, any ability to distinguish a sentence which *says* something from one which is empty and dull. For this is not something which can be explained in terms of synonyms and paraphrases. It is the force of the words which escapes a literal translation.

But the words in the poem, or the novel or play, could not have the force there which they do without the rest of language, if they were never used anywhere but in literature. When, for example, Defoe wished to depict the spiritual barrenness of Moll Flanders' world, he did so by having her describe this world in words and phrases which normally have their life in economic and commercial contexts. It is this which gives irony to, for example, the account of Moll's first marriage:[14]

> It concerns the story in hand very little to enter into further particulars. ... Only to observe that I had two children by him, and that at the end of five years he died. He had been a very good husband to me, and we lived very agreeably together; but as he had not received much from his parents, and had in the little time he lived acquired no great matters, so my circumstances were not great, nor was I much mended by the match.

In a discussion of Defoe's use of phrases like 'received much', 'acquired no great matters', 'my circumstances were not great' in this and other contexts, one critic remarks that they 'are as limited in meaning as a mathematical sign' and that 'by their frequency they compose a picture of Moll's mentality and sensibility'.[15] What should be noted is that it is the life of these phrases *outside Moll Flanders*, their use in predominantly commercial contexts, which gives them their ironic force when Moll applies them to her life with her husband and to his death. Normally, of course, such phrases are not used in this way. Certainly Moll's words would not strike us as they do if this were at all a commonplace form of expression. Nevertheless, the effect of the book depends on the

---

[14]   It has been argued that the irony is unintentional, and that Defoe's choice of words merely depicts the barrenness of his own life. Whether or not this is so, it does not affect my point, only the appropriateness of my example. I do not claim that Defoe's language has the sort of force suggested above; only that if any use of language has this sort of force, then this is the way in which it has it.

[15]   Dorothy Van Ghent, *The English Novel* (New York:, Harper Collins, 1953) p. 37.

fact that the words Defoe uses are not limited to literary contexts, but are, on the contrary, a part of his readers' lives. And though a child may learn the meaning of some of these words by reading *Moll Flanders*, generally he does not. If he did, I do not see how he could ever appreciate what he reads.

This shows why my earlier analogy between literature and chess, though it had a point in that it drew attention to the importance of standards in both activities, was also in many ways unsatisfactory. For making a move in chess is quite unlike writing a line of poetry. The significance of the pieces which the chess player uses is defined by their role in the game. The king, for example, just *is* that piece which can make such-and-such moves, and which stands in such-and-such a relationship to the other pieces. The poet or the playwright, on the other hand, uses words whose significance cannot be explained simply by their role in what he writes, but which on the contrary are normally used in the course of activities which are quite intelligible without reference to literature. This is what is so profoundly wrong with Ezra Pound's remark:

> Really one DON'T need to know a language. One needs, damn well needs, to know the few hundred words in the few really good poems that any language has in it.[16]

Discussing this remark, F.R. Leavis comments that Pound's view goes with a 'conception of Culture as something apart and aloof, forming a special consecrated realm and having only external contacts with profane living'.[17] By now it scarcely needs remarking that I agree with Leavis in regarding such a view as mistaken. My point is that the falsity of Pound's ideas about language proves false the conception of culture which Leavis attacks. It is precisely this conception of culture which lies behind the views of those writers whom I have called autonomists.

Quoted by F.R. Leavis, *Anna Karenina and Other Essays* (London: Chatto & Windus, 1967) p. 150.
Ibid.

5

Art and Understanding

I

It may be thought that in what I have said so far two important questions have been either overlooked or intentionally ignored. One fairly obvious criticism will be that, though I have rejected two common accounts of the way in which a work of art may be said to tell us something about morality,[1] I have as yet failed to give any detailed account of my own. This objection would be, to some extent, a fair one. Central to my criticisms of both moralist and autonomist writers has been the claim that they fail to see that what an artist reveals about morality cannot be distinguished from the manner in which he does so. But clearly there is more to be said about this, and perhaps more important, what I *have* said requires to be defended against objections which many would regard as overwhelming. This then is an issue which must be considered in the present chapter.

The second issue is also one which I have so far omitted to discuss, but in this case the omission may at first appear to be no mere contingent matter. Rather, it may be considered a necessary consequence of my remarks in the previous chapter, where I emphasised the artist's relation to both the artistic tradition within which he works and to the society of which he is a member, that my account should avoid any discussion of the nature of artistic originality. For, it may be asked, are not originality and an adherence to tradition just the sorts of things which are normally regarded as incompatible in any artist's work?

This latter objection does, of course, have a point. For it is true that any discussion of what distinguishes a great creative artist

---

[1]   Or, to be more precise, one such account, the moralist's, and another, the autonomist's, which denies that such a thing is possible.

from his less talented contemporaries, or of the respects in which the artistic contributions of two original contemporaries differ, will be concerned with just the sorts of aspects of these artists' work which cannot be explained solely by reference to its social and artistic context. Thus, though Shakespeare's history plays stand in a close relation to a long history of Tudor and Stuart morality plays, it is not just this relation which we have in mind when we discuss the originality which is displayed in them. Again, though both Shakespeare and Marlow worked within the same literary and social contexts, the differences in their writings, the greater complexity and solidarity of Shakespeare's delineation of character, for instance, cannot be explained by the contexts in question, but only by reference to the writers themselves and to what they brought to the development of Elizabethan drama.

Despite this, it would, I think, be a confusion to suppose that my account rules out the possibility of such an explanation. For the fact that a creative artist may introduce innovations into the traditions within which he works does not entail the conclusion that his innovations can be understood independently of these traditions. Certainly, originality cannot be regarded as one mode of adherence to tradition. It is nevertheless true that originality is possible only for someone who works within certain traditions. Thus, for example, it is sometimes noted that Swift's work, in particular *Gulliver's Travels*, has often been misunderstood through a failure to appreciate its relations to 'a tradition of wit which provided for a free play of fictitious attitudes'.[2] By ignoring his mastery of this tradition, his skill in developing outrageous arguments which do not directly represent his beliefs, his critics have, for example, been led to equate Swift's moral viewpoint with that of Gulliver and thus have tended to neglect one level of satire in the book (the level at which Gulliver himself is being satirised). Nevertheless, though Swift's work does depend on such a tradition, though we are likely to fall into error unless we notice its relationship to the work of, say, Dryden or the metaphysical poets, it does not follow from *this* that there is no difference between these writers, that Swift was a mere plagiarist. For it is clear that if this were so then the error in question would have

---

[2]   D.W. Jefferson, 'An Approach to Swift', in Boris Ford, *The Pelican Guide to English Literature*, Vol. IV: *From Dryden to Johnson* (Harmondsworth: Penguin, 1970) p. 249.

been impossible. What does follow is that the difference between a writer like Swift and the plagiarist does not lie in the one's working within certain traditions while the other ignores all traditions, but in Swift's being able to do what the plagiarist cannot, namely extend and contribute to these traditions.

The second of the above objections is then less powerful than it might at first appear, and it may now seem appropriate to turn to the other issue which I mentioned at the beginning of this chapter, that is, the question of how it is possible for a work of art to tell us anything about morality. There are, however, reasons why the two issues cannot be separated in this way. What I mean is that in art the concept of originality and the idea of 'having something to say' run together. When, for example, I referred earlier to the difference between a mediocre writer and an original artist, I might equally well have spoken of the difference between a writer who 'has something to say' and one whose work tells us nothing. For if originality were thought of as unimportant in art, if writers, composers and painters were content to go on writing, composing and painting in the same old way, and if their audiences did not care about this (a state of affairs which is by no means inconceivable), then I think that one consequence of this would be that it would no longer make much sense to speak of our learning anything from their work, or of art having anything to contribute to the life of the community.

This is not, of course, meant to imply that great artists consciously strive after originality. For originality can be found only where the artist has something to say, and the painter or poet who consciously pursues it is likely to be concerned with how his work will be seen in relation to the work of other painters or poets rather than with what he has to say. Still, it would clearly show a confusion for someone to say: Forget what it is for an artist to show originality. Forget those aspects of his work which lead us to regard it as something out of the ordinary. Simply explain how it is that this work can teach us anything. And I want therefore to begin by indicating two characteristics which a work of art must possess if it is to be seen as original, that is, two central differences between the creative and the mediocre artist.

(i) In the previous chapter, I discussed Tolstoi's comparison between the portraits of Vronsky, who we are told possessed merely 'a gift for imitating', and Mihailov, who is represented as an artist of some creative ability. Now the first thing to notice about this distinction is that, as Tolstoi draws it, it is a difference of kind and not just of degree; that is to say, Mihailov does something *quite* different from what Vronsky does, not merely the same thing but with greater ability. His portrait of Anna tells his audience something new about her, whereas Vronsky's says nothing.

Vronsky, of course, does not recognise this. And it is, I think, significant that *he* thinks of the difference as simply one of *technique*. For it is characteristic of skills or techniques that differences in ability among those who practise them are differences in degree. If Vronsky and Mihailov had been concerned with making prints from an engraving of Anna, then Vronsky's account of the differences might not have been misleading. Both the expert and the third-rate printer aim at the same kind of result, a print which will match the artist's specifications, and both work according to a set of rules or standards calculated to bring about this result. Where the expert printer differs from his slipshod competitor is in having the patience or the ability to adhere to these rules and thus to bring about the desired result.

But though we may praise the printer's accuracy, patience or precision, we do not praise him for originality. And when we do praise an artist's originality, his imagination, it is not for attaining some predetermined end which his inferiors cannot attain, but for breaking new ground, for doing something out of the ordinary, something which could not have been specified in advance. Unlike the printer, the nature of whose task is determined by what the artist has done, Mihailov's problems are those of *deciding* what he wants to say. These are not the problems which an artist like Vronsky faces at all. He has nothing to say. He imitates, but he does not create. He does not aim at, and miss, a target which Mihailov hits. The target which Mihailov hits, Vronsky cannot even see.

(ii) Let us turn to another passage from the same section of *Anna Karenina*. Vronsky and Anna have been discussing Mihailov's work with him in his studio:

> When they had gone, Mihailov sat down in front of his picture of Christ and Pilate and went over in his imagination what his visitors had said of it. ... He suddenly saw something wrong about the foreshortening of Christ's leg, and taking up his palette he set to work. As he was working he kept gazing at the figure of John in

the background, that had seemed to him so absolutely perfect—
and his visitors had not even noticed it.[3]

The theme of Mihailov's painting was a hackneyed one, and no
one would have attached much importance to his work if his treatment of it had not differed from that of others. What this passage
brings out, however, is that Mihailov's work is not *merely* different. Had he painted in a purely capricious manner, the result
would probably have been novel, but it would not have shown
imagination or originality. And in fact Mihailov's painting is not
capricious, but subject to a critical control which enables him to
reject the foreshortening of Christ's leg as wrong, and to appreciate the perfection of the figure of St John.

A similar point comes out in the passage which I quoted in the
previous chapter. Tolstoi tells us that those who saw Mihailov's
portrait of Anna discovered something new about her from it,
something which was not to be found in Vronsky's portrait. But
what they marvelled at was not simply that an artist could show
something different from what others had shown. There would
have been nothing to marvel at in that. For to paint differently
from others, one need only know how others have painted and
avoid those ways. And a child who knew nothing about art would
certainly not have painted Anna's portrait in the same way as
Vronsky. Mihailov's originality lay in his being able to create
something which was different and yet *right*—'so true that everyone who saw it thought that they had known it all before'.

What these examples show is that in the sphere of art 'original'
cannot be equated with 'novel' or 'different'. For the concept of
originality brings in a reference to standards, a distinction
between 'right' and 'wrong', in a way that the concept of novelty
does not. The importance of this distinction in the field of
literature, the concern of the artist to find just the right form of
expression, is well illustrated in Maupassant's account of
Flaubert's manner of composition:

> Possessed of an absolute belief that there exists but one way of
> expressing one thing, one word to call it by, one adjective to
> qualify, one verb to animate it, he gave himself to super-human

---

3   Tolstoi, *Anna Karenina*, p. 39.

labour for the discovery, in every phrase of that word, that verb,
that epithet.[4]

That 'there exists but one way of expressing one thing' would not,
as I pointed out earlier, be true of all uses of language, of a
commentary on a horse-race, for instance, or of the directions I
give someone to enable them to reach my house. But it is true of
writing a novel or a poem. It errs only in being too limited. I do
not mean that Maupassant has not described how a painter or a
composer works, for that was not his intention, but that what he
says does not cover even literature. When, for example, in *The
Rape of the Lock*, Pope wished to deepen our understanding of the
scale of values of the Augustan age, to comment upon a society
where the cutting of a girl's hair could take on the importance of a
rape, he did so partly by the words he selected. An example of this
would be his reference to the scissors which the Baron uses in his
assault as a 'glittering Forfex', where the adjective 'glittering'
brings out the triviality of the incident by comparison with the
sort of event for which the solemn Latin term 'Forfex' would be
appropriate. But this effect of diminution is not carried only (in a
narrow sense) by the words which Pope chooses. It is to be found
also in the tone of the poem, in the constant alternation between
heroic and conversational diction, and especially in the balancing
of one line against another which the couplet form makes possible:

> For a moment Pope sustains the grander tone of *Absolom and
> Achitophel*
>> 'Even then, before the fatal Engine clos'd …'
> but with the next line
>> 'A wretched Sylph too fondly interpos'd'
> he restores the scene to scale.[5]

If one said, rightly I think, that Pope's moral criticism, what he
reveals about morality in the poem, lies in his choice of just the
right words, one would have to recognise that it lies also in his
choice of the right tone and the right poetic form; that Pope did
not just happen to write in pentameters, any more than he just
happened to refer to the cutting of Belinda's lock as a 'rape'.

But whatever precise form it may take, the distinction between
right and wrong, between the successful and the unsuccessful

---

4   Quoted in Walter Pater, *Appreciations* (London: Macmillan, 1910) p. 29.
5   R.A. Brower, *Alexander Pope* (Oxford: Clarendon Press, 1963) p. 144.

treatment of an artistic theme, is an important one, for if it is ignored, one is likely to confuse the creative imagination of an artist like Pope or Flaubert and mere idle fancy[6] or even the ravings of a madman. And though we do use the term 'imagination' in all of these cases, though children given to flights of fancy are sometimes said to have 'vivid imaginations' or to be 'highly imaginative', and to someone whose grip on reality is slipping one may protest 'But it's all in your imagination', the connections should not blind us to the differences which I have indicated. The poet is in some sense concerned to 'get things right'. But this is not a notion which plays any part in the sphere of fantasy, and the madman is precisely someone who, in one way or another, has lost the sense of the distinction between right and wrong, between what makes sense and what is mere caprice.

Nevertheless, in the sphere of art the distinction itself is not without its difficulties. For one is inclined to ask what sense it can have to speak of the right word, the right verse-form, the right expression for the face in a portrait, where what is being discussed is the work of an *original* artist. The difficulty in question arises from my earlier point, that the difference between the first-rate artist and the mediocre is a difference in kind. It would not arise if this were merely a difference in degree, if the greater artist had simply mastered some skill which eluded the lesser. For we know what it means to say that there is a right and wrong way of producing a print, or that the skilled printer carries out his task successfully. It means quite simply that he has obeyed the rules and that his final product accords with the artist's intentions as embodied in the original engraving. But if, as I have suggested, the work of a great artist, say Donne's comparison of parted lovers to a pair of compasses in 'A Valediction: Forbidding Mourning', or Pope's use of the rhyming couplet in *The Rape of the Lock*, is something which goes *beyond* the rules, something unusual or out of the ordinary, if the success of such treatments does *not* consist in their

---

6   For an example of this fault, see Freud's essay 'The Relation of the Poet to Day-Dreaming', in *Collected Papers*, Vol. IV (London: Hogarth Press, 1949), where he argues that the fantasies of human beings may be used as a model by which to understand 'the creative powers of imaginative writers'. The only difference, Freud suggests, is that the fantasies of ordinary men are generally rather repulsive, whereas it is the poet's job to make his attractive. 'The essential *ars poetica* lies in the technique by which our feeling of repulsion is overcome' (ibid., p. 183).

according with some pre-established blueprint or recipe, then what sense can be given to the notions of 'right' and 'wrong', 'success' or 'failure' here?

It is, I think, obvious that any answer to this question will bring us back to the first of the issues which I mentioned at the beginning of this chapter. If one is to explain what it means to speak of the shape of a figure in a painting, or of a word in a poem, as 'right' or 'wrong', one cannot ignore the question of what it is for a work of art to reveal something to us. For the right word or phrase *is* the word or phrase which can show us something, where an alternative, which in other circumstances might serve equally well, cannot. The comparison of the lovers to a pair of compasses is not merely novel, though it is that. It also tells one something about love, enables one to see it in a new light, as, for example, the comparison to a pair of pruning-shears would not.

II

This brings me to a difficulty which is central to this essay. For throughout I have asserted that if we learn anything from a painting or from a novel, then we learn from the painter or the novelist having selected precisely the right word, the right colour, the right image. Donne's 'Valediction' can bring me to a deeper understanding of love because he chooses just the right image, and the only right image for the two lovers. Vronsky discovered something from the trueness of the expression on Anna's face in Mihailov's portrait. We can learn from Pope's Rape of the Lock, because the poet chooses just the right words to describe the scissors in the Baron's hand. And in all these cases, what we learn could not be expressed in any other way. As Wittgenstein remarks:

> If a theme, a phrase, suddenly means something to you, you don't have to be able to explain it. Just *this* gesture has been made accessible to you.[7]

But, my critic is likely to say, clearly this is unsatisfactory. If a work of art, a novel or a painting, is to teach me anything, if I am to learn from it, then what I learn cannot be limited to the particular case in this way. True, when I read a novel, I expect the writer

---

[7]   L. Wittgenstein, *Zettel*, eds. G.E.M. Anscombe & G. von Wright, trans. G.E.M. Anscombe (Oxford: Blackwell, 1967) para. 158.

to find the right words in which to describe characters and incidents. But what he tells me cannot be limited to the way in which
he describes these things. It must be something which can be
applied elsewhere, to other characters or events, and it must therefore involve some sort of general principle or rule. After all, when
I learn to open a tin or to fire a gun, I do not learn to open only *that*
tin or to fire only *that* gun, but any tin or gun which is reasonably
similar. When a child learns that the object in the corner of the
living-room is called a 'piano', we should not say that he had
learned the meaning of the word 'piano' unless he were able to
recognise other objects in different situations as pianos. In short, it
seems to be the case that 'Whenever we learn to do something,
what we learn is always a principle'.[8] Must not the same be true
also of what we learn from art or literature?

Apparently then, on this account, what a novel or a poem
teaches me must be either new principles or at least modifications
to my old principles. Of course, no one would maintain that it
does this simply by *stating* principles. No novel is merely a list of
general rules, nor would any theory which suggested that it was
be taken seriously. Fortunately for the account I am considering,
this is not the only possibility. For, it may be argued, a novel presents us with human beings in certain situations, with the sorts of
choices they make in those situations, the difficulties they face, the
consequences of their choices, and so on. And we may learn from
their experiences in the same way that we learn from our own,
namely by crystallising what we learn in a principle or rule 'of a
not too specific or detailed form so that its salient features may
stand out and serve us again in a like situation without need for so
much thought'.[9] Thus, reading about the situations in which
fictional characters find themselves is to some extent a substitute
for actually experiencing these situations ourselves (situations,
perhaps, which we should *never* in the normal run of things
experience):

> Sir Alan Herbert in the course of his protracted campaign for the
> liberalisation of the divorce laws, wrote a novel called *Holy Dead-
> lock* which was a sympathetic account of the tribulations of some
> unhappy people caught up in them. The effectiveness of this novel

---

8   R.M. Hare, *The Language of Morals* (Oxford: Clarendon Press, 1952) p. 60.
9   Hare, *Freedom and Reason*, pp. 41–2.

as an argument for a liberal position depended on its power to awaken the sympathetic imaginations of its readers.[10]

What Hare means when he speaks of literature as awakening our sympathetic imaginations seems to be a sort of superimposition of the lives of fictional characters on to the lives of those we know or on to our own lives. And though the fit is presumably never perfect, often it will be close enough for me to realise what it would be like for me or my friends to live similar lives, to be, say, victims of barbaric divorce laws, close enough for me to realise the misery which such laws might bring us. As a result, my attitude towards the law or towards divorce may be influenced, my principles changed.[11]

I speak of 'literature' here and not of art in general, because I think it is obvious that the above account is not going to help us much if what we are concerned with is how someone can learn from a portrait or a symphony. And this might be thought to be a difficulty in Hare's account, though it is one which he recognises. But there are deep confusions in what he says about literature too.

Presumably Sir Alan Herbert had experienced, been acquainted with, or at least thought deeply about the sorts of difficulties which may surround love and marriage, and he presented these difficulties in his novel. The same is true of other writers, Tolstoi in *Anna Karenina*, Zola in *Thérèse Raquin*, Hardy in *Jude the Obscure*, Ibsen in *A Doll's House*. What they have given us are stories of men and women wrestling with the problems which marriages can create. Probably the authors learned from writing these stories, certainly many of the characters are represented as learning things from their experiences, and we too can learn from reading about them. The issue between Hare and myself concerns not whether these sorts of learning are possible, but what they involve; in particular, what it means to speak of our learning from the life of a fictional character. And one consequence of the account which *he* gives would seem to be that I can learn from the life of Anna Karenina or of Ibsen's Nora, from their problems and

---

[10]   Ibid., p. 181.

[11]   I think that the account which I have outlined above is, both in its general form (as an explanation of what is involved in *all* learning) and as an account of how we can learn from works of art, a fairly widespread one. My quotations are all taken from Hare's writings because his is the most explicit statement of the view with which I am acquainted.

the way in which they solve them, only in so far as those problems and the situations which rise to them are like my own or those of people I know:

> It is true that these situations are not thought of as actually occurring; but they are claimed to be like situations which do actually occur — otherwise their relevance to moral thought would be small.[12]

But learning from the treatment of problems in literature is nothing like learning from experiencing those problems, and often the problems an author describes are such that no one else *could* experience them. In Ibsen's play, for instance, Nora and her husband face difficulties in their marriage, just as my wife and I might. But they are not *our* difficulties, and the problem for someone who holds that we can learn from them only if they are like ours is that in *that* sense they could not even be like ours in the relevant respects. Nora's problems arise from the way she feels towards her husband, her marriage, her children, and from her attempts to understand these feelings. They are inexplicable except by reference to the particular people involved and the particular relationships between them, and it is never *these* relationships with which someone else is concerned. Even if my wife is also trying to understand her feelings for me, her problem is not the same as Nora's, any more than I am Nora's husband.

True, not all moral problems are like the above, and in some cases reading a novel may help in the way Hare suggests. Certainly this is true outside morality. I imagine that, for example, a man living on a desert island would find that reading *Robinson Crusoe* solved many of his problems. Discovering himself in a like situation to Crusoe, he might learn what Crusoe (and presumably Defoe too) had learned about fending for oneself. *Within* morality, I suppose that Hare's own example is in many ways a good one. If I had never realised the misery which outdated divorce laws could cause, then a novel might change my opinion of the desirability of such laws. Just as, if I had never realised the human evils involved in processes of rapid industrialisation, I could discover a great deal from reading *Hard Times*. What must be noticed, however, is that in so far as we are concerned with the use of literature to change people's principles, then what is learned has nothing to do

---

12   Hare, *Freedom and Reason*, p. 183.

with the artistic merits of the works in question. The man on the desert island would find a do-it-yourself manual more help than *Robinson Crusoe*, you learn as much (in this sense) from the poorer parts of *Hard Times* (the scenes involving Stephen Blackpool, for example) as you do from the better sections, and you learn less from both than you do from Engels' *Condition of the British Working Class in 1844*.

This aspect of Hare's account is adequately illustrated if we consider what is involved in one of his claims which I mentioned earlier, namely that I can learn from a fictional character only in so far as his life has points of contact with my own. For it would seem to follow from this that the more the characters in any novel are generalised, the more likely we shall be to learn from them. A story of typical people facing typical situations will be *most* likely to be relevant to our moral thought. On the other hand, it is, of course, by no means the case that characters who typify certain human traits, or certain types of lives, are necessarily *artistically* superior to those who do not. Goldsmith, for example, is often *criticised* for creating characters (in, *e.g.*, *The Vicar of Wakefield*) of whom this is true, and though Uriah Heep and Squire Western are types in a way that, say, Heathcliff and Othello are not, this does not make them finer creations. Probably Hare would not deny this. He himself says of poets and novelists that 'their contributions to moral thought may not make them better artists',[13] and presumably he would think that these were cases in point. Unfortunately even this does not seem to be true. Do I learn less from Heathcliff's life than from that of Uriah Heep, for example? Or again, consider Turgenev's criticism of Balzac:

> All of his characters are so marvellously *typical*, they are exquisitely worked out and finished to the last detail — and yet ... not one of them possesses even one particle of the truth which makes the characters of Tolstoi's Cossacks, for instance, so vitally alive.[14]

For Turgenev, the lack of types among Tolstoi's Cossacks did not prevent us from learning from them, nor did the typicalness of

---

[13]   Hare, *Freedom and Reason*, p. 181.
[14]   Quoted in R.G. Kappler, 'Turgenev and French Literature', in *Comparative Literature* X (1968) p. 133.

Balzac's characters prevent Turgenev from accusing their author of a 'total lack of comprehension of artistic truth'.[15]

Hare's account, then, with its emphasis on the *general* nature of learning, on rules and principles, has the disadvantage of cutting off what makes something a great work of art from what enables one to learn from it. The novelist and the dramatist, he tells us, 'have claims on their skill, which have nothing to do with moral thinking but arise from the pursuit of artistic perfection for its own sake'.[16] And he can make such a distinction because he thinks of a novel or a play as simply an illustration of a certain type of problem in such a way that we become aware of those features which the artist regards as important. Nothing of what he says explains how literature and art may themselves *contribute* to morality. It explains only how problems and principles which have risen independently of art can be illustrated in works of literature. There is no conception that what an artist can contribute to morality may lie in precisely what makes him a creative artist. On this account, the only function of his creativeness is to enable him to dress up sets of antecedently established moral principles in situations which will bring home their force to his readers. At best the artist becomes merely a good public relations man for his own moral position.

If, however, this account is to be rejected, then it is necessary to show that the general account which provides its rationale, the theory that all learning is the learning of principles, is also mistaken. In particular, it is necessary to show that it is mistaken with respect to morality. For if it *were* the case that all moral learning is the learning of principles, then it would follow that all that art can contribute to morality would be further principles or general rules.

Fortunately, it is, I think, clear that this view is mistaken. That there are types of activity of which it would be a justifiable account is not, of course, denied. The learning of skills or techniques would seem to be one such sphere. If, for example, I teach someone to use a gun, then I teach him to do certain things and to refrain from others. The pupil is taught always to keep his eye on the target, to squeeze and not jerk the trigger, and so on. And, in one sense, this is all that he ever learns. Once he has learned the

---

[15]   Ibid.

[16]   Hare, *Freedom and Reason*, p. 181.

rules and can apply them, then he has learned all that I can teach him.

True, there will be things which as a matter of fact he does not learn by learning rules. There are generally limits to what can be taught in this way, and though one may learn how to load the gun by memorising certain simple principles, this method would hardly be appropriate if what was involved were, say, learning to judge distances or learning to make allowance for the wind. In many such cases the pupil is normally taught by demonstration, not by precept. But the limits in question are practical ones. They do not indicate a point beyond which it would be a sign of confusion to govern one's conduct by principles, but rather a point beyond which principles become so complicated that though in theory they could be imparted to a pupil, as a matter of fact this is never done. It is also the case that when a man has mastered the rules, he may then cease to make explicit reference to them in his shooting. A skilled marksman may score a bull's-eye without ever being able to formulate any general principles governing this operation. Nevertheless, what he does *is* governed by general rules, and to discuss, assess or criticise what he does is to apply these rules. In firing a gun there is nothing which the rules do not cover. To shoot well is to obey these rules.

But morality is not a skill, and though a man cannot learn anything without being taught some principles, without his being taught that some actions are good, others evil, he will not have learned much if this is *all* that he learns. In Theobald Pontifex (in Butler's *Way of All Flesh*) we see how a man may have learned and live by principles and yet be a moral failure. For Theobald, as for his wife Christina, morality is comprised in a list of actions and principles of action. They have learned that there are certain things which they may do, and others which they may not do. Like Hare, they think of moral development, both their own and that of their children, as the adoption or inculcation of new or modified principles. Christina's advice to her son, Ernest, we are told, 'came invariably to the same result, namely, that he ought to have done something else, or ought not to go on doing as he proposed',[17] and her attitude towards her own virtues and vices displays the same limitations. When, shortly after her marriage,

---

[17]   S. Butler, *The Way of All Flesh*, The Travellers' Library (London: Jonathan Cape, 1926) p. 230.

Christina suffers doubts about her own moral purity, these doubts lead, not to any increased moral insight or understanding, but to the adoption of a new principle, to a prohibition on the eating of certain foods.

Theobald and Christina can justify all their actions in terms of the principles which they possess. 'They had', says Butler, 'chapter and verse for everything they had either done or left undone.'[18] And though there are elements of self-deception in their characters, neither is simply a cheap hypocrite like Theobald's father, George Pontifex. By contrast with him, Theobald is a tolerably sincere man. According to Hare, then, I think that one would have to say that Theobald and Christina had learned all that they could about morality. But to me this seems quite clearly a mistake. Indeed the picture with which Butler presents us is, on the contrary, of two people who are remarkably lacking in moral understanding. Their lives, far from being perfectly virtuous, show a particular kind of perversion of morality.

In saying that the Pontifexes are examples of moral corruption, I am not saying that they live by corrupt principles, that they do one thing where I should be inclined to do another. I imagine that Theobald's beliefs would be shared by many people who would nevertheless want also to say that he presents an unfavourable moral spectacle. For the corruption is more deeply-rooted than this, and though we see it in Theobald's immediate decision to dissociate himself from his son, Ernest, when the latter is sent to prison, we see it also when he reverses this decision. Theobald's own explanation of the change is illuminating. 'I am unwilling', he tells Ernest, 'to have recourse to a measure which would deprive you of your last connecting link with respectable people.'[19] If one were asked why this remark shows a moral corruption, one would of course think of its self-righteousness. But if someone thought that were all that was wrong with it, then I should also want to point to the way in which Theobald's principles, his horror of doing what is in an external sense wrong, exert a tyranny over him here and stifle what feeling he has for his son. To say this, however, would not be to say that he should have adopted some *other* principles here. For it is clear that if Theobald's attitude were

---

18   Ibid., p. 280.
19   Ibid., p. 300.

thought of as stemming solely from obedience to *any* principles, it would show just the same corruption.

The distinction which I have in mind here comes out in another rather different example. In Alexander Kuprin's novel *The Pit*, a story of the lives of prostitutes in Tsarist Russia, a student, Likhonin, tries to save a peasant girl, Liubka, from her life in a brothel. He does so, however, not from any kindness towards the girl herself, but only from an, admittedly sincere, concern for certain egalitarian principles. 'You'll see,' he tells a friend, 'in a year or two, I shall give back to society a fine, worthy, industrious, human being, with a virginal soul.'[20] And it is this lack of true kindness or affection towards Liubka, his view of her as simply one of a class of people towards whom he has a moral duty to be kind, which corrupts their relationship, a corruption which becomes apparent in the small details of their life together:

> He put his arm around Liubka's waist and looked at her with tender, almost loving eyes. Yet at the same time he was thinking that his look was a paternal one.[21]

Like Theobald Pontifex, Likhonin's error lies, not in the principles which he accepts, but in supposing that morality is simply a matter of principles, simply a matter of doing one action rather than another. When Theobald 'forgives' his son, when Likhonin takes Liubka from the brothel, both see themselves as doing their moral duty. Certainly, they act in accordance with their principles. But what both fail to see is that there is more to morality than this, that it concerns also the spirit in which a man acts. Both, I should say, lack moral understanding. Perhaps some people would disagree. *They* may demand no more of a man than that he should live by the rules. But if they go on to suggest that there *can be* nothing more to morality than living by the rules, nothing more to the growth of moral understanding than the learning of principles, then I think that this is a confusion. It is a confusion which stems from a false analogy between moral understanding and the mastery of a skill, between insight and expertise.

---

[20]   Alexander Kuprin, *The Pit*, trans. B.G. Guerney (New York: Modern Library, 1959) p. 161.
[21]   Ibid., p. 154.

III

Unlike Theobald Pontifex, Likhonin learns from his experiences, comes to see the way in which his relationship with Liubka is a moral failure. But if, as I have maintained, he does not learn any new principles, what does this learning consist in? One thing, I think, is that he comes to see what is morally possible for him. Lacking, as he does, any real feelings for the victims of prostitution, he realises that it is not possible for him to do anything for them, or at least that any attempts to help them must be through channels which he had formerly despised as half-hearted, through organised charities and homes for fallen women. He realises that any personal intervention in their lives is fated to become merely cheap melodrama.

Now, though it must not be pressed too far, there is I think some analogy here with what can be learned from art. What the right word or phrase can do is to extend my notions of what is and what is not morally possible. Earlier in Kuprin's novel, Platonov, a journalist, is discussing with Likhonin how the evils of prostitution might be brought home to those who are at present willing simply to accept them. Likhonin asks why the journalist does not write a novel:

> 'I did try,' answered Platonov with a wry grin. 'But nothing came of it. The descriptions seemed banal, the words had no warmth. But I believe that some time, not now and not soon, perhaps fifty years hence, a writer of genius will appear. He will understand and absorb the agony and the wickedness of this life and will interpret it for us in simple, subtle images. And we shall say then, "Why we have seen and known all this, only we never thought that it *could* be so horrible".'[22]

The work of a great writer might show us just how it was possible for prostitution to be seen as horrible. But there would be no question here of this possibility being brought out in some *other* way. Platonov is not speaking of the mere depiction of something which anyone would see as horrible. Discussing Charles Kingsley's *Alton Locke*, one critic has remarked that the novel

> suffers from almost every fault in the vocabulary of literary criticism; yet its total impact continues to impress. Part of the interest is no doubt purely sociological: the descriptions of the

---

[22] Ibid., pp. 84–5.

tailor's sweat-shops, like comparable passages in a twentieth-century novel, *The Jungle*, do not depend for their effect on any special intensity of imaginative treatment, but simply on the revelation of facts, the horror of which speaks for itself.[23]

But this is not what Platonov has in mind. Those to whom he is speaking are quite well aware of the facts about prostitution. And a 'writer of genius' is needed precisely because the horror of these facts does *not* speak for itself. On the contrary, they are an accepted part of his contemporaries' lives. Where Kingsley simply draws our attention to things which we cannot help seeing as morally outrageous (and which would seem so, *however* they were presented to us), the writer of whom Platonov is thinking would show his audience how it was *possible* to see the familiar details of a prostitute's life as terrible. He would do so by virtue of his creative ability, his ability, as Platonov says, to 'interpret some insignificant little trifle, some pitiful little trait in such a way as to expose a reality so terrible, so frightening to the reader that his jaws would drop'.[24]

The distinction is an important one. For there is a tendency to suppose that if a writer can tell us anything about reality, about vice, or about war or love, then what he tells us must be a matter of fact. If a child reads a story like *Martin Chuzzlewit*, and supposes it to contain an account of some historical character, then he makes a conceptual mistake, a mistake about the logical grammar of what he reads. But if, on discovering his mistake, the child goes on to suppose that Dickens's novel has nothing to tell him, that there is nothing in it, he makes another conceptual mistake. For when a writer tells one something, this need not mean that he imparts new facts. If I said that Dickens's portrait of Pecksniff tells one something about hypocrisy, one might be misled into supposing that he gives one new information. But this is not the way in which critics talk:

> He can give us a couple of lines that say as much about the ruling vice of Mr Pecksniff as the rest of the hypocrites' adventures together. I am thinking of chapter III when Mr Pecksniff is having that conversation with Mrs Lupin in the Blue Dragon. He pulls off

---

[23]   Arnold Kettle, 'The Early Victorian Social-Problem Novel', in Boris Ford ed., *The Pelican Guide to English Literature*, Vol. VI: *From Dickens to Hardy* (Harmondsworth: Penguin, 1969) p. 184.
[24]   Kuprin, *The Pit*, pp. 83–4.

his gloves to warm his hands before the fire — warming them, says Dickens, 'as benevolently as if they were somebody else's, not his', and his back 'as if it were a widow's back, or an orphan's back, or a back that any less excellent man would have suffered to be cold'.[25]

If it were a matter of imparting information, then though a couple of lines might sum up a great deal (as, for example, statements about the average Welshman may condense a mass of information about Alun Jones, Owen Davies and others), they will always be a substitute for a more detailed account. But if I say that Dickens's words say what could not otherwise be said in a whole book, that they show how hypocrisy can be found in small details of a man's behaviour, or the evil which may lie behind a seemingly insignificant gesture, I do not mean that these words say succinctly what could nevertheless be said with greater accuracy by a more comprehensive account. In *that* sense, this would be simply untrue, for all that Dickens says in the lines in question is that Pecksniff warmed his hands in a certain manner, whereas elsewhere we learn of the hypocrite's life, his relations with his family and acquaintances, and of his ultimate unmasking. One thing which I should mean is that the lines themselves are worth reading. They are 'food for thought' in a way that a straightforward statement of fact never is. I may say of a man of my acquaintance, 'The Reverend Pecksniff preaches hell fire and damnation for mortal sin, but he keeps a mistress', and then I *do* tell you a fact about the minister's hypocrisy, something perhaps which you did not know. But if you are already aware of it, then you gain nothing from my telling you, any more than you gain something from yesterday's weather reports. By contrast, the remark about Mr Pecksniff could not tell you anything (in the sense with which we are here concerned) if you got nothing out of it on the second reading. For what you get comes from the way it is said.

The point which I wish to make is that though artists do not (or at least do not *qua* artists) present us with new facts, do not tell us how things are in that sense, it does not follow that there is *no* sense in which they are concerned with how things are. This conclusion has, however, seemed sufficiently obvious to some writers, writers of whom it has been said that 'indifference to truth' is 'part

---

[25]   R.C. Churchill, 'Charles Dickens', in B. Ford ed., *The Pelican Guide to English Literature: From Dickens to Hardy* (Harmondsworth: Penguin, 1963) pp. 122–3.

of their definition of the aesthetic'.[26] One example of this confusion is to be found in the article which we considered in the previous chapter, namely J.O. Urmson's 'What Makes a Situation Aesthetic?' As we saw, Urmson's alleged intention is to explain the difference between the approaches of an architect and a painter, or between those of a playwright and of a psychologist. And he wishes to equate these distinctions with the distinction between a preoccupation with appearances, with how things look, and on the other hand a concern with how they really are. What makes a painter's sketch of a building different from an architect's blueprint is that the former 'is concerned with a thing's looking somehow without concern for whether it really is like that; beauty, we may say, to emphasize the point, is not even skin-deep'.[27]

If I were to say that an architect's work shows a building only as it appears (as opposed to showing it as it really is), you would be justified in concluding that he is an indifferent architect. The projection is all wrong, perhaps, so that one could not build a house according to his specification, though it looks as though one could. Probably it would require a competent architect to correct his mistakes.

The distinction has a similar force within art and literature. If, for example, one says that the work of Dickens is concerned only with appearances (concerned only with how Mr Pecksniff's actions appear, not with how they really are), then this is a criticism. One implies that his writing is superficial ('not even skin-deep'). His approach, we might say, is a shallow one; he is concerned only with effects. And of course there are elements in his writing of which this would be true. It has been said, for instance, that the comedy of novels like *The Pickwick Papers* lacks depth compared with that of *Martin Chuzzlewit*. And there are aspects of the latter novel of which similar criticisms might be made—the plot, for example, with its use of old Martin Chuzzlewit's fortune as a *deus ex machina* to ensure a happy ending. But if one said that this was an example of shallowness, one would not say the same of *all* of *Martin Chuzzlewit*. It could not be said of the passage which Churchill quotes, for instance. And

---

[26]   R.W. Hepburn, 'Contemporary Aesthetics and the Neglect of Natural Beauty', in B. Williams and A. Montefiore eds., *British Analytical Philosophy* (London: Routledge & Kegan Paul, 1966) p. 305.

[27]   Urmson, 'What Makes a Situation Aesthetic?', p. 89.

this shows that the distinction between reality and mere appearance, between how things are and how they look, is one which is drawn *within* literature. It is not one which can be drawn between literature (or art in general) and any other form of activity. If one says that Dickens is sometimes (even always) concerned only with how things appear, not with how they really are, then, whether true or false, this is at least intelligible. But if one adds 'as compared with a writer like Freud', then it becomes nonsense. Dickens or Goya does not fail to do what the psychoanalyst or the architect succeeds in doing. They do not try to do it. No architect could show Goya where he had gone wrong. Only another painter could do that.

The great artist, then, does not impart new facts about hypocrisy or about love or about human degradation. Nor does he draw attention to facts which have been previously ignored. This is not what he tells us. What he does is to bring us to a clearer apprehension of these things; he shows us that it is possible to see them in a new light. And though this may lead to a change in the rules by which we govern our lives, this is not the artist's intention either. What we gain from his work is not information, nor new principles, but understanding. I think that an example may, to some extent, bring out what is involved here.

Some time in 1945, Malcolm had written a letter to Wittgenstein in which he spoke of the war as a 'boredom'. Wittgenstein replied:

> I want to say something about the war being a 'boredom'. If a boy said that school was an intense boredom, one might answer him that, if he could only get himself to learn what can really be learned there, he would not find it so boring. Now forgive me for saying that I can't help believing that an enormous lot can be learned about human beings in this war — if you keep your eyes open. And the better you are at thinking, the more you'll get out of what you see. For thinking is a digestion. If I'm writing in a preaching tone I'm just an ass. But the fact remains that if you're bored a lot it means that your mental digestion isn't what it should be. I think that a good remedy for this is sometimes opening your eyes wider. Sometimes a book helps a little, *e.g.* Tolstoi's *Hadshi Murat* wouldn't be bad.[28]

---

[28]   N. Malcolm, *Ludwig Wittgenstein — A Memoir* (Oxford: Oxford University Press, 1958) p. 41.

One might say that Malcolm's remark, like that of the child whom Wittgenstein mentions, showed a lack of imagination. Malcolm had a limited notion of what was involved in war, and of what could be learned from it. Presumably he wanted only that it should finish.

In his reply, Wittgenstein did not try to teach Malcolm any new principles. He thought that it would be stupid to write in a 'preaching tone'. Nor did he think that *Hadshi Murat* would teach Malcolm principles. It has often been remarked by critics that unlike many of the author's later works, *Hadshi Murat* is relatively uninfluenced by his moralist views,[29] and it is clear that the lack of dogma, the absence of a 'preaching tone', was precisely one of the things which Wittgenstein valued in the book. Malcolm himself later quotes Wittgenstein as saying that 'when Tolstoi just tells a story, he impresses me far more than when he addresses the reader'.[30]

But nor, of course, did Wittgenstein try to impart to Malcolm new facts about war, to turn his attention from what he now found boring to other things which might interest him. If he had regarded Malcolm as simply ill-informed, then Wittgenstein might have advised him to read the newspapers or to study military strategy. This would have been one way to change Malcolm's attitude, but again if this were the sort of change which Wittgenstein had had in mind, he would scarcely have recommended *Hadshi Murat*. The story of a mid-nineteenth-century Tartar chieftain would have been unlikely to give much information about a mid-twentieth-century war.

Nevertheless, Wittgenstein certainly thought that a work of literature could have some influence on a man's ideas about war, that reading *Hadshi Murat* might open Malcolm's eyes in some way. And I hope that my remarks in this essay have given some idea of how this might be so. Reading *Hadshi Murat* might help because in the way Tolstoi described the life and death of Hadshi Murat—in, for example, the comparison which runs throughout the story between the warrior's death and a thistle crushed by a plough—Malcolm might have found a new idea of how it is possible to think and speak of war and of its relationship to a host of

---

[29]   This is presumably what led Tolstoi to comment in a letter that he wrote it 'partly with pleasure, partly against the grain and with shame'.
[30]   Ibid., p. 43.

other things, to love, to power, to fear, and to life and death. In this way, Malcolm's concept of war would have been enriched and extended, so that there would be new things which he would say about it, and things which he would no longer say — like perhaps that it was all a boredom.

His idea of war would have been enriched in the way that our ideas about love may be enriched by seeing how parted lovers may be compared to a pair of compasses, so that we now see what the parting amounts to, what it is really like, or what it can be like, to be separated from one's loved one. Or as our ideas of hypocrisy may be enriched by discovering how it can show itself, not just in a man's treatment of his friends or the way he brings up his children, but in a man's dress or the way he warms his hands. In each of these cases what we gain is a new conception of some aspect of our lives, a new idea of what it makes sense to say about war or love or hypocrisy, and thus a new idea of the significance which they may have for us. And if someone then asks (like the sceptic whom I mentioned at the beginning of this essay), 'But does all this matter?', then the answer is that it does matter, not because it will necessarily make men more virtuous, and in particular not, as moralists like Tolstoi have supposed, because it will bring them into conformity with anyone's preconceived ideas of virtue, but because it is a part of knowing what kinds of things hypocrisy and war and love are.

Bibliography

Anderson, John, 'Art and Morality', *Australasian Journal of Philosophy and Psychology* 19 (3) 1941.

Bell, Clive, *Art* (London, Arrow Books, 1961).

Bradley, A.C., 'Poetry for Poetry's Sake', in *Oxford Lectures on Poetry* (London, Macmillan, 1914).

Brower, R.A., *Alexander Pope: The Poetry of Allusion* (Oxford: Oxford University Press, 1963).

Bullough, E., *Aesthetics*, ed. with an introduction by E.M. Wilkinson (London, Bowes & Bowes, 1957).

Butler, S., *The Way of All Flesh* (London, The Travellers' Library, 1926).

Cary, Joyce, *Mister Johnson* (Harmondsworth, Penguin Books, 1962).

Chesterton, G.K., 'Dombey and Son', in *Appreciation and Criticisms of the Works of Charles Dickens* (London, Dent, 1911).

Churchill, R.C., 'Charles Dickens', in *From Dickens to Hardy: A Guide to English Literature* (London, Cassell, 1961).

Hampshire, S., 'Logic and Appreciation', in *Aesthetics and Language*, ed. with an introduction by W. Elton (Oxford, Basil Blackwell, 1959).

Hare, R.M., *Freedom and Reason* (Oxford, Oxford University Press, 1963).

-----, *The Language of Morals* (Oxford, Oxford University Press, 1952).

Hepburn, R.W., 'Contemporary Aesthetics and the Neglect of Natural Beauty', in *British Analytic Philosophy*, ed. Bernard Williams and Alan Montefiore (London, Routledge & Kegan Paul, 1966).

Jefferson, D.W., 'An Approach to Swift', in *The Pelican Guide to English Literature*, vol. IV: *From Dryden to Johnson*, ed. Boris Ford (Harmondsworth, Penguin Books, 1970).

Kettle, Arnold, 'The Early Victorian Social Problem Novel', in *The Pelican Guide to English Literature*, vol. VI: *From Dickens to Hardy*, ed. Boris Ford (Harmondsworth, Penguin Books, 1970).

Kierkegaard, S., *Purity of Heart*, trans. and with an introduction by Douglas Steere (London, Fontana Books, 1966).

Lawrence, D.H., 'John Galsworthy', in *Selected Literary Criticism*, ed. Anthony Beal (London, Heinemann, 1955).

Leavis, F.R., *Anna Karenina and Other Essays* (London, Chatto & Windus, 1967).

Malcolm, Norman, *Ludwig Wittgenstein: A Memoir* (Oxford, Oxford University Press, 1958).

Marcus, Steven, *Dickens: From Pickwick to Dombey* (London, Chatto & Windus, 1965).

Mochulsky, Konstantin, *Dostoevsky: His Life and Work*, trans. with an introduction by M. Minihan (Princeton, Princeton University Press, 1967).

Moore, G.E., *Principia Ethica* (Cambridge, Cambridge University Press, 1960).

Orwell, George, 'Benefit of Clergy', in *Decline of the English Murder and other Essays* (Hamondsworth, Penguin Books, 1965).

-----, 'Mark Twain: The Licensed Jester', in *The Collected Essays, Journalism and Letters of George Orwell*, vol. II (London, Seeker & Warburg, 1968).

Pater, Walter, *Appreciations* (London, Macmillan, 1910).

Reid, L.A., *A Study in Aesthetics* (London, Allen & Unwin, 1931).

Rhees, Rush, 'Art and Philosophy', in *Without Answers* (London, Routledge & Kegan Paul, 1969).

Saw, R., 'Art and the Language of the Emotions', *Proceedings of the Aristotelian Society*, supp. vol. 36, 1962.

Sidney, Sir Philip, 'An Apology for Poetry', in *English Critical Essays, 16th–18th Centuries*, ed. E.D. Jones (The World's Classics, Oxford, 1922).

Stocks, J.L., 'The Limits of Purpose', in *Morality and Purpose*, ed. with an introduction by D.Z. Phillips (London, Routledge & Kegan Paul, 1969).

Tolstoi, Leo, *Anna Karenina*, trans. R.S. Townsend (London, Everyman's Library, 1939).

-----, 'Schoolboys and Art' and 'What is Art?', in *What Is Art? and Essays On Art* (Oxford, The World's Classics, 1930).

Twain, Mark, *Pudd'nhead Wilson* (London, Zodiac Press, 1955).

Urmson, J.O., 'What Makes a Situation Aesthetic?', *Proceedings of the Aristotelian Society*, supp. vol. 31, 1957.

Van Ghent, Dorothy, *The English Novel* (New York, Rinehart, 1953).

Whistler, J.M., 'The Ten-O-Clock Lecture', in *The Gentle Art of Making Enemies* (London, Heinemann, 1890).

Wilde, Oscar, 'The Critic As Artist' and 'The Decay of Lying', in *Complete Works of Oscar Wilde*, with an introduction by Vyvyan Holland (London, Collins, 1966).

-----, *The Picture of Dorian Gray* (Harmondsworth, Penguin Books, 1968).

Wittgenstein, L., *Remarks on the Foundations of Mathematics*, eds. G.E.M. Anscombe, R. Rhees & G. von Wright, trans. G.E.M. Anscombe (Oxford, Basil Blackwell, 1956).

-----, *Zettel*, eds. G.E.M. Anscombe & G. von Wright, trans. G.E.M. Anscombe (Oxford, Basil Blackwell, 1967).

Part 2

Art

1

Learning from a Novel[1]

There is always a danger in philosophy, that what is intended initially as simply one explanation of some form of activity, should come to be regarded as the only possible form of explanation. Nor does this danger seem to be diminished where a philosopher's aim is itself that of attacking limited notions of what is possible as an explanation. This is one, though not the only, reason why it is often the case that what at first appears as a revolutionary and illuminating solution of certain philosophical difficulties, later gives rise to even more intractable problems of its own.

When Gilbert Ryle wrote *The Concept of Mind*, he numbered among his aims that of curing what he saw as a traditional obsession among philosophers with propositional knowledge as the form of knowledge *par excellence*. More generally, he wished to attack a limited view of the nature of qualities of mind, the view that all intelligent activity, all forms of learning, knowledge, understanding were to be explained as forms of intellectual activity, as different species of knowledge that something is the case.

> There are many activities which directly display qualities of mind, yet are neither themselves intellectual operations nor yet effects of intellectual operations. Intelligent practice is not a step child of theory.[2]

Intelligent practice is not a matter of propositional knowledge, or 'knowledge that' at all. It is a matter of 'knowledge how'. To speak of a man's powers of reasoning, his knowledge of football or his skill at cards is not to refer to a list of facts which he possesses.

---

1   First published in G.N.A. Vesey ed., *Philosophy and the Arts* (London: MacMillan, 1972).
2   *The Concept of Mind* (London: Hutchinson, 1949) p. 26.

Rather it is to credit him with the ability to perform tasks in accordance with certain rules of procedure. Knowledge how is exercised in the observance of these rules. Its absence lies in their breach.

With the distinction between knowledge how and knowledge that in his hands, Ryle proceeds to wreak havoc among traditional theories of knowledge, the will, emotion and the intellect. And in this he has been both praised and condemned. But it is not to my purpose in this paper either to praise or to condemn Ryle's application of the distinction. Nor, at least in one sense, shall I be concerned to criticise the distinction itself. Despite suggestions to the contrary, Ryle's contrast between propositional and executive knowledge may be a perfectly illuminating account of the differences between certain cases of learning, discovering, understanding. My objection is that it has been presented as more than that. What should be a flexible distinction between certain forms which intelligence may take has, in the hands of certain philosophers, shown signs of hardening into a rigid dichotomy. There are indications that the disjunction 'either knowledge how or knowledge that', 'either theoretical or practical' is itself tending to become a model for the form which any example of knowledge or understanding must take, so that philosophers like R.M. Hare[3] are now found assuming that since, for example, what we learn from reading a novel or a poem is manifestly not to be explained as a list of facts, it must be explicable in terms of a list of principles of conduct.

In this paper I shall try to show that such attempted explanations inevitably lead to failure. The dichotomy of knowledge how and knowledge that, at least in the form given by Ryle, is unable to account for certain cases with which we are all perfectly familiar. In particular I shall suggest that the case which I have just mentioned is of this sort, and that an unbiased study of what it means to speak of a man's learning from literature leads to the destruction of the dichotomy in question.

I

The seeds of this destruction are to be found in the account given by Ryle himself, particularly in the account of what is variously

---

3   *Freedom and Reason* (Oxford: Oxford University Press, 1963) ch. 9.

termed 'executive' knowledge, 'practical' knowledge, and 'knowledge how'. As we have seen, it is a pervasive theme of Ryle's book that intelligence is to be explained not (or at least not primarily) as the knowledge or ignorance of this or that truth, but as the possession of 'know-how'. Of course, in itself this is sufficiently vague, but it can, I think, be rendered more precise if we turn our attention to a collection of terms which feature predominantly in Ryle's account of knowledge how. I have in mind his equation of 'acting intelligently' with 'acting efficiently', 'skilfully', 'melodically', 'shrewdly', 'competently', his failure to distinguish between 'teaching' or 'education' and 'training', his continual reference to the different forms of intelligence as 'skills' or 'competences', and so on. For what is obvious about these ways of speaking is that they are most naturally used when what we are discussing is a man's mastery or a method or technique, that is, his ability to employ a set of established procedures in order to bring about certain predetermined results. Thus, to take what is obviously one of Ryle's central examples, the intelligent marksman, the man who knows how to shoot accurately, is not someone who can call to mind numerous facts about the use of small arms, but someone who shoots according to the rules. And when we speak of rules in these sorts of context, what we are thinking of are primary recipes for achievement within the sphere of activity in question — that is to say, rules of skill. What we expect from a crack shot is perfect technique.

That Ryle's is an adequate account of the sort of intelligence manifested in some forms of activity is of course undeniable. It is, for the most part, a good account of his own central examples, of those with which he chooses to deal in any detail. Bur it is I think evident that the account is in many cases not being offered by Ryle as merely an analysis of certain forms of intelligent activity but as an account of the nature of intelligent activity itself. Were this not made clear in a series or explicit statements of quite unrestricted generality — 'Intelligence lies ... in the ability or inability to do certain things', 'Understanding is a part of knowing how' — it would nevertheless be apparent from the examples to which the account is successively applied — pruning trees, tying a reef knot, having skill at cards or prudence in investment, planning military strategy, obeying one's conscience, writing poetry, and so on. Thus, when on page twenty-eight Ryle asks rhetorically, 'What is involved in our descriptions of people as knowing how to make and appreciate jokes, to talk grammatically, to play chess, to fish, or to argue?' his question at least suggests that there is *one* thing involved in these different activities, that *one* model will serve to explain the type or excellence appropriate to each of them. And on the face of it, this might not seem particularly plausible. For why *should* it be assumed that what is to be found in the ability to make or appreciate jokes will also be found in the ability to talk grammatically or the ability to fish? Indeed at first sight it might appear that one thing which characterises the ability to make jokes, that is to say originality or creativity, is fairly conspicuously lacking from a mastery of English grammar or skill with a fishing rod. Normally success in either or the latter activities depends on the agent's acting in pretty firmly established ways. A man will not be said to speak grammatically until he constructs sentences in *precisely* the ways laid down by certain authorities, teachers, parents or perhaps television newsreaders. And it would be the height of irrationality for an angler to think of departing from the traditional techniques at least until he had acquired very con-siderable understanding of, or competence in those techniques. The techniques might, it is true, be poor ones. Still, it would be quite irrational for anyone to begin by assuming this to be so.

With a joke it is quite different. One of Whistler's barbed wise-cracks once elicited from the young Oscar Wilde the admiring response, 'I wish I'd said that'. It is said that Whistler, who had no great regard for Wilde, replied grimly, 'You will, Oscar, you will.' I do not know what Whistler's original remark was, or the context in which it was made. But presumably one important aspect of it lay in its unpredictability. Just this quality would be what was lacking from Wilde's subsequent plagiarisms. Wilde, Whistler was implying, was the sort of man who would turn original remarks into clichés. By contrast, Whistler's reputation for wit rested upon his ability to avoid well-trodden conversational paths, his ability to turn a conversation in unexpected directions. One might say that Whistler's remarks were humorous at least in part because they went beyond any of the rules governing polite conversation.

Unlike the ability to fish or to speak grammatically, the possession of a sense of humour does not seem to rest on the mastery of established rules or techniques. Indeed, the fact that it is natural to speak of the 'rules of grammar' though not of the 'rules of humour', of the 'rules of fishing' but of the 'ability to make jokes' rather than the 'rules for making jokes' should give pause for thought here. For it is worth noting that though Ryle makes considerable capital from the initial implausibility of supposing that the wit simply knows certain facts of which his audience is unaware, precisely such an implausibility is to be found in the suggestion that he alone has been initiated into some method, some set of rules which they have not mastered. To talk grammatically or to fish competently is to obey established rules in a way that making or appreciating jokes conspicuously is not.

Now Ryle, obsessed as he is to fit any form of intelligent activity into his preconceived model of 'executive knowledge' is forced to deny just these sorts of difference. This is especially apparent in a passage which might at first seem to point the opposite conclusion.

> The wit, when challenged to cite the maxims, or canons, by which he constructs and appreciates jokes, is unable to answer. He knows how to make good jokes and how to detect bad ones, but he cannot tell us or himself any recipes for them.[4]

One might be forgiven for supposing that in this passage Ryle is in fact denying that there are any such recipes. But this would be a mistake. For according to Ryle the reason why the wit is unable when challenged to cite the rules of wit is not that there are no such rules but that they are unformulated. And this of course is a possible case. As Ryle remarks elsewhere, methodologies presuppose an application of the methods of which they are the products. It is possible for a man to fish according to the principles formulated in Walton's *Compleat Angler* without himself being able to formulate them. What is curious is that Ryle seems automatically to assume that what is true here of fishing will also be true or humour, that whenever an activity is carried on without reference to rules this will be merely because the rules are (as yet) unformulated, and to ignore a rather more obvious possibility, namely that the wit is unable to formulate the principles of humour for the simple reason that there is nothing to formulate.

Now, one reason for Ryle's failure to consider this possibility lies in his recognition that the sphere of humour is one within which it makes sense to speak of a man's having performed correctly or incorrectly, well or badly. For one of the main attractions of the notion of a rule, as Ryle uses it, is that where it is applicable, it enables us to explain what it is for a performance to fail or succeed. Thus, for example, the marksman condemning a

---

4   *The Concept of Mind*, p. 30.

pupil's use of the rifle can defend or explain his judgement by an appeal to those rules contravened by his pupil's practice. So it is tempting to assume that if it is possible, as it clearly is, to identify among a comic's performances those which fail and those which succeed, if it is possible to appreciate a good joke and to distinguish it from a bad one, then here as well there must be rules, albeit unformulated, in terms of which the distinction is made.

And of course it *is* true that a knowledge of rules may also be relevant to the appreciation of humour. For a joke is made within the context of the rules governing language, and the man who fails to grasp these rules will miss the point of the joke. What does not follow is that the rules in question can be regarded as constituting a technique for appreciating jokes, or that they will be any help in explaining why one joke is good and another bad. In *Pudd'nhead Wilson*, Mark Twain begins his portrait of the hero of the story with an example of the latter's 'deadpan humour':

> He made his fatal remark the first day he spent in the village, and it 'gaged' him. He had just made the acquaintance of a group of citizens when an invisible dog began to yelp and snarl and howl and make himself very comprehensively disagreeable, whereupon young Wilson said, much as one who is thinking aloud —
> 'I wish I owned half of that dog.'
> 'Why?' somebody asked.
> 'Because I would kill my half.'
> The group searched his face with curiosity, with anxiety even, but they found no light there, no expression that they could read. They fell away from him as from something uncanny, and went into privacy to discuss him. One said:
> ' 'Pears to be a fool.'
> ' 'Pears?' said another. '*Is,* I reckon you better say.'
> 'Said he wished he owned *half* of the dog, the idiot,' said a third. 'What did he reckon would become of the other half if he killed his half? Do you reckon he thought it would live?'[5]

The way in which language is used in Wilson's joke does stand in some relation to certain rules, namely to the rules governing the uses of the words 'half', 'kill', etc. One could not understand the joke unless one understood the way in which these words are normally used. If one wished I suppose one could say that the

---

[5]   M. Twain, *Pudd'nhead Wilson* (London: Zodiac Press, 1955) p. 37.

normal use, the rules for their use in *other* contexts, lends itself to the sort of joke that Wilson makes. But this is far from saying that the joke is itself an application of these rules. Indeed Wilson's audience regard him as an idiot precisely because his remark is so plainly not an application of the linguistic rules which they have all been taught, but on the contrary breaks them. And though an understanding of these rules is certainly relevant to an understanding of Wilson's joke, though for example one way (and indeed so far as I can see the *only* way) in which one might explain the joke to someone who failed to understand it, would be to indicate the relationship of Wilson's comment to the rules ('But, don't you see? You *can't* kill half a dog'), this can scarcely be regarded as itself a rule or method for appreciating the joke. Wilson's audience understood this relationship perfectly, though they were unaware that a joke had even been made. And while a similar relationship would have been involved if Wilson had remarked that he wished to breed half of the dog or enter half of it into a dog-show, his remark would no longer have constituted a joke at all, or at best an extremely pointless one.

When Ryle speaks of the rules, maxims, canons, methods or techniques according to which jokes are constructed or appreciated then, it is by no means clear what application his remarks have. Whatever rules or principles may be relevant to the appreciation of humour, they do not themselves seem to provide a criterion for distinguishing between good and bad jokes. Nor can this conclusion be avoided by arguing, as some seem to wish to, that since the creative comic cannot be understood by recourse to any established rules, then his remarks must be seen as bringing with them their own rules, or as involving an appeal to rules which he himself has invented. For this would be merely an attempt to retain the vocabulary in question where it has already been shown to be inapplicable. If on entering a restaurant I am told that the establishment has a rule against serving philosophy lecturers, then I shall probably be both surprised and displeased. But if I am then told that this is a rule which has been specially invented to suit my particular case, I shall certainly not conclude that the rule in question is one of that particular species which characterises creative acts. On the contrary, I shall assume with good reason that there is in fact no such rule and that the proprietor is simply indulging a private whim.

Ryle's own example of humour brings out certain characteristics of his philosophical procedure in *The Concept of Mind*. We have seen that, faced with any example of intelligent activity, Ryle is inclined to explain the activity as an instance of knowledge how, or the application of a method for attaining certain results, as a set of rules or principles of skill. And we have also seen that he shows precisely the same inclination even where the examples with which he is faced will not support such an interpretation but on the contrary underline its inadequacies. What we are faced with here, therefore, is explicable only as a philosophical prejudice about the nature of intelligence, a prejudice which, I have suggested, is to be seen at work in Ryle's discussion of the form of intelligence manifested in making or appreciating jokes.

Of course, in saying this I am not criticising the negative part of Ryle's thesis. I am not, for instance, suggesting that the possession of a sense of humour is explicable as a type of factual knowledge. My point is that there are types of learning, understanding and knowledge which cannot be understood as *either* the knowledge of facts *or* the grasp of principles or techniques. And I want now to turn to the main example of my paper, which, unlike those I have so far discussed, is not mentioned by Ryle except in passing. I shall try to show that this oversight is no merely contingent matter, but is on the contrary necessitated by the sort of account offered by Ryle, and to this end I shall begin by indicating certain characteristics of the types of learning, knowledge and under-standing discussed in *The Concept of Mind*, which are not, I think, shared by the examples which I have in mind.

II

When a man learns a fact or a technique, learns that something is the case or learns how to perform some task, then what he learns is only contingently related to the source of his information. For example, he learns the history of the Trade Union movement from a course of lectures, where he might have learned the same facts from a history book. Or he is taught to mend a fuse while apprenticed to an electrician, where a do-it-yourself manual could have imparted the same technique. In a way it is even a matter of indifference for what is learnt whether a man is taught by a good or bad teacher. Presumably we shall not be inclined to describe a teacher as good unless pupils tend to learn more thoroughly under his guidance, remember what he has taught them more easily. Nevertheless, there is no contradiction in the assertion that though my first history teacher was a wonderful teacher, he did not impart to me as much information as did the unimaginative drudge who succeeded him. And in neither case need an account of what I have learned involve a reference either to my teacher or to anything which he has said to me. Indeed, it is often true of these sorts of learning (what Ryle continually suggests is true of *all* learning) that a pupil's proficiency depends at least in part on his *ceasing* to pay attention to his teacher's precise words. If he has been well taught, he will have learnt to concentrate on the activity in which he is engaged, rather than on describing that activity. So that, if asked to put the knowledge he has acquired in to words, he may even be unable to do so.

Let us now contrast this with a rather different case. Let us imagine a man who finds that his life has gone sour on him. By this I do not mean that he regrets the particular course which his life has taken, so that a change in his fortune might immediately bring about a new perspective, but rather that he fails to see interest or significance in anything. Like Mill in his youth, he has 'worn out all pleasures' and feels that 'life, to all who possess the good things of it, must necessarily be a vapid, uninteresting thing'.[6]

Such a man may ask himself or others how he can go on living. But it is important for my purpose to notice that this question is unlikely to be a request for information, or for a method of overcoming his difficulties. This is connected with the point that unlike problems relating to the acquisition of knowledge or the mastery of a technique, problems about the meaning of life are personal problems, not general ones. There is, for example, no such thing as 'finding meaning in someone's life for him' as we may speak of obtaining information for someone, nor would it show much intelligence in the face of such problems to reply, 'Well, you'll just have to try to snap out of it', or 'Why don't you take up golf?' Such remarks would have a sense only when one suspected that the man in question was insincere, or perhaps deceiving himself about the depth of his problem. They would not be ways of dealing with a serious case of despair.

Nevertheless I do not think it senseless to speak of ways in which such despair might be overcome. Let us suppose, for example, that by chance the man in my example one day picks up a novel or a poem. Absorbed by what he reads he goes on, reads it

---

6   J.S. Mill, *Autobiography* (London: Longmans, Green, Reader & Dyer, 1873) p. 146.

again, possibly many times. And afterwards he is no longer inclined to think or speak of the world in the same way. The significance which events have for him is changed, and he now sees a new meaning in life. Perhaps he is inclined to say, 'I never thought that it could be possible to get much out of this life, but Wordsworth or Tolstoi has shown me that it is'.

Now it seems to me clear that this example differs quite radically from the examples of learning which I have mentioned so far, the learning of facts or of techniques. For though we may speak in this case also of the man having learnt something — of his having learnt what life is really like, or of his having learnt that certain things are possible for him — it no longer makes much sense to speak of alternative ways of learning these things. If someone tells me that it is possible to drive a car up a wall, say by a discussion of the laws of gravity and the principle of the internal combustion engine, then he may change my ideas of what is possible in this way. But just the same change might have been brought about in another way, for instance by his driving the car up a wall in front of my very eyes. On the other hand, though we may speak of a novel or a poem's bringing a man to see what is possible for him, we can no longer conceive of these possibilities existing independently of the way in which he was brought to recognise them. If asked what he has learned from the novel or the poem, the man may tell me to read it more carefully. Or he may read it himself emphasising what he takes to be the correct expression. But if this is unsuccessful, then he will not offer an alternative statement of the work. For what it has to tell us is internally related to the work itself.

Precisely what this claim amounts to can be seen in another rather more specific case. In his autobiography, Edwin Muir recalls how [writing] a poem [*Ballad of Hector in Hades*] once broke the hold which certain memories had over him. As a child he had been chased home under humiliating circumstances by a school-friend, and had thereafter been unable to think of the incident without shame and terror.

> I got rid of that terror almost thirty years later in a poem describing Achilles chasing Hector round Troy ... The poem cleared my conscience. I saw that my shame was a fantastically elongated shadow of a childish moment imperfectly remembered ... and I could at last see the incident whole by seeing it as happening, on a great and tragic scale, to someone else. After I had

written the poem the flight itself was changed, and with that my feelings towards it.[7]

This differs from my earlier example in that the agent learns from creation rather than contemplation, but the cases are similar in that in both a man is brought to see a new significance in his life. I speak of an agent's seeing a new significance 'in *his* life' rather than 'in life' or 'in the world', because, at least in the case of Muir, I think that this is more natural. But I doubt whether the distinction could be pressed very far. In a radio discussion, Dylan Thomas once remarked that, 'A good poem helps to change the shape and significance of the universe, helps to extend everyone's knowledge of himself and the world around him.'[8] But to suppose that understanding the world around one and understanding oneself or one's own life can be regarded as distinct in this context would show a failure to grasp Thomas's point. Part of what would be meant by speaking of Muir's having learned from writing *Ballad of Hector in Hades*, would be that the poem made a difference to his life, made a difference to the significance which be attached to the incident from his childhood for instance. Nor could this change be understood except by reference to the sort of man Muir was, to the difficulties and problems in his life, and to the sort of understanding which he brought to the poem.

This understanding is something which will differ with different people. It may even be completely absent, for the sort of learning which is involved here is not possible for everyone. I do not mean that not everyone is capable of writing poetry, though that is of course true, but rather that the way in which literature contributes to a man's understanding depends partly at least on what he brings to the study of a novel or a poem. This is why it may deepen one man's understanding where it says nothing at all to another. 'Lessing', Goethe is reported to have said, 'was of the very highest understanding and only one equally great could truly learn from him. To a half faculty he was dangerous.'[9] On a rather more mundane plane, parents and teachers may wonder whether a play or a novel is not beyond the grasp of a child of a certain age, while recognising that it would present no difficulties for older children.

---

[7] E. Muir, *An Autobiography* (London: Hogarth Press, 1980) p. 42.

[8] D. Thomas, 'On Poetry: A Discussion', *Encounter* III, November 1954, p. 23.

[9] J.P. Eckermann, *Conversations of Goethe* (London: Everyman, 1973) p. 110.

Yet though people may differ in what, if anything, they learn from the same work of literature, it does not follow that what is learnt can be specified independently of the work itself, though this is a tempting conclusion. To see why the temptation should be resisted, we must recognise that the sort of learning from literature which I have mentioned is possible only where the poem or the novel is good of its kind. The man in my first example would not have spoken of coming to see a new significance in his life, had he regarded what he read as an artistic failure. Muir's poem could not have brought him an insight into his childhood cowardice, has it not been an example of artistic care, has he not laboured over the form of the poem. For its form of expression, the vividness or power of the language in a poem, is bound up with what enables us to learn from it.

The same is not true of the forms of learning on which Ryle concentrates. For here the linguistic formulation, the way in which things are said, does not have the importance which it does with a work of literature. Of course, this does not mean that it has *no* importance. If a pupil is to benefit from his teaching, it is important that he should be given correct information, or that the principles which he is taught should be adequate to the situation which he is likely to face. But when one speaks of a piece of information as false or of the statement of a maxim or principle as inadequate, then one rejects a form of words because, though they *might* be used to make a true assertion, *as it happens* they are being used to make a false one. If someone tells me that the President of the United States is a Red Indian, or that it is advisable to swim the breast stroke with one's legs motionless, then I shall reject what he says, not on the grounds that it would be a misleading account of any conceivable situation, but on the grounds that it is inapplicable to a particular situation, namely that in which we find ourselves. The man tells me something. But he tells me something which, it so happens, is false.

These sorts of considerations will not take us far if we are trying to explain what, if anything, it means to speak of truth or falsity in literature. For here the particular words which are used have an importance which they do not in the statement of facts or of rules. When a man formulates a principle incorrectly, asserts for example that gooseberry bushes should be planted 3'6" apart, we may be inclined to say that, though wrong, what he says is not far wrong. 'Actually', we reply, 'they should be planted 4' apart, but still, what you say is close enough.' But though a man's

understanding of literature may come out in the way he reads to
his wife or children, if he misreads a line of poetry, say, and when
corrected, replies, 'Oh well, I wasn't far out', we shall have difficulty in seeing how he could ever have got anything from it. Our
inclination would be to say that he had missed the point of the
line. A man who appreciates the truth in a poem, shows a concern
with the particular words which the poet uses. For him it is not
merely a contingent matter that these words are capable of telling
him something.

In the same way, the falsity in a poem or a novel is something
which comes out in the writer's style, in its tendency to run to
cliché for instance, or in the use of phrases simply for cheap
effects. Muir speaks of the way in which a man's understanding
may be corrupted by literature. 'There is', he tells us, 'as well as
exquisite wit, a sickly, graveyard strain in Heine's poetry. It was
this that attracted me now. I battened on tombs and shrouds.'[10]
But when he comes to characterise the falsity in Heine's thought,
he does not present us with some statement or some principle
which he regards as mistaken. Rather it is Heine's style, the
repetitive nature of his poems which he emphasises.

> The word *einsam* ('lonely') recurs over and over again in Heine's
> poetry; the lonely cottage, the lonely man in his grave, the lonely
> pine-tree, and always the lonely Heine. I steeped myself in that
> sweet poison.[11]

One might contrast what Muir says here with the way in which,
for example, people speak of the harmful effects of television
violence. It is sometimes said that the portrayal of violence in
people's homes will eventually prove harmful to them. But I do
not imagine that anyone has ever supposed this to be the only way
in which such corruption can be brought about. Television
violence is generally supposed to corrupt in much the same way
as exposure to, say, real-life violence, or as violence in the cinema.
But when Muir spoke or the way in which a study of Heine's
writings might corrupt or cheapen a man's understanding of
death, and later went on to contrast him with Baudelaire, a man
who was genuinely possessed by death and not merely coquetting

---

10   *An Autobiography*, p. 144.
11   Ibid., p. 146.

with 'the shroud and the tomb',[12] he did not have in mind something which might have been induced by different means. The falsity of Heine's thought, its capacity for corruption, was a falsity in the way he wrote, the falsity or a writer who thinks in stereotypes ('the shroud and the tomb'), whose words and phrases have lost their force through constant repetition in literary contexts. It was presumably this force which he *found* in Baudelaire. I think that this would be what was meant if one spoke of the truth in the latter's work.

Certainly it is this sense of 'truth' and 'falsity' of which Joyce Cary is thinking when he says that a man who reads a great novel like *Lord Jim* must feel, 'That is important, that is true', and then contrasts this sense with the sense in which one might say, 'I suppose that is true, but I've heard it before.'[13] If the man who reads *Lord Jim* were to say, 'I suppose that is true, but I've heard it before', then he could not be speaking of artistic truth. For here what makes it true and what makes it original, memorable, striking, cannot be distinguished in this way. This would be inexplicable if we were thinking of the truth of a factual statement or of a principle or maxim, for when a man imparts information or new techniques, then what makes his words memorable or important is the context in which they occur. It is likely that a swimming instructor who emphasises a pupil's first lesson by throwing him in the deep end, will give the pupil cause to remember his words. And I shall probably remember the first man who tells me my name is to appear in the New Year's Honours Lists in a way that I shall not remember the fifth. Though both will say something equally true (or false), it is possible here to distinguish the truth of what is said and its importance, what makes the statement striking or memorable on a particular occasion. A true statement may be of the utmost importance or trivial in the extreme.

It would make no sense to speak of a trivial or everyday artistic truth. Because it is not the occasion of its utterance, but the character of the language itself which makes the poem memorable, it will still be capable of fixing our attention at other times and places. And though it is true that a man may remember his first

---

[12]   *An Autobiography*, p. 146.
[13]   Joyce Cary, *Art and Reality* (Cambridge: Cambridge University Press, 1958) p. 4.

contact with the work or Milton or Coleridge for the rest of his life, it would be a mediocre poem where what impressed him could not survive a second reading. Thomas Mann brings out how an artist's concern for the words he uses goes with what makes his work important for us:

> And a sentence which must be heard twice must be fashioned accordingly. It must—I do not speak of beauty—possess a certain high level, and symbolic suggestion, which will make it worthy to sound again in any epic future. So every point becomes a standing ground, every adjective a decision, and it is clear that such work is not to be produced off-hand.[14]

Mann was I suppose speaking here primarily of his own work. But although it would obviously be false to say that all literature displays *this* degree of care, his remarks are not merely an indication of the attitude which *he* brought to his writing. They are philosophical rather than biographical. For they indicate the *sort* of concern for detail which makes it possible for a novel to teach us something. Similarly, the failure to see what a writer has to tell you, is a failure to grasp the importance which details have in his work, a failure to see why only the particular words which he uses will do. In his first lecture on Shakespeare, Coleridge brings out perfectly how these things go hand in hand.

> I was (he says) one day admiring one of the falls of the Clyde; and ruminating upon what descriptive term could be most fully applied to it, I came to the conclusion that the epithet 'majestic' was the most appropriate. While I was still contemplating the scene a gentleman and a lady came up, neither of whose faces bore much stamp of superior intelligence and the first words the gentleman uttered were 'It is very majestic'. I was pleased to find such a confirmation of my opinion, and I complimented the speaker upon the best choice of epithet, saying that he had used the best word that could have been selected from our language. 'Yes Sir,' replied the gentleman. 'I say it is very majestic; it is sublime; it is beautiful; it is grand; it is picturesque.' 'Ay (added the lady) it is the prettiest thing I ever saw.' I own that I was not a little disconcerted.[15]

---

14   Quoted in D.H. Lawrence, *Selected Literary Criticism* (London: Heinemann, 1955) p. 126.

15   S.T. Coleridge, *Seven Lectures on Shakespeare and Milton* (London: Chapman and Hall, 1856) p. 10.

By treating the words 'majestic', 'sublime', 'picturesque', and so on, as if they were interchangeable, Coleridge's acquaintances showed their failure to understand what he himself had seen, namely that only the word 'majestic' possessed the right force to bring out the true character of the scene before them. This is not something which one might find in another word, even in a synonym, and for this reason I think it unfortunate to try (as many writers do) to explain it as a matter of the 'association' of words. Joyce Cary shows signs of this confusion when he notes, quite correctly, that 'the word "seaman" carries a quite different meaning from "sailor", a tougher, more versatile and grimmer meaning', but then goes on to characterise this difference as a matter of mere subjective associations. The very fact that it is possible for Cary to appeal to the difference between the words 'sailor' and 'seaman' in the way that he does, and to be confident of his example being understood, the fact that Coleridge could rely on his readers' sympathising with his consternation at the sightseers' remarks, shows that what is involved here is no merely subjective matter, not just a question of the associations which a word may happen to have for a man, but something which is part of a shared life and language. Of course, the various words which Coleridge's sightseer used may well have had similar associations for him. Probably they were all words which he associated in some vague way with impressive examples of natural beauty. But to admit this is quite compatible with the assertion that the words have nevertheless very different forces, that though in some cases their meaning is fairly close, in another sense they all have quite different meanings. In this latter sense of 'meaning' there are no synonyms. There are no synonyms for the force of a word.

When a man's contact with literature enables him to discover meaning in what had before seemed pointless and boring, when Muir's poem brought him to see his fears in proper perspective, when Coleridge settled on the epithet 'majestic' to describe the falls of the Clyde, then the new understanding involved was bound up with the way in which each came to speak of these things. Unlike the sort of learning which Ryle discusses, unlike the acquisition of factual knowledge or the mastery of a technique, what is learnt in the cases I have discussed could not have been learnt in any other way, by any alternative means. It was, for example, only when Edwin Muir found precisely the right words in which to express his fear that he came to see it in a new way.[16]

I speak here of literature bringing men to see their lives or events in their lives in a different way. And indeed this is how Muir himself speaks of his experience. Nevertheless, I should perhaps make it clear that in this context 'seeing' cannot be equated with perception.[17] When Muir tells us that after writing his poem he could 'at last see the incident whole by seeing it as happening, on a great and tragic scale, to someone else', he is making a remark of a logically quite different sort from the man who says, 'I could at last see the needle, though without my son's sharp eyes, I might have missed it completely.' In the latter case, the ability to see something depends on acuteness of visual powers. It is a quality which might be displayed by a well-trained gun dog or a hawk, though not by a bat or by an oyster. When, on the other hand, one speaks of a poet's ability to open one's eyes to what one had overlooked, one is thinking of something which could happen only to a human being, and indeed only to a human being brought up within a certain cultural life. Within that cultural life it might happen to a blind man.

The difference becomes apparent, if one compares the change which I have just mentioned with another which Muir discusses later in the book. After an unhappy period in Glasgow he had moved to Prague, where:

> I began to learn the visible world all over again. In Glasgow the ugliness of everything—the walks through the slums, the uncongenial work—had turned me in upon myself, so that I no longer saw things, but was merely aware of them in a vague way. In Prague everything seemed to be asking me to notice it; I spent weeks in an orgy of looking; I saw everywhere the visible world before my eyes.[18]

Muir's life in Glasgow had bred in him the habit of ignoring his surroundings. When in Prague he began to break himself of this

---

[16]   The matter is complicated because Muir's own explanation of the situation is partly influenced by psychoanalytic theory. But I think that my own account is nevertheless for the most part correct.

[17]   The temptation is, of course, considerably greater in respect of the visual and plastic arts, that is, when one speaks of a painter or a sculptor bringing someone to see something. I think that it is to be resisted equally strongly here, and for similar reasons.

[18]   *An Autobiography*, p. 189.

habit, began to 'learn the visible world all over again', the change
which came over him can be explained by saying that he now saw
things whose presence he had before failed to notice. He had
failed to notice his surroundings in Glasgow because, for fear of
seeing what was unpleasant or distasteful, he had simply refused
to look. It is easy to imagine a change of the sort which Muir
mentions being contrived in a quite different manner, perhaps by
a television documentary on the city, or even by a spell of good
weather. For the change was not a change in the significance
which Muir's environment had for him. He had simply become
more observant of that environment.

When he came to see his childhood terrors in proper perspective by writing of them, there is also a sense in which Muir
now saw things whose presence he had before failed to notice. But
this sense cannot be explained by saying that he discovered facts
about the incident which he had hitherto failed to appreciate, or
that he remembered new aspects which he had forgotten. Apart
from the doubtful sense of speaking of a man's imparting information to himself by writing a poem, Muir makes it clear that as a
biographical source the poem in question would have been quite
unhelpful. 'I imagined Hector', he remarks, 'as noticing with
intense, dreamlike precision certain little things, not the huge
simplified things which my conscious memory tells me I noticed
in my own flight.'[19]

What the poem brought him to see was nothing which a
television documentary on childhood or a cine-film of the incident
might have shown him. Rather it was a change in the significance
which the whole event came to have for him, a change bound up
with the way in which he was inclined to think and speak of it.
'After I had written the poem', he tells us, 'the flight itself was
changed and with it my feelings towards it.' One might speak of
this as a difference in the way Muir interpreted the event or a
difference in his viewpoint, were it not for the fact that normally
when one speaks in this way one has an idea of some independent
standpoint or state of affairs of which the different points of view
or interpretations may be shown to be adequate or inadequate
accounts. 'There is a lot to be said for his point of view', we say, or
'That interpretation is quite indefensible.' And to say that an interpretation is mistaken or inadequate will be to say that the state of

---

[19]   *An Autobiography*, p. 43.

affairs in question really possesses characteristics which the interpretation cannot explain. As we have seen, Muir *might* have
spoken in this way of the change which came over him in Prague.
But if writing *Ballad of Hector in Hades* had led him to condemn his
earlier attitude towards his childhood as mistaken, this would not
have been because the poem brought out features of his life which
it could independently have been shown not to possess, but
because he no longer felt any inclination to speak or think of it in
the same way as before. Just as, having seen how Shakespeare
expresses Romeo's love for Juliet, the way in which I have become
accustomed to speak of my love for my wife may lose its hold over
me, so Muir's terror lost its hold over him, when he learnt how to
talk of it. This is why what he learnt cannot be seen as a matter of
either the knowledge of facts or the knowledge of a technique.
What we are faced with here is not a case of either *learning how* or
learning that, at least in Ryle's sense. If such a phrase is necessary, I
think that this case might best be described as a case of *learning
from.*

III

So far I have discussed certain situations in which literature may
be said to be responsible for changes in men's lives, in order to
bring out the limitations in one account of the nature of learning
and knowledge. Unfortunately, it might be thought that in one
way my choice of examples has been ill-considered. For it is
noticeable that for the most part they involve situations which
might justifiably be referred to as instances of moral change.

To some extent this is of course predictable, since it is likely
that any really fundamental change in a man's life will have a
moral dimension. Nor do I think it unimportant that when men
speak of what they have learned from literature, often their
discussions will be couched in moral terms. Clearly moral considerations enter deeply into the sort of importance which literature has for us, so that it would be a mistake to try to explain how
one can learn from novels and poems, and then to discuss, as a
quite different matter, what it is for a man's moral understanding
to be deepened.

Nevertheless, a recognition of these points may lead to confusion. For it may lead one to suppose that any situation where
one might speak of learning from literature will *necessarily* possess
a moral aspect, that the form of learning involved will *always* be

describable in moral terms. Thus, D.H. Lawrence has suggested that 'Every work of art adheres to some system of morality', though he recognises that within that morality it may constitute a revolutionary force, may, as he says, 'contain the essential criticism of the morality to which it adheres'.[20] And even a writer like Joyce Cary, who is unwilling to make any generalisation about the nature of art itself, nevertheless accepts Lawrence's thesis as applied to literature. 'When we speak of the novelist and poet's revelation of truth', he says, 'we mean that it is essentially moral, that it asserts a moral meaning.'[21]

These remarks do of course have some value in so far as they indicate that morality stands in a relationship to literature which other aspects of our lives do not. For a novel or a play may embody a moral vision, may be spoken of as contributing to the moral life of society, in a way in which it would make no sense to speak of its embodying a *scientific* vision or of its contributing ideas to the economic life of the society or to its civil engineering. But they are confusing if they are taken to imply that literature need always involve moral notions, and not simply because a work of literature generally contributes to aspects of our life other than morality—to religion, to politics, to love—but also because we can speak of learning from a novel or a poem even where it would no longer be helpful to speak of *any* specific form of activity to which it contributes. When Oscar Wilde wished to indicate how art may influence men's lives, he did not find it necessary to discuss changes in their moral or religious ideas. But nor did he speak of *any* activity on which the work of artists might throw new light. He spoke only of the importance which natural beauty may have for men.

> At present people see fogs not because there are fogs, but because poets and painters have taught them the mysterious loveliness of such effects.[22]

Of course, it may be thought that this example tilts the scales rather heavily in my own favour. For it is notorious that, for quite bad philosophical reasons, Wilde was particularly concerned to emphasise the independence of art and morality. Moreover, it

20 *Selected Literary Criticism*, p. 185.
21 *Art and Reality*, p. 144.
22 G.F. Maine ed., *The Works of Oscar Wilde* (London: Collins, 1948) p. 986.

might well be argued that there is in any case no necessary incompatibility between an artist's treatment of nature and his concern with moral issues.

> Dickens, at the beginning of *Bleak House*, gives us only the London fog. But that fog is the keynote of the whole. It gave Dickens back all the time whenever he needed it, the sense of a dark, dirty and muddled world, of the confusion and despair of lost souls.[23]

Despite this, I see no reason to suppose that *any* artistic treatment of natural beauty must be of the above sort, and to maintain that literature always involves a moral perspective would be to run the risk of blurring important differences. One might compare here the sorts of cases of *moral* change which I discussed earlier with what Ford Madox Ford found in the novels of W.H. Hudson:

> It is years and years since I first read *Nature in Downland*, yet, as I have already said somewhere or other, the first words that I there read have become a part of my life. They describe how, lying on the turf on the high, sunlit down above Lewes in Sussex, Hudson looked up into the perfect, limpid blue of the sky ... Now that is part of my life.[24]

If one were comparing what Ford found in Hudson's novels with what, say, Muir learnt from his own poem, or from the writings of Baudelaire, then one might speak in very similar ways. One might say, for instance, that both were brought to a deeper understanding of some aspect of life, or that both came to see what the world was like. And one would emphasise that in neither case could this recognition be regarded as distinct from the way in which Ford or Muir was brought to it. Coming to see what life or the world is like cannot be compared with finding out what an ammeter is like. If I have found out what an ammeter is like, then I shall be able to tell you. 'It's a sort of metal box', I may say, 'with a dial on it.' On the other hand neither Ford not Muir could have *said* what they had learned from literature, from their own writings or from those of others. Muir did not try to explain what he found in Baudelaire, and when Ford wishes to characterise the difference which reading Hudson made to him, he says only that the first words of *Nature in Downland* have become a part of his life. I doubt whether

---

[23] Joyce Cary, *Art and Reality*, p. 100.
[24] *The Bodley Head Ford Madox Ford* (London: Bodley Head, 1962–3) vol. 3, p. 297.

anyone who failed to see these similarities could have understood much of what was involved in either example.

This having been said, it is then important to notice the differences. One is bound, that is, to mention that, though in the case of Muir what was learnt had a moral dimension, with Ford this was not so. Muir came to a new idea of the significance of certain events in his life which it is difficult not to see as moral. Ford simply learnt what it was like to lie on the downs, looking up at the sky, so that though he had never done this, yet 'that is I, not Hudson, looking up into the heavens'.[25] It would be absurd to suggest that this is not an important difference between the examples. But given the similarities between them already indicated, it would seem sheer philosophical prejudice to go on to argue with Lawrence and Cary that, since Hudson's novels brought about no moral change in Ford's life, Ford cannot be said to have learned from them. If one were willing to speak of learning in the case of either Ford or Muir, then I fail to see why one should not speak of it in both.

At this point I can imagine someone wishing to push the argument rather further. 'You have denied', they may say, 'that reference to the artistic worth of a novel or poem need necessarily involve reference to a moral vision. And you have indicated cases where a man might speak of learning from a work of literature, even though it is not possible to identify any moral aspect to what he learns. But have you gone far enough? May there not be cases in which a work of art is recognised as having artistic merit, whilst involving a corrupt or evil vision? And if you deny that this may be so, are you not then guilty of a mere philosophical prejudice of the sort which you have attacked in the views of Lawrence and Cary?'

The man who asks these questions may for instance be impressed by the way in which qualities which are normally regarded as morally blameworthy may nevertheless, in the hands or a great artist, become acceptable. He may remember how Orwell, having condemned Swift for a world-view so diseased that it 'only just passes the test of sanity', was led then to admit that he regarded *Gulliver's Travels* as a 'great work of art'.

---

[25] Ibid., p. 297.

> From what I have written it may seem that I am *against* Swift, and
> that my object is to refute him and even to belittle him. In a
> political and moral sense I am against him, so far as I understand
> him. Yet curiously enough he is one or the writers I admire with
> least reserve, and *Gulliver's Travels*, in particular, is a book which it
> seems impossible for me to grow tired of.[26]

I doubt whether anything *general* could usefully be said about this
sort of case. Clearly much will depend, with the example I have
chosen, on whether Orwell is interpreted as saying on the one
hand that Swift's work is good *despite* the pernicious moral viewpoint which it embodies, or on the other that it is good *as well as*
pernicious or even good in its perniciousness. As it happens, the
first interpretation does seem to some extent a plausible one.
Many of Orwell's remarks indicate that he does not see himself as
praising (from an artistic viewpoint) Swift's moral failings, but
rather those qualities which override these failings, the 'power
and simplicity of Swift's prose', for example, which he says, 'has
been able to make not one but a whole series of impossible worlds
more credible than the majority of history books'.[27] It would therefore seem to me correct to say that, in this respect at least, Orwell
regards Swift's work as good *despite* its moral corruption. Furthermore, I think that this could be the *only* correct description of any
case in which a writer's vision was thought of as being morally
trivial in some way. For instance, a work of literature could only
be good *despite* its sentimentality.

On the other hand, I should not wish to deny that there are
many aspects of Orwell's discussion of which the above would not
be a correct account and where it would perhaps be more appropriate to say that he finds Swift's work both artistically good *and*
morally corrupt, that he responds to the expression of a moral
viewpoint which he nevertheless regards as diseased and evil.
What is to be noted here is that Orwell does not find Swift's
viewpoint *merely* diseased and evil. He himself says that he cannot
imagine himself responding to any moral position of which this
was true, for example that of 'spiritualist, a Buchmanite or a
member of the Ku-Klux Klan'. Swift's moral position differs from
theirs in that, though it is one which most people would regard as

---

[26] G. Orwell, *Inside the Whale and Other Essays* (Harmondsworth: Penguin
Press, 1962) p. 142.
[27] Ibid., p. 139.

distorted, even dangerous, it is also one which most people could imagine themselves holding. It is not merely trivial or crazy. Swift, Orwell tells us:

> remains permanently in a depressed mood which in most people is only intermittent ... But we all know that mood, and something in us responds to the expression of it ... Swift falsifies his picture of the world by refusing to see anything in human life except dirt, folly and wickedness, but the part which he abstracts from the whole does exist, and it is something which we all know about while shrinking from mentioning it.[28]

There are then two sides to Orwell's regard for Swift. To some extent he admires Swift's work in spite of its immorality. To some extent it is the immoral position embodied in Swift's work to which he responds. On the other hand, it is worth remarking that for those who mistakenly believe that *all* art embodies a moral viewpoint, there may be considerable temptation to ignore this distinction, and to suppose that however evil or even trivial a writer's moral viewpoint, it must always be by virtue of this viewpoint, rather than in spite of it, that he is admired. Thus, faced with Orwell's example, if they do not simply write it off as confused, they will be inclined to argue that since Orwell regarded Swift as a great writer, and since it is *only* in respect of the moral viewpoint which it embodies that any work can be of artistic worth, it follows that Orwell, who recognised the corruptness or Swift's moral vision, must have thought him a great writer solely by virtue of a corrupt moral vision.

The fallacy in this argument should be apparent from what I have said already. What makes a writer's work valuable for us need not be thought of in *moral* terms at all. As a matter of fact, Orwell *was* impressed by aspects of Swift's work quite unconnected with morality. Once the supposition that art must always embody moral ideas is rejected, then there is no reason why we should continue to deny that a work of literature may possess artistic excellence in spite of its embodying a morally outrageous or even trivial theme. It is just that where this is so, it will not be this aspect of the work which impresses us, but other non-moral aspects.

---

[28]   Ibid., p. 140.

It should, however, be clear that my position here is to be sharply distinguished from another to which it is, at least in this respect, apparently similar. For what I have argued is that when we learn from a work of literature, then what we learn, the content or the work, is essentially bound up with the way in which the writer expresses himself, bound up, that is, with the author's style. And I have also indicated that I regard it as a mistake to assume that the content of the work will always be of a moral nature.

Now, those who do *not* reject this assumption, but are on the contrary *very* strongly influenced by it, are sometimes led to suppose that in cases where a work has apparently *no* moral content, or no moral content worthy of consideration, the artist's merit, if any, must lie simply in his style, in a sense in which style *is* distinguishable from content. Thus, for example, G.K. Chesterton, recognising that Milton was 'a man of magnificent genius', but nevertheless finding his moral vision hackneyed and unoriginal, felt himself forced to locate Milton's greatness 'in a style and a style which seems to me rather unusually separated from its substance'.[29]

The sense of 'style' which Chesterton has in mind here, the sense in which one can distinguish an artist's style from what he has to tell you, is, as his subsequent remarks make plain, simply a matter of the architecture of a poem or a novel, of its word-arrangement or rhyme-scheme. It is the sense in which school-teachers often speak when they compare Pope's style with that of, say, Coleridge, or when they distinguish blank verse from rhyme. And indeed, a schoolteacher might bring a child to see these sorts of differences even if the child were incapable of learning anything from poetry or literature, or cared nothing for either. The teacher need only communicate certain rules or methods, need only teach the child to count the number of iambic feet in a line, or to notice how often the writer uses the word 'and'.

But, though we might say that in one sense the child understands Pope's style or understands certain stylistic differences, this would be a superficial, a trivial sense of 'style' and of 'understanding'. The child would never see what was great about Pope's writing for example, nor would he see why Pope's use of certain rhyme-schemes differed from that of mediocre, but competent,

---

[29]   W.H. Auden ed., *G.K. Chesterton: A Selection from His Non-Fictional Prose* (London: Faber and Faber, 1970) p. 86.

imitators. To make him alive to this difference you would have to point to far more than rules or methods. You would have to bring him to see what Pope had to say about life. A knowledge of rules and canons might enable him to recognise that the *Epistles* are written in heroic couplets, or perhaps where Pope breaks the rules of this poetic form, but if that were all that he found in Pope's style, there would be no reason why he should marvel at it (except as you might marvel at a man's skill in composing tongue-twisters). And he would never learn anything from it.

It is this last sense of 'learning' which I have tried to explain in this paper. And I have tried to show why Ryle with his emphasis on training and skills, on rules and on the transmission of techniques, does not even notice that there is such a sense. This is why I do not find it surprising that whenever Ryle refers to the appreciation of literature or poetry in *The Concept of Mind*, his references are always couched in the terminology of rules and canons. I have said that such references involve a trivial conception of style. But then, it is a limitation of the account of learning and knowledge offered by Ryle that it could not explain any sense of 'literary style' which was *not* trivial. Ryle refers somewhere to his task in the book as that of 'mapping the logical geography of the concept of mind'. It is as though, the task having been completed to Ryle's satisfaction, he and certain of his followers then proceeded to mistake the map for the country and simply forgot those places which had never been entered on the map. My suggestion is that the cases of learning from literature which I have discussed in this paper constitute just such a Shangri-La.

2

Two Trends in
Analytical Aesthetics[1]

Of late the idea that morality can best be understood in terms of
some external element of commendation rather than by reference
to the kinds of action commended has come in for some hard
criticism. By contrast a comparable programme in aesthetics,
involving the identification of some unique aesthetic attitude,
distinct from, say, religious or scientific attitudes and capable of
being characterized without reference to any of the possible
objects of aesthetic appraisal, has until fairly recently enjoyed
considerable immunity from philosophical objections. Indeed, for
many years it was quite customary for writers in the field to
deplore those who, like Collingwood, Croce, Tolstoi, Richards,
concentrated their attention upon works of art at the expense of
the many other sorts of objects which may be seen aesthetically.
For it is of course a consequence of the view in question that the
appraisal of *any* object is a suitable subject for philosophical specu-
lation. E.F. Carritt, for example, is ruthless with those writers who
in their discussions neglect natural beauty in favour of artistic
merit, 'since our experience in face of both is of the same kind and
may well be indistinguishable',[2] a criticism echoed by, amongst
others, Edward Bullough[3] and for slightly different reasons R.W.

---

[1]   Based on paper read to *The British Society of Aesthetics*, 2nd May 1973, and
first published as 'Two Trends in Contemporary Aesthetics', *British Journal of
Aesthetics*, 13 (4), 1973. © British Society of Aesthetics, 1973.
[2]   E.F. Carritt, 'Croce and his Aesthetic', *Mind* 62 (248) 1953, p. 456.
[3]   Edward Bullough, *Aesthetics: Lectures and Essays*, ed. E.N. Wilkinson
(London: Bowes and Bowes, 1957).

Hepburn.[4] Perhaps predictably, this line of reasoning has even led one writer to question whether a study of works like *Hamlet* is helpful even for those philosophers concerned specifically to understand the arts and whether it would not be methodologically advisable to concentrate on natural beauty, which presents all the characteristics of great works of art save only their complexity and certain other optional extras such as insight into human nature, which we tolerate in Shakespeare's writings only because they are thrown in *gratis* alongside the poetry and are not easily detachable from it.[5]

Within the last few years, however, the picture has changed somewhat. For various reasons it has come to be doubted whether the notion of a distinctively aesthetic attitude is philosophically fruitful. And in this respect two recently published books are important. For they contain what are perhaps the most well-known statements of two lines of argument which are becoming increasingly prevalent in contemporary aesthetics, arguments which are connected with one another in various ways, and which may jointly be seen as constituting a powerful, but I believe radically misconceived attack on the position which I have out-lined. They are Richard Wollheim's *Art and its Objects* and John Casey's *The Language of Criticism*.

I

Wollheim's argument seems simple. Carritt, Bullough, Urmson, have all got it precisely the wrong way round. Our understanding of art cannot be explicable as one variety of an attitude which we adopt primarily towards natural objects, if only because the aesthetic contemplation of nature is itself an extension of an attitude established on the basis of works of art.

> A serious distortion is introduced into many accounts of the aesthetic attitude by taking as central to its [sic] cases which are really peripheral or secondary.[6]

R.W. Hepburn, 'Contemporary Aesthetics and the Neglect of Natural Beauty', in B. Williams and A. Montefiore eds., *British Analytic Philosophy* (London: Routledge & Kegan Paul, 1966).

[5]   J.O. Urmson, 'What Makes a Situation Aesthetic?', *Proceedings of the Aristotelian Society*, Supp., Vol. 31, 1957.

[6]   R. Wollheim, *Art and its Objects* (Harmondsworth: Penguin, 1970) p. 83.

Wollheim gives as examples, Kant's discussion of the beauty of a rose and Bullough's of a fog at sea. Both are attempts to identify the characteristics of aesthetic appreciation. And as such both are confused.

> It would be a parody of this kind of approach, but involving no real unfairness, to compare it to an attempt to explicate an understanding of language by reference to the experiences we might have in listening to a parrot 'talking'.[7]

Wollheim's discussion here is sketchy, and nothing which he says suggests that he is alive to what is nevertheless a serious ambiguity in his use of the phrases 'aesthetic attitude' and 'aesthetic viewpoint'. By concentrating his attention at this stage on the notion of an attitude or viewpoint, he is blinded to the complexity of the term 'aesthetic' in these and other contexts. Nevertheless, it is, I think, clear that we do use this term in at least two rather different ways and part of the difficulty in criticising Wollheim's position stems from his failure to draw attention to this.

One way in which the term 'aesthetic' is employed is in order to indicate those activities, objects, interests or attitudes which are in some way directly connected with the arts, with painting, sculpture, literature and so on. It is this narrow sense of the word which Hepburn has in mind when he condemns those writers who define aesthetics as 'the philosophy of art'.[8]

What Hepburn does not mention is that there is no reason why someone who uses the term in this way should be precluded from speaking of the aesthetic appreciation of objects other than works of art. They may do so because it is possible to treat something which is not in fact a work of art (a piece of driftwood, for example) as if it were. Thus schoolboys and middle-aged adolescents sometimes jokingly protest that their interest in strip-shows and obscene photographs is purely aesthetic. And what they mean, I suppose, is that they view these spectacles, which are not, after all, primarily artistic exercises, as though they were. So when Wollheim claims that an aesthetic attitude towards nature is possible only within the context of an artistic culture, it is possible that what he means is quite simply that one can treat a piece of

---

[7]   Ibid., p. 84.

[8]   Hepburn, op. cit., p. 285.

driftwood or a strip-show (say) as a work of art only if one already has the concept of a work of art. And this is of course true. It is in fact a rather unedifying tautology, which could have philosophical significance only if it were implicitly denied. Unfortunately, it is by no means clear to me that those writers whom Wollheim takes to task *did* deny it, even implicitly. Certainly it was no part of Bullough's purpose to make the obviously absurd claim that natural objects are the paradigm cases of works of art, but rather to discuss the appreciation of natural beauty, which he felt had important affinities with and could throw important light on art appreciation.

Now it is clear from Wollheim's subsequent discussion that he would wish also to reject *this* claim. And this suggests another interpretation of his own argument, according to which what is alleged to be parasitic upon the notion of a work of art is not merely the ability to see natural objects as works of art, but rather *any* appreciation of natural beauty. Wollheim would, that is to say, be using the term 'aesthetic' not in the narrow sense which Hepburn criticises and in which it is limited to what concerns the arts, but in the wider sense in which it is sometimes said that one can adopt an aesthetic attitude towards anything (and in which a love of art is only *one* form of aesthetic concern). And he would be claiming that the adoption of such an attitude is possible only in a society where men are already engaged in artistic activities.

Whether or not this is a correct interpretation of Wollheim's argument, it certainly expresses a view which seems to have some attraction for philosophers. It is, to take examples almost at random, implied by Margaret Macdonald's suggestion that when one admires something for its own sake, a garden or the lines of a yacht, one admires it as a work of art[9] and by Nelson Goodman's claim that, 'Nature is a product of art and discourse.'[10] Most recently Karl Britton has argued along similar lines that the appreciation of natural beauty is possible only because we are faced

9 Margaret Macdonald, 'Art and Imagination', *Proceedings of the Aristotelian Society*, 1952–3, p. 206.
10 Nelson Goodman, *Languages of Art: An Approach to a Theory of Symbols* (New York: Bobbs Merrill, 1968) p. 33.

with something which, though it is not in fact a work of art, *might* nevertheless have been.[11]

What these views have in common is the claim that the appreciation of nature or of the lines and style of non-artistic artefacts is possible only by analogy with the appreciation of artistic qualities,[12] together with the corollary that we could not have a feeling for natural beauty unless we already had a feeling for works of art. And, if true, then this is of course a fundamental criticism of the views of Bullough, Kant, Urmson, etc. Their mistake would be that of offering what are merely peripheral or borderline instances of aesthetic appreciation as if they were paradigm cases.

Unfortunately, the claim does not seem to be true. In an article called 'England, Your England', George Orwell once noted two characteristic traits of the English, traits which he maintained 'would be accepted by almost all observers'.[13] They were 'the English indifference to the arts' and the 'English love of flowers'. Though these traits may seem to be contradictory, he remarked, in fact they are not. For the latter, the love of flowers, is to be found even in people who care nothing at all for art and know nothing about it. Now on the face of it these remarks seem to be both plausible and incompatible with the thesis I am discussing. And it is worth noting that one reason why they seem plausible is that there is a natural tendency to think of the love of nature, of flowers, sunsets, birds, as being among the prerequisites of artistic creation and appreciation rather than as being parasitic upon them. When Britton argues that to contemplate the aesthetic characteristics of a flower is to view it as if it were a work of art there is a temptation to ask: And how does an artist view a flower? There is a temptation, that is, to suppose that unless a painter could already view flowers aesthetically, unless he were able to

---

[11]   Karl Britton, 'Concepts of Action and Concepts of Approval', *Proceedings of the Aristotelian Society*, 73, 1972–3, p. 116.

[12]   It is worth remarking that this view is also implied by the writings of some very much earlier writers. For example, both Clive Bell and R.G. Collingwood doubted whether there *could* be an aesthetic appreciation of nature because they were unable to find in natural objects the qualities which they regarded as important in works of art. Obviously, this argument will only make sense on the assumption that works of art are the paradigm cases of aesthetic objects.

[13]   *The Collected Essays, Journalism and Letters of George Orwell*, eds. Sonia Orwell and Ian Angus, Vol. 4: *In Front of your Nose 1945–1950* (Harmondsworth: Penguin, 1970) p. 65.

see something striking or novel in their appearance, then there
would be something lacking in his artistic treatment of this subject
matter. Anyhow, this is the way in which Joyce Cary speaks of
Monet's work:

> For instance, you go walking in the fields and all at once they
> strike you in quite a new aspect; you find it quite extraordinary
> that they should be like that. This is what happened to Monet as a
> young man. He suddenly saw the fields, not as solid flat objects
> covered with grass or useful crops and dotted over with trees, but
> as colours in astonishing vivacity and subtlety of gradation. And
> this gave him a delightful and quite new pleasure.[14]

One might say, as Cary does, that Monet's contributions to painting were possible only because he had already been struck by an
aspect of nature to which others had been blind. Certainly, it could
scarcely be said that the recognition of this aspect was parasitic
upon, or an extension of, any artistic traditions (though this is in
fact precisely what Wollheim does say about this case),[15] for
Monet was himself on the point of creating the traditions in
question. Even if it is true that an acquaintance with his work
brought others to an awareness of this aspect of nature, this is
something which could not be said of Monet himself.

Of course, this is not to say that there are no cases of which
something similar might be said, cases where a man's attitude
towards nature *is* parasitic upon artistic traditions, that is. But this
is not the only possibility. You might think, for example, of the
way in which St. Francis's view of nature was an extension not of
any artistic traditions but of his religious beliefs. And even where
the relationship is of the sort that Wollheim discusses, it is by no
means clear what precisely isolated examples could prove. Mark
Twain, for instance, is sometimes said to have seen nature as a
series of paintings, a characteristic which comes out in his
descriptions of Lake Tahoe in *Roughing It*:

> The forest about us was dense and cool, the sky above us was
> cloudless and brilliant with sunshine, the broad lake before us was
> glassy and clear, or rippled and breezy, or black and storm-tossed,
> according to nature's mood; and its circling border of mountain
> domes, clothed with forests, scarred with landslides, cloven by

---

[14] Joyce Cary, *Art and Reality: Ways of the Creative Process* (New York:
Doubleday, 1961) p. 1.
[15] Wollheim, op. cit., p. 89.

canons and valleys, and helmeted with glittering snow, fitly framed and finished the noble picture.[16]

It is not simply that Twain refers to the scene as a picture, but the whole manner in which he describes it which suggests the influence of artistic conventions here. One might say of Twain's vision of nature what Wollheim says generally, that it would be inexplicable except by reference to certain artistic traditions, in this case traditions of landscape painting. What is interesting about such a case, however, is that far from supporting Wollheim's general thesis, it is intelligible only if that thesis is false. Writers have thought it worth while mentioning this aspect of Twain's character only because in this respect he is exceptional, just as one would scarcely single out St. Francis's attitude towards nature had it been the general rule in his society. Were Wollheim's thesis correct, then it would have been inconceivable that anyone should fail to view nature in the way that Twain did.

The general argument of which I have used Wollheim's work as an illustration has, then, no great initial plausibility. But at this stage this is not a line of criticism which I wish to press, not because I do not think it is important, but because I do not think it is necessary. This can be seen if one remembers that Wollheim is attacking a thesis according to which the appreciation of art is best understood by reference to the appreciation of nature. Against this he argues that the situation is precisely the reverse, that our appreciation of nature can be understood only by reference to the sphere of artistic activity. But the truth of the matter seems to be that both are best understood independently. This is not to say that they are not related in various ways, but simply that there are aspects of art appreciation which cannot be understood if one thinks of our reactions to a play as a complicated version of our reactions to a rose. And there are aspects of the love of nature which make no sense if one has before one's mind the way in which people respond to paintings and sculptures. It is some of these aspects of art and nature which I wish to recall in this paper.

II

Perhaps the most obvious way in which the appreciation of, say, a novel differs from that of a rose or a sunset is that it makes sense

---

[16] Op cit., p. 120.

to speak of learning from the novel in a way in which it makes no sense to speak of learning from the rose. One reason why this difference is often overlooked is that there are many philosophers who would say that it makes no sense to speak of learning from either. And in a way this is not difficult to understand. One begins to understand it when one looks at the words of those who have tried to explain what this sort of learning involves. Compare, for example, Renford Bambrough's observation that: 'In literature, as in other media in which philosophy of life may be conducted, we often learn without learning anything new',[17] with Orwell's remark that literature can 'open up a new world for us, not by revealing what is strange, but by revealing what is familiar'.[18]

I do not find it hard to see why a certain sort of philosopher may be impatient with such claims. For what, he will ask, can it mean to speak of a man's learning where there is nothing he learns which he did not know already, or of something with which he is already familiar being revealed to him? Do not both of these ways of speaking look dangerously close to contradictions?[19]

In the abstract of course they do. What is required to render such remarks intelligible are examples of the sorts of learning to which they apply. Clearly, however, such examples had better not be examples of learning from literature. For this would be likely merely to invite the charge that what is involved in them is not correctly describable as 'learning'. For this reason I shall take an example which has no particular connection with art and literature and about which there will, I hope, be no disagreement. Towards the end of the war George Orwell had entered Stuttgart as foreign correspondent for a British newspaper, in the company of a Belgian journalist.

> The Belgian had been broadcasting throughout the war for the European service of the BBC, and, like nearly all Frenchmen or Belgians, he had a very much tougher attitude towards 'the Boche' than an Englishman or an American would have. All the main bridges into the town had been blown up, and we had to enter by a small footbridge which the Germans had evidently made efforts to defend. A dead German soldier was lying supine at the foot of

---

[17] *Reason, Truth and God* (London: Methuen, 1969) p. 120.
[18] George Orwell, *Inside the Whale and other essays* (Harmondsworth: Penguin, 1969) p. 11.
[19] I do not of course intend to imply that either of these writers is unaware of the apparent paradox of his remarks.

the steps. His face was a waxy yellow. On his breast someone had laid a bunch of the lilac which was blossoming everywhere. The Belgian averted his face as we went past. When we were well over the bridge he confided that this was the first time he had seen a dead man ... For several days after this, his attitude was quite different from what it had been earlier ... His feelings, he told me, had undergone a change at the sight of '*ce pauvre mort*' beside the bridge: it had suddenly brought home to him the meaning of war.[20]

I doubt whether anyone, except in the interests of defending some philosophical thesis, would deny that Orwell's journalist had learned from his experience. After seeing the dead soldier his attitude towards war and towards the people he had regarded as his enemies had changed. Actions which before might have seemed impossible to him now came naturally:

When he left he gave the residue of the coffee we had brought with us to the Germans on whom we were billeted. A week earlier he would probably have been scandalised at the idea of giving coffee to a 'Boche'.[21]

Nevertheless, it is, I think, clear that any attempt to say what he had learned, as if this were a piece of information which he might perhaps have imparted to others, would end in platitude. What is one to say? He had learned that men die in wars. But this, of course, he knew already. He knew, Orwell says, that the war had already produced perhaps twenty million dead, of whom he had seen only one. Or should one say that he had learned what a soldier's death is like? But then one would have to recognise that there could be no answer to the question: And what was it like, then? What death is like, was something which came out in the pathetic scene to which he had been a witness. Unless you had seen the soldier lying by the bridge you could not know what it was like.

This may tempt those of a reductionist persuasion to equate 'Knowing what it was like' and 'Being there'. Of course, they may object, one cannot *explain* what the Belgian learned from his experience for he had learned nothing. He had simply lived through it. And were he to say that unless you or I had been there,

---

[20]   'Revenge is Sour', *The Collected Essays, Journalism, and Letters of George Orwell*, Vol. 4, p. 6.
[21]   Ibid.

we could not know what it was like, then this would be simply a roundabout way of asserting that we were not there. The move is tempting. Unfortunately, the reductionist's equation cannot be maintained. 'Learning from the scene on the bridge' cannot mean 'Witnessing the scene on the bridge' since it would have been quite possible for Orwell's journalist to have witnessed the dead soldier without learning anything. Had he merely remarked: 'Well, that's one less to bother with', then I think that Orwell would have said that he remained blind to the meaning of war.

Still, it is worth asking how it is possible for us to be blind to the meaning of something which is a part of our lives, as war is; how one can *fail* to see what war is like. One way in which this may happen springs from the very nature of social life. I have in mind the tendency of any form of social life to give rise to forces which obscure reality, forces, that is, which are of their very nature forces of deception. Now Orwell says of his Belgian journalist that he had for several years been engaged in allied propaganda work. And this is important, for propaganda is just such a force. No one speaks of himself as a propagandist (just as no one speaks of himself as a hypocrite) because propaganda is essentially an activity aimed at concealing the true nature of things. So for several years the Belgian had been engaged in an activity whose aim was that of hiding from himself and from others the nature of the war which was being fought (and perhaps of war generally). It is a part of this that he thought of the men against whom he was fighting simply as 'the enemy' or 'the Boche', thought of them, that is, not as individual human beings with aims and desires but as a collective obstacle to the attainment of his own goals and those of his allies. It was this that changed when he saw the dead soldier on the bridge. He now saw the people against whom he had struggled for years, the 'Boche' of his imagination, as they really were. I do not want to say that he could now see things from their point of view, for no doubt this was as distorted as his own. It is rather that, though in one sense he had known all along of the vast loss of life, both amongst his own countrymen and amongst those against whom he was fighting, the significance of this fact had been brought home to him by an event in his life in such a way that one might speak of the change in him as internally related to this event. The change in him was that when he thought of death in action he would think not of the death of certain men standing in the way of allied victory, or of a series of statistics, but of a young soldier lying by a footbridge beneath a wreath of lilac.

Let us now compare this with another example which again comes from Orwell. Orwell is here discussing what can be learned from a play, from Shakespeare's *King Lear*:

> Shakespeare starts by assuming that to make yourself powerless is to invite an attack ... If you turn the other cheek, you will get a harder blow on it than you got on the first one. This does not always happen, but it is to be expected, and you ought not to complain if it does happen. The second blow is, so to speak, part of the act of turning the other cheek. First of all, therefore, there is the vulgar commonsense moral drawn by the Fool: 'Don't relinquish power, don't give away your lands.' But there is another moral. Shakespeare never utters it in so many words, and it does not matter very much whether he was aware of it. It is contained in the story which, after all, he made up, or altered to suit his purposes. It is: 'Give away your lands, if you want to, but don't expect to gain happiness by doing so. Probably you won't gain happiness. If you live for others you must *live for others*, and not as a roundabout way of getting an advantage for yourself.[22]

As with the earlier example, what is learned here cannot be stated without becoming banal. It seems that we all know what *King Lear* means until we are told. Indeed, in the above passage almost every sentence expresses a statement of parallel triviality to the remark that men die in wars, and in particular both of the 'morals' which Orwell takes as being central to the play are trivial. The first, that to relinquish power is to invite attack is, as Orwell says, simply a piece of common sense. It could scarcely be something new which we learn from reading *King Lear*, simply because no one of sufficient intelligence to read *King Lear* could fail to be aware of it. Indeed, with many of the activities in which men engage it is a *precondition* of the performance of those activities, and for this reason scarcely needs to be formulated, except for the benefit of those who are new to the activities in question. Thus, officers discussing military strategy will normally find it sufficient to remark that a certain deployment of forces will weaken their defences. They will not find it necessary, except just possibly when addressing raw recruits, to add that to weaken one's defences is to invite attack, since even a basic knowledge of strategy pre-supposes this consequence.

---

[22] 'Lear, Tolstoi and the Fool', in *Collected Essays, Journalism and Letters of George Orwell*, Vol. 4, p. 298.

The second of Orwell's 'morals' fares even worse as a candidate for novelty. For it is clearly a tautology. It is, I have said, possible (though very difficult) to imagine circumstances in which it might be necessary to warn someone of the dangers of relinquishing power; when speaking to a small child, for instance. But it is well-nigh impossible to imagine needing to tell someone that living for others is not a form of self interest. Or even if one might again say this to a child, the reason is different. For it will not be that, knowing what morality is, the child is nevertheless unaware of some basic techniques for living a moral life, but rather that the child does not yet understand the nature of morality. One is teaching a conceptual truth.

Yet it is this conceptual truth, a truth presupposed by any understanding of the nature of renunciation, which Orwell claims Shakespeare tried to impart in *King Lear*. Nor, though Orwell does not mention this, is Shakespeare unique in this respect. For we find much the same theme in a much later work, Tolstoi's *Father Sergius*. Like Lear, the brilliant young officer, Prince Kasatsky, renounces his worldly possessions in order to gain some personal advantage. His vanity wounded by the discovery that his bride-to-be has already lost her virtue as mistress to the Czar, Kasatsky decides to enter a monastery. But, again as in the case of Lear, he is merely exchanging one form of egoism for another, and the story centres around his gradual awakening to this truth. His sister's words bring out perfectly the deception in the life of the man who has by now adopted the name of Sergius:

> By entering the monastery he showed his contempt for all the things which had seemed so important to him while he was in service, and he placed himself on a new height from which he could look down on those he used to envy.[23]

Clearly one might say equally well of *Father Sergius*, what Orwell says of *King Lear*, that it 'points out the results of practising self-denial for selfish reasons'.[24]

Now I have mentioned these particular examples because we have in Shakespeare and Tolstoi two men who are at least arguably unsurpassed in their respective fields, and we have in *King*

[23] 'Father Sergius', in *The Short Stories of Leo Tolstoi* (New York: Bantam Books, 1960) p. 442.
[24] Orwell, op. cit., p. 298.

Lear and *Father Sergius* what are among the finest examples of their work. Yet if you thought that the aims of these writers were to impart information, then you might well ask why they should have bothered to tell us what everyone knows already. True, *King Lear* and *Father Sergius* have more in them than the statements of Orwell might suggest, and I suppose someone might argue that in some way their 'morals' are more impressive, more convincing, when dressed up as the life of Lear or of Sergius. But then these are not things whose truth *needs* impressing on us, so the effort seems wasted. Yet nobody, I imagine, *would* make this criticism. And though I have said that we find the same truths in both works, nobody is likely to say that this makes Tolstoi's story superfluous. Nor would they speak of Tolstoi's treatment of the theme superseding Shakespeare's (as we might speak of one answer to a technical problem, say in metallurgy or in carpentry, superseding another), unless this meant only that developments, changes in literature or in people's lives, had made it impossible for Tolstoi to write in the way Shakespeare did.

Now one reason for this is that where certain sorts of issues are concerned, those in technology for instance, we can speak of someone's learning something, learning how to make stronger wood joints or learning what will remove the stain from the carpet, in a way which has nothing to do with a particular technologist's statement of the problem. If someone has spilt port on the Axminster, then my problem is the same whichever way I express it (even if I express it in another language), and so too with its solution. So that if one thought that all learning were a matter of obtaining information of this sort, then one would not see why the same was not true of what one learns from Tolstoi or from Shakespeare. And one might then ask oneself why such great artists should have chosen to communicate such banal messages, and perhaps conclude that nothing can be learned from literature. To see why this conclusion must be resisted it is worth recalling Orwell's earlier example. I said that to understand what Orwell's journalist learned from his wartime experience, one must recognise the role which this experience came to play in his thought. That is, one must recognise that what the journalist learned was internally related to the experience, and could not without lapsing into vacuity be expressed independently of it. If we now turn to Shakespeare's *Lear* or Tolstoi's *Sergius*, a similar point can be made. One reason why it is possible to speak of 'learning' here, despite the resultant banality when one tries to state what has been learned, is that once again what one can learn from either is internally related to the works in question. But there is a difference, a difference, that is, in the *sort* of internal relationship which is involved. This brings me to the second of the arguments which I want to discuss in this paper.

III

Writers who have wished to deny that art can be explained by reference to an aesthetic attitude which may be adopted towards any set of objects whatsoever, often emphasise what they call the 'intensionality' of the feelings or experiences arising from works of art. It has been felt that in this respect emotions like fear and grief are the appropriate models, rather than sensations such as nausea and pain. Unlike pain or nausea, which may be occasioned by any sort of objects whatsoever, the feeling of fear is inseparable from a certain sort of object, namely one which threatens. Thus, to characterise the fear is necessarily to characterise the object of the fear. A terrible fear is the fear of some terrible threat. Similar considerations, it is said, apply to our reactions to plays and novels. Speaking of the emotions or reactions to which *King Lear* may give rise in those who read it, John Casey says:

> We cannot describe these emotions without describing the play (emotion words are 'intensional' in that they are essentially directed to objects); it is logically impossible that they should be produced by a drug or by *Macbeth*.[25]

Elsewhere in the book Casey makes the comparison quite explicit. His view is that the 'way of seeing' which a play expresses is related to its object (the play) in the way that an emotion is related to *its* objects.[26]

Now it seems to me that this comparison is confusing. And it is worth noting straight away that even in the brief passages I have mentioned it involves Casey in a non-sequitur. For it does not follow from the claim that the 'way of seeing' which a play expresses is related to its object in the way that an emotion is related to its objects, that two plays, *Macbeth* and *King Lear* for example, could not both give rise to the *same* 'way of seeing'.

---

[25]   John Casey, *The Language of Criticism* (London: Methuen, 1966) p. 132.
[26]   Ibid., p. 115.

Indeed, far from entailing this conclusion, Casey's premise contradicts it.

This will become clearer if one remembers that the intensionality of emotions like fear or grief lies in their being directed towards *objects of a certain kind* and not towards particular objects. The creaking of my stairs at midnight may awaken in me a nameless terror, but one reason why it is possible for a terror to be nameless is that in the circumstances it need not matter whether the creak is brought about by an escaped leopard or by an axe-wielding psychopath. In either case the terror may be the same. So that if in this respect plays or novels were the same, then it would perhaps follow that what one learns from a play could not be learned from, say, a newspaper report (which would, I suppose, be comparable to the claim that one can feel grief for one's father but not for someone one has never heard of). But it would not seem to follow that it is logically impossible for a man to learn the same from two plays (cf. one can fear both a leopard and a mad axe-man). Nor would it follow, and this is also important, that changes in a play need make much difference to what we learn from it (cf. the leopard would scare the life out of me even without its spots).

Now, to be fair, Casey is not completely blind to these consequences of the comparison which he has drawn. Indeed, in places he seems willingly to embrace them (though he is not consistent). Thus, while admitting that '*Oedipus Coloneus* and *The Tempest* have their place in such immensely different contexts'[27] that it would be very difficult indeed to imagine someone getting the same from both (as it would be very difficult indeed to imagine a man-eating tiger and a mounted butterfly giving rise to the same emotions), he is nevertheless not averse to the suggestion that there might be a play from which we do learn the same as from *The Tempest*, though he thinks it extremely unlikely. And much as one might say 'I don't care if the leopard has any spots or not, it still terrifies me', so Casey remarks of *King Lear*: 'Of course, lines even scenes can be left out without seriously damaging the effect of the play.'[28]

What is interesting here is that Wittgenstein, the philosopher most commonly appealed to in support of the thesis that emotions

---

[27]   Ibid.
[28]   Ibid., p. 131.

are intensional, and from whom the comparison between emotions and our reactions to works of art is, I believe, derived, certainly did not accept Casey's conclusions about art. For example, in his lectures on aesthetics he remarked:

> You *could* select either of two poems to remind you of death, say. But supposing you had read a poem and admired it, could you say, 'Oh, read the other, it will do the same?' How do we use poetry? Does it play this role—that we say such a thing as: 'Here is something just as good as... ?'[29]

Wittgenstein's question is rhetorical. It does not *make sense* to speak of learning the same from any other play as from *King Lear*, for here what we learn is internally related to the particular play itself. For the same reason Wittgenstein notes that to change a work of art is to change what we learn from it.[30] This, as we have seen, Casey denies. Scenes can be left out of *King Lear*, he claims, without damaging its effect. But it is worth asking of which scenes this might be true. Not the scenes on the heath, I imagine. But let us admit that parts of the play are otiose. What Casey fails to see is that this is a criticism. It can show nothing about the nature of art, for what it refers to is an artistic failing. Discussing Tolstoi's famous condemnation of the play, Orwell admits:

> Tolstoi is right in saying that Lear is not a very good play as a play. It is too drawn-out and has too many characters and sub-plots. One wicked daughter would have been quite enough, and Edgar is a superfluous character; indeed it would probably be a better play if Gloucester and both his sons were eliminated.[31]

Orwell does not *argue* that the irrelevancies in *Lear* are grounds for condemnation. He takes this for granted, for it is a presupposition of literary criticism that any unexplained irrelevancy in a work detracts from it artistically. And Orwell's subsequent remarks make it plain that what such irrelevancies detract from is the meaning or significance of the work, what we can learn from it. This is why, when Orwell wishes to reject Tolstoi's ridiculous claim that there is no justification for the presence of the Fool in the play, he does so by showing that the theme of the play would

---

[29] L. Wittgenstein, *Lectures and Conversations on Aesthetics, Psychology and Religious Beliefs*, ed. Cyril Barrett (Oxford: Blackwell, 1967) p. 34.

[30] Ibid., p. 35.

[31] Orwell, op. cit., p. 292.

become unintelligible (or at least less intelligible) were the Fool absent. And this is also why Casey's claim that certain lines or scenes in the play cannot be justified does nothing to support his general contention that what we learn from a play is to some extent independent of its precise form. Just in so far as the former claim is true it will for that reason be true that there is nothing to be learned from the play. What we learn we learn from the precise way in which the author expresses himself, from the way he writes.[32] And the recognition that the play might have been written in a different way, or that one was mistaken in one's assessment of its qualities, is tantamount to the admission that there is nothing to be gained from reading it, or at least that what is to be gained is very different from what one had thought.

Nothing similar can be said of emotions generally. The following is a passage from John Braine's *Life at the Top*. The 'hero', Joe Lampton, has just told his wife and father-in-law that he intends to leave her for good and drive to London:

> She looked at me appealingly. 'Joe, you're tired. You've had something to drink. Wait until morning at least, dear.'
> Brown snorted. 'Dear!' he said. 'He's leaving her and she calls him dear. Let the bastard kill himself and good riddance! ... I'll deal with him. I'll make him suffer. You're too softhearted, Susan, that's your trouble ...'
> 'Do you know why he's leaving me?'
> 'You needn't tell him, Susan,' I said.
> She stamped her foot. The childish gesture was oddly shocking. 'I've been having an affair with Mark,' she said.
> Brown's face seemed to grow smaller; he swayed forward, then checked himself. 'I don't believe it,' he said.
> 'It's true. Ask Joe.'
> He clenched his fist. 'It's your fault,' he said to me. 'You can't have been a proper husband to her. It's your fault.'[33]

Abe Brown's recognition that he had misjudged his son-in-law shows only that his anger was misdirected. What it does not show is that the anger was not genuine. The harsh words, the contempt, were evidence of its genuineness. This is why, recognising that his rage was nevertheless unfounded, he is forced to seek another justification for it, though one of the same type. He has to pretend

---

[32] For a fuller discussion of this point see *Art and Morality* [Part 1 above] and 'Learning from a Novel' [Part 2, Ch. 1 above].

[33] Ibid., p. 216.

that the rift in his daughter's marriage is nevertheless her husband's fault. If he has not deceived her, then he has driven her to deceive him.

In part because one's reaction to a work of art is directed not to an object of a certain kind, but to a particular object, the same move is no longer possible with a novel or a play. The recognition that one has attributed qualities to the work which it does not possess involves a reassessment of one's reactions to it. It may, for instance, necessitate the recognition that the understanding imparted by the work was not a genuine understanding. 'It wasn't a great novel as I thought but simply a cheap thriller', is another way of saying: 'I learned nothing from it, though I thought otherwise.'

What I am saying here is not, I think, incompatible with my earlier remarks about the possibility of learning the same thing from *King Lear* and *Father Sergius*. For I have already commented on the triviality of this latter sense of 'learning' as applied to art. The sense in which one can learn the same from both plays is the sense in which what one learns can be stated in independence of either. And, as we have seen, if one thought that this were the *only* sense, then one would never see why literature should be thought to be of any importance. For one would not see why *King Lear* and *Father Sergius* were anything but long-winded ways of stating the obvious, or why either is any more profound than *Uncle Tom's Cabin*.

That there is another sense is, I think, shown by an earlier example. It is true that in one way Orwell's journalist did learn at the bridge outside Stuttgart only something which he knew already, something obvious to everyone. But in another sense he had to see the soldier lying there to understand what he and everyone knew. He had to be *shown* what death was like. And his experiences changed him, not by contradicting anything which he had previously regarded as a fact, but by replacing the picture which he had held of the death of an enemy with a new picture, by showing him what a soldier's death is really like.

Now in many ways a novel or a play may do something very similar. The story of Lear or Sergius can bring one to a new understanding of what one knows already in a way that a statement of fact never could. Tolstoi and Shakespeare do not *tell* you that there is a corruption in certain forms of renunciation where you might have thought otherwise. Rather they *show* you the corruption. The lives of Lear and Sergius show you what is meant by saying that renunciation is not a form of self-interest. Not that their lives are examples or anything like that. *King Lear* is not an allegory. And Lear himself is not self-interest anthropomorphically endowed with the form of a king. If you wished to find an example to illustrate this notion, you would choose the life of someone typical or representative of most men. You would not choose a king or a hermit. There are, however, more illuminating models to enable us to understand the role of the figure of Lear in our thought than that of an example. It is, for instance, sometimes worth bearing in mind Chesterton's comparison between the power of a poet's words and the power of myth. Chesterton's remarks about the myth of Father Christmas may be compared with what I said above about *King Lear*:

> Father Christmas is not an allegory of snow and holly; he is not merely the stuff called snow afterwards artificially given a human form, like a snow man. He is something that gives a new meaning to the white world and the evergreens; so that snow itself seems to be warm rather than cold.[34]

Further analogies come out in Wittgenstein's discussion of the myth of the King of the Wood at Nemi. Wittgenstein says:

> Put that account ... together with the phrase 'the majesty of death', and you see that they are one. The life of the priest-king shows what is meant by that phrase. If someone is gripped by the majesty of death, then through such a life he can give expression to it. Of course, this is not an explanation; it puts one symbol in place of another. Or one ceremony in place of another.[35]

The ceremony shows the majesty of death for what it is in the same way that the lives of Sergius and Lear show renunciation for what it is. Adopting one of Wittgenstein's remarks one might equally well say: 'Put the phrase "Renunciation is not a form of self-interest" together with Shakespeare's account of the life of Lear and you see that they are one.' It is this relationship which enables Orwell to speak of the phrase as the 'moral' of the story. And it is also this relationship which makes it possible for us to speak of learning from the story. The point is that reflection on the

---

[34] G.K. Chesterton, 'Man and Mythologies', in W.H. Auden ed., *G.K. Chesterton: A election from his non-fictional prose* (London: Faber & Faber, 1970) p. 214.

[35] L. Wittgenstein, 'Bemerkungen uber Frazers "The Golden Bough"', *Synthese*, 17 (3) September 1967, p. 236.

life of Lear may *replace* reflection on the phrase, much as in Orwell's earlier example I said that reflection on the dead soldier had replaced reflection on the statistics of dead in the journalist's thought. The difference is that *any* dead soldier might have brought about the same change. It was merely a coincidence that this was the first dead soldier he had seen. So that if one said that the change was internally related to the event which gave rise to it, then one would have to recognise that it was only a contingent matter that this particular event came to play such a role in his life. But when it is reading *King Lear* which changes a man then there will no longer be any sense in saying that such a change might have been brought about in some other way, by *Father Sergius* for example. Certainly the life of Sergius might *also* replace the phrase 'Renunciation is not a form of self-interest' in a man's thought. But it does not follow that he will then have learned the same as he would have learned from Shakespeare's play. Having read *Lear* a man may be captivated by Tolstoi's story, so that when he thinks of renunciation he thinks of it in connexion with the life of Sergius. We may still speak of a *change* in his idea of the nature of renunciation, of its being deepened or trivialised. He will not simply be a man who has sat through the same lesson twice.

To see this is to see why what a man gets out of either story can be explained only by reference to that particular story and not, as Casey's view sometimes suggests, by reference to a story of a certain type. To see this, however, is also to see what is wrong with the position which both Casey and Wollheim are attacking, that is the idea that the appreciation of art can be explained by reference to the appreciation of nature. For the possibility of the form of learning I have discussed constitutes a radical dissimilarity between the appreciation of art and the appreciation of natural beauty.

In this, of course, I am not denying that people *do* speak of learning from nature, nor that this way of speaking is perfectly intelligible. What Orwell's journalist learned from the sight of the dead soldier might be regarded as an example, though for various reasons I am uneasy about describing this as an instance of the aesthetic appreciation of nature. Nevertheless, there are more clear-cut cases. One might think, for example, of the way in which Coleridge's ancient mariner is saved from the curse brought upon him by his gratuitous slaughter of the albatross when he recognises the beauty of the sea-snakes which surround the ship. Earlier he had despised them as creatures of horror, 'a thousand thousand slimy things', resenting the fact that what is repulsive to him should live while his ship-mates lay dying. But now, captivated by their beauty, he comes to respect their independent existence:

> O happy living things! no tongue
> Their beauty might declare
> A spring of love gushed from my heart
> And I blessed then unaware.

Coleridge's story could not be understood by someone who failed to see that the mariner had learned something from the sea-snakes, that his moral insight had been deepened by the appreciation of their beauty. If one ignored this, then one would be unable to understand why the curse was lifted from him.

> The self-same moment I could pray
> And from my neck so free
> The Albatross fell off, and sank
> Like lead into the sea.

But nor could one understand the story unless one recognised that what the mariner learns is nothing like what one might learn from a work of art. There is nothing about the sea-snakes in particular which enables the mariner to learn from them. The same understanding might have arisen from an appreciation of the beauty of any living creature. Indeed it is essential to the story that had he recognised the beauty of the albatross, the tragedy need never have occurred.

There is nothing in the experiences of the mariner, nor in my appreciation of a sunset, which need illuminate the way in which someone might learn from reading *King Lear*, and any attempt to assimilate the one to the other could lead only to a blurring of differences. Unfortunately, there is a way of expressing these differences which may also lead to confusion, and to confusion of much the sort of which Wollheim and others are guilty. For one may be tempted to emphasise the form of understanding which characterises the appreciation of art, though not the appreciation of natural beauty, by suggesting that when a man reads a novel he is appreciating both its form and its content, whereas when he marvels at a sunset or the tranquillity of a forest he is merely appreciating its form in the trivial sense in which its form is thought of as a pattern of lines and colours, pleasant, perhaps, but of no significance. And this in its turn may lead to confusion. For in its implication that there is nothing to be found in natural beauty which is not to be found in artistic beauty it may lead one to suppose that the appreciation of the former is merely a less complex form of the appreciation of the latter. So that it is at least plausible to suppose that a grasp of the beauty of nature is already implicit in the appreciation of art.

The truth is that the whole picture is a simplification. Certainly, there is something in the suggestion that the man who watches in wonder as the sun sinks over the forest does not normally look for significance in what he sees. We may, for instance, contrast him with the farmer whose scrutiny of the same scene stems from practical concerns and for whom the tones of the sky, the clouds, the haze on the horizon are seen as signs, as warnings of bad weather, perhaps, the distant fox merely a threat to his poultry. And though, like the man who sees a picture of a sunset, he may wonder at what he sees, at the kaleidoscope of colours, the lines and shapes, unlike the latter he will never have to wonder what to make of it. Nevertheless, it does not follow that what he admires is simply a pattern of colours, a painting minus the ideas. Were this the case, then a photograph would be an adequate substitute for the sunrise.

When someone is captivated by the mysterious tranquillity of a forest, when Coleridge's ancient mariner marvelled at the sea-snakes, the wonder comes from living through the scene, from its being a part of one's life. A photograph would be nothing by comparison, though the colours and shapes will be there even in the photograph, for what is important is the contact with nature. It is this background, the fact that I have been brought up in contact with trees and animals, know how they live and grow, what the rain does to them, and how they look in winter, which makes it possible for me to be impressed by *this* scene, lit in this way, and with the shadows thrown in this way. Even where, as in Coleridge's story, what is witnessed is something the like of which I have never seen before, it is against the background of our lives, our knowledge of other more familiar living things, that what I witness now is wonderful. When the mariner marvelled at the beauty of the sea-snakes, at their 'blue, glossy green and velvet black', or at the 'elfish light' which 'fell off in hoary flakes' when they reared from the water, this was not all he admired, for he might have found the same in a firework display. What made the scene wonderful was their being living creatures which 'coiled and swam' around the boat.

Again there is nothing in the pattern of colours and shadows which would give us this background, though the pattern would mean nothing without it. 'Green trees might be the withering ones, and brown trees the flourishing ones ... You cannot read these things off from the patterns or colour-combinations.'[36] Without a background of experience of nature the patterns or colour-combinations would mean nothing to us. Of course, I do not say that it is this background which makes the forest wonderful. A scene which was banal or horrifying, the destruction of the forest by fire, or the same forest on a wet, foggy day, would have the same background. But without it the scene could evoke neither wonder nor horror. It is the forest which moves me, but were I not part of the scene, and were it not a part of my life, then there would be nothing to move me.

Yet there is nothing of this in a work of art, and a discussion of stories and paintings will not bring us to see what men find wonderful in nature. When Oscar Wilde referred to a sunset shown him by his landlady as 'only a second-rate Turner' he was, of course, only half serious. Certainly, there are similarities and connexions. This was what prevented the joke from being simply pointless. We have, for instance, seen the impossibility of rendering either the story or the sunset in a description. In either case the description will leave out what really matters. Asked to say what there is in *King Lear* I shall say that it shows the impossibility of practising self-denial from selfish motives. Asked to describe the sunset, no doubt I could do better, though again what I say will miss what is really important. But as we have seen, the reasons for the inadequacy of my remarks in each case are different. With *King Lear* the banality stems from the attempt to bring out what can be learned only in Shakespeare's words. With the sunset there is nothing to learn. It is just that however well I describe the scene, it is not a part of *your* life but of mine. You may see from my description what it must have been like, but you were not there.

Of course the experience of art and nature are normally not independent of one another. We are surrounded by novels and plays, and it is understandable that a love of beauty in nature should often go along with a love of art. It is this contingent fact which may make it seem plausible to suppose that the one is a

36   B. Bosanquet, *Three Lectures on Aesthetic* (London: Macmillan, 1915) p. 44.

variety of the other, or that both are aspects of the same thing, as do the writers I have considered in this paper. But this would be a mistake. One further observation may help to make this clear.

I can imagine a society in which men are untouched by any form of artistic activity and yet still possess a love of nature which one might call aesthetic. I can imagine this because it is to some extent true of children in our own society. This may be obscured if one thinks chiefly of the more sophisticated forms of the love of nature, the appreciation of landscapes and sunsets, which in our society are characteristic of adults, and which are of course closely connected for many adults with the appreciation of art. But this is a one-sided view of nature. Chesterton remarks somewhere that though nature may present itself to the poet as consisting of stars and lilies, these are not poets who live in the country. One might add that they do not seem to be poets who remember their own childhood very well. For it is generally what is fantastic in nature and not what is serene or magnificent which appeals to children. For them nature consists of cows and pigs, top-heavy toadstools and monstrous jelly-fish. Even where a child is attracted by sunsets or the sky at night, it is what is odd or surprising in these scenes which attracts them. They are enchanted by the curious spectacle of a silver disc suspended in the sky which changes in shape from night to night and which disappears in the daytime, rather than by anything you find described in the work of a lake-land poet.

There is little enough temptation to see in a child's love of what is grotesque or surprising in the shape of a toadstool, the influence of artistic tradition. No more than there is a temptation to say when a child is amused by someone's slipping on a banana skin, he is amused only by virtue of his contact with music-hall conventions of humour. But there should be even less temptation to deny that this love has its aesthetic aspects. Because the form of a toadstool surprises us, gives us a start when we see it, we are likely to see it in a way which we do not see more familiar objects, associated as these are with everyday activities and characteristics.

There is much of this love of what is fantastic, contorted in a child's attitude towards fairy-tales too, and later in his life a man may find such characteristics in literature or in sculpture. A poet's words may again bring us to see things as they really are by emphasising their bizarre side. Once again I quote Chesterton:

> If we say 'a man is a man' we awaken no sense of the fantastic, however much we ought to, but if we say, in the language of the old satirist, 'that man is a two-legged bird without feathers', the phrase does, for a moment, makes us look at man from the outside and gives us a thrill in his presence.[37]

But when the child comes to appreciate poetry, he comes to appreciate much that he did not find in nature. What makes him look twice at the toadstool is its form. The form of the satirist's language is striking too. Say instead 'A man is an animal in some respects different from others' and the line no longer impresses. But in poetry *what* is said is important. Say 'A man is a small elephant, without a trunk' and you have the same form but nothing is said which would impress you. Because of these differences you are going to come seriously unstuck if you try to explain why the line is striking by comparing it to what a child finds in a toadstool. But if you try to explain why the child loves the toadstool by referring to an adult's love of poetry or sculpture, then I think that you may have forgotten what it was like to be a child looking at a toadstool.

---

[37] 'Browning as Literary Artist', in *G.K. Chesterton: A selection from his non-fictional prose*, p. 29.

3

The Limits
of Imagination[1]

> We may compose, paint and describe monsters and chimeras of
> every extravagant variety of form; but still, if we analyse them, we
> shall always find that the component parts, how much soever they
> may be distorted or disguised, have been taken from objects or
> qualities of objects, with which we have previously been
> acquainted throughout the organs of sensation.
>
> Richard Payne Knight, *An Analytical Inquiry into*
> *the Principles of Taste*[2]

Writers of an empiricist persuasion have traditionally paid equal
attention to the powers and to the limitations of the human
imagination. For it has been customary for them to emphasise that
while the imagination, unlike the memory, is not restricted simply
to *recording* what happens or has happened, there is, nevertheless,
a sense in which it is bound by past experience. I can remember a
man with green skin only if I have met a man with green skin,
whereas I can imagine such a man whether I have met one or not.
Still, I can imagine such a man, so the argument goes, only
because I have seen men with more conventional complexions and
have seen many objects, though not men, which are green: green
grass, green trees, green moss. My idea of a man with a green skin
is simply a complex construction from more simple observed
elements. *Any* such creation must be. It is in this way that limits
are imposed on the imagination.

[1] First published in *British Journal of Aesthetics*, 20 (2) 1980. © British Society
for Aesthetics, 1980.
[2] Richard Payne Knight, *An Analytical Inquiry into the Principles of Taste*, p.
141.

But the limits are more apparent than real. Some of Hume's remarks point to the difficulties. 'Suppose a person to have enjoyed his sight for thirty years and to have become perfectly well acquainted with colours of all kinds, excepting one particular shade of blue ... Now I ask whether it is possible for him, from his own imagination, to supply this deficiency.'[3] Though Hume brushes the example aside, were he to be consistent, he would presumably have to say that this new shade of blue is itself a complex of the other shades which have been observed, or that it has elements in common with them. But then one wonders what it could mean to say that one shade of blue is composed of another, or that different shades of blue have something in common. And if it is said that all that is meant is that we can imagine a new shade of blue only if we can already apply the word 'blue', then the thesis reduces to triviality. It is scarcely a restriction on the creativity of a poet or novelist or upon our ability to appreciate his creations that his imagination must be exercised in a language the meaning of whose words we are both able to understand.

All the same I think that there are many today who would maintain that it is the only restriction. Impressed perhaps by the failure of empiricist and other accounts to furnish substantial limits to the powers of human imagination many people are inclined to suppose that whatever can consistently be described can also be imagined, and to use 'unimaginable' as equivalent to 'logically impossible' or 'self-contradictory'.

It seems evident to me that this is an artificial construction of the sort characteristic of philosophical theory, rather than an account of how the concept of imagination is actually employed in everyday contexts. For the most part, where it is appropriate to speak of what can be imagined, it also makes sense to speak of what can barely be imagined, what it is difficult to imagine, of someone's limited imagination, and so on. But it is clear that such locutions cannot be construed as covert ways of referring to what is or is not self-contradictory. For it makes no sense at all to speak of what is barely logically possible, or of what is almost self-contradictory. And it therefore remains to ask whether the ways in which we ordinarily speak of the imagination do have any sense. This question is of some especial importance in the present state of

3   David Hume, *An Enquiry Concerning Human Understanding*, ed. C.W. Hendel (New York: Oxford University Press, 1955) p. 29.

aesthetics. For it seems to me that the general rejection by philosophers of talk about the limits of the imagination is mirrored in
much contemporary aesthetics and particularly in recent studies of
the language of fiction. This has led to some confusion.

I

In order to explain what I mean, I should like to look closely at an
extremely influential article by Margaret Macdonald, 'The
Language of Fiction'.[4] In this article Miss Macdonald's aim, to
which I am for the most part sympathetic, is to emphasise the
deceptive nature of the language of fiction. Confusion is liable to
arise precisely because in one sense the language of fiction is not a
distinct language at all, even in the sense that the language of
religion or mathematics is. If I open the New Testament or a textbook of geometry I shall find at least some terms which appear
only or mainly in religious or mathematical contexts. If a man
speaks of God, of reverence, of omnipotence, or of radii, tangents,
hypotenuses, then it is likely that he is discussing religious or
mathematical questions. I say 'likely' and not 'certain' because of
at least one other important possibility, namely that the man in
question is engaged in telling a story or writing a novel. For there
is no sentence, scientific, religious, mathematical, which could not
of its nature appear in a work of fiction. And any of the sentences
which compose *Anna Karenina* or *Portrait of the Artist* could have
occurred outside fiction, for instance in biography.

Nevertheless, the title of Miss Macdonald's paper is not wholly
misleading. For in fiction, sentences which might have occurred in
biography, in a newspaper editorial, or in Hansard, are used in a
quite distinct way. In particular, Miss Macdonald wishes to
distinguish this use of language from its descriptive or informative
use. 'To tell a story', she says, 'is to originate, not to report.' Fiction
involves a creative use of language, not an informative use. In
Miss Macdonald's account of the difference the notion of choice
occupies a central place.

> When someone reports a fact he may choose the language or
> symbolism of his report. He may choose to use this carefully or
> carelessly. But there is a sense in which he cannot choose what he
> will say. What is truly said of Charlotte Bronte must be controlled

---

[4]   M. Macdonald, 'The Language of Fiction', reprinted in C. Barrett ed., *Collected Papers on Aesthetics* (Oxford: Blackwell, 1965) p. 107.

by what she was and what happened to her. But Jane Austen was
under no such restraints with Emma Woodhouse. For Emma
Woodhouse was her own invention. So she may have any qualities
and undergo any adventures her author pleases.[5]

Unfortunately, this way of expressing the difference carries with it
its own dangers of confusion. For to say that the creation of a
fictional character is marked by an absence of restraints, or that a
character in fiction can say or do what its author pleases, may
make it appear that character construction is a completely arbitrary activity, an activity in which the notion of a mistake is quite
out of place. To say in some context that I may do as I please is a
way of saying that nothing I do can be wrong.

It is clear that such a conclusion would be unwelcome to Miss
Macdonald: 'There is certainly a sense in which every work of
fiction is a law unto itself. Nonetheless, I think that there is a
general notion which governs these constructions, though its
application may give very different results. This is the Aristotelian
notion which is usually translated "probability", but which I
prefer to call "artistic plausibility".'[6] Miss Macdonald does not
explain this notion of artistic plausibility except to say that the
plausible is what convinces us, which is scarcely illuminating.
Rather more illuminating are the examples which she gives of the
concept's application. She continues:

> It is quite plausible that Alice should change her size by drinking
> from magic bottles, but it would be absurd that Emma Woodhouse
> or Fanny Price should do so. Or to make such an incident
> plausible, Jane Austen's novels would need to be very different.
> For it would have needed explanation in quite different terms
> from the conventions she uses. This also applies to more important
> plausibilities. Emma Woodhouse could not suddenly develop a
> Russian sense of sin, without either destroying the novel's plausi-
> bility or bringing about a complete revolution in its shape.[7]

If one asks why such incidents would be impossible in these contexts, one recognises that though in a sense a novelist can choose
what he will say, as a biographer for example cannot, in another
sense he is subject to even greater restrictions. For the form of the
narrative, its construction is important in literature in a way in

---

5   Ibid.
6   Ibid., p. 123.
7   Ibid., p. 124.

which it is not important in biography. Miss Macdonald is right to emphasise this and to see it as imposing restraints of a quite distinct kind on a novelist. An example from Joyce Cary brings out the nature of these constraints.

> When Proust was writing his masterpiece, he had a letter from Mme. Schiff to complain that he had made Swann ridiculous. Proust answered that he had no wish to make Swann ridiculous, far from it. But when he had come to this part of the work he found it unavoidable. That is to say, he had been compelled by the logic of the craft to do what he had not intended or imagined himself doing. For if he had not made Swann ridiculous, the whole work would have suffered.[8]

If he had been writing a biography of a man called Swann, then Proust could have ignored Mme. Schiff's complaint. Or he might have replied, '*I* didn't make Swann ridiculous, that is how he *was*.' But because Proust was in fact engaged in writing a novel, it was open to him either to introduce the character of Swann or not to do so. And having introduced Swann he was then in many respects free to decide what character Swann should have. Nevertheless, as Cary emphasises, this does not make character construction an arbitrary process. For what happens in a novel, the developments in its characters for instance, must be intelligible in terms of, must follow naturally from, what has gone before. And what has gone before may sometimes be such as to rule out any alternative developments. Proust represented Swann as ridiculous not because he was ridiculous, but because he had to be. Had he not done so, then the unity of the novel would have suffered; we should have been presented with an artistic failure.

Miss Macdonald imagines hypothetical examples of such failures. Cary gives us a real example. The writer is Flaubert, and the novel *Madame Bovary*, chapter III, book III.

> We are [Cary says] in the middle of Emma Bovary's love affair with Leon, the clerk at Rouen. Her excuse for visiting Rouen is to prepare a power of attorney with the lawyer, on which Leon as lawyer's clerk is to give his advice. We have then a whole chapter of their romantic love affair. They part and Leon is left with his intoxicated memories of the day. Then suddenly we have the passage: 'But why', he asks himself afterwards, while he goes home alone through the streets, 'is she so keen on this power of

---

8   Joyce Cary, *Art and Reality*, p. 87.

attorney.' This sentence about the power of attorney checks the reader at once. There is no reason on earth why the clerk should think at that moment about the power of attorney. It is quite out of key with his mood.[9]

The fault for which Cary condemns Flaubert could only be a fault in a work of fiction. Were *Madame Bovary* biography, then there would be no reason why Leon's romantic mood should *not* have been interrupted by quite unrelated thoughts. 'Actual young men', Cary remarks, 'may be as scatterbrained as you please.'[10] Indeed it would be a serious fault in a biographer to suppose that people can never act in an arbitrary or eccentric manner, do things which are out of character. But it is not clear what would be meant by speaking of a fictional character, Leon or Swann, acting out of character, unless this were intended as a criticism of their creators' work. This does not mean, of course, that there can be no surprises in a novel. No one could have predicted the development in Swann's character to which Mme. Schiff objected. Proust himself could not have done so. For his conception of Swann's possibilities had been changed, perhaps deepened by this development. Nevertheless it is essential that in retrospect such developments should be intelligible in terms of what has preceded them and not appear contrived or forced. This is why critics have uniformly condemned the surprises and coincidences which facilitate the satisfactory denouement of a novel like *Martin Chuzzlewit*, in a way that they have not, for the most part, condemned similar coincidences in, for instance, *Tess of the D'Urbervilles*. The series of accidents which lead to Tess's death can be understood in terms of Hardy's main theme in the novel, that of an innocent woman's life destroyed by blind fate, whereas the unexpected return of old Martin Chuzzlewit which ensures a happy ending to Dickens's novel has no important relation to the theme of selfishness and hypocrisy around which the story centres.

If I am writing a biography, I may learn of events in a man's life and of circumstances surrounding it, which are surprising to me. And it need not matter that these discoveries are incongruous with what I know of him. It will not necessarily be a fault in a biography of, say, Hitler that I am forced to present him in a less unified, coherent way because of the discovery that he was Jewish,

---

9   Ibid., p. 123.
10   Ibid.

or that he did not commit suicide in the Berlin bunker. What would be a fault would be to suppress or ignore facts about Hitler in the interests of a unified, coherent account. But if I were to conclude that there were faults in Dickens's or Flaubert's novels, these would not be mistakes *about* Martin Chuzzlewit or Leon. Flaubert did not make a mistake about Leon. He made a mistake in the construction of Leon.

II

So far I have been concerned to develop the view of fiction which is implied by Margaret Macdonald's article. It would not be, I think, unfair to represent this view as fundamentally that of Oscar Wilde. In his essay 'The Decay of Lying', Wilde says: 'If a novelist is base enough to go to life for his personages, he should at least not boast of them as copies. The justification of a character in a novel is not that other persons are what they are, but that the author is what he is.'[11] As I have indicated, Miss Macdonald is concerned, as Wilde is not, to emphasise the importance of the conventions within which a novelist works. A novelist may be criticised for internal incoherencies or irrelevancies in the construction of character. The difficulty is that, like Wilde, she seems to allow no other possibilities. For it is central to her distinction between the language of fiction and the language of information that in the case of fiction no check of external reality is desirable or possible. What this implies is that a novel which involves no internal incoherencies cannot be criticised. Miss Macdonald is thus in agreement with Wilde's dictum that 'No great artist ever sees things as they really are',[12] if this is taken to mean, as it was no doubt intended, that it is never a criticism of an artist that he does not see things as they really are.

It is this claim which I now wish to examine, and I shall begin by indicating one sort of criticism which it would, on the face of it, appear difficult to reconcile with Miss Macdonald's viewpoint. The example[13] comes from a review by George Orwell of Graham Greene's novel *The Heart of the Matter*, and Orwell begins by

---

[11]   Oscar Wilde, 'The Decay of Lying', in *Intentions*, p. 12.

[12]   Ibid., p. 44.

[13]   I am indebted to Professor D.Z. Phillips for drawing my attention to this example.

giving an outline of the story, which it is necessary for me to quote at length:

> The time is 1942 and the place is a West African British Colony, unnamed but probably the Gold Coast. A certain Major Scobie, Deputy Commissioner of Police and a Catholic convert, finds a letter bearing a German address, hidden in the cabin of the captain of a Portuguese ship. The letter turns out to be a private one and completely harmless, but it is, of course, Scobie's duty to hand it over to higher authority. However, the pity he feels for the Portuguese Captain is too much for him, and he destroys the letter and says nothing about it. Scobie, it is explained to us, is a man of almost excessive conscientiousness. He does not drink, take bribes, keep Negro mistresses, or indulge in bureaucratic intrigue, and he is, in fact, disliked on all sides for his uprightness, like Aristides the Just. His leniency towards the Portuguese Captain is his first lapse. After it his life becomes a sort of fable on the theme of 'Oh, what a tangled web we weave', and in every single instance it is the goodness of his heart which leads him astray. Actuated at the start by pity, he has a love-affair with a girl who has been rescued from a torpedoed ship. He continues with the affair largely out of a sense of duty, since the girl will go to pieces morally if abandoned; he also lies about her to his wife, so as to spare her pangs of jealousy. Since he intends to persist in his adultery, he does not go to confession, and in order to lull his wife's suspicions, he tells her that he has gone. This involves him in the truly fearful sin of taking the Sacrament while still in a state of mortal sin. By this time, there are other complications, all caused in the same manner, and Scobie decides that the only way out is through the unforgivable sin of suicide. Nobody else must be allowed to suffer through his death; it will be arranged to look like an accident. As it happens, he bungles one detail, and the fact that he has committed suicide becomes known. The book ends with a Catholic priest hinting with doubtful orthodoxy that Scobie is perhaps not damned. Scobie, however, had not entertained any such hope. White all through, with a stiff upper lip, he had gone to what he believed to be certain damnation out of pure gentlemanliness.[14]

Though Orwell rightly insists that his account is no mere parody of the plot of Greene's novel, it does, I think, give a fairly clear idea of Orwell's assessment of it. The story is ludicrous. 'It gives the impression', Orwell says, 'of having been mechanically

---

[14]   George Orwell, Review of *The Heart of the Matter*, in *The Collected Essays, Journalism and Letters of George Orwell*, Vol. 4, p. 239.

constructed, the familiar conflict being set out like an algebraic equation, with no attempt at psychological probability.'[15] Now it is interesting to ask whether the philosophical account which we have been considering could accommodate this sort of criticism. And, as I have said, the implication of Miss Macdonald's remarks is that Orwell's criticism could be legitimate only if it were an internal one, a criticism of incoherences *within* the story. Thus Orwell might object to Greene's work on the grounds that we are not adequately prepared for the developments in Major Scobie's character, or that these developments are contrived or forced, or that there are elements of the story which do not contribute to these developments, or that some of these developments themselves do not contribute in any significant way to the theme of the novel. And these are all criticisms which would be supported, if at all, by an examination of the relation between different elements of the story.

What is interesting, however, is that none of these is among the reasons given for Orwell's condemnation. Nor is it merely that, despite its internal coherence, Orwell has some other reason for attacking Greene's story (which would in itself be difficult enough to reconcile with Miss Macdonald's account), but that he finds it 'ridiculous' precisely because of its coherence. It is not, for example, that there is a difficulty in seeing how the Major Scobie with whom we are presented at the beginning of the novel could end up committing suicide, but that there is all too little difficulty. It is not that Scobie's suicide is inadequately explained by what has preceded it, but that it is too adequately explained to be real. The development of Scobie's character is somehow too systematic, too coherent. And the chief reason for this is that the explanation of his problems and of his final solution to them is to be found solely in his own thoughts and actions. 'In every single instance', Orwell remarks, 'it is the goodness of his heart that leads him astray.' The other characters in the novel are merely devices for advancing the plot. 'The novel is set in Africa, but the Africans are present only as an occasionally mentioned background. The date is 1942 but Scobie thinks about the war only insofar as it impinges on his dilemmas. He seldom thinks about his work. His mistress and wife are mentioned only insofar as they contribute to Scobie's

---

15   Ibid., p. 239.

downfall.'[16] For, of course, adultery requires both a wife and a mistress.

Orwell's point is not, of course, simply that Greene makes use of minor characters. One might compare *The Heart of the Matter* with *Anna Karenina*, another story which culminates in the suicide of the central character. Here also there are minor characters, whose lives are subordinated to the central theme of the book. Indeed, when attacking Henry James's claim that Tolstoi ignores principles of composition in the book, F.R. Leavis is at pains to emphasise the interrelatedness of its elements, the way in which what might at first appear to be digressions from the story of Anna and Vronsky — the romance between Kitty and Levin, the troubles in the Oblonsky household — in fact contribute to the final tragedy. Throughout the subordinate scenes, Leavis says, 'the terrible logic moves like an accelerating mechanism to the catastrophe'.[17] It is of course a consequence of this that many of the minor characters are left undeveloped, except in so far as they have a bearing on Anna's dilemma, but while in a real-life situation there is always more to a man than his relationship to a certain situation, in a novel this need not be so. Thus, at the opening of *Anna Karenina*, we are told that the Oblonsky household is in a state of confusion owing to the discovery of Stephan's adultery with their French governess, for this is crucial to the development of the novel. We are not told the age of the governess, since this would be irrelevant. To argue that any woman must have an age and that Tolstoi should therefore have decided upon the age of Stephan's mistress would be simply absurd. Mercifully, no such considerations lead Leavis to speak of a lack of reality in Tolstoi's writings.

Nevertheless, it does not follow that all the subordinate characters in a novel could be similarly attenuated without the work's suffering. In *Anna Karenina* they are plainly not. Anna's dilemma, the possibilities open to her, stem at least in part from the nature of her relationship with Vronsky, with her husband Alexei, with Kitty and others. It is not just because of the sort of woman that she is, but also because of the sort of man that Alexei is, that her marriage breaks down. But with Scobie it is different. What is possible for him, and what is not, is determined solely by

---

16   Ibid., p. 240.
17   F.R. Leavis, *Anna Karenina and Other Essays*, p. 26.

what he has done and what he feels. He faces problems because he has both a wife and a mistress. But the sort of people that his wife and mistress are, their thoughts and feelings, are irrelevant to the nature of the problems. It is just this which leads Orwell to condemn the novel's lack of reality. It lacks reality precisely because it exemplifies what Miss Macdonald claims is true of all literature. 'Characters', she tells us, 'play a role, human beings have a life.'[18] Orwell's point is that the characters in *The Heart of the Matter* do merely play a role in the central theme of the novel, the progress of its central figure towards damnation. They have no life of their own. They are simply the background against which Scobie's problems unfold; and human problems, Orwell wishes to say, are not really like that.

I think it fair to say that we can make sense of the sort of criticisms that Orwell directs against Greene's novel, only in so far as we recognise that they refer not to the story's internal construction, to breaches of the conventions within which it is written, but to some conception of reality external to the story. This notion of reality is not, however, without difficulties. One reason why I feel reservations about its introduction is that it may lead us to suppose that within literature there is some one way of distinguishing what is in accord with reality from what is not. We may, that is, attempt to erect one standard of realty against which all literature from *War and Peace* to *The Fall of the House of Usher* may be measured, and ignore the very different conventions within which these works were written. What I have in mind is well illustrated by some of the views of John Hospers. Hospers's main aim is to establish that it is always a criticism of a work of literature to say that it is untrue to human nature. In itself this might not be objectionable. But though it is never spelled out in detail, Hospers clearly has a limited conception of what being true to human nature amounts to: 'If the novelist's main character were presented as a well-adjusted average human being; not given to excessive guilt-feelings or morbid introspection, who suddenly joins some obscure sect devoted to constant penance and self-flagellation, we should condemn such a characterization as wildly implausible and untrue to human nature.'[19] What this passage

---

[18]   Macdonald, op. cit., p. 118.
[19]   John Hospers, 'Literature and Human Nature', *Journal of Aesthetics and Art Criticism*, Vol. 17, p. 48.

strongly suggests is that Hospers is using the conventions peculiar
to one genre of literature as the standard by which to assess all
literature. Roughly, what this amounts to is a demand for veri-
similitude in literature. And though he goes on to say that on
examining 'major characters in admittedly great works of literature',[20] he is unable to find any which offend against his own
implied canons, one can only assume that he is here operating
with a persuasive definition of the phrase 'great works of literature'. Indeed the hypothetical conversion described in the passage
quoted above is scarcely less remarkable than that undergone by
Ebenezer Scrooge, and considerably less remarkable than the fate
of the character developed in one of Virginia Woolf's novels, who
is an adult in the Elizabethan age, hardly older in the 1920s, and
who, starting as a man becomes a woman halfway through the
book.

Miss Macdonald is very alive to the dangers of the sort of
monolithic conception of reality exemplified by Hospers's
account. We must, she tells us, be wary of assuming that all literature should, for example, be realistic or naturalistic. For such an
assumption may lead us to condemn whole genres of novels,
ghost stories, fairy tales, science fiction, not because of the individual characteristics of the works we classify as belonging to
these genres, but simply because they do belong to them.

Miss Macdonald's argument on this point seems to me sound.
What it proves, however, is not that the notion of reality has no
relevance to the sphere of fiction, but that it cannot be applied
without allowance being made for the very different forms which
fiction may take. Thus it would be quite wrong to suppose that if
we are to criticise Greene's portrayal of Scobie as unreal, we must
for similar reasons necessarily be willing to reject out of hand a
story like *The Black Cat*, or *The Fall of the House of Usher*. Nor does
Orwell make any such assumption. Writing of Poe's novels, he
notes that 'they do not convey a feeling of falsity'. They are, he
continues, 'true within a certain framework, they keep the rules of
their own peculiar world'.[21]

What Orwell, unlike Miss Macdonald, is willing to say is that
even when due allowance has been made for the conventions
within which a story is written, it may nevertheless lack reality. To

---

[20] Ibid.
[21] George Orwell, *Inside the Whale and Other Essays*, p. 44.

understand the force of this claim, we shall be led to rather more general reflections on the nature of our response to literature.

III

If one were to ask what it is to appreciate the portrayal of a character in fiction, one answer which one might receive is that implicit in the account given by Margaret Macdonald. To respond to the characterisation in Tolstoi or Dickens, it might be said, is to respond to certain aspects of the construction of their novels, to the way in which certain passages are composed and their relation to other passages. No doubt there would be much to be said for such a view. Consider the following passage:

> Sharing a tent with a man who was crazy wasn't easy, but Nately didn't care. He was crazy too, and had gone every free day to work on the officers' club that Yossarian had not helped build. Actually, there were many officers' clubs that Yossarian had not helped build, but he was proudest of the one on Pianosa. It was a sturdy and complex monument to his powers of determination. Yossarian never went there to help until it was finished; then he went there often, so pleased was he with the large, fine, rambling, single-storied building. It was truly a splendid structure, and Yossarian throbbed with a mighty sense of accomplishment each time he gazed at it and reflected that none of the work that had gone into it was his.[22]

In this book, *Catch 22*, the portrayal of Yossarian's character depends for much of its force on the way in which it is expressed and this is especially true of what seems to me the really decisive touch in the whole passage, the last sentence. What strikes one first about this line is its construction. But it is not easy to say what is striking about this. What is easy is to say how it might be rendered innocuous. This would consist simply in changing the word 'none' to 'all' or 'most' or 'some'. Yossarian would then be presented as the sort of man who takes pride in his part in some important enterprise. To understand how Yossarian's attitude differs from this, one must recognise that very often such people's pride is unaffected by the recognition that what they have accomplished is itself worthless, or positively evil. Thus, the man who is fond of remarking that if a job is worth doing it is worth doing well, often fails to notice that his motto only enjoins effort directed

---

22   Joseph Heller, *Catch 22* (New York: Simon & Schuster, 1961) p. 17.

towards what is worth while, and has nothing to say about the diligent pursuit of worthless goals. Yossarian, however, is in a situation, an American military campaign where he is surrounded by objectives, the furtherance of the war effort and various less comprehensive military and non-military goals, which he regards as not merely worthless but insane, and by people who, recognising the insanity of these objectives are nevertheless willing to risk their lives for them. The paradoxical nature of the situation comes out in Colonel Dunbar's conversation with Dr. Stubbs.

> 'Do you really want some more codeine?' Dr Stubbs asked. 'It's for my friend Yossarian. He's sure that he's going to be killed.'
> 'Yossarian? Who the hell is Yossarian? What the hell kind of a name is Yossarian, anyway. Isn't he the one who got drunk and started that fight with Colonel Korn at the officers' club the other night?'
> 'That's right. He's Assyrian.'
> 'That crazy bastard.'
> 'He's not so crazy,' Dunbar said. 'He swears he's not going to fly to Bologna.'
> 'That's just what I mean', Dr Stubbs answered. 'That crazy bastard may be the only sane one left.'[23]

Where a man's only possible objectives are worthless, then the inference from 'He made an effort', to 'He has a right to feel proud' is a dubious one. And its dubiousness is brought out in the portrayal of Yossarian. Yossarian throbs with a mighty sense of accomplishment precisely because he has done nothing at all.

What should, however, by now have become clear is that an appreciation of this portrayal is possible only in so far as one grasps not merely the form of the portrayal, the character of the sentence-construction, and the way in which the passage I have quoted is related to other passages in the book, but also the content of the beliefs and values which it embodies. An appeal to the formal qualities of the writing will allow us to explain what makes certain of the sentences, particularly the last one, surprising or unexpected. What such an appeal will not do is to explain why there is in these sentences something which seems appropriate as well as surprising, why what is well said may also be worth saying, why what is clever may also be more than clever. To

---

explain this one must appreciate the beliefs and attitudes of which Yossarian's character is an expression.

Now it is a commonplace observation that where the beliefs embodied in a work of art are too far removed from those of its audience, then the work will hold no fascination for them. Thus, in the above example, someone who made a point of handing out white feathers to conscientious objectors, or who stood for the kind of patriotism which finds expression in the motto, 'My country, right or wrong', could not be expected to respond to the joke around which *Catch 22* centres.[24] And many other examples could be mentioned. But perhaps the best way to illustrate the point is to draw attention to the bewilderment which we feel where it does not appear to hold good. A well-known instance is that attitude of the reading public towards Charles Dickens. For what is curious about Dickens is that he became a national institution in a country almost every aspect of whose life he had violently attacked in his writings. As someone once remarked, it would surprise no one to learn that *Little Dorrit* is a best-seller at the Home Office, for just the very people who are ferociously satirised in Dickens, stupid officials, hypocritical industrialists, insensitive teachers, are often just those very people who have taken him to their hearts. This has led many critics to question whether there is not something unreal in Dickens's attack on society.

It is worth asking why this does seem a natural assumption to make, why we do naturally assume that if someone appreciates the literary merit of works embodying beliefs and values which are the very antithesis of those which they themselves stand for, then there must be something superficial or unreal in these values. No doubt, of course, many would say that such an assumption raises issues of no philosophical interest, or is simply mistaken. Writing of the feeling that what one finds horrifying or terrible cannot be aesthetically moving, Renford Bambrough in a recent paper suggests that there is simply no contradiction between these elements. 'A beauty', he says, 'may be a terrible beauty. A horror may be horrible, and still sublime.'[25] Often there is the temptation to add that any conflict one feels between these elements is merely

[24]   I am indebted for this point to an unpublished paper by Mr. H.O. Mounce.
[25]   Renford Bambrough, 'Literature and Philosophy', in R. Bambrough ed., *Wisdom: Twelve Essays* (Oxford: Blackwell, 1974) p. 283.

psychological. It is merely a psychological matter that lawyers do not appreciate jokes against lawyers, that the Czar had no high opinion of *Resurrection*, and that retired Colonels are blind to the merits of *Catch 22*. The term 'psychological' is, of course, scarcely self explanatory, and if one says that the lawyer's failure to respond to jokes about lawyers is psychological, then I do not see what this adds to the claim that lawyers do not respond to jokes about lawyers, though it certainly *sounds* more scientific. On the other hand, if what is implied is that there is never any explanation of the lack of response except perhaps irrational prejudice, then this seems to me an over-simplification. It is an over-simplification because, as I have tried to show, beliefs and values which do not have their source in literature, may nevertheless have an important part to play in what makes a work of literature profound, or humorous, or moving. And it would seem to follow that where a man's viewpoint is such as to rule out a certain set of beliefs as incomprehensible when he encounters them outside literature, then this may well present an insuperable obstacle to the appreciation of a work of literature which embodies these beliefs.

That such breakdowns in comprehension can occur outside literature seems to me undeniable. A particularly striking example occurs in a novel by Isaac Babel. *Red Cavalry* is the story of a Jew drafted into a Cossack regiment and its theme is that of the clash of beliefs between two alien cultures. This conflict comes to a head in one chapter where a Cossack has been mortally wounded in battle, and to escape torture at the hands of the Polish army begs the Jew to kill him. The latter refuses, and at that moment another Cossack appears on the scene.

> They spoke briefly; no words reached me. Dolgushov held his papers out to the platoon commander, and Afonka hid them away in his boot and shot Dolgushov in the mouth. 'Afonka,' I said … 'I couldn't, you see.'
> 'Get out of my sight', he said, growing pale, 'or I'll kill you. You chaps in specs have as much pity for us as a cat has for a mouse.' And he cocked his rifle.[26]

In his introduction to the book, Lionel Trilling speaks of the conflict here as a conflict between a vision of peace and a vision of

---

[26]   Isaac Babel, *Red Cavalry* (London: Alfred A. Knopf, 1929) p. 117.

violence. One way of explaining this would be to say that it is a conflict between a view of life in which the important distinction is between one's friends and one's enemies, and a view of life in which this distinction has no significance. For the Cossack, Afonka, the only consideration governing how one treats a man is whether he is friend or foe. If he is a friend, then one is justified in killing, stealing, lying, to help him. For the Jewish narrator, these things are ruled out whoever is concerned. Since the distinction between friend and enemy is not one around which his life centres, he can see the willingness to kill an injured comrade as a manifestation of violence, of the brutality of the Cossack's life. Afonka by contrast cannot see it as anything but pity.

This conflict which lies at the heart of Babel's novel, seems to me to illustrate a point made by Wittgenstein. It is important, Wittgenstein says, to recognise that: 'One human being may be a complete enigma to another. We learn this, when we come into a strange country with entirely strange traditions; and, what is more, even given a mastery of the country's language, we do not understand the people ... We cannot find our feet with them.'[27] When such a conflict occurs (and of course not *all* disagreements are of this sort, for otherwise we should never understand anyone who did not share our viewpoint), then each party may be inclined to say of the other that he cannot see how people *can* see things as they do, or how people *can* feel like that. We might speak of this as a failure of imagination, were it not that this might imply a criticism. But in Babel's example, it is not that either the Cossack or the Jew is making a mistake, but simply that they see things differently. And it is perhaps better to speak here of a limit to the imagination. Limits are drawn to what we can imagine by our natures, by our beliefs and values, by what we think and feel. This is why Wittgenstein goes on after the passage I have quoted, to say: 'If a lion could speak, we could not understand him.'[28]

None of the things which are important in our lives are important (or important in the same way) for lions. Lions do not vote in elections, pray to God, feel remorse, or carry round in their wallets snapshots of their children. If a lion could speak we could not understand him, not because we could not know when and how a

---

[27] L. Wittgenstein, *Philosophical Investigations*, ed. G.E.M. Anscombe & R. Rhees, trans. G.E.M. Anscombe (Oxford: Blackwell, 1953) p. 223.
[28] Ibid.

lion uses a word and perhaps use it in that way ourselves, but because we could make no sense of the way he sees things. We could not for instance know the difference between what is for him merely conventional and what comes from the heart. For us there could be no such difference. I wish at this stage merely to indicate one corollary of this. It is that if a lion could write a novel then we could see nothing in it.

But one may feel doubts about the significance of this corollary. One may, that is, feel doubts about whether it has any implications for the understanding of novels written by human beings. 'Surely', someone may say, 'when you mentioned the activities in which human beings (though not lions) engage, you ignored the most important difference. For you neglected to mention that lions do *not* write novels. Nor do they sing, tell one another stories or paint pictures. They have in fact no cultural traditions at all. Were they able to speak, it would be this more than anything which would constitute a barrier to an understanding of their lives. For it is from a study of their culture that we can best come to understand those peoples whose lives are at first an enigma to us.'

Such an objection has its point. The point is that it is a mistake to say without qualification that whether or not we can appreciate a novel will depend on whether we think it possible to take seriously the moral viewpoint which it embodies. For the novel itself may bring us to a new awareness of what it is possible to take seriously. For a reader in our present society the first impression of the Cossacks whom Babel describes may be, as no doubt it was for Babel, merely one of violence. Yet the stories themselves may bring us to a deeper understanding of the Cossacks, may bring us to see that it is possible for men to see the violence of their lives as more than mere mindless brutality.

By this I do not mean that the novel may show us that people do in fact adopt such attitudes (as the man who lifts 300 pounds before my eyes shows me that it is possible to lift such weights). Rather, it is the way in which Babel's stories are written that may make such attitudes convincing to us, may enable us to see how they can be taken seriously, even perhaps where we might not agree with them. The difference between these two senses of 'possible' is crucial here. If what I have witnessed leads me to conclude that it is possible to lift 300 pounds, then I mean that any rational person would draw this conclusion, that no alternative judgement can be made. But if I am brought by Babel's stories to see the violence of the Cossacks' lives as 'having a primitive energy, passion and virtue', I may have to recognise that this does not rule out the possibility of alternative viewpoints. It does not show that it would be possible for anyone to view the Cossacks' lives in this way. Whether this is possible will depend on the sort of attitudes which the reader brings with him. In his introduction Trilling suggests that if it is possible for us to see the violence of Babel's Cossacks as anything but a 'very ugly brutality', then this will be because we are already inclined to respond to the ethical qualities of violence, to its simplicity, its straightforwardness. I should not wish to deny this. All that I should wish to add is that there may also be those in whom no such inclination exists, who see the violence perhaps as something merely disgusting or obscene. I do not see how such people could respond to Babel's stories. It would be like trying to respond to a novel written by a lion.

IV

Now the novel which Orwell reviewed for the *New Yorker* was not written by a lion, but by a Catholic novelist named Graham Greene. Still, Orwell found it unconvincing. He was unable to 'find his feet' with the characters portrayed by Greene and found their lives, their beliefs, their problems incredible and unreal. To understand this, one must look at the idea around which the story revolves. Orwell refers to this as 'the cult of the sanctified sinner'. 'The central idea of the book', he tells us, 'is that it is better, spiritually higher to be an erring Catholic, than a virtuous pagan.' Greene appears to share the idea, which has been floating around since Baudelaire, that there is something rather *distingué* in being damned; Hell is a sort of high-class night-club, entry to which is reserved for Catholics only, since the others, the non-Catholics, are too ignorant to be held guilty, like the beasts that perish.'[29] Now it is important to see that Orwell rejects the cult of the sanctified sinner, not because it is an intelligible view with which he is nevertheless in disagreement, but because he is unable to understand how anyone could hold such a view. In this, he is not chiefly concerned to deny the sincerity of men like Greene. True, he obviously had his doubts about this. 'When people really believe

---

[29]   Orwell, op. cit., p. 441.

in hell,' he remarks, 'they are not so fond of striking graceful attitudes on its brink.'[30] But this, he says, is not to the point. What is to the point is that Orwell was quite unable to come to terms with any view founded on the principle that some human beings are superior to others. Now, in Greene's case, the superior beings were Catholics. Of course, even Greene could not with any plausibility maintain that non-Catholics are in all respects just like the beasts that perish. Non-Catholics are capable of 'ordinary human decency'. They may be kind to their wives, keep their promises, love their children. But compared with distinctively Catholic concerns, these things are of no importance. It is not pretended that Catholics are any better than others in these respects. They may be worse. But they are worse in respects which are unimportant. The only truly important issues, the issues of personal salvation and damnation, are ones which Catholics alone even understand.

Now it was just this distinction between the really important and exclusively Catholic concerns of damnation and salvation, and the pagan values of ordinary human decency, which Orwell found embodied, 'clothed', as he says, 'in flesh and blood' in the character of Major Scobie. Orwell found himself unable to respond to the portrayal of Scobie, because of just such a distinction; a distinction between, on the one hand, the important problems in Scobie's life, which centre around his progress towards damnation and, on the other, his relations with other people, which raise no really important problems and simply constitute a background to his theological concerns. 'Scobie', Orwell says, 'is incredible, because the two halves of him do not really fit together.'[31]

When Orwell condemns the portrayal of Scobie as incredible, he clearly does not mean that it involves an internal inconsistency, that, for example, Scobie's problems are not coherently developed. What is incredible is that anyone should have these problems, that anyone should think of problems in the way that Scobie does. The problems in Scobie's marriage, the problems surrounding his affair, are like those of a shepherd with his flock. The shepherd's problems may be caused by his sheep, but the nature of those problems is not determined by the ideas and values of the sheep, who do not have ideas and values, but only by his own ideas of what is important. For Orwell this was just the respect in which

---

[30] Ibid.
[31] Ibid., p. 442.

human beings differ from sheep. And Orwell's condemnation of the portrait of Scobie is an expression of this gulf between his own beliefs and those embodied in Greene's story. If one asks what the standard against which the story is being assessed is, then the standard is that of Orwell's own beliefs. The story is being tested against the limits of what Orwell can imagine, and found wanting. Given this, any internal coherence in its construction is quite by the way. The story might be a supreme example of literary crafts-manship. For Orwell it lacks reality.

In so far as the above is a fair account of Orwell's criticisms, then I do not see what *philosophical* objections there can be to them. What they amount to is a condemnation of a story, not by reference to its internal construction, but by reference to the beliefs and values which the critic brings to bear on it. One may not agree with the criticism which Orwell makes, but if someone wished to reject the very idea of such criticism, then he could do so only by advocating a conception of literary criticism as artificial and one-sided as that implied by the account of Margaret Macdonald. I refer to this conception as artificial because it is an attempt to explain literary creation and literary criticism without reference to the sorts of limits placed on the imagination by the beliefs and values of both critics and writers. Dostoevsky once remarked: 'I am a novelist so that I can invent.' The last word on the subject, however, was Tolstoi's. 'Psychology', said Tolstoi, 'is the one thing an artist must *not* invent.'[32]

---

[32] I have been unable to trace the source of the two quotations. [Editors: The Dostoevsky remark is quoted without source by E. Lampert in 'Dostevsky', in J. Fennell ed., *Nineteenth-Century Russian Literature* (Los Angeles: University of California Press, 1973) p. 240. The Tolstoy quotation is reported by Chekhov in a letter to Gorky (dated Moscow April 1899) in which he writes 'The day before yesterday I went to see Lev Tolstoy. He praised you highly and called you "a remarkable writer." He likes your "Fair" and "In the Steppe" and doesn't like "Malva". He said a writer can invent whatever he pleases, but he can't invent psychology, and Gorky occasionally goes in for such psychological inventions. He describes things he has never felt'; see *Anton Chekhov's Life and Thought: Selected Letters and Commentary*, trans. M.H. Heim & S. Karlinsky (Evanston, IL: Northwestern University Press, 1973) pp. 355–6.]

4

Literary Examples and Philosophical Confusion[1]

It is by no means unusual in works of philosophy for writers to make use of examples from literature or (like *e.g.* Peter Winch[2] and Eugene Kamenka[3]) to bemoan the lack of literary examples in the work of other philosophers. Nor is it unusual for philosophers to write substantial tomes without ever mentioning any work of literature or (like R.M. Hare[4] and C.W.K. Mundle[5]) to condemn the use of literary examples as a threat to clarity of thought. This contradiction in practice and principle might lead us to suspect that what we are here dealing with is at least to some extent a philosophical disagreement, and I believe this to be the case. Unfortunately, what is extremely unusual is any direct discussion of the philosophical issues involved, that is to say any discussion of what philosophers are doing when they appeal in their writings to works of literature, and of what if anything is lost by those who fail to do so.

I

As I say, direct discussion of the role of literary examples in philosophy is not common. Nevertheless, there *is* one view which,

[1]   First published in A. Phillips Griffiths ed., *Philosophy and Literature* (Cambridge: Cambridge University Press, 1981).

[2]   P. Winch, 'The Universalizability of Moral Judgment', *Monist*, 49, 1965, pp. 199–200.

[3]   E. Kamenka, *Marxism and Ethics* (London: Macmillan, 1969) p. 35.

[4]   R.M. Hare, *Freedom and Reason* (Oxford: Oxford University Press, 1977) p. 183; and *Moral Thinking* (Oxford: Oxford University Press, 1981) pp. 47–9.

[5]   C.W.K. Mundle, *A Critique of Linguistic Philosophy* (London: Clarendon Press, 1970) p. 14.

while not often explicitly acknowledged, does seem to underlie the remarks of many philosophers on this issue and in particular of those who are most conscious of the (alleged) dangers of a preoccupation with literary examples. Indeed, so much is the view in question taken for granted that many may see any discussion of this topic as superfluous. 'Is it not obvious', they will ask, 'that the role of literary examples in philosophy is simply identical with that of other non-literary examples?' Both, so the argument goes, are either illustrations of general philosophical theses or counter-examples to general philosophical theses. It is, for example, a widely held view that all moral reasoning is in the final analysis utilitarian and that what is right or wrong is determined by the consequences of our actions. On the present account, someone who (like myself) found this claim unconvincing might present as a counter-example Sheriff Hampton in Faulkner's *Intruder in the Dust*, who, faced with a demand that be hand over Lucas Beauchamp, a negro accused of murder, to a lynch mob, refuses, though he knows full well that in doing so he faces the likelihood that he and many others will die in a fruitless attempt to protect the man. On the other hand they might equally well point to the example of General De Gaulle's refusal to sanction the use of torture in Algeria in the face of the perfectly plausible claim by his military advisers that the information so obtained was saving French lives. For both the literary and the real-life examples present us with the same problems — whether to sacrifice one's moral values for the sake of beneficial consequences — a problem which according to at least some versions of utilitarianism, should not exist.

Whether, and if so how far, you agree that what we have here are counter- examples to the utilitarian thesis, all this might so far seem pretty unexceptional. And no doubt, so far as it goes, it is. The main difficulty from my point of view is that it seems to present literature with a rather limited role to play in philosophy. There is, for example, no suggestion that great literature might have something to offer philosophy which what is inferior does not, nor any sense that the distinctively literary qualities of litera-ture might have a role to play in philosophy. For in so far as fictional characters and their problems are regarded as examples or counter-examples, but anyway as examples, they are not being treated in the way we normally treat characters in works of litera-ture. When I read *Macbeth* or *Alice in Wonderland* I do not think of Macbeth or Alice simply as examples. And perhaps we can start to see what literature might have to offer the philosopher by observing that when it is claimed that fictional and real-life examples have the same role to play in philosophy because they can present us with the same problems, the use of 'same' here is by no means unproblematic. It will be so only for a philosopher who wishes to maintain that there are no important logical differences between our responses to fictional situations and to those in real-life, no important differences between the significance which each has for us.

Some of the difficulties here come out in a recent Aristotelian Society symposium, 'How can we be moved by the fate of Anna Karenina?'[6] In his contribution to the discussion Colin Radford emphasises the possibility of our responding emotionally to purely fictional characters. We are, for example, moved by the fate of Anna Karenina while recognising that no such person ever existed. And this recognition makes a difference to the nature of our response to her fate. We do not, for example, try to intervene or offer solace. Of course, this is not to say that there are no important similarities between our responses to Anna and to a real person. Pity for characters in fiction is in some respects similar to feeling pity for people we know. For example we may, if we are prone to tears, cry over the fate of Anna as we may cry over the fate of our sisters or aunts, and whether prone to tears or not, we are likely to be upset by their respective fates, discuss with others how the problems arose and how things might have been different. Nevertheless, as Radford emphasises, these similarities should not blind us to important conceptual differences. In this Radford seems to me to be right as against one of his critics, Barrie Paskins, who wishes to maintain that our responses to characters in fiction are really to be construed as responses to human beings in the same situation.

> When you are moved to tears by Anna, you are not moved by her, at least not really, but by the similarly awful fate of Mrs Muriel Parsons of Belsize Park ... who in 1937, etc.[7]

Apart from the wild implausibility of Paskins's claim, which Radford mentions, it is also obvious that Paskins does nothing to

---

6   *Proceedings of the Aristotelian Society*, Suppl. Vol. 49, 1975, pp. 67–93.

7   B. Paskins, 'On Being Moved by *Anna Karenina* and Anna Karenina', *Philosophy*, 52, 1977, pp. 344–7.

explain the sense of 'the same situation' or 'similarly awful fate' and in consequence simply begs the question in what respects the problems of fictional characters can be the same for us as those of real-life people.

This is not, of course, to say that the way in which Radford presents this question is always clear or even coherent. Paskins is himself led into confusion partly because he is responding to Radford's presentation of the difference as involving some sort of paradox: 'Given that pity is what we feel for real human beings, how can we feel pity for fictional characters, who we recognize do not really exist.' Paskins's mistake is to attempt to answer this question by suggesting that pity for fictional characters is really pity for human beings, whereas it is clear that granted the truth of Radford's premise the question is unanswerable. Given that pity is what we feel only for human beings, then obviously we cannot feel pity for characters in fiction, and that is that. What Paskins misses is that no answer is needed, since the premise is patently false. Just as it is a matter of fact about human beings that they feel pity for other human beings in distress, so it is equally a matter of fact about human beings that they feel pity for characters in fiction. Radford seems to see this as in some way irrational. But it is so only in the (dubious) sense in which the pity we feel for human beings is irrational. In neither case can the feelings we have be justified, but they are nevertheless an almost universal feature of human life. And in neither case should we know how to deal with people who did *not* react in these ways. When I say to a child 'You'll make Mommy cry if you do that—and you don't want Mommy to cry, do you?', I do not expect the answer 'Yes, that would be nice' except from a child precocious in its use of sarcasm. And if I were to come across a child who *genuinely* did not feel pity for those in distress, I should be at a loss to know how to speak to the child about morality or indeed human relationships generally. In the same way, I shall be amazed to come across a child who when presented with the story of Rumpelstiltskin finds the plight of the princess amusing. Certainly, unless a child reacts in certain ways—laughs at funny stories, cries over sad ones, shudders at what is horrible—we shall, in the absence of special circumstances, simply conclude that it does not understand the stories we tell it. And then we shall certainly not present it with more sophisticated stories, but rather simpler ones in the hope of eliciting the appropriate response—'the appropriate response' being here the response which would be normal where we are not dealing with fiction. What Radford seems to ignore is that it is a *precondition* of understanding literature that we should react to certain fictional situations in partly the same ways as we do to their real-life counterparts.

Where he is, I think, right is in his emphasis on the differences. With real-life problems we do not expect people merely to be upset or indignant. We also expect them to meet problems with compassion, try to help (or sometimes tactfully to refrain from helping), offer advice, ask for explanations and so on. But it would be a confusion about the logic of fiction to suppose that any of these responses were appropriate with literature. Still it does not follow, except with the most unsophisticated reader or the most unsophisticated forms of fiction, that people's responses are limited simply to emotional responses. With *Anna Karenina* or *Macbeth* interest and enlightenment occupy the place which in real-life problems is occupied by advice and help. A work of literature is presented as an object of contemplation in which we may find profundity and originality, whereas a situation in real life can only be unexpected or different.[8]

Now if you hold the sort of account of the role of literature in philosophy with which I opened this paper, you are not likely to attach much importance to these differences. True, on any account fictional examples will have advantages and disadvantages over real-life examples. On the credit side, since the novelist, unlike the historian or biographer, is not bound to recording what actually happens, he is likely to furnish us with a wider range of problems, situations, possibilities with which to illustrate and test our philosophical theories. 'In a good work of fiction', it has been suggested, 'the reader enters imaginatively into actions and experiences for many of which no opportunities occur in real life and which he could not actually perform.'[9] But there is a price to be paid. For:

---

[8]   I am not, of course, denying that the sort of enlightenment which characterizes fiction, can sometimes be found in the description of non-fictional events — for example, in great journalism. I have in mind, for instance, Orwell's account of a hanging or the shooting of an elephant in Burma. But it would be important to note here that Orwell does not just state what happened, but tells a story.

[9]   S. Ducasse, 'Taste, Meaning and Reality in Art', in S. Hook ed., *Art and Philosophy* (New York: New York University Press, 1966) p. 190.

story-books, though they help to stimulate our imaginations, do not by themselves help us, very much, to separate what is really likely to happen from what is not, nor to assess the probable frequency of its occurrence. For this, some experience of actual moral perplexities, and of the actual consequences of certain moral choices, is a necessity.[10]

Given the assumptions which Hare and Ducasse appear to share, then reason would seem to dictate that, like Hare, we err on the side of caution. For, if the value of literature to philosophy lies simply in its ability to present the novel or the fanciful, problems and dilemmas which are merely *different* from those we encounter in real life, then it is so far unclear why the variety it offers should be of interest to philosophers. For, on the face of it at least, to imagine the application of a familiar concept in a wildly fanciful context is more likely to blind us to those features of our lives which give that concept its sense, than to illuminate them. Certainly, some of the examples used by philosophers do fit just this specification.

> Imagine a Robinson Crusoe asleep on an island about to be wiped out by a tidal wave, he is ignorant, experiences no suffering, can do nothing about the outcome ...[11]

Gombay uses the example to show that there are cases where knowledge is unarguably a bad thing, and its artificiality stems from its having been set up in such a way as to provide a case which excludes any other possible view of the matter. Of course, deciding what we want to say about imaginary Robinson Crusoes is part of the modern philosopher's stock in trade. But it is, I think, worth comparing Gombay's Crusoe with Defoe's. I take it that a major part of Defoe's difficulty in writing the novel would have been to present us with a picture of an unusual situation, that of a man removed from his normal background of social relations, which while unusual is nevertheless convincing. But since Gombay is not writing a novel but merely engaging in an exercise of philosophical fancy, he does not even have to bother about such things. We see the difficulties if we ask now the episode he describes might be incorporated into Defoe's story. Obviously,

---

[10]   Hare, op. cit.
[11]   A. Gombay, 'What You Don't Know Doesn't Hurt You', *Proceedings of the Aristotelian Society*, 79, 1978, pp. 239–49.

since *Robinson Crusoe* is written in the first person, it cannot be. Crusoe cannot know that unbeknownst to him nothing can save him. But perhaps this point is trivial, for there might be someone else in the story who knows it, for example Man Friday. Remember, however, that what we are being asked to imagine is not a situation of the sort which is familiar to us (and which might be expected to be familiar to Man Friday), where we might say 'nothing short of a miracle can save him'. For here there is still room for the man who believes he ought to fight against hopeless odds, die with his boots on, and hence room for the man who says 'Better for him to know'. If there is to be no argument that he should have been kept in ignorance, then it has to be known that whatever he does (hiding in the caves, climbing the mountains, putting his affairs in order) can make no difference to anything — even to the way in which Crusoe views his own life and death. So what is needed is not Man Friday but a narrator possessing divine omniscience, that is to say a device whose artificiality is such that it guarantees that we shall be unable to take this aspect of a novel seriously. It is this, for example, for which Sartre once condemned the work of Mauriac. The central fault in Mauriac's style, Sartre suggests, lies in the introduction of God's standpoint into the narrative.

To be able to take Defoe's *Crusoe* seriously, we do not have to believe that he is describing actual events. It is more a matter of knowing what we are supposed to be imagining, being able to respond to the characters and see their problems as real ones. Whether we are able to do this or not will in part decide whether what we are presented with is a work of stature or, for example, mere escapism. But obviously, if like Hare and Ducasse you think of fiction (at least in so far as it is relevant to philosophy) as simply a source of novel situations, you are not going to be able to see the importance of this distinction. For there are novel situations in both the *Iliad* and *Tarzan of the Apes* or *From Russia with Love*. 'As a consumer of fiction', Ducasse remarks, the philosopher 'does not and should not attend to and contemplate aesthetically the technique of the story, since this would to a greater or lesser extent distract from the content of the story.'[12] And Hare also thinks it important to draw a firm distinction between the pursuit of artistic perfection and the pursuit of clarity of thought.

---

[12] Ducasse, op. cit.

Commonly, of course, the practice of philosophers does not cohere with this principle to ignore literary qualities in favour of content. For it is not, I take it, mere coincidence that their examples tend to come from the work of people like Tolstoi or Shakespeare, rather than that of Edgar Rice Burroughs or Ian Fleming. And this seems to suggest that in practice at least they recognise the difference between the profound and the merely fanciful, between the original and the merely novel. But I believe that the most illuminating discussion of the principles behind this difference is to be found in the writings of Wittgenstein.

II

A central theme, perhaps the central theme, of the notebooks now translated under the title *Culture and Value* makes its appearance in one of Wittgenstein's earliest entries where he speaks with approval of Tolstoi's claim that the significance of the greatest art lies in its being universally understood. In his *Memoir* Norman Malcolm mentions how impressed Wittgenstein was by this theme in Tolstoi's writings. But on the face of it Tolstoi's views seem not only paradoxical, even stupid, but also inconsistent with Wittgenstein's repeated observations both in the *Lectures and Conversations* and in *Culture and Value* that we may appreciate the art of one culture and yet be *completely* at sea with that of another. And Wittgenstein himself remarks that Tolstoi's claim is 'both true and false'.[13] The falsity is apparent even in Tolstoi's own favoured examples. For instance, everyone, he says whatever their social background, can understand the story of Abraham and Isaac. But far from this being the case, it is in fact extremely difficult for a member of our own society to understand this story. What, for example, is it for a man to sacrifice his own child to God? If I were to take my daughter (or even my dog) for a walk, with the expressed intention of making a sacrifice to God, the reaction of most people would be to call the police and try to get me committed. They would regard my conduct not as the expression of religious dedication, but as symptomatic of mental disturbance. Or again, why was it so important that Isaac was Abraham's first-born son? Except in rather special circumstances (among the Royal

---

[13]   *Culture and Value*, ed. G.H. von Wright, trans P. Winch (Oxford: Blackwell, 1980) p. 17. I am grateful to the editor of the *British Journal of Aesthetics*, Dr T.J. Diffey, for permission to quote extensively from my review of this work.

Family, for instance, where questions of title and inheritance are involved) we tend no longer to attach a greater importance to our first child than to our second, nor to sons rather than daughters. So it appears that Tolstoi's claim that what is important in art can be understood by everyone is not only false, but obviously false. Where another culture, its standards and values are sufficiently remote from our own, we are likely to have difficulty in understanding the art of that society. And it is the possibility of such a lack of knowledge as understanding which Tolstoi tends sometimes to deny.

What Wittgenstein sees, however, is that there is a deeper truth in Tolstoi's claim. To appreciate this we need to remember that Tolstoi's claim is specifically a claim about *great* art. In this it differs from the point I have been making so far which is a general one. When I find difficulty in understanding the art of another society it will not be only work of their finest artists, but also of those they regard as mediocre, which puzzles me. I remember once reading of a Chinese mandarin in the last century, who on observing the painted shadow on the face in a Gainsborough portrait asked whether it was the custom of English ladies to wash only one side of their faces. The mandarin would have faced the same difficulty presented with the work of any British portrait painter of the period, good, bad or indifferent. For his problem was, at least in part, that he was ignorant of the standards and conventions of British portrait painting. By contrast what Tolstoi sees is that the puzzlement which any of us may face when presented with a *great* work of art, is not a matter of knowledge, of the intellect at all (and in that sense not a matter of the understanding) but as Wittgenstein says, of the will—not a matter of what it is hard to see in the sense of 'requiring intelligence or specialised knowledge', but of what it is hard to see in the sense of 'requiring courage'. Courage, the courage of the great creative artist, or the courage required of an audience in coming to terms with his work is emphasised by Wittgenstein throughout. What he had in mind here is not a matter of holding on to one's views in the face of powerful opposition as when, for example, Kenneth Tynan once used a certain old English verb on television. For though what Tynan did was different from what had been done before and perhaps (in one sense) required courage, it would be simply absurd to suggest that he had done anything profound or even original. The courage of which Wittgenstein speaks is not the courage to go against received opinion (though it may certainly involve that), but the willingness to question what is simply taken for granted, even by oneself. An artist who is profound or original will be difficult to understand not because we lack the intellectual capacity, but because in order to do so we shall be forced to throw over what is dear to us, because it will appear to us as a threat.

I think that this is what Wittgenstein has in mind when he says that the difference between Mendelssohn and Brahms is that 'there is perhaps in Mendelssohn no music that is hard to understand' or 'difficult'.[14] The conflict which gives rise to the difficulty here is a conflict between what the music can bring us to see and 'what most people want to see'.[15] But unlike the difficulty facing the mandarin in my previous example it has nothing to do with taste, with an education in or understanding of the standards of one's own or any other culture. Reviewing the first Impressionist exhibition of 1875, Albert Wolff, critic of *Le Figaro*, remarked that it would be as difficult to explain to Renoir that a woman's torso is not a mass of green and violet patches as to explain to a madman that he is not the Pope. Wolff's difficulty with Renoir's work was not an intellectual difficulty, a lack of education in art. On the contrary, he was a man of highly cultivated taste. But he had been faced with a conception of representation, a new artistic style, which questioned the very principles on which his taste rested, and, unable to accept this questioning, he was forced to represent it as a fraud. Again, it was only by having the courage to question the principles of the French schools that Renoir had himself been able to reach the conception of nature as patterns of light and colour which Wolff condemned. As Wittgenstein says, 'The faculty of taste cannot create a new structure, it can only make adjustments to one that already exists.'[16]

I have illustrated the point by referring to music and painting, but it is more to my purpose, and I think even more obvious, that in literature the difficulty of appreciating an original style is bound up with the difficulty of questioning our most deeply rooted ideas. It is, for example, clear that the problems faced by many of his contemporaries in coming to terms with what they saw as the brutality and disagreeable nature of D.H. Lawrence's style cannot be separated from Lawrence's emphasis on the

---

[14]   Ibid., p. 28.
[15]   Ibid., p. 17.
[16]   Ibid., p. 58.

instincts and passions as opposed to the life of reason. For instance it is no coincidence that a writer of the previous generation like John Galsworthy with his emphasis on reasonable thought should have found *The Rainbow* aesthetically detestable, nor that T.S. Eliot, while remarking that Lawrence 'can reproduce for you not only the sound, the colour and form, the light and shade, the smell, but all the finer thrills of sensation' should nevertheless comment, 'This is not *my* world, either as it is, or as I wish it to be.'[17] For the power of Lawrence's style lay precisely in its ability to question the current ideas of what the world is like.

Now it is evident that if what I have been saying about the relationship of style and content in art and literature is correct, then those writers who I discussed at the beginning of this paper will be forced to say that there is a fundamental difference between literature and philosophy. For, as we saw there, many writers hold questions of style to be irrelevant in philosophy and if so this difference would be important. What is interesting is that the philosopher I have been discussing does not appear to have held this. For throughout his writings, and especially in *Culture and Value*, there are comparisons, both explicit and implicit, between the originality or profundity of an artist and that of a philosopher, between the difficulty of finding (and understanding) a new form of artistic expression and that of solving a philosophical problem. Of course, in itself this proves nothing. Wittgenstein could simply have been wrong. But let us begin by asking whether in saying that in literature a new mode of expression may bring about a change in the way we see things, we are describing something which is wholly unfamiliar in philosophy. I think that it is obvious that we are not. Consider for example F.H. Bradley's claim that 'Time is unreal'. In his article 'The Conception of Reality', G.E. Moore says of this claim:

> If Time is unreal, then plainly nothing ever happens before or after anything else; nothing is ever simultaneous with anything else; it is never true that anything is past; never true that anything will happen in the future; never true that anything is happening now; and so on.[18]

---

[17] From 'The Contemporary Novel' quoted in R.P. Draper ed., *D.H. Lawrence: The Critical Heritage* (London: Routledge, 1997) p. 276.

[18] G.E. Moore, 'The Conception of Reality', *Proceedings of the Aristotelian Society*, 18, 1917–18, pp. 101–20.

Here as elsewhere Moore held such claims to be preposterous, held that when they had been expressed in this way they would be claims which we should wish to reject. Still, I should not be surprised to learn that Bradley was not too impressed by Moore's response to his theory. For the attraction of the claim that Time is unreal and the arguments which led Bradley to it cannot be recaptured by a list of claims about whether so and so had breakfast before lunch, or whether such and such happened at the same time as the clock struck three. Again, I have discovered that one philosophical thesis which seems to hold a great deal of attraction for my students is the paradoxical claim that two people can never really know when they look at physical objects whether they see the same colours. Expressed in this way the claim strikes them as both true and exciting. Unfortunately, what they soon discover is that it is impossible to express the claim in any other way, and still preserve its appearance of embodying a fascinating insight. For if you *ask* any two people what colour they see when they look at a sample door or lampshade, they will, except in special circumstances, agree in calling it 'red' or 'blue' or 'green'. So it appears that they *do* generally see the same colour, and the thesis is false. And if the student then replies (as he or she usually does), 'Yes, but it's just that we've been taught to call it "red" or "blue" or "green"' (with the implication that they do not really believe it to be so), then one has only to ask 'So what colour do you really think it is?' to elicit the response 'Well, "red" (or "blue" or "green").' So again the thesis turns out to be false. In the long run, of course, the student will normally be forced to some claim which does express a truth, for example, 'Whenever I see a colour, it is always *me* and not another person who does the seeing.' But the trouble is that this claim turns out to be as completely boring as the claim that it is always me and not another person who nods my head. True, this is not normally how the student sees it. He or she is likely to feel that when translated in this way, the point of the philosophical thesis has been lost. And of course in one sense this is true, just as the point of a joke will be lost if we try to explain it in other words, or just as a poem will lose its force when translated into prose. For the fascination of the original claim lies in part in the language in which it is expressed.

If this were not so, if the attraction of general philosophical theses owed nothing to the way in which they were expressed, then one would find it difficult to understand why apparent counter-examples do not always seem to destroy this attraction.

One would, for example, expect F.H. Bradley to have retracted his claim that Time is not real when presented with the known truth that G.E. Moore really had breakfast before dinner. Or to return to an earlier example, one would expect De Gaulle's refusal to sanction the use of torture while recognising its socially beneficial consequences to destroy the utilitarian claim that what is held to be right or wrong is determined by its consequences. But anyone who does expect this has obviously little acquaintance with philosophical discussions. For notoriously what generally happens is that the alleged counter-example is explained in terms of the theory, so that the theory remains intact and the philosopher holds on to the form of language which embodies the original confusion.

Nevertheless, what does not follow from this is the sceptical conclusion that counter-examples can never be effective in philosophy. For what I have been (purposely) ignoring is that the examples may themselves have a force, that they may be expressed in language whose power is such as to break the hold on us of other ways of expressing ourselves. And just as I said in literature a new mode of expression may bring about a change in the way we view the world, so it may have the same function where the way we view the world is one which has been distorted by philosophical confusion.

As an example of a view distorted by philosophical confusion let me return to the case of utilitarianism. Though it is an oversimplification, it is only a slight over-simplification to say that the attraction of utilitarianism is the attraction of the idea of a calculation. This is apparent in the very terms in which writers like Bentham and Mill express their fundamental task, i.e. as that of finding the 'measure' of virtue, or of founding a 'science' of morality dealing in generalisations (that is, in amounts).[19] So it is not surprising that what the theory 'measures' is numbers, nor that the generalisations which it discovers should state *how often* such things as honesty or murder harm or benefit people and *how many* people they harm or benefit. Of course, numerical considerations may make some difference on any account of morality. That my actions will harm more people rather than less may make *some*

---

[19]   It may be said that Mill breaks decisively with this aspect of his introduction of qualitative considerations. But it is worth noting that in the last resort Mill is forced to explain even this aspect as a matter of what *most* qualified judges would choose, i.e. as a matter of numbers.

difference whatever my moral viewpoint. But in the various versions of utilitarianism, these considerations have become all-pervading. For the utilitarian *all* moral decisions are in the final analysis calculations. 'That it be made a matter of reason and calculation, and not merely of sentiment is', according to Mill, 'what renders argument or discussion possible.'[20]

Given that you do think of morality in mathematical terms, it will of course appear to you that only *certain* judgements, *certain* viewpoints are possible, even intelligible. For the language in which you have chosen to describe morality (or rather, feel obliged to do so) will determine for you which aspects of our lives make sense. Suppose that the question is whether it is permissible to torture or even kill a terrorist in order to save, let us say, 100 lives. The inclination will be to present this as a sum and then to subtract from the 100 lives the one terrorist's life, thus ending with a credit balance of 99 lives in favour of this particular atrocity. So that the man who like De Gaulle refuses to permit the sacrifice will appear to be ignoring one element in the calculation, the 100 lives, or supposing that somehow one life is more than 100, and hence to be guilty of an error in calculation. The only way out of this absurd conclusion is to pretend that De Gaulle had really got the right answer, but to a different sum. What he had done was to subtract the 100 lives from the net total of lives saved by a general ban on the ill-treatment of terrorists. And so the argument continues.

What the man gripped by this theory needs to be brought to see is that numerical considerations *need* play no part at all in someone's moral deliberation, or to put it another way, that many of the considerations which are central in morality have no numerical aspect. And I suggested earlier that one way of combating utilitarianism would to be appeal to a work of literature like Faulkner's *Intruder in the Dust*. Faulkner's novel is not, of course, his greatest, and it is not always convincing, particularly in the later chapters, where he employs long polemical speeches by the lawyer Gavin Stevens to preach to the reader. What *is*, in my opinion, convincing (as in most of Faulkner's writing) is the portrayal of individual characters and their relationships. And it is such portrayals which can help break the hold on us of the

---

[20]   J.S. Mill, 'Essay on Bentham', in *Dissertations and Discussions Vol. 1* (London: Parker & Son, 1859).

abstract and mathematical account of human relationships embodied in the theory of utilitarianism. Thus we are presented with the picture of Will Legate, the hunter who is willing to risk his life to protect Lucas Beauchamp, because he has been paid to do a job, or the jailor who has taken an oath of office and will not be able to live with himself if he lets a 'passel of no-good sonabitches' take a prisoner away from him, or the young narrator who will prevent the lynching if he can 'not because he was himself, Charles Mallinson junior ... but because he alone of all the white people Lucas would have a chance to speak to between now and the moment when he might be dragged out of the cell and down the steps at the end of a rope, would hear the mute, unhoping urgency of the eyes ...'[21]

Unlike the relationship of a man's actions to the happiness of the greatest number (or some other variant), none of the relationships by which characters are impelled to act in Faulkner's novel, a man's relationship to his job, or to a particular human being (father, mother, friend), has any numerical or mathematical aspect, and this is why utilitarians have traditionally had difficulties with these aspects of morality and have often been forced simply to deny their reality.

Whether, when we read Faulkner, such relationships do strike us as real, whether we are capable of responding to the characters in the novel, is, as I have tried to show earlier, a literary and stylistic question. But it is not, however, a question which is irrelevant to philosophy. For it may be that by seeing how Faulkner writes and thinks of human beings we are brought to think of them in that way ourselves, and in this way to see the artificiality of the utilitarian preoccupation with quantities. In this respect the relation between counter-examples and philosophical thesis is comparable to the relation between one artistic style and another which I discussed earlier.

III

'But now', someone may say, 'are you not in danger of blurring the differences between literature and philosophy. For, whatever its faults, one merit of the account of the relationship between the two which you have criticised is that by claiming that literary

---

[21] William Faulkner, *Intruder in the Dust* (London: Chatto & Windus, 1949) pp. 68–9.

qualities are philosophically irrelevant, it does at least make clear why we distinguish the two subjects in the first place. Whereas on your account this becomes quite mysterious, so that it now appears as though one way of doing philosophy is to write novels and plays.'

There is certainly a danger that by rejecting the mistaken idea of a conflict between literature and philosophy we shall fall into the opposite error of over-emphasising the similarities. This seems to me to have happened to some extent in the writings of Renford Bambrough and especially in his paper 'Literature and Philosophy' where he is concerned to emphasise the unity of the two subjects. According to Bambrough this is necessary because of an artificial separation of the two subjects which he lays at Plato's door.

> His struggle to separate them would have been unnecessary if he had not recognized that both in principle and in ancient practice, philosophy and literature were modes of one substance.[22]

We see this unity in their subject-matter. For both subjects centre around the same range of topics:

> Man, God, Nature, Arts, Will, Fate, Necessity, Chance and Freedom; Knowledge and Ignorance; Truth and Falsehood, Good and Evil.[23]

Since it seems impossible to imagine *any* problem which could not plausibly be subsumed under one of these categories, or indeed the first four, one might be forgiven for thinking that it is Bambrough's unity, rather than Plato's separation, which has been artificially imposed. But it would be premature to suppose that Bambrough's thesis is merely vacuous, for he claims to detect not simply a unity of subject-matter, but also of method. In both 'the understanding moves in dialectical paths'.[24] That is to say, in both we find a procedure aimed at removing paradox and confusion engendered by generalities through an examination of particular cases, by 'a process of examining more minutely and particularly

---

[22] In R. Bambrough ed., *Wisdom: Twelve Essays* (Oxford: Blackwell, 1974) p. 274.
[23] Ibid., p. 275.
[24] Ibid.

the minute particulars concerning which the opposed generalities are in conflict'.[25]

This is similar to what I have said about the way in which a study of examples may break the hold on us of abstract philosophical theories. And of course Bambrough is right to say that the problems, puzzles, paradoxes which torment philosophers are also to be found in literature. But there is a difference which may be expressed by saying that though works of literature may involve such problems, philosophy *starts from* them. Wittgenstein once remarked[26] that in his later life Russell had lost his sense of philosophical problems, so that everything now seemed simple to him. And he identified this process with the trivialisation of Russell's thought. Whether or not one agrees with Wittgenstein's assessment, it is, I think, clear that he was right to equate the two things. For without a sense of puzzlement, there is no philosophy.

Unfortunately, when Bambrough speaks as if problems had the same part to play in literature, he is in danger of over-intellectualising our responses here. I said earlier that it is among the most general feature of human beings that they tend to respond to certain portrayals in fiction. Given this response, then through his characters a novelist may present us with general problems and ideas. But we can still speak of a work as literature even where there are *no* problems. In a well-known essay Ford Madox Ford recounts his reactions on receiving the manuscript of Lawrence's 'Odour of Chrysanthemums' for publication in the *English Review*. He read, so we are told, the first few sentences and knew that he was in the presence of a great writer. Yet these sentences present us with no problems, indeed nothing of any generality at all. They describe a train pulling into a station, watched by a woman on the platform. Ford recognised literary talent in Lawrence's ability to outline character and situation with 'a casual word here and there', because in a few lines he could bring people to life. But where the characters are mere abstractions, where we are unable to respond to them as living things, the problems and the ideas will lack force for us. [As Joyce Cary notes]:

---

[25]   Ibid., p. 276.

[26]   Wittgenstein, *Zettel*, eds. G.E.M. Anscombe & G. von Wright, trans. G.E.M. Anscombe (Oxford: Blackwell, 1967) p. 82.

> Take *Everyman* where the hero, Everyman, threatened by death, first asks Fellowship for help and Fellowship deserts him. Then he goes to Kindred, and Kindred also backs out. At last he falls back on Good Deeds, who finally saves him from Hell ... The failure of *Everyman* is a defect of characterization. How are we to take any interest in such lay figures as Good Deeds and Kindred? But we don't object to Christian and Faithful Byends or Giant Sloth in *Pilgrim's Progress*, or to Sir Wilfull by Congreve. These are like real people subject to whim and moods, but the characters of *Everyman* are mere conceptions.[27]

It should be clear from what I have said so far that in so far as I understand it, I believe Plato's characterisation of literature as a device which bewitches the intelligence by appealing to the emotions to be simplistic. Even so, by assigning drama and poetry to the realm of the feelings and philosophy to that of reason, Plato was at least pointing to an important difference which Bambrough with his emphasis on unity is in danger of blurring. For a problem presented in a work of literature can be made real to us, only if we are first capable of responding to the characters there, that is to say, if our feelings are involved. In this sense it is the feelings which are fundamental in our appreciation of literature. My aim in this paper has been to show that it is by making problems and ideas real to us in this way, that literature can be of service to philosophy. But it will do this only if we feel the force of the problems in the first place. Without the problems there would be no philosophy. And so, in this sense, it is the problems which are fundamental in philosophy.

---

[27]   Joyce Cary, *Art and Reality* (Cambridge: Cambridge University Press, 1958) pp. 154–5.

5

The Censorship of Works of Art[1]

When Hume remarked 'generally speaking the errors in religion are dangerous, those in philosophy only ridiculous',[2] he was expressing what is on the whole a fairly recent view of philosophy. Certainly it is not a view which would have recommended itself to those Athenians who put Socrates to death for corrupting the youth. And one might be tempted to attribute it to a peculiarly Anglo-American view of the relevance of the arts and humanities to everyday life. I think that it was Peter Ustinov who once countered a television interviewer's complacent remarks about the tolerance of the West towards its poets and novelists with the suggestion that the correct name for this 'tolerance' is 'indifference'. In Russia, he observed, they may indeed censor the work of their greatest writers, but there is also a town called Gorki. There is no Dickenstown in England, nor to the best of my knowledge a Clemenstown in America.

Nevertheless it would be ungenerous to suggest that the popularity of Hume's view among present-day philosophers is due simply to indifference to the humanities, and perhaps rather too generous to Hume to attribute it solely to his own influence. For one reason why there has been a tendency, especially in this country, for philosophers to fight shy of any attempt to use philosophy to criticise human institutions is the influence, or assumed influence, of a far greater philosopher; I mean Ludwig Wittgenstein.

---

[1]   First published in P. Lamarque ed., *Philosophy and Fiction: Essays in Literary Aesthetics* (Aberdeen: Aberdeen University Press, 1983).

[2]   David Hume, *A Treatise of Human Nature*, p. 272.

In *Philosophical Investigations*, *On Certainty* and elsewhere, Wittgenstein warns against the danger of supposing that there are certain language-games which are a necessary feature of the life of *any* society. We can, he suggests, imagine people who have no counterparts to ways of speaking which are fundamental in our society. Nor can it be demonstrated that these people's language would be deficient. Since any language-game is based on ways of acting for which reasons are neither required nor possible, it follows that language-games can neither be justified by reasons, nor rejected by showing that they are irrational.

Now much of what we make of this argument will depend on what we take Wittgenstein to have meant by 'language-game'. And if, for example like Thomas Morawetz in his book *Wittgenstein and Knowledge*, we take Wittgenstein to mean simply *any* practice in which men engage, we shall swiftly be led to the conclusion that philosophy is irrelevant to human life: 'Philosophy can neither justify nor criticise language-games; all human practices are language-games; *ergo* …'[3]

Whether Wittgenstein intended it or not, the conclusion which I have suppressed on the ground of obviousness is palpably false. In our own society, judging people's character by their birth signs and employing alleged psychic powers to foretell the future are fairly common practices and are often taken seriously. Yet it is clear that both are vulnerable to philosophical argument. For, in the case of the former it is easy enough to show that, though self-styled astrologers commonly assess my character having been told my date of birth, no one ever responds to the challenge to estimate my date of birth from an assessment of my character, and consequently that any claim to a unique correlation between the two is without justification. And in the case of the latter, it is noticeable that claims to foreknowledge are always either of such generality as to be impervious to falsification or are simply reinterpreted or ignored where they turn out to be false. A Dallas housewife with alleged psychic powers recently claimed to have foreseen the assassination of President Reagan. She was, it turned out, over a month out in her prediction so that by the time Hinckley's shots were fired, she had decided that the psychic warning referred to

---

[3]   *E.g.* 'I shall speak of practices where Wittgenstein speaks of language-games,' T. Morawetz, *Wittgenstein and Knowledge: The Importance of on Certainty* (Amherst: University of Massachusetts Press, 1978) p. 5.

the death of her own brother some weeks earlier. Even if we ignore the obvious difficulty that the President was not, as we now know, assassinated, it is still obvious that *someone* will die at least every month, especially in Dallas.

True, any philosopher will be well-advised to use arguments of this sort with caution. For confused sceptical attacks on human institutions are considerably more common in our history than are confused human institutions; so it is a counsel of prudence to suspect the argument rather than an institution, especially if the institution is itself part of an alien culture where the risk of misunderstanding is great, or like religion is a part of our own culture but one which many find difficulty in understanding.

Nevertheless, whatever Wittgenstein and some of his followers may have thought, there is no reason why a human practice, even a relatively common one, should not rest on confusion, and in this paper I hope to show that one practice which is of considerable importance, and perhaps even fundamental to the maintenance of certain kinds of social order, is a case in point. I have in mind the practice of censoring works of art.

I

In our society the issues of censorship seem more naturally to arise in connection with works of literature and to some extent films. There is, I suppose, no necessity about this. Plato after all held that music could corrupt, and paintings as well as books have been banned. Still it ought not to be surprising that many people see art as a threat, which it is tempting either to ignore or suppress. For, though an important part of our lives, it is also a force which may sometimes lead us to question those things which we simply take for granted. Taking things for granted is not, of course, to be seen as simply a regrettable tendency which rational men would do well to eradicate, as many philosophers have implied. It is, as Wittgenstein emphasised in his later writings, a precondition of the possibility of rational thought itself.

> Lavoisier makes experiments with substances in his laboratory and then concludes that in combustion such and such happens. He does not say that of course another time it might happen differently. He goes by a particular world-view, and of course he has not invented this but learned it is what goes without saying as the

foundation of his research, and this is also why it is never mentioned.[4]

We could not say that Lavoisier was careless or slipshod because he did not question or perhaps even notice this feature of scientific method, nor is it something which a more careful approach in science might show to be simply mistaken. For unless a man *does* take it for granted that results obtained on different occasions under laboratory conditions will be uniform and that they will have a significance outside the laboratory, then we shall not understand what is meant by 'laboratory conditions' or by 'an experiment'. What Wittgenstein describes as a feature of Lavoisier's world-picture is something without which *any* sort of scientific method would be impossible and without which any talk of scientific error would lack sense. It is not, as writers like Russell have sometimes suggested, a mere assumption which must be questioned if our knowledge is to rest on secure foundations.

There will be many things which we take for granted in other areas of our lives—in morality, religion, mathematics too—and were this not so, various aspects of the way in which we discuss these things would also lose their sense. But the example that Wittgenstein gives may be misleading when we turn to consider other cases. For while it is difficult, if not impossible, to imagine anything which might lead scientists to give up the sort of assumption of uniformity which Wittgenstein mentions, what this shows is that there need be nothing idle or irrational in taking things for granted, and that it would itself be a confusion to think of these things as simple errors or mistakes (not that what is taken for granted can *never* be questioned). And it is here that art may have a part to play in bringing to light and challenging what is taken for granted. Let me give an example.

In 1971 Francis Ford Coppola's film *The Godfather* was released, but only after considerable public protest and in the face of many attempts, some of them involving acts of physical violence, to suppress the film. Part of the reason for this public reaction stemmed, as is well known, from the feeling that the film constituted a slur on the Italian-American community, but another objection which I have commonly heard made is that Coppola presents violence as a natural and indeed inescapable response in

---

4   L. Wittgenstein, *On Certainty*, p. 24.

certain sorts of social situation, and ultimately shows violence as triumphing over the forces of justice.

Now it is interesting that in this respect *The Godfather* can scarcely compare for sheer sadism with several other films released over the past few years — *Straw Dogs, The Exorcist, Soldier Blue* — which, though lacking much redeeming artistic merit, did not draw as much adverse public comment (or if, as in the case of *The Exorcist*, they did, did so for rather different reasons). Nor is it hard to see why. Part of the reason is illustrated by the tendency of many people to talk of violent crime, and perhaps of crime in general as a 'problem'; to speak of the 'problem of the violent offender'; to suggest methods of ridding society of the criminal element; to advocate a return of 'law and order', and so on. What is generally presupposed by these ways of talking is the notion, never explicitly stated but rather taken for granted, that it is possible to locate in *any* sort of society an area of activity which is criminal or unjustifiably violent and which can be distinguished from what is not criminal, or if violent, then justifiably so. Now like any work of art *The Godfather* does not state that this notion must be rejected. Rather, it portrays, through the life of Don Vito Corleone and his family, and in particular through the constantly frustrated attempts of his son Michael to escape from the life of the Mafia only to be forced back into crime by a corrupt police force, racial prejudice, the indifference of law-abiding citizens, that there may be sorts of society so shot through with corruption that the distinction between the criminal and the forces of law and order is an unreal or perhaps pointless distinction, and where fundamental injustices (racial prejudice, economic inequality) are so much a part of the fabric of the society that it is merely idle to distinguish the just man from the unjust man. Obviously, to the advocate of law and order or of a strengthening of the arm of the law as an 'answer' to the 'problem' of crime, such a suggestion, if it is not merely ignored, will be a disturbing one. And so it is not surprising if one response is to attempt to suppress the suggestion. As G.K. Chesterton once remarked, 'If you make any sentient creature jump, you render it by no means improbable that it will jump on you.' Nevertheless, though natural, it by no means follows that the reaction is a rational one. To show this let us begin by examining some of the forms which this reaction may take.

In 1898 Count Leo Tolstoi completed the essay called *What is Art?* in which, notoriously, he issues a blanket condemnation of some of the most respected works of art of his, or indeed of any, time. Claiming to judge art from the standpoint of the 'religious perception'—that is, the prevailing moral ideal of his age—Tolstoi notes that one after another alleged masterpiece stands condemned because it transmits neither feelings of love for God and one's neighbour nor feelings which 'unite men in the joys and sorrows of life'.

> "What, the Ninth Symphony not a good work of art?" I hear exclaimed by indignant voices. And I reply: Most certainly it is not.[5]

The conclusion, Tolstoi thinks, is obvious. Bad art 'deserves not to be encouraged but to be driven out, denied and despised' and 'the efforts of those who wish to live rightly should be directed towards the destruction of this art'.[6] Tolstoi's essay was itself censored in several Russian versions before its publication in its original form in English.

Almost fifty years later George Orwell, who had himself condemned Tolstoi's views as 'worthless', reviewed Salvador Dali's *Secret Life*, an autobiography with illustrations drawn by Dali. Dali's work, Orwell remarks, is 'a direct, unmistakable assault on sanity and decency; and even—since some of Dali's pictures would tend to poison the imagination like a pornographic postcard—on life itself'.[7] And this is apparently at least a *prima facie* case for saying that the book should be censored. True, Orwell thinks that Dali's work casts a useful light on the decay of capitalist civilisation and for this reason it would be 'doubtful policy' to suppress it. But it is clear that for Orwell the case for refraining from censorship is one that has to be made. Just as a wall may be a good wall and yet deserve to be demolished if it surrounds a concentration camp, 'so it ought to be possible to say, "This is a good book or a good picture and it ought to be burned by the public hangman"'. What is again of interest here is that the essay 'Benefit of Clergy' was itself subsequently suppressed on the grounds of obscenity.

Now, though these two cases, in which the prospective censor is himself the subject of censorship, would be just the kind that would in ordinary parlance be called 'paradoxical', there is in fact

---

5   L. Tolstoi, *What is Art?*, p. 248.

6   Ibid., p. 261.

7   George Orwell, 'Benefit of Clergy: Some Note on Salvador Dali', p. 159.

no genuine logical paradox involved. We can, that is to say, describe what transpired without contradiction, either explicit or implicit. Still, there is something about the institution of censorship which has led some writers to ask whether it does not involve some form of conceptual oddity, whether there is not some confusion involved in, to use Orwell's own example, the attempt to infer from, 'This is a morally evil book or picture' to the conclusion, 'This book or picture ought to be burned.'

Of these, undoubtedly the most famous is John Stuart Mill in his essay *On Liberty*. Like many political philosophers before and after him, Mill's aim is to outline the 'nature and limits of the power which can be legitimately exercised by society over the individual', but for my purposes what is important is a corollary which Mill draws from his own account of these limits. For one thing about which Mill is clear is that any interference with freedom of expression, any form of censorship, is well outside them. Though Mill's argument is complex, it can, I think without parody, be said to rest on the claim, common to empiricists from Locke to Ayer, that since it is possible to imagine circumstances in which *any* judgement whatsoever may turn out to be false, there are no judgements whose truth can be claimed to be certain.[8] We can never attain certainty in our judgements, only satisfy ourselves that so far as possible we have considered and shown to be false any contrary judgements. But, this being so, it follows that censorship can never be justified, since of its nature it removes the conditions under which such a process is possible. If the judgement that we censor is true, then we are left with error. If the judgement that we censor is erroneous, we are left with what is as bad, a judgement which, because we cannot know how it will fare in the face of contrary evidence, can never be *known* to be true. And to rest content with such a judgement is to be satisfied with mere convention and dogma.

It would be a mistake to underestimate the initial plausibility of Mill's argument, a plausibility attested by the fact that since the publication of *On Liberty* much of the discussion of the issues of censorship has been conducted on Mill's terms. Despite this, it seems to me that the empiricist assumption which lies at the basis of his attack on censorship is patently false. Strangely, however,

---

[8]   Mill excepts mathematical judgements, but for reasons which do not affect my argument.

when the precise nature of this falsity is established, the case against censorship, far from being weakened, becomes unanswerable.

II

Let me begin by indicating certain cases where Mill's thesis *is* false — cases, that is, where it does not seem possible for my judgements to be fallible. As an indication of one sort of judgement which I have in mind I will mention my certainty that my wife is not an agent of the KGB. I purposely do not express this by saying that my wife is a 'paradigm case' of someone who is not a KGB agent, since whatever the merits of paradigm case arguments in other contexts, I find it difficult to understand what, in this field at least, paradigms are supposed to be. (I would have thought that anyone who was a KGB agent would try very hard to avoid any of the features of a paradigm.) Rather what I mean is that the possibility of my wife's working for the Russian Secret Service is not one that I can seriously entertain. True I can *imagine* what future events could lead me to suspect her and to question my judgement. The discovery that my wife spent her teens in Russia, apparently for no good reason, or that her life with me was punctuated by the occasional trip to the Russian Embassy in London would obviously cast some doubt on my claim to certainty. Fortunately, I am equally certain that I shall discover no such things. I met my wife in her teens, along with numerous friends who had shared her childhood in Wales, and though she has not spent all her life in my company since meeting me, she has certainly not spent enough time apart from me to allow for even occasional day-trips to the Russian Embassy. Again, I am not saying that you or, for the matter, the men from MI5 might not entertain doubts on this matter. But this does not affect my certainty. For I am in a much better position to know than either you or MI5. She is, after all, *my* wife.

To say that I am in a better position than others to judge this issue is not of course to say that I have better reasons for my claim than do others. Once I allow talk of reasons for and against my wife's credibility as a loyal citizen, then it is open to someone of Mill's persuasion to question the worth of my reasons, offer reasons against and in this way cast doubt on my claim to certainty. But the truth is that I have *no* reasons for my belief. Admittedly it is easy enough to find propositions from which the proposition 'My wife is not a KGB agent' can be derived—for example, 'My wife has had no contact with any official of the Russian Communist Party at any time' or 'My wife would never do anything to further the cause of the USSR'—but it is obvious that these are not reasons for my claim, since I am as a matter of fact considerably less certain of their truth than of my original claim. And this is the point. I am as certain of *that* claim as I am of anything in this life. Consequently the idea of using reasons either to support it or to convince me of its falsity is ruled out by the logic of argument. For in any argument we use claims of which someone is more certain to convince them of something of which they are less certain.

What we have here then is, like the example from Wittgenstein mentioned earlier, something whose truth goes without saying. But of course, so far my argument, even if accepted, may seem of doubtful relevance to Mill's points, or to the question of censorship. 'After all,' someone may say, 'the interest of Mill's position, at least for your purposes, lies not in its relevance to factual claims, such as your wife's security status, but in its relevance to moral questions. And here the situation is very different, for even if it is admitted that people are sometimes in a position to judge with certainty on factual issues, when we turn to moral issues no one is in any better position to judge than anyone else, and consequently any claims to certainty will be unfounded. The application of moral concepts is, after all, as many contemporary philosophers never tire of pointing out, "essentially contested".'

Now there is some truth in this objection, to which I shall return later. What is not true is that there is no certainty in the sphere of morality comparable to that which we find with some factual claims. Let me illustrate this by returning to Orwell's criticism of Salvador Dali's autobiography. Orwell's assessment of the book rests largely on various incidents from Dali's life which he relates. These include, from Dali's early childhood, kicking his young sister in the head for fun and throwing a small boy from a suspension bridge for no apparent reason, and in his late teens half-killing a small girl and, for the feeling of power which it gives him, sexually teasing a young woman who is in love with him for five years and then deserting her. On the basis of these and other similar examples of sadism, Orwell claims that Dali is a 'dirty little scoundrel' and his autobiography 'disgusting', and I might as well say at this point that not only do I agree with Orwell's judgements, but that if anything they seem to err on the side of leniency.

I am, that is, certain that Dali's attitude towards the particular people he mentions was despicable. And I say 'the particular people he mentions' not because I have in mind some features which distinguish them from other people (for I have no doubt that the examples he gives are illustrative of Dali's lack of concern for people generally), but simply to rule out the imaginable cases where those kicked, tormented, or otherwise are Hitlers or Ghengis Khans and where my certainty might (*might*) be less. Such cases are imaginable but they do not affect my case here, for I am equally certain that Dali's victims were young children and teenage women and not tyrants or mass-murderers, and that they were abused for fun and not, for example, because of their potential or actual danger to humanity. Indeed, as Orwell points out, it hardly affects the case whether or not the incidents mentioned actually occurred since they are obviously things which Dali would have *liked* to do, and it is the delight in acts of horrific cruelty, imagined or otherwise, which is one of his most repellent features and which justifies Orwell's assessment of the book as disgusting. Nor am I denying that we can imagine others who might disagree with these judgements. Indeed, we scarcely need to imagine this, since we can safely assume that, at least until his alleged conversion to Roman Catholicism, Dali himself would have disagreed. But, as with my previous case, the possibility of others disagreeing, and perhaps being able to offer reasons for so doing, does not affect my own certainty. For again, my certainty that it is despicable to cause suffering to others for the sake of one's own enjoyment or even, as Dali might claim, for the sake of one's artistic development, is not one which either admits of or requires reasons, since it is among the most fundamental of my moral convictions.

There is, however, an important difference between the two cases, and this brings me back to a point which I indicated earlier. For, when discussing the possibility of my wife's being a KGB agent, I mentioned that my certainty here is a function of my being in a better position to judge than others. The conceptual connection between these notions, that of being in a position to judge and that of certainty, comes out most clearly (though not only) in those cases where we might be inclined to introduce the notion of expertise. If my car will not start, or if I suffer from recurrent headaches, often what I shall do is to consult an expert, an automobile engineer or a doctor. Probably I shall simply leave them with the problem. 'I haven't time to tinker around with the car', I say to the garage mechanic, 'You find out what's wrong.' I leave the doctor to carry out some tests and try to forget about the headache. And I shall be certain of their verdicts, primarily to the extent that I suppose them to be in a position to judge. Thus, if my doctor informs me that in his opinion the headache is tension, but that he is referring me to a specialist, my judgement that I am suffering from tension will be more tentative than when the specialist finally confirms the doctor's opinion. For after all the specialist, having been through a certain training, is therefore in a better position to judge. And there will be many things, such as that the earth is approximately round or that there exists such a city as New York, whose certainty I *never* question, not because I have ever checked myself, but simply because *all* the experts, everyone who is in a position to judge (scientists, astrologers, ship's captains), agrees on them.

Now, it seems clear to me that when we turn to moral issues, the concept of certainty is no longer connected with that of being in a position to judge or to answer questions or to solve problems, for the simple reason that these notions have no sense here. I have indicated that part of what gives the mechanic or the doctor their expertise is their familiarity with a certain *kind* of problem. And this goes along with certain problems being pretty much the same whoever has them. The motor mechanic can help me with my burnt-out clutch because burnt-out clutches are similar in important respects, the doctor with my heart attack because my heart attack and yours are not too dissimilar.

With many moral problems there is nothing like this. In Camus' novel *The Plague* we are presented with the story of various men and women trapped in Oran, a plague-stricken town in Algeria, and central among the book's themes is the different conceptions which people can have of their lives and those they share them with. Some of these are brought to the fore in the relationship of the journalist Rambert and his friend Dr Rieux. Rieux's attitude towards the plague is partly one of resignation. At worst the quarantine laws, which prevent his leaving Oran, and the enforced isolation from his wife who is in a nearby sanatorium, are necessary evils. At best they are a blessing since they protect her from the plague and provide an opportunity for Rieux to devote himself to relieving the suffering in the town. Either way 'the law was law, plague had broken out, and he could only do what had to be done'.[9]

For Rambert on the other hand, the quarantine laws are simply an obstacle to his reunion with his girlfriend in Paris. Where Rieux sees the restrictions imposed by the plague as facts to be accepted, Rambert sees them as barriers to be overcome. This disagreement is brought to a head by Rieux's suggestion that Rambert should join the volunteers engaged in the dangerous task of fighting the plague. Rambert replies:

> Personally I've seen enough of people who die for an idea. I don't believe in heroism; I know it's easy and I've learnt that it can be murderous. What interests me is living and dying for what one loves. (pp. 135–6)

Though one might say that in a superficial sense Rieux and Rambert face the same problem, separation from a loved one, this *would* be only in a superficial sense. For the nature of their problems stems from the particular circumstances of their relationships and the particular role which these play in their lives. Rambert sees in the request to join Rieux's campaign, or indeed in the suggestion that he reconcile himself in any way to imprisonment in Oran, a demand that he sacrifice his relationship with his girlfriend for the sake of an empty piece of heroism, for an 'idea'. That is to say, he thinks of his life apart from her, his work, as something independent of their relationship, a point brought out earlier in the book when Rieux suggests that the plague at least offers Rambert an unparalleled opportunity to employ his journalistic talents, and Rambert remarks tersely:

> The truth is that I wasn't brought into the world to write newspaper articles. But it's quite likely that I was brought into the world to live with a woman. (p. 72)

Rieux, by contrast, does not see his dedication to medicine as something which stands in the way of his relationship with others, but as a part of what makes him the person he is and hence makes those relationships what they are. But in neither case can the problems faced be separated from the people involved and those they are involved with. And this is generally true of problems connected with personal relationships. That this is one of Camus'

---

9   Albert Camus, *The Plague*, trans. S. Gilbert (London: Penguin, 1960) p. 73.

main points in the book is shown by his account of how finally preoccupation with the plague and fear of catching it 'killed off the faculty not only of love but even of friendship' in the inhabitants of Oran.

> For the first time exiles from those they loved had no reluctance to talk freely about them using the same words as everybody else, and regarding their deprivation from the same angle as that from which they viewed the latest statistics of the epidemic ... Obviously all this meant giving up what was most personal in their lives. Whereas in the early days of the plague they had been struck by the host of small details that, while meaning absolutely nothing to others, meant so much to them, personally ... now, on the other hand, they took an interest only in what interested everyone else, they had only general ideas and even their tenderest affections now seemed abstract, items of the common stock. (pp. 149–51)

As Camus observes, the uniqueness of a relationship is involved in what makes it one of love or friendship. And it is a corollary of this that where there are problems in such relationships, the problems will themselves be unique. If I have problems in living with my wife and you have problems living with yours, we do not share the same problem. I might have *no* problem living with *your* wife.

True, not all moral problems will be of this sort. And there will be many where we *can* give some sense to the notion of others facing the same problem, so that we may turn to them for advice and help. Sometimes this will be so where, for example, people face problems like unemployment or conflicts between professional ethics and personal values. But even here no sense can be given to the idea of someone's being in a better position than I to judge. I may ask another's advice, but whether I take it or not is up to me. With a medical problem, I may simply follow the doctor's advice, and if things do not turn out as expected I can disclaim responsibility. ('Don't blame me—the doctor told me just to keep on taking the tablets'.) But it would be simply a bad joke (or the mark of an extreme conventionalist) if, when faced with a serious moral problem, I were to say to someone 'I'm no good at facing up to these sorts of difficulties, so you tell me what the answer is, and then I shan't need to think about it myself.' As we have seen, with factual issues my certainty often stems from my having taken on trust what those who are in a position to judge have told me. With moral issues, by contrast, my judgement will count as a genuine moral judgement only in so far as it is not taken on trust but is one which I have reached for myself. And this is to say that in morality the notion of being in a better position to judge lacks sense.

III

So far the relevance of all this to the issue of censorship may not be obvious. But it becomes clearer when one notices that any form of censorship, in so far as it is justified on moral grounds at all, *can* be justified only on the assumption that some people *are* in a better position to judge than others. Thus, when Orwell suggests that if we share his condemnation of Dali's autobiography we must, even if only imaginatively, be willing to consider the possibility of suppressing the work in question, he is asking us to accept that we should be willing (even if only imaginatively) to countenance a situation in which others allow the judgement that the work is 'debased and disgusting' to be made for them — a situation in which, that is, it makes sense for someone to say 'I think Dali's work is disgusting because George Orwell says so.' Again, when Tolstoi recommends the suppression of what in his opinion offends against the moral ideals of his age, he not only pre-supposes a degree of moral consensus which there is no reason to suppose actually obtains, but also implies that his judgement of what is morally offensive is one which others should take on trust. The general point is concisely made by John Anderson. The advocates of censorship, he notes, always 'imply in professing to be able to censor, that they themselves will take no harm from examining what they proceed to suppress; in other words they imply that there is a line of social demarcation between protectors and protected'.[10]

What Anderson emphasises in his writings on censorship, and what others who have dealt with the subject both pro and contra have generally ignored, is that the institution of censorship involves not merely a relation between those who censor and those whose works they censor, but also and more importantly a relation between the censor and those whose access to the censored works is thus impaired. Orwell, for instance, makes considerable play of those features of Dali's work which he finds morally objectionable and, as we have seen, uses these features as

---

[10]   John Anderson, 'Art and Morality', p. 280.

grounds for censorship. What he does not discuss is the question whether anyone has the right to prevent others examining these features for themselves and reaching a judgement on them.

Similarly, in recent political discussions about the wisdom or moral propriety of placing limits on free speech, the issue has been expressed almost exclusively in terms of whether or not there are political views so far beyond the pale that no one ought to be allowed to express them, rather than whether there are views which only certain people should be allowed to hear. A few years ago, Professor Roy Edgeley illustrated this perfectly in an article[11] intended to show that the notion of completely free speech is incoherent as an ideal. Edgeley took the specific case of a demonstration at Sussex University in which he was himself involved, and whose object (and result) was to prevent a lecture by the American academic and Vietnam War advisor Thomas Huntingdon, and pointed out that those who opposed the demonstration on the grounds of freedom of speech were themselves, more or less explicitly, proposing various sorts of constraints on this freedom.

> Let's list the various constraints imposed or proposed by different parties in the whole complex of the Huntingdon affair: (1) by some members of Sussex University against Huntingdon, shouting and heckling sufficient to prevent him from speaking on 5 June (2) by some members of Sussex University against Huntingdon, withdrawal of the invitation for 5 June (3) by Huntingdon, against millions of Vietnamese, the direct application of mechanical and conventional power on such a massive scale as to force a massive migration from countryside to city (4) by Crossman against the academics proposing (5) loss of job.[12]

Edgeley goes on to remark that the form of constraint actually imposed by himself was mild compared with the others. What is interesting is that he carefully avoids listing (and indeed at no point in his article mentions) *one* constraint which, mild or severe, might be thought to be at least worthy of notice. What he does not mention is that in preventing Huntingdon from speaking he was

---

[11] Roy Edgeley, 'Freedom of Speech and Academic Freedom', *Radical Philosophy*, 10 (9), 1975.

[12] Ibid., p. 11. R.H.D. Crossman had suggested in a letter to the *Times* that it should be a condition of employment in a University that one neither prevents nor seeks to prevent freedom of speech.

also preventing anyone who might have wished (in this case presumably students) from listening.

Though the proponents of censorship whom I have mentioned —Tolstoi, Orwell and Edgeley—differ widely both in the moral standpoints from which they propose censorship, and in the range of objects which they propose to censor, what is common to them is that despite an emphasis on the relationship of their own moral beliefs to the subjects of their moral appraisal (works of art, lectures) none of them discusses the relationship of these moral beliefs to the moral beliefs of those who will be the victims of their proposed censorship. Nor is this surprising, a mere oversight. On the contrary, it is necessary to the whole notion of protecting others from corruption which is central in any defence of censorship that the censor should refuse to judge his own moral beliefs in the same terms which he applies to those of others. He must, to use the terms which I have hitherto employed, regard himself as in a better position to judge. As Anderson indicates, this can be established by a *reductio ad absurdum* argument. For let us suppose that it is admitted that the censor is morally on precisely the same footing as those he claims to protect. This being so, we can only assume that either he never comes into contact with any corrupting material, in which case he remains uncorrupted but without a function and the institution of censorship is pointless, or he comes into contact with corrupting material, in which case, since he *alone* does so, he is the member of society most in danger of corruption and hence least suited to the post of censor—in which case, the institution of censorship is dangerous rather than pointless. Thus Edgeley, who was evidently acquainted with Huntingdon's views and uninfluenced by them since he claimed to object to them, was seeking to prevent his students from hearing these views, presumably on the grounds that they *would* be influenced by them, would be unable to see them for what they were. But a simpler way of expressing this point would be to say that according to any view of censorship, the censor's view of what is immoral is to be taken on trust by those whom he claims to protect. Not having been given the opportunity to consider the alternatives, they are to accept that certain works are obscene, depraved, and evil simply because the censor says so. The censor is given, that is to say, the role of an expert in a field where expertise, relying as it does on the notion of 'being in a better position to judge' has been shown to have no sense.

Now it is at this point that the proponent of censorship can generally be relied upon to reveal what he regards as his trump card. 'For,' he will ask, 'is it not obvious that whatever arguments may be offered to the contrary, the notion of being in a position to judge *does* have a part to play, and indeed a vital part, in morality. For is it not obvious and admitted by all, that whether Orwell and Tolstoi are in a better position to judge the moral acceptability of art than you and I, whether or not Professor Roy Edgeley is in a better position to judge the acceptability of certain political views than the students of Sussex University, all of us — Tolstoi, Orwell, Edgeley, University students, you and I — are in a better position to judge on all these issues than (say) a four-year-old child.' Put briefly, the objection is that censorship is both justified and indeed essential in the case of children. And since most works of art are accessible to very young children, is not then censorship necessary to protect them from corruption?

The answer to this objection is that, far from its being the case that censorship is justified when it has as its aim the protection of young children, it is of doubtful significance to speak of censorship in this context at all. I have said that censorship occurs where in one way or another limitations are placed on those viewpoints which are to be given a hearing. But it seems to me a precondition of these limitations constituting censorship that the audience under consideration should consist of human beings capable of forming judgements on the basis of what they hear. Or again, I have said that the incoherence of defences of censorship lies in the supposition that sense can be given to the notion that in morality one person may be in a better position to judge than another; but it is a presupposition of this objection that the beings in question are capable of judgement in the first place.

Now where what we have in mind are very small children, it should be obvious that neither of these conditions is satisfied. As we saw at the beginning of this paper, judgement is possible only where certain things are taken for granted, accepted without question. And it follows that if a child is ever to be capable of judging for itself in morality, there will be a stage where it must simply accept certain judgements without question. I may discuss with a ten-year-old child whether stealing is not sometimes justified — for example whether it is not sometimes justified to steal from the rich to give to the poor. But such a discussion can make sense only against a background of the child's having been brought up to accept without question, as say a four-year-old, that

stealing is something wrong, something which requires justification. And bringing the child to accept this will no doubt have both
its positive and its negative aspects. For it will involve both telling
the child that stealing is wrong (and brooking no opposition on
this) and keeping the child away from those who would lead it to
think otherwise. For a parent or teacher to try to protect young
children from those people, those films, those books, which they
see as obscene or corrupting cannot intelligibly be condemned (or
indeed commended) as an example of censorship, as an interference with the child's freedom of choice, since this would presuppose precisely what is in question, that the child is in a
position to choose.

I should, however, emphasise that in saying this I am not
repeating one of the points made by Mill in his essay. Mill is
emphatic that his opposition to censorship is 'meant only to
human beings in the maturity of their faculties', but where I have
made the conceptual point that it is coherent to speak of censorship only in respect of a person already capable of reasoned judgement, Mill appears to rest his case on a moral judgement. Censorship, so the argument goes, is an evil. But though still an evil even
where young children are involved, in this case it is justified by
the child's overriding need for protection. Unfortunately, since it
is not only children whom we may regard as immature and in
need of protection, this argument leads Mill to recommend the
most far-reaching censorship.

> It is, perhaps, hardly necessary to say that this doctrine is meant
> only to apply to human beings in the maturity of their faculties ...
> Those who are still in a state to require being taken care of by
> others, must be protected against their own actions as well as
> against external injury. For the same reason we may leave out of
> consideration those backward states of society in which the race
> may be considered as in its nonage ... Despotism is a legitimate
> mode of government in dealing with barbarians ... ('On Liberty',
> pp. 135–6)

Mill's discussion of these issues is confusing in the highest degree.
When I say, that a child who is being taught the moral standards
that will form the basis of his judgement, is immature, I am
making a factual judgement about the stage of development which
the child has reached, and about which there would be no disagreement except perhaps in borderline cases. By contrast, to say,
as Mill does, that certain *adults* in other societies, or perhaps in our

own society, are immature, is, if it means anything at all, to make a moral judgement, and one about whose correctness there may be *moral* disagreement.[13] And to say, again as Mill does, that in such cases censorship is permissible, while admittedly a legitimate use of the concept of censorship, involves, like all defences of censorship, the elevation of one set of moral judgements, in this case judgements about maturity, to a privileged position. It is again to adopt the stance of an authority in a context where the notion of an authority has no place. Where the notion does have a sense is in the relationship of parents and teachers to young children. But then, what they do cannot without logical impropriety be termed censorship.

But to say that the relationship of parents and teachers to immature children cannot be characterised as censorship is not to say that this relationship may not itself be the subject of censorship. You cannot subject young children to censorship. What you can do is to subject to censorship the views of parents and teachers vis-à-vis their charges' moral education. Thus when the censors of film and television prevent the portrayal of certain subjects or viewpoints on the grounds that they may corrupt the youth, they are guilty of usurping the role of parents and teachers in a child's education. And in so far as any defence is offered for this interference the advocate of censorship will once again be committed to the idea that some people are in a better position than others to judge on moral issues—in this case the moral issue of what influence parents should have over their children.

My point here is perfectly illustrated by one of the counsel for the prosecution's opening remarks to the jury in the notorious *Lady Chatterley* trial:

> Would you approve of your young sons, young daughters— because girls can read as well as boys—reading this book? Is it a book that you would have lying around in your own house?

Mr Griffith-Jones was at this point, of course, trading on the jury's understanding that such questions are ones which it is appropriate for parents to ask, and presumably answer in different ways. What he failed to see was that it was being asked in the course of an argument designed to show that such questions should be

---

[13] I can attach no sense at all to the suggestion that a race or society, as a whole may be immature.

asked and answered, not by parents with regard to their own children, but by the twelve just men and true to whom it was addressed. For if the prosecution were successful, then the net result would be to rob parents of choice in this matter.

I said at the beginning of this essay that the institution of censorship does not involve any contradiction, explicit or implicit. But it looks as though the apparent contradiction implicit in Griffith-Jones's argument, can be avoided only on the assumption that the jury were in a better position to judge on this moral question than other parents. But here, as elsewhere, the notion of being in a better position to judge morally is without sense.

6

Wittgenstein on Tolstoi's What is Art?[1]

It is customary in any account of the development of Wittgenstein's thought to give some mention to the influence of Tolstoi's writings. Wittgenstein was, we are told, impressed, and his views on religion influenced by *The Gospels in Brief* and the tales for peasants, generally known as *The 23 Tales*. He also held some of the writer's novels in high esteem — Malcolm in his *Memoir* mentions *Hadshi Murat*, though he also claims that Wittgenstein did not like *Resurrection*, which may be the source of A.N. Wilson's curious observation that *Hadshi Murat* was one of the few of Tolstoi's works which Wittgenstein could admire.[2] Rather less commonly biographers and critics draw attention to the fact that the philosopher had, as a young man, read and admired Tolstoi's essay *What is Art?*

Despite this, and despite the vast amount of attention which has over the past forty years been paid to Wittgenstein's work, there has nevertheless been relatively little discussion of the precise nature of the influence which Tolstoi exercised on his thought, both in respect of *What is Art?* and of the other works. For the most part writers content themselves with a few relatively general comparisons between the writers' respective views of religion. Or they draw superficial links between Tolstoi's attitude towards peasant life and Wittgenstein's retreat to the peasant community of Trattenbach in the Austrian Alps. But it is particularly strange that there does not seem to be any detailed discussion of the influence of Tolstoi's aesthetic theory on Wittgenstein, since the

[1] First published in *Philosophical Investigations*, 14 (3) 1991.
[2] A.N. Wilson, *Tolstoi*, p. 497.

existence of such an influence is no mere conjecture, nor even hearsay. On the contrary Tolstoi is one of the very few writers mentioned by name in the notes now translated as *Culture and Value*, and he is mentioned not once but three times. Of these, the second is a reference to Tolstoi's version of the expression theory of art, and while it is plainly incorrect to say bluntly, as P.B. Lewis does,[3] that Wittgenstein finds the theory repellent — what he says is that 'there is a lot to be learned from Tolstoi's bad theorising about how a work of art conveys "feeling"'[4] — it would, even so, be odd to present this passage as evidence of Tolstoi's influence. For in the first place, it is clear that Wittgenstein believes that we can learn from Tolstoi here, by seeing what is wrong with his account. And in the second place, his remarks concern a theory which has been expounded, and expounded in a more sophisticated manner, by writers other than Tolstoi. The first and third references, how-ever, *appear* to be concerned with a theme which is distinctively Tolstoi's own and which seems on the face of it to be the most outrageous claim in a book which has never been famed for the tameness of its conclusions — I refer to Tolstoi's view that the significance of the greatest art lies in its being universally under-stood. This fact is interesting, since we have it on the authority of more than one of Wittgenstein's biographers that this was a theme in Tolstoi's writings which had particularly impressed the young Wittgenstein.

I

In chapter 10 of *What is Art?* Tolstoi paints a striking picture of the effects wrought in art by the system of patronage.

> When a great universal artist (such as were some of the Greek artists and Jewish prophets) composed his work, he naturally strove to say what he had to say so that it should be intelligible to all men. But when an artist composed for a small circle of people placed in exceptional conditions, or even for a single individual and his courtiers — for popes, cardinals, kings, dukes, queens, or for a king's mistress — he naturally aimed only at influencing these people, who were well known to him and lived in exceptional conditions familiar to him. And this was an easier task, and the

---

[3]   'Wittgenstein on Words and Music', *British Journal of Aesthetics*, 17 (2) 1977, p. 112.
[4]   *Culture and Value*, p. 58.

artist was involuntarily drawn to express himself by allusions comprehensible only to the initiated.[5]

According to Tolstoi, such developments had disastrous consequences for the way in which artists viewed their own work.

> As soon as ever the art of the upper classes separated itself from universal art, a conviction arose that art may be art and yet be incomprehensible to the masses. As soon as this position was admitted it had inevitably to be admitted that art may be intelligible only to the very smallest number of the elect and eventually to two, or to one of our nearest friends, or to oneself alone — which is practically what is being said by modern artists.[6]

But for Tolstoi this is simple nonsense.

> To say that a work of art is good but incomprehensible to the majority of men, is the same as saying that some kind of food is very good but most people can't eat it. The majority of men may not like rotten cheese or putrifying grouse, dishes esteemed by people with perverted tastes; but bread and fruit are only good when they are such as please the majority of men. And it is the same with art. Perverted art may not please the majority of men, but good art always pleases everyone.[7]

This conclusion that good art always pleases everyone plays an important role in Tolstoi's discussion here. For it is what enables him to characterise the development which he has described as a process of deterioration, of increasing decadence, in art. And it may well have appeared to Tolstoi a natural consequence of his version of the expression theory. For if, as Tolstoi believed, the aim of an artist is to transmit to others feelings which he had experienced, then it may have seemed plausible to conclude that where an artist fails in this aim, where there are those to whom the feelings are not transmitted, then this must be a reflection on the value of his work. Unfortunately what Tolstoi fails to notice, or perhaps ignores, is that arguments of this form, though possessing a force in a particular context, cannot simply be abstracted from that context. We may criticise a writer of children's stories, if his audience is found to be indifferent to his work, but we do not criticise Dostoevsky if he fails to make an impression on the same

---

5   *What is Art?*, p. 156.
6   Ibid., p. 175.
7   Ibid., p. 176.

age group. Similarly it is no reflection on Enid Blyton that most adults find her work wearisome. Implicit in any assessment of an artist's success in communicating with an audience are certain assumptions about the degree of receptiveness of that audience. We *are* justified in condemning a writer who fails to communicate his ideas to *those capable of appreciating them*. Who such people are will depend on the particular context.

It is just this reference to a particular context which Tolstoi's argument ignores. For what he maintains is that there is a corruption in art which fails to communicate to *anyone*, under any circumstances whatsoever. 'Good art always pleases everyone.' But this can only be because he has from the beginning decided to exclude from the discussion any question of intelligence, receptiveness, appreciation. So that it can scarcely be legitimate to present the exclusion of such considerations as the consequence of the argument.

Similar remarks apply to what may be Tolstoi's more funda-mental, though admittedly less explicit, reason for rejecting the suggestion that there are those who cannot appreciate certain sorts of art, namely that such a claim displays arrogance, involves the sort of elitism in which the speaker adopts a position of superior-ity towards others. For this idea, though common enough, is also mere confusion. One could equally say that it is Tolstoi's own position which displays the arrogance. For if there is no such thing as greater or lesser understanding, better or worse taste in art, then my own understanding must be as great as any, my own taste unimprovable. But the truth of the matter is that both con-clusions are equally unjustified. For, once again, accusations of arrogance or conceit draw their sense only from a particular context of appreciation, where one wishes to suggest that the agent overrates, say, his own understanding of the Romantic poets or of post-Impressionist art. Elitism consists in the attribution to certain groups—the rich, owners of art galleries, fashionable critics—an understanding whose existence cannot be demon-strated. To say of Tolstoi's proposal to dispense quite generally with all talk of what can or cannot be understood that it displays either humility or arrogance is quite simply senseless.

Like sceptical arguments generally, Tolstoi's scepticism about the role of understanding in art, relies on precisely that feature of our lives which it is intended to destroy. For in so far as Tolstoi uses arguments to defend his conclusion, they can be seen to involve notions which rest on our common understanding that people do differ among themselves and from one group to another in what they are capable of appreciating. But perhaps in the final analysis what gives Tolstoi's argument its power to convince is not any explicit argument, but rather his tendency to substitute for a discussion of the particular circumstances in which someone may or may not appreciate a particular novel, painting, poem, a discussion couched in terms of human responses. For there is certainly a superficial plausibility in the suggestion that it is not necessary to understand something in order for it to evoke a response in us. The following passage makes it plain what Tolstoi has in mind:

> What distinguishes a work of art from all other mental activity is just the fact that its language is understood by all, and that it infects all without distinction. The tears and laughter of a China-man infect me just as the laughter and tears of a Russian; and it is the same with painting and music, and also with poetry when it is translated into a language I understand.[8]

What Tolstoi is offering in this passage is, once again, his version of the expression theory, the so-called theory of art as infection, which sees music, painting, even literature as involving the communication of feelings without the mediation of understanding. The term 'infection' is, despite its unfortunate ring, appropriate here. For Tolstoi's suggestion is that just as it does not require understanding for me to become infected with your cold or someone else's typhoid, so in art feelings are communicated without the understanding being brought into play. And Tolstoi is, of course, quite correct to say that there are areas of our lives in which feelings can be transmitted in this way. Human beings tend, for example, to respond to tears and laughter with tears and laughter. And their reacting in these ways need not depend on any understanding of the circumstances which have occasioned the sorrow or joy. Laughter is infectious, so that I may join in the mirth even when I have not understood the joke. And the small child may be upset by its mother's tears, even where the tears are a response to something (say, a court summons) which the child could not understand. Similar remarks apply to depression, anger (I tend to lose my temper with people who lose their tempers with me), fear and so on. In this sense it may be said that there are

---

[8]   *What is Art?*, p. 177.

human responses which transcend cultural barriers. But, as Wittgenstein continually emphasises in his lectures on aesthetics, this is of little help when we turn to art. 'When we make an aesthetic judgement about a thing, we do not just gape at it and say "Oh? How marvelous!" We distinguish between a person who knows what he is talking about and a person who doesn't.'[9] Another way of expressing the point would be to say that with a work of art what is of interest is not a mere response, but a response which involves understanding. If I wonder whether you have seen the humour in a story, for instance, I am not interested only in whether you laugh, for you may laugh without under-standing. And it is just in respect of their *understanding* of humour that people differ. Consider the following passage:

> Everything about this boy was curious—everything turned out differently for him from the way it does to the bad (little boys) in the books.
>
> Once he climbed up in Farmer Acorn's trees to steal apples, and the limb didn't break, and he didn't fall and break his arm, and get torn by the farmer's great dog, and then languish on a sickbed for weeks and repent and become good. Oh no; he stole as many apples as he wanted, and came down all right; and he was all ready for the dog, too, and knocked him endways with a brick when he came to tear him. It was very strange—nothing like it ever happened in those mild little books with marbled backs, and with pictures in them of men with swallow-tailed coats and bell-crowned hats, and pantaloons that are short in the legs, and women with the waists of their dresses under their arms and no hoops on. Nothing like it in any of the Sunday-school books.[10]

Twain's target here is a certain sort of moral tale, designed to convince children that virtue has its own reward in this world as well as the next. Such stories, Twain is suggesting, are not merely implausible, they are *obviously* implausible, and are given to children in the vain hope that they will be too naive, too unworldly to notice the implausibility. So that their distribution by Sunday-school teachers amounts to a variety of cheating, where one would have least expected it.

The point is not itself humorous—anything but, in fact. The humour lies in the intentional contrast between Twain's mildly

---

9   *Lectures and Conversations*, p. 6.
10   Mark Twain. 'The Story of the Bad Little Boy', in *The Complete Short Stories of Mark Twain* (New York: Bantam Books, 1981).

racy prose and the tone of the Sunday-school books, which he is mocking. For what Twain has noticed is that the implausibility of the stories in the Sunday-school books goes hand in hand with an inappropriateness of tone. There is nothing that *real* bad little boys do which could appropriately be described as 'languishing' or 'repenting'. So whereas in the Sunday-school books the dog tears the bad little boy who languishes and repents, in Twain's story the dog is knocked endways with a brick.

This being so, it is obvious that the wit is capable of being appreciated only by those who have some familiarity with the particular stories and the particular style which Twain is satirising. In my own case, and probably that of most people of my generation, this familiarity is slight, so that there are no doubt nuances and allusions which pass me by. (For instance, I suspect, but cannot precisely identify, some irony in the description of the illustrations in the Sunday-school books.)

But it is not difficult to imagine another people or another generation on whom the whole point would be lost. True, it could probably be explained to them, for instance by presenting them with examples of the sort of religious tract being satirised. But then there is an obvious difference in response between someone who responds to a joke only after explanation and someone who responds immediately. Indeed there could be only one greater difference, namely between both these reactions and that of the person who does not respond at all.

Faced with the difficulty some writers have been inclined to discount such differences. There are, they admit, elements in literature which are intelligible to members of one society, but not to those of another. But, so the argument goes, this is true only in so far as what we are dealing with is not of literary value. A story has real value only in so far as it does not deal with what is particular to the experience of a certain age or a certain society, but with what is typical of everyone's experience. My suspicion is that it would not take very much argument to show that it is this view or something very like it which often lies behind the apparently ubiquitous theory that what is truly important in art and literature is what stands the test of time, the general idea being that if Shakespeare's plays are admired in the twentieth century as they were in the seventeenth century, then they must deal with issues which are so fundamental as to be common to the lives of very different societies. But anyhow it is clear that such a view plays a central role in Tolstoi's essay. To be classified as great art, he tells us, a work:

> must not transmit feelings accessible only to a man educated in a certain way, or only to an aristocrat, or a merchant, or only to a Russian or a native of Japan, or a Roman Catholic, or a Buddhist and so on, but must transmit feelings accessible to everyone … such as feelings of merriment, of pity, of cheerfulness, or tranquility and so forth.[11]

One's first reaction on reading what Tolstoi says here may be to wonder what can be meant by speaking of feelings which are accessible to *everyone* or to ask in what way a story can be typical of the experiences of *everyone*. But it is important to see that the difficulty here is not empirical but conceptual. It lies not in Tolstoi's having mistakenly believed himself to have identified some common elements in the lives of Roman Catholics and Buddhists, merchants and aristocrats, but in his having failed to give sense to the idea of a common element. If someone asks me what is common to ships, sealing-wax and kings, my puzzlement will stem not from my inability to find *something* in common, common that is from some standpoint or other (I could do *that* easily enough, *e.g.* they are all pretty hard to find in the middle of the Kalahari desert), but in my failure to grasp the standpoint from which such a question is asked.

The point is presented dramatically by the figure of Temple Drake in Faulkner's *Sanctuary*. Trapped by her boyfriend Gowan Steven's need for alcohol into visiting a delapidated antebellum mansion known locally as 'the old Frenchman's', Temple finds herself menaced by the sinister collection of bootleggers who live there, and unwisely attempts to manipulate them with the sort of flirtatiousness which had been successful with the college boys at Ole' Miss. Unfortunately, she fails to recognise that her own ideas of love, ideas which involve strict, and within her own group, generally accepted limits on what is permissible between a man and a woman, have no sense for the inhabitants of 'the old Frenchman's' where any such relationship has to be sexual. The conflict between these views is noted, if rather unsympathetically portrayed by the prostitute Lee, who lives with one of the bootleggers.

---

[11]   *What is Art?*, p. 177.

Take all you can get and give nothing. 'I'm a pure girl. I can't do that.' You'll slip out with the kids and burn their gasoline and eat their food, but just let a man so much as look at you and you faint away because your father the judge and your four brothers might not like it.[12]

In the particular context with which the novel is concerned — Temple's inability to control her relations with others — to say that she has something in common with Lee because they are both capable of experiencing love, would be as pointless as insisting that they have something in common because they both have two hands. Someone who spoke in this way would simply have missed the point of the story. This is not to say that in a different context, from the standpoint of a different set of interests, it might not be relevant to point to what the two women share. If, for example, Faulkner's novel had been intended as a treatment of the social problems facing the gay community, it might be important to emphasise that Temple and Lee both take it for granted that love is a relationship between man and woman. But this simply shows that questions about common features cannot be divorced from a context of interest. For the same reason Tolstoi's attempt to assess stories on the basis of whether their characters embody feelings common to all mankind is, in the absence of some specified context, merely a dead-end.

II

Given my criticisms so far, it may now seem rather difficult to explain why Wittgenstein thought Tolstoi's thesis worthy of attention. And the puzzlement may well be increased rather than diminished, when one reflects that many of these criticisms are of a sort normally associated with Wittgenstein himself. For example, my last point about Tolstoi's misuse of the notion of 'what is common' can easily be seen to be an application of Wittgenstein's remarks in *Philosophical Investigations* about the use of '*same*',[13] when it is noticed that the common feelings which Tolstoi needs to identify will be those which are the same for all human beings. Nor does Wittgenstein himself simply accept Tolstoi's thesis at this point. It is, he says, 'both true and false'.[14]

---

12 *Sanctuary.*
13 *Philosophical Investigations* paras. 185, 208, 215–6, 223–7.
14 *Culture and Value*, p. 59.

To see why this is so, to see why Wittgenstein believed that the apparent silliness of Tolstoi's views masked an important truth, we must, I think, begin by paying attention to a distinction which appears both in Wittgenstein's *Lectures on Aesthetics* and in *Culture and Value* but which has to date been largely ignored. In both works the point is made in the context of a discussion of the nature of taste, which Wittgenstein identifies as an appreciation of the standards involved, either explicitly or implicitly, in some cultural activity. In the lectures Wittgenstein was concerned to attack a false disjunction, which arises primarily because philosophers have concentrated their attention on wholly uncharacteristic examples of aesthetic judgement—'This is beautiful', 'This is ugly', etc. What is significant about these examples is that, though they have the form of subject-predicate propositions, closer examination reveals that they are in fact employed more as interjections or as expressions of reactions. So it is not difficult to see that an emphasis on such examples can easily lead us into confusion. Impressed by their surface similarity to judgements like 'This is red' or 'This is round', certain philosophers conclude that all aesthetic judgements attribute features to physical objects in accordance with universally accepted standards. Impressed more by the actual role of such expressions in our lives, observing perhaps, as Wittgenstein notes, that the word 'beautiful' could often simply be replaced by a gesture like rubbing one's stomach to indicate that one's desire has been satisfied, others conclude that aesthetic judgement is merely subjective. But as Wittgenstein sees, there is no reason to accept either of these alternatives. For the idea of universal standards of artistic excellence makes little sense when we realise that we may appreciate the art of one culture and be *completely* at sea with that of another. Still it does not follow that the only alternative is subjectivism. For *within* different cultures, there will still be many agreed standards of taste. At this point Wittgenstein draws an analogy with the activities of a tailor making a suit. Just as the tailor's judgement is shown by his recognising that the sleeves are too long, the lapels too wide, so in painting one shows one's taste by, for example, seeing that the background would have been more effective had the artist used more muted shades, in observing that the central figure should have been drawn a little more to the left, and so on.

'Taste', Wittgenstein remarks, 'makes adjustments.'[15] And the ability to make such adjustments is not simply a subjective matter, but something which we learn. We learn to judge in accordance with the accepted standards of our society. Since, however, these are the accepted standards of *our* society, they may give us little help when we turn to another society. I may have no difficulty in seeing that the sleeves of the jacket which I have just tried on are too long, but this will give me no help in judging the coronation robes of Edward the Confessor. The difficulty here is (in one sense) that of ignorance. I do not know what counted as 'too long' in that society.

Much of Wittgenstein's argument so far had been prefigured in the work of Hume in his essay 'Of the Standard of Taste'. In particular the importance which Hume attaches to comparisons can be seen as a corollary of Wittgenstein's observations. For just as the tailor in making adjustments is by implication comparing the suit on which he is working with another more perfect suit, real or imagined, so in seeing how a particular poem might be improved, we are by implication comparing it with other poems, real or imagined. There is, however, an important difference between Wittgenstein and Hume here. For the centrality of such comparisons to the nature of taste leads Hume to suppose that in taste he has identified the distinguishing feature of aesthetic judgement. All aesthetic judgement involves taste. Taste will allow us access to all works of art from the mediocre to the works of genius, all of which may be ranked on a scale of increasing refinement and perfection, just as at a dog show the principles employed by the judges enable them to rank the entrants in order of merit. This conclusion is, however, one which Wittgenstein resists. Referring back to the analogy with the tailor, he remarks:

> A good cutter won't use any words except words like 'Too long', 'All right'. When we talk of a symphony of Beethoven, we don't talk of correctness. Entirely different things enter. One wouldn't talk of appreciating the *tremendous* things in Art. In certain styles in architecture a door is correct, and the thing is to appreciate it. But in the case of a Gothic cathedral what we do is not at all to find it correct — it plays an entirely different role with us. The entire *game* is different.[16]

---

15   Ibid., p. 63.
16   *Lectures and Conversations*, pp. 6/7.

To suppose that there is some scale on which we rank all works of art would be to suppose that great works of art differ from the mediocre only in degree, in doing what the latter do, but superlatively. But this is sheer confusion. In the magazine *Private Eye*'s satirical column, 'Dear Bill', a series of fictional letters written by the Prime Minister's husband Dennis, Margaret Thatcher is at one point depicted as having decided, on the advice of her public relations advisors that she needs to present a more cultured image and embarks on a study of Dostoevsky's work. After a few hours with *The Brothers Karamazov*, she gives as her opinion that it is 'not a patch on *Murder on the Nile*'.[17] The intended effect of this remark is, of course, to present Mrs. Thatcher as a philistine. But it attains its effect not, as one might at first imagine, by representing her as having ranked the two works in an order which we all know to be incorrect. For it would be equally a mark of philistinism to have suggested that *Murder on the Nile* was not a patch on *The Brothers Karamazov*. The crassness of the comparison lies, that is to say, in the desire to draw a comparison at all, in the supposition that we can speak of *Murder on the Nile* and *The Brothers Karamazov* in the same terms.

For Wittgenstein there is a fundamental difference in the way we can speak of or respond to, on the one hand the general run of works of art, and on the other great works of art. And this raises the possibility that what may be truly said of great works of art would be incorrect as an account of art in general. More specifically it raises the possibility that what Tolstoi says of the relation between art and understanding, though false as a thesis about art in general, would have a point had he restricted it to great art.

But does he so restrict it? Unfortunately, the answer is ambiguous. Tolstoi's discussion is just not consistent. Sometimes, as in the passages I have quoted so far, the point concerns art in general. A work of art — any work of art — in so far as it is not an example of corrupt, exclusive art, can be understood by everyone. Sometimes, however, it *is* specifically a claim about 'great art', 'the highest works of art', 'the very best works of art'. Consider the following passage, where Tolstoi is once again presupposing the view that art's function lies in the expression of emotion.

---

[17]   I owe the example to a discussion with Dr. T.J. Diffey, who, as I remember, used it to make a somewhat different point.

> The hindrance to an understanding of the best and highest feelings
> lies not at all in deficiency of development and learning, but on the
> contrary in false development and false learning.[18]

In so far as Tolstoi restricts his claim, as he does in these passages,
then the criticism on which I concentrated in the first half of this
paper—criticisms which concern the barriers to an understanding
of art—become not false but misdirected. For when, for example, I
find difficulty in understanding the art of another society, it will
not be only the work of their finest artists, but also of those they
regard as mediocre, which puzzles me. I remember once reading
of a Chinese mandarin in the last century, who, on witnessing the
work of certain British portrait painters, asked whether it was the
custom of English ladies to wash only one side of their faces. The
mandarin would have faced the same difficulty with the work of
any British portrait painter of the period, good, bad or indifferent.
For the problem was, at least in part, that he was ignorant of the
standards and conventions of British painting, in particular those
concerning the representation of shadow. By contrast, what
Tolstoi sees is that the difficulty which any of us may face when
presented with a *great* work of art, is not a matter of knowledge or
of taste at all—and in that sense not a matter of understanding,
but of the will. The point is a general one, not restricted to the field
of art:

> I know that most men—not only those considered clever, but even
> those who are very clever—can seldom discern even the simplest
> and most obvious truth if it be such as to oblige them to admit the
> falsity of conclusions they have formed perhaps with much diffi-
> culty; conclusions of which they are proud, which they have
> taught to others, and on which they have built their lives.[19]

In their general form Tolstoi's views bear a striking similarity to
Wittgenstein's own, as witness his repeated observations in
Culture and Value that with philosophical problems it is cleverness,
rather than silliness which blinds us to their solution. Or consider
the remainder of the paragraph referred to earlier, where Wittgenstein is outlining the truth which he finds in Tolstoi's views.

> What makes a subject hard to understand—if it's something
> significant and important—is not that before you can understand

---

[18]   *What is Art?*, p. 179.
[19]   Ibid., p. 218.

it, you need to be specially trained in abstruse matters, but the contrast between understanding the subject and what most people want to see. Because of this the very things which are most obvious may become the hardest of all to understand.[20]

Restricted to the case of art, the claim is that what stands in the way of our responding to great art is not a lack of taste, a lack of education in or understanding of the standards of one's own or some other culture, but rather, as Wittgenstein continually emphasises, a lack of courage, a lack of willingness to question what is taken for granted, even by ourselves. An artist who is profound or original will be difficult to understand not because we lack the intellectual capacity or taste to do so, but because in order to do so we shall be forced to throw over what is dear to us, because his work will appear to us as a threat. It will be hard to understand not in the sense that we are unable to understand it, but rather in the sense that we cannot bring ourselves to understand it. Indeed, far from its being lack of taste which stands in our way, it is often taste itself which is threatened and so constitutes the bar to understanding. Tolstoi himself inadvertently provides us with an example when he quotes the reactions of his daughter, Tatiana Sukhotin, to the Paris exhibitions of 1894:

> The first exhibition, that of Camille Pissarro was comparatively the most comprehensible, though the pictures were out of drawing, had no content, and the colourings were most improbable. The drawing was so indefinite that you were sometimes unable to make out which way an arm or a head was turned …
>
> In the colouring bright blue and bright green predominated. And each picture had its special colour with which the whole picture was, as it were, splashed … In the same gallery—that of Durand-Ruel—were other pictures: by Puvis de Chavannes, Manet, Monet, Renoir, Sisley, who are all Impressionists. One of them, whose name I could not make out—it was something like Redon[21]—had painted a blue face in profile. On the whole face

---

[20]   *Culture and Value*, p. 17.

[21]   It is worth noticing that Mme Sukhotin had inherited her father's literary device of making something appear ridiculous by concentrating the reader's attention on irrelevant details. For it has no relevance to the painting's merit that Redon's signature was barely legible. If it was necessary to identify the painting, she needed only to ask an attendant or consult a catalogue. Notice also the other feature of this technique—exemplified, no doubt, by this footnote—that it has the effect of making anyone who draws attention to it look like a pedant.

there is only this blue tone, with white of lead. Pissarro has a water-colour all done in dots. In the foreground is a cow entirely painted with various coloured dots. The general colour cannot be distinguished, however much one stands back from or draws near to, the picture.[22]

Tatiana's reaction to the work of the Impressionists had been mirrored in the writings of critics throughout Europe some years earlier, and though Tolstoi represents it as an example of an untutored and unsophisticated response to corrupt and exclusive art, its true nature becomes more apparent if we ask just what it was in the work of, say, Pissarro or Monet to which his daughter objected. The answer seems simple enough. She thought that the Impressionists could not paint. They did not draw objects — faces, human figures, cows — as they really were. By contrast here is another contemporary critic speaking of their work:

The Impressionists abandoned the three illusions by which the academic painter lives — line, perspective and studio lighting. Where the one sees only the external outline of objects the other sees the real living lines, built not on geometrical forms but in a thousand irregular strokes which, at a distance establish life.[23]

Laforgue's response to the sort of criticism we have been discussing should alert us to the possibility that what is involved here is not a dispute between an aesthetically neutral conception of what it is to draw an object and someone who, either from lack of ability or from choice, ignores that conception, but rather between two different conceptions of what it is to draw an object. And it is not necessary for us to enter into this dispute to notice the possibility that Tatiana, who had, it turns out, studied painting at the Moscow School of Art, faced in Pissarro's work a conception of representation which questioned the very principles on which her own understanding of art, her own taste, rested, and unwilling to accept this questioning, she was forced to reject the Impressionists work. So that, far from illustrating, as he imagined, Tolstoi's confused thesis that genuine art can be understood by all, in reality her comments illustrated the claim, shared by both Wittgenstein and Tolstoi, that what stands in the way of understanding great art is not the understanding, but the will.

---

[22] *What is Art?*, p. 170.
[23] Jules Laforgue, quoted in Phoebe Poole, *Impressionism* (London: Thames & Hudson, 1967).

III

It would, however, be misleading, were I to fail to draw attention to what is at least a difference of emphasis between the two writers.[24] And perhaps the best way to see this difference is to notice that whereas in *What is Art?* Tolstoi tends to represent what stands in the way of understanding as a matter of what has been learned, of conclusions which men have reached and on which they have built their lives, Wittgenstein does not appear to see learning as the only obstacle. He speaks more generally. 'What makes a subject hard to understand … is … the contrast between understanding the subject and what most people want to see.' So it may be objected that by restricting my discussion to cases where it is someone's taste which stands in the way of their responding to great art (as in the case of Tatiana Sukhotin), I have unwittingly given support to Tolstoi's views in so far as those differ from Wittgenstein's. I hope that my last example will dispel this impression.

In 1886 under the influence of the view of art expounded in *What is Art?* Tolstoi published a short story entitled 'How Much Land Does a Man Need?', a story regarded by many as amongst his greatest works, and incidentally much admired by Wittgenstein. Most of Tolstoi's critics have commented on the extreme simplicity of the tale's style and content. Two sisters are discussing life in the city and life in the country. The younger sister, the wife of a peasant, criticises the greed and vanity of city life. In the country, by contrast, all genuine human needs are met. She and her husband, Pakhom agree that if they had only a little more land, then they would be content. Overhearing the conversation, the devil lays his plans.

Later Pakhom gains more land, and still more, but is not satisfied, realising, for example, that he can farm more efficiently if he has more land, so that one field in two may be left fallow. Eventually he is told that among the people of Bashkir land can be purchased very cheaply. He visits the Bashkirs and strikes a deal with their chief. He will pay 1000 roubles for as much land as he can encompass on foot in a single day. At daybreak the Bashkirs gather on a hill to mark the beginning and end of his journey. Unfortunately Pakhom is overcome by greed and travels too far.

---

[24] I am grateful to D.Z. Phillips for having drawn my attention to the importance of this point.

Seeing the sun sinking he breaks into a run, though by now completely exhausted. With one last desperate effort he reaches the hill just as the sun touches the horizon, collapses and dies. His servant measures his master and digs a grave for him. The grave is six feet long.

As an example of a story which could not be misunderstood, 'How Much Land Does a Man Need?' seems an extraordinarily bad candidate. For, despite its simplicity, this seems often to have been its fate. Both in Tolstoi's time and in the writings of later critics it has often been taken either as a warning about the dangers of land ownership or an attack on the greed of the Russian peasants. But neither of these interpretations makes very much sense. For, if we take the former, then it must surely have struck Tolstoi that a desire to own land need not be an example of greed, which is certainly what the story is about. And if the latter interpretation were correct, then the title should have read 'How Much Land Does a Peasant Need?' for the story would not be about men in general, but only about peasants. Indeed, it is striking that in offering interpretations of the story which link it to a specific group or to a specific aspect of human life, Tolstoi's critics bear a remarkable resemblance to Pakhom's wife, whose words delight the devil. For she too believes greed to be the preserve of a certain group or characteristic of certain activities though not others. It is simply that the groups, the activities are different. The desire for fine clothes of the city dwellers is to be contrasted with the genuine needs of the peasants. The greed of tradesmen to be contrasted with the contentment of a farmer's life. What she and Pakhom fail to see is that the insidious form of greed lies not in our desiring what we ourselves regard as luxuries, mere idle wants, but rather presents itself as the attempt to obtain what we need. Unlike some others we could name, *we* do not want a mansion: if we just had a larger garden, then we should be content. So that the greed of others, being all too visible, conceals from us the extent to which we too are its victims. It is his failure to see this which leads to Pakhom's death. For we are most at the mercy of greed, where we do not even recognise it as such. The answer to the question, 'How much land does a man need?' is not 'Six feet', nor as Chekhov suggested, 'The whole world?' For there is no answer which will ensure that so long as we only seek to justify our needs, we shall not fall prey to greed.

In what sense, then, was the story hard for Tolstoi's critics to understand? Certainly not in the sense that it would have been hard for a member of another society which did not possess the concept of land ownership to make anything of it. The Sioux Indians who led a nomadic life following the bison, appear to have had difficulty in understanding the desire of white settlers to purchase land. For the same reason we can imagine that they would have been at a loss to make anything of Tolstoi's story. And in a clear sense, their difficulty would have been an intellectual one. This was not, however, the problem facing Tolstoi's critics. The story was hard for them to understand in that they did not want to understand it. For to do so would have shown them, as it may show us, something unwelcome about the nature of their own greed. So that if we ask what it was that stood in the way of their understanding, the answer is not, as Tolstoi's views would imply, their learning. For you do not need to be learned to be prey to greed. It was rather the fact that they were men. The barrier which they, like us, needed to overcome was the barrier of their own humanity.

7

Art and Family Resemblances[1]

When Tilghman's book *But Is It Art?* was first published,[2] I was asked by the *Times Higher Education Supplement* to review it, along, as I remember, with two other books. At the time, 1984, I was engaged in a considerable amount of reviewing, generally in the field of aesthetics, and I have to say that I had become rather blasé about the standard of what I was being invited to read. So Tilghman's book came as a delightful surprise. When I read it recently, for the third time, I was again surprised, not this time that Tilghman had managed to shed so much light on the problems of aesthetics and on the application of Wittgenstein's ideas to those problems, for I had by then become accustomed to *that* thought, but by the extent to which my own thinking on the subject had been influenced by his writings. It may therefore appear ungrateful of me to present an essay in which I try to show some limitations in the argument which he develops in *But Is It Art?* I stress limitations, since fundamentally I think that we are in agreement. If, however, it does strike you as ungrateful to emphasise the disagreement in an essay intended to honour Tilghman, then I think that this will simply show that philosophy is not your subject. For philosophy is above all the area in which it is disagreement and not imitation which is the sincerest form of flattery.

If one had to identify an orthodoxy among those whose aim was to reveal for aesthetics the importance of Wittgenstein's ideas concerning language, then this orthodoxy would for a long time have been exemplified by the views of Morris Weitz. In its

---

First published in *Philosophical Investigations*, 18 (3) 1995.
[2] Ben Tilghman, *But is it Art?* (Oxford: Blackwell, 1984).

essentials Weitz's account, as developed for instance in his paper
'The Role of Theory in Aesthetics',[3] consists in a fairly straight-
forward application to the case of art of a certain interpretation of
Wittgenstein's views on language popularised by Renford
Bambrough in his paper 'Universals and Family Resemblances'.[4]
According to this view, Wittgenstein, in certain paragraphs of
Philosophical Investigations had solved what Bambrough calls 'the
problem of universals'. He had, that is to say, solved the problem
of how it is that we are able to apply a general term such as 'table',
or 'number' or 'language' or 'game' to different instances of tables,
numbers, languages, games. And he had solved this problem by
rejecting the answer offered by writers such as Locke, according to
which general terms are applied by virtue of some property
common to all their instances, and by suggesting an alternative
account. The rejection in question consists in Wittgenstein's
challenge to find some property common to all games or numbers,
and his observation that if we 'look and see', we shall realise that
there just is no such common property. The alternative account
consists in his identification of what he refers to as a pattern of
'family resemblances', threads of similarities, between the different things which we call 'games' and 'numbers'. Wittgenstein
insists that if we examine what we call 'games', without philosophical prejudice, then:

> We see a complicated network of similarities, overlapping and
> criss-crossing: sometimes overall similarities, sometimes simi-
> larities of detail.[5]

It is, according to Bambrough, on the basis of the identification of
such similarities that we apply or withhold the word 'game'.

Now, as I say, Morris Weitz's aesthetic theory consists almost
completely in a straightforward application of this account of
Wittgenstein to the special case of the word 'art'. For Weitz the
confusion in traditional theories of art, traditional attempts to
explain why we apply the term 'art' to a very diverse range of

[3]   Morris Weitz, 'The Role of Theory in Aesthetics', *Journal of Aesthetics and
Art Criticism*, 15, 1956.
[4]   Renford Bambrough, 'Universals and Family Resemblances', in G. Pitcher
ed., *Wittgenstein: The Philosophical Investigations* (New York: Anchor Books,
1966) pp. 186–204.
[5]   L. Wittgenstein, *Philosophical Investigations*, §66.

human activities, is once again that of trying to find some essence of art, some property common to all these activities.

> The problem of the nature of art is like that of the nature of games, at least in these respects: if we actually look and see what it is that we call 'art', we will also find no common properties — only strands of similarities. Knowing what art is is not apprehending some manifest or latent essence, but being able to recognise, describe and explain those things we call 'art' in virtue of these similarities.[6]

It may appear from this passage as though Weitz's view is that when we recognise something as a work of art, we do so because of its similarities, its 'family resemblances' to other works of art. But put *that* generally, the view would be of dubious coherence. If I say that x is a work of art because of the similarities it shares with y, then presumably y must already be accepted as a work of art. It cannot be that whenever we are doubtful about whether something is to be regarded as a work of art our doubt is dispelled by noticing the similarity of this case to another of which we are equally doubtful. It is, I suppose, for this reason that Weitz introduces the notion of the 'paradigm case', a notion which does not, so far as I can see, play any obvious role in Wittgenstein's discussion. In explaining why we classify something as a work of art, Weitz tells us:

> certain (paradigm) cases can be given, about which there can be no question as to their being correctly described as 'art'.[7]

Where, however, a question does arise, and in particular when it arises as a result of some radical departure from tradition in painting, or music, or literature, then, according to Weitz:

> what is at stake is no factual analysis concerning necessary and sufficient properties, but a decision as to whether the work under examination is similar in certain respects to other works, and consequently warrants the extension of the concepts to cover the new case.[8]

What I have just given is the interpretation of Wittgenstein against which Tilghman develops the argument of his book *But Is It Art?*

---

6   Weitz, op. cit., p. 31.
7   Ibid.
8   Ibid., p. 32.

And I do not think that it would be an overstatement to say that Tilghman rejects it wholesale not merely as an interpretation of Wittgenstein, but as an account of *any* aspect of our use of language. Perhaps the easiest way in which to see the nature of this rejection is to note that for Tilghman the so-called 'problem of universals' from which Bambrough and Weitz start their respective enquiries into the nature of games and art, that is the question 'Why do we call all the different things that we do "games" or "art"?' simply lacks sense. For this question pre-supposes that there is some activity, classifying things as games or as art, which is itself independent of any particular human interest or activity. We are asked why 'we' (all of us, all the time) classify certain things as games or as art, regardless of any particular reason we might have, any particular contrast which we may wish to make, any importance that the classification might have. But, as Tilghman says, such a question 'posed in abstraction from any particular circumstance and concern is simply another instance of language gone on holiday'.[9] Of course in a particular context I may say that the children are playing a game in order to emphasise the harmlessness of what they are doing (they did not, for instance, mean to frighten the baby), in another context I may say of the same activity that it is not a game, in order to emphasise the pointlessness of it and lack of formalised rules (where, let us say, another child asks me to teach it how to play the game, or asks why the children are playing it). But it is precisely because the question 'Is this a game?' can be raised in different contexts, where different criteria of what makes something a game are involved, that the above remarks cannot be taken to involve a self-contradiction. And it is for this same reason, that any talk of the *general* question 'Why do we call the things that we do "games"?' or any idea of some *general* standpoint from which we classify certain things as games, others not, is a mere confusion.

   Though it may not be immediately apparent, the argument just given is in effect an application of Wittgenstein's observation at *Investigations* §255 that the word 'same' has sense only when used in conjunction with some rule or criterion of identity. For, of course, to classify just is to treat as being of the same kind. It therefore follows that to speak of how 'we' classify independently of any specified criterion is to talk nonsense, and that the so-called

---

9   Tilghman, *But is it Art?*, p. 27.

'problem of universals' is a pseudo-question. But, as Tilghman sees, and indeed emphasises, for the same reason, to offer either the essentialist position or the 'theory of family resemblances' as answers to this problem must also be to talk nonsense. For just as it makes sense to speak of classifying games only by reference to some specific standpoint which involves criteria of classification, so it makes sense to speak of identifying what is common to different games only by reference to some specific standpoint, and of identifying similarities between games only by reference to some specific standpoint.

If one is impressed by Tilghman's arguments so far, as I certainly am, then what is impressive is the range of that attack. For it seems that by the development of an argument drawn from Wittgenstein's writings, he has at the same time shown to be confusions, on the one hand an account of the problem which Wittgenstein faced in *Philosophical Investigations* (the 'problem of universals') together with an account of the answer which he offers to it (the 'theory of family resemblances'), and on the other an extremely influential account of the application of that answer to the study of aesthetics, namely that of Morris Weitz.

There is, however, as Tilghman sees, a difficulty. Ben illustrates one of the most familiar varieties of this problem, at least in the twentieth century, by imagining what he refers to as a 'plain gentleman' who enters a gallery to be confronted by Karl Andre's firebricks, Marcel Duchamps's urinal entitled *Fountain*, or some such work. Ben says:

> When he is told that it is art ... he is puzzled. That piece of information is not enough; he wonders how this can be. His puzzlement arises out of his previous understanding of art. He is not put off by any lack of representation because he knows and enjoys abstract art, but this doesn't seem to have any of the characteristic virtues even of abstract art. There is no formal arrangement worthy of being called a design, there are no interesting colour relationships, there is no texture worthy of attention, nor is it apparently symbolic of anything and no doubt the artist or his critic tout would deny the relevance of any or all those things.[10]

Faced with this puzzle, Tilghman's plain gentleman may be inclined to ask of the work on display 'But is it art?' Unfortunately, this may tempt one to suppose that what is required here is

---

10   Ibid., p. 54.

just what Tilghman has ruled out, namely some general principle according to which such objects and activities are to be classified as art or as something else. And then it may appear that precisely what will fit the bill is the sort of account which is offered by Morris Weitz. For, as we have seen, one of the features of Weitz's position is that it appears to offer an explanation of something which seems genuinely puzzling, namely how it is that we decide when faced with some new development whether or not to classify it as art. So that, according to Weitz, the problem facing Tilghman's plain gentleman will be solved, when he discovers in the urinal or the firebricks, not some property common to all works of art, since that possibility has been rejected, but rather sufficient similarities with what are for him paradigm cases to justify these particular things as works of art.

It is, however, at this point where Tilghman's position seems to face most problems that its real strength becomes apparent. For, Tilghman insists, it is surely wrong to present the plain gentleman faced with what is sometimes called the 'shock of the new' as standing in need of a classification. His problem, when faced with Duchamp's *Fountain*, he protests 'But is it art?', is not that he wishes to know how this thing is to be classified, as though the answer 'Yes, that is how we classify it', would somehow solve his problem. In this he is like two other cases which Tilghman mentions, that of the person who, presented with an apparently incomprehensible form of activity, asks 'Is it a game?' and that of the person who, presented with an apparently incomprehensible remark, asks 'Is that a joke?'. For in these cases as well, it would be merely silly to suppose that what is in question is a classification. The person who can make nothing of mahjongg is obviously not going to be any the less bewildered if they are told that this is what is classified as a game in China. Nor is the person who wonders whether the remark was a joke going to have their puzzlement removed by the solemn reply, 'Yes that *was* what I call a joke'. For in all these cases, what is required is not a classification, but an explanation. The person does not understand what has been presented to them as a work of art, or they cannot make anything of the game, or they do not see the humour in what has been said. So our plain gentleman's difficulty on encountering the urinal or the firebricks will not be resolved by getting him to classify what he sees in a certain way. For he may, after all, be willing to accept that this is the sort of thing which people do classify as art. He may even, though Tilghman does not mention this, be willing in some contexts to classify it in this way himself. For example, in the company of a small child, inclined to play with the firebricks (I have tried not to imagine what the small child might do with Duchamp's exhibit), he may point out that this is one of the works of art and so should not be touched. His problem is that he does not understand what there is about the object which merits this kind of attention.

Can his question then be answered? I think that Tilghman's view here can probably be summed [up] by saying that whether it can or not will depend on what the plain gentleman is looking at. For the history of art is full of examples of plain gentlemen, being initially bewildered by new developments in art, and subsequently being brought to see these developments as just that, legitimate artistic developments. One familiar case concerns Roger Fry's attempt to explain the work of the post-impressionists to an Edwardian audience whose first inclination when faced with the work of, say, Cezanne was to respond with contempt. Fry is generally thought to have argued convincingly that the mistake was to try and see Cezanne as though he were painting (unsuccessfully) within the tradition of Landseer, whereas his work should rather be seen as an attempt to recapture in painting qualities possessed by Giotto but lost in the subsequent development of painting. Unfortunately, if what puzzles the plain gentleman is not the work of Cezanne or Matisse, but rather that of Duchamp or Andre, then though it might seem that in principle the puzzlement might be removed in a similar fashion, Tilghman thinks that as a matter of fact this is not possible. For the arguments which are offered to bring us to understand the work of these alleged artists, turn out on examination to be worthless. They rest on a series of confusions—for the most part, conceptual confusions. The attempt to enlighten the plain gentleman turns out to be a complete failure.

If I do not examine in detail Tilghman's arguments at this point, it is not because I do not find them convincing. On the contrary, I find them completely convincing. What I wonder, however, is whether they are necessary, or rather whether they are always necessary. For I said earlier that for Tilghman whether the plain gentleman's perplexity can be removed depends on what he is looking at, Cezanne or Duchamp. Unfortunately, I think that Ben is at this point inclined to leave out of the discussion another factor, which will have a bearing on this question, namely who the plain gentleman is. For it seems to me to depend on who the plain

gentleman is whether or not the shock which he feels when confronted with the new signals a request for explanation. As we
have seen, one way to express Tilghman's disagreement with
writers like Morris Weitz is to say that he wishes to replace the
idea that when confronted by the shock of the new what is
required is a classification with the view that what is required is
explanation. And the notion of explanation plays a large part in
Tilghman's argument. My only difficulty lies in the suspicion that
it plays too large a part, or perhaps too exclusive a part. And one
way to see this is to ask whether when one views something with
the sort of suspicion which is suggested by the question 'But is it
art?', it is always explanation that one needs. I use the word
'suspicion'. For though the plain gentleman is Tilghman's
creation, and so may have whatever qualities Tilghman chooses to
endow him with, there do seem to be other plain gentlemen who
are not so much puzzled as sceptical. For example me. I wonder
whether, when presented with Duchamp's *Fountain* or other
works of that ilk it would be quite right to represent my state of
mind as that of someone puzzled by something and seeking an
explanation. In what follows I shall try to develop another
possibility.

At §69 Wittgenstein asks and answers the following question:

> How should we explain to someone what a game is? I imagine that
> we should describe *games* to him and we might add: 'This *and
> similar things* are called "games".'

Writers such as Morris Weitz have taken this passage as con-
firming their view that what he holds is what I have called 'the
family-resemblance theory'. They have, that is to say, held that
what Wittgenstein is saying here is that the ability to apply the
word 'game' depends on our recognising in different activities
strands of similarities to those things which we have already
learned to call 'games'. And Tilghman seems to find the passage
puzzling because he also thinks that it must be interpreted in this
way, but finds it ludicrous as an explanation of how children learn
to use such a word.

> The word 'game' … is not applied or withheld on the basis of simi-
> larities or the lack of them to some paradigm in order to achieve a
> classification.[11]

No doubt the passage is puzzling. After all, Wittgenstein talks of
explaining the word 'game', but gives no indication of why or for
whom the explanation is being given. Are we supposed to be
explaining the word to a foreigner, in which case why do we need
to *describe* games to him rather than simply telling him that cricket,
football, contract bridge are games, hoping that he will latch on
that 'game' is the translation of some term in his own language?
Or are we dealing with someone who lacks the concept of a game,
for some reason, in which case, as Tilghman notes, there would
not be much point in describing to him what will inevitably seem
to him rather bizarre activities. Tilghman, himself takes Wittgenstein to be thinking of an explanation given to a child and he
insists that the only way in which we can teach a child what a
game is by, among other things, teaching the child how to play
games.

It may be that like Morris Weitz, Tilghman assumes that when
Wittgenstein imagines saying to someone 'This and similar things
are called games', the force of 'and similar things' is the same as
that of 'things which are similar in some respect or other', and so
concludes that he is saddled at this point with some version of the
family-resemblance theory. But this is not how I would have read
the passage. Rather I had taken that the point of the phrase 'similar things' was simply to indicate that what are being given are
examples of games and that the application of the term is not
exhausted by the instances to which it is here applied, as it would
be were someone explaining the use of a proper name like
'Everest' or a word which identified some limited set such as 'the
Disciples'. Now there is no doubt that Tilghman is right to say that
such an account could not be a *complete* account of how a child
learns the concept 'game' and that if Wittgenstein is implying in
the passage in question that it could, then he is guilty of confusion.
For as Tilghman says, the child will need also to understand
games, and normally the way in which this is brought about is by
teaching the child to play them. Nevertheless, it does not follow
that learning to identify something as a game is the same as

---

[11]   Ibid., p. 33.

having the game explained or understanding the game, nor does it follow that there is no room in the teaching of a child for simply identifying something as a game in the way Wittgenstein indicates. Imagine, for instance, that a young child, having recently graduated from Cowboys and Indians to football, asks what its father is doing and receives the answer that he is playing a game called poker with his friends. I can see no reason to say that the child is unable to apply the word 'game' in this case until it receives an explanation of how the game is played, which in the nature of things it is unlikely to receive for some years to come. And why assume that what would normally be forthcoming is an explanation of any type. For sometimes we just tell the child that such-and-such is a game and leave it at that. The child now knows that it is a game, because we have told it so. Of course, if we are to bring the child to understand the game, rather than simply telling the child that it is a game, then we shall have to do something like teach it the rules. But it does not follow that even in adults the ability to apply or, more importantly for my purposes, withhold the word 'game' depends on understanding and so on explanation. I have almost no understanding of American football, but no difficulty in identifying it as a game (a game which is pretty incomprehensible to me), nor do I have much grasp of what went on in bearbaiting (whether there were any rules, for example), and not much more of what goes on nowadays in bullfights, and I have certainly little inclination to find out, though I should, in many contexts, refuse to call them games or sports. Nor is my remark that I have little inclination to find out about bearbaiting or bullfighting intended merely as a sardonic aside. I mean that I should not like to open myself to the possibility of coming to see bearbaiting or bullfighting as games or sports.

Of course, in saying this, I am not disagreeing with Tilghman's claims about the inappropriateness in thinking of such examples as 'borderline cases', as cases where, though it is not in doubt that they present us with some of the characteristics of games, some similarities with more paradigmatic cases, nevertheless a decision is called for as to whether these constitute sufficient reason for applying the word 'game' or 'sport' in this case. Tilghman is, in my view, right to reject the suggestion that, quite generally:

> there is really nothing at stake in calling something a game or any-
> thing else for that matter, except possible alternative schemes of
> classification, and that in troublesome borderline cases one can say

what one likes so long as one is clear about what is being said, that
is the extent to which it is the similarities or the dissimilarities to
some selected paradigm that are being appealed to.[12]

The absurdity of this account is particularly apparent in the sorts
of case which I have just mentioned. For obviously, if what strikes
one about, say, the bullfight is that it involves the slaughter of a
tormented animal, then one is unlikely to find particularly compelling any series of comparisons between the skill of a jockey and
of a picador, or between the accuracy and fleetness of foot of a
footballer and that of the bandarilleros. Indeed, faced with a
certain sort of objection to bullfighting, such comparisons will
have no more point than the corresponding comparisons with the
horsemanship displayed in a cavalry charge, or the accuracy and
fleetness of foot of someone throwing a hand-grenade into a
machine gun nest. They will, that is to say, as little have the effect
of showing that bullfighting is a sport, as they would of showing
that warfare is a sport.

Nevertheless, it does not follow that in rejecting Weitz's
account at this point, we are forced in the direction of adopting the
view that what is at stake is a need for explanation. Of course, it is
true that even here someone may attempt an explanation, and it is
even true that such an explanation may bring me to see it as sport,
in the sense of seeing that that is how *they* think of it, and perhaps
in the sense of seeing what their reason for this might be. But
though it is not impossible, in many cases it does not seem likely
that *any* explanation will work and sometimes it would be simply
pointless. I once took my young daughter to a variety of bullfight
which is found in the Gascony region of France and which is
generally called the 'course landaise'. The variety is one in which
the bull is not killed or indeed hurt in any way. The matadors, by
contrast, are apparently injured. It became obvious after a while
that my daughter was in tears, and, assuming that she thought the
bull was being mistreated, I pointed out that as far as I could see
the animal could take care of itself. I tried, that is to say, to explain
what was going on in a way which would remove the barrier to
her seeing it as sport. Unfortunately, it soon transpired that she
was upset, not by what was happening to the bull, but by what
was happening to the matadors. She could not respond to what

---

12   Ibid., p. 31.

she saw as a sport or a game, precisely because she found it terrifying. As I remember, I lied and told her that the matadors were really pretending (as in all-in wrestling) in order to stop her crying. But I did so, precisely because there remained no true explanation which would enable her to see the spectacle as sport. The matadors really were being injured, and so what she saw really was too frightening for her to see it as sport. And though it may be said that in such cases the reaction of fear is more likely in a child than in an adult, fear is not the only reaction which can prevent one seeing an activity as a sport or game. It will be much the same if someone finds boxing simply brutal, or is sickened by the spectacle of a bullfight. In such a case, the nature of one's reactions may be such as to lead one to reject any explanation which might bring one to see the activity in question as a sport.

A similar point may be made if we now turn our attention to what is for Tilghman a rather more central example, that of the appreciation of jokes. Here again explanation may have an important role to play, but it is not the end of the story and often not even the beginning. Oscar Wilde once said, *a propos* of Dickens' *Old Curiosity Shop*, that it would take a man with a heart of stone to read the story of the death of little Nell without immediately bursting out laughing. If like me, you find this remark mildly humorous, then, as with many jokes, this will no doubt be connected with the unexpectedness of the punch line. We expect Wilde, that is to say, to finish the sentence with the words 'without bursting into tears', but to our surprise he finishes with the words 'without bursting out laughing'. The joke trades on the fact that the normal way to continue the phrase 'It would take a man with a heart of stone…' is to mention some appropriate reaction or other. Wilde, by contrast, mentions what is perhaps the most inappropriate reaction to the tragic death of a young girl, namely spontaneous mirth. This, however, can scarcely be the whole story. For though it explains what makes Wilde's remark unexpected, it does not go far towards explaining why we may find it humorous. To see this, we need to recognise that although Wilde's response is from one perspective inappropriate, from another it may be thought far from inappropriate. For laughter is certainly a perfectly normal and appropriate response to over-sentimentality, and Dickens' description of the death of little Nell is to many people a particularly grotesque example of over-sentimentality. Indeed it is written in a style which no great writer would ever again dare to employ for fear of provoking laughter in his audience. Wilde recognised this fact, that is to say recognised that Dickens could rely on a response in his audience which would not be forthcoming from a later and in some ways more sophisticated, or at least more cynical, audience (one to which Wilde himself might be expected to appeal). And he makes the point by beginning his remark in a way which might appeal to Dickens' audience, and then ending it in a way which would appeal to his own. The joke consists in Wilde's juxtaposing these two perspectives in the same line, and thereby mirroring a particular stage in the history of literature.

What I have just given is what would normally be counted as an explanation of Wilde's joke. Nevertheless it is quite obvious that, whether such an explanation can be expected to work, will depend on who receives it. My point here is not that such an explanation will not necessarily bring someone to laugh. For, as Ben says, the explanation generally makes the joke rather artificial, so that even if the person to whom it is given now sees Wilde's remark as a joke, the explanation is not likely to elicit laughter (or at best only rather forced laughter). Rather, what I have in mind is an ambiguity in the phrase 'to see as a joke'. For there is still the fact that when a joke has been explained to me, I may still not see it as funny. Of course, I see the joke in the sense that I see that it is intended to be funny, or even in that I see why the person thinks that it is funny. But I do not see the joke in the sense of seeing it that way myself. Tilghman sees this, and presents it as a failure to react. But this may, I think, be to oversimply the reaction (or lack of it). For though from the point of view of the person making the joke, I may be said not to see the humour, from my own perspective it may be that there was no humour to be seen. Nor need this stem from a lack of understanding on my part. On the contrary it may be a function of the way in which I do understand, not in this case a joke, but I suppose one might say, life. The fact that there are certain things in my life which I take seriously means that there are certain things which I do not see as a subject for humour. Faced with a joke about these things, my understanding of their seriousness will manifest itself in what may, from the point of view of the person making the joke, be a failure to react, but what is, from my point of view, a different kind of reaction, shock, say, or indignation.

It might be said that all we have described here is the way in which external factors may interfere with our appreciation of a joke. But this way of expressing the point would, I think, be unfortunate since it ignores the involvement of such factors in the appreciation of the joke itself. This can be seen in the example which I have just given. For as we saw, the possibility of appreciating Wilde's remark is dependent on our seeing that there is something both inappropriate and appropriate about laughing at the death of a young girl. Someone who did not see both the impropriety and the propriety could not understand the joke. But, one way of expressing this lack of propriety is to say that it is a lack of moral propriety. It is immoral, indeed outrageous, to laugh over the death of a young girl, even a fictional one. So that we can, I suppose, imagine someone whose response to Wilde's remark would simply be to react to its immorality, perhaps with outrage. Indeed this seems the only likely response from a member of the audience for whom Dickens wrote, some of whom wrote to Dickens accusing him of being an unfeeling monster for having dared to kill off little Nell.

Now it is at this point that Tilghman draws a direct comparison with the case of art. The situation of someone who, faced in the art gallery with firebricks or urinals can, Tilghman says, be profitably compared to that of someone with a good sense of humour who does not see the point of some particular joke. In this I do not disagree with him. For it is not merely that in many ways the understanding of a joke is a good *model* for the understanding of a work of art. In one obvious respect the appreciation of humour is just a form of aesthetic appreciation. For to see the point of many plays, novels, poems, pictures and even pieces of music, from Fielding's *Tom Jones* to Stoppard's *Jumpers* just is to see, among other things, the humour. Indeed a joke itself can often be thought of as a very short humorous story. Rather it is the limited nature of the comparison which Tilghman draws, the fact, if you like, that he does not push the comparison far enough, which gives rise to my misgivings. For his aim is to show that just as we may hesitate to call something a joke because we lack an explanation, so our plain gentleman puzzled by the *avant garde* fails to respond because he stands in need of an explanation.

> When he asks 'But is it art?' his question is a demand for explanation of the thing as art and a plea to be shown what is relevant to an understanding and appreciation of it as art.[13]

---

13   Ibid., p. 55.

If the analogy with jokes is to be pressed, then it may be that, the explanation having been given, he will even so still remain bewildered. He will know why it is that people, or perhaps some people, see this as a work of art, but it by no means follows that he will be able to see it in this way himself. In this I am not denying Tilghman's point that the explanations which are given him may be inadequate. It is rather that given the way in which the plain gentleman sees things, the adequacy or inadequacy of the explanations which he is offered may be purely incidental.

Part of what obscures this possibility in Tilghman's discussion is the limited nature of his account of the plain gentleman. Tilghman describes him in the following way:

> Let us picture him as knowledgeable and discerning with respect to the history of art and thoroughly at home in twentieth century art; he knows and appreciates a wide range of periods and styles from Lascaux to abstract expressionism.[14]

What this man brings to the appreciation of art is explained here in purely aesthetic terms. So, if there is something to which he is blind, then the temptation will be to explain that in aesthetic terms and the blindness will be overcome, if at all, by an aesthetic explanation, though as Tilghman sees, such an explanation may not be forthcoming, or adequate, even if it is. So it is no accident that when he considers what explanations may be available to the plain gentleman, he limits the candidates to those which concern purely aesthetic properties of the work. But as my remarks about the appreciation of jokes show, what we are capable of appreciating is not limited to what is explicable in aesthetic terms, but also involves values which have a life independent of their life in jokes. And by analogy, and more generally, what Tilghman's plain gentleman brings to his appreciation of art will not be limited to the aesthetic, but will include other sorts of considerations. Nor is the point limited to the artistic.

Somewhere Renford Bambrough mentions the case of a friend of his who had been afflicted by the recurring memory of a scene which he had witnessed during the battle of Britain. During an air battle he had seen a friend's Spitfire struck by machine gun fire from an enemy fighter, burst into flames against a beautiful sunset. He had subsequently been tormented by the thought that this

---

14   Ibid., p. 54.

was both one of the most wonderful and also one of the most terrible sights that he had ever seen. Bambrough's view is that the answer to his friend's problem was that the apparent conflict was an illusion. The scene was both wonderful and terrible. And I should not, of course, wish to deny that it might be possible for someone to see it in that way. Still there may also be someone for whom that is not a possibility. For imagine someone who asks 'but how could there be anything wonderful about watching the agonised death of a friend?' Though such a question might stem from a genuine puzzlement, might be a straightforward request for explanation, in such a case it will normally be rhetorical. The force of the question will not be that of a plea for explanation, at least not if explanation is thought of as concerning the aesthetic, but rather to indicate that for the speaker there is precisely no room for such an explanation. What leaves no room for explanation in such cases is, as I say, not primarily an aesthetic matter. But it is only by an artificial separation of what is aesthetic from other aspects of our lives that we can represent it as irrelevant to aesthetic appreciation.

When someone's moral or religious or political viewpoint carries implications for their aesthetic judgements, this will often take the form of imposing limits on what they can take seriously as an explanation. As we have seen, my moral opposition to bull-fighting may be such as to prevent me taking seriously the remarks of those who see bullfighting as a sport. My moral or political or religious views may be such as to rule out my finding humour in certain subjects, and so such as to render pointless explanations of the humour. In the same way I see no reason why certain aspects of the plain gentleman's view of life may not be such as to rule out any attempt to bring him to see as works of art some of the creations which have decorated our art galleries for the past eighty years.

In saying this, I am of course neither accepting nor rejecting the explanations which may be offered for such things. Consider the work of the environmental artist Robert Smithson, of which *Asphalt Rundown* and *Surrounded Islands* are examples, the former a truckload of asphalt poured down a rock face and the latter eleven miles of pink plastic netting draped over some small islands in the Pacific. I have heard these defended on the grounds that they are an affront to nature, the idea being, so far as I can gather, that just as it is an affront to nature to attempt to capture it in a landscape, so it is an affront to pour asphalt over it. This explanation may strike one as poor, even stupid. For the form of the 'affront' (if that is not simply the wrong word) in the work of, say, Monet lies in the attempt to bring out what is wonderful in nature, whereas in *Asphalt Rundown* there is the attempt to destroy it. My point is that this may be just by the way. For imagine that when our plain gentleman is presented with, or indeed told of, *Asphalt Rundown* the word which springs into his mind is simply 'desecration'. What role is left for the explanations of Smithson's work to play? Nor does this case seem to me to be far removed from that of Duchamp's *Fountain*. For it is difficult not to notice that what Duchamp placed in an art gallery was not, say, a saucepan or a steam-engine, but rather, with apparently deliberate offensiveness, a urinal. I do not want to generalise here. It may be, as Tilghman says, that someone, faced with an explanation of something which he sees in this way may pay serious attention to the explanations which he is given and conclude that he finds them unconvincing. But nor do I want to rule out as prejudiced, or as an example of a closed mind, the plain gentleman who will have no truck with any such explanations.

Part 3

Morality and Human Nature

8

Consequences and Moral Worth[1]

I remember once reading a story (I no longer remember where), in which the reader was presented with the case of a young French-woman faced with the following dilemma. During the German occupation of France, her husband, a member of the resistance, is seized by the Gestapo and thrown into prison. On the same day a high-ranking German officer who has been billeted with the family comes to her with a proposition. He tells her that one of two things will happen to her husband. Either he will be executed immediately for crimes against the Reich, or he will be imprisoned for an indefinite period. The officer can use his authority to see that her husband is not executed, but will do so only if she agrees to become his mistress. To save her husband the woman agrees.

Not everyone would regard her choice as the right one. We can imagine many possible moral reactions to her solution. But I wish to consider only two.

1. Many people would say that the woman was right to become the officer's mistress, even that her action was morally commendable. Nevertheless, they will not deny that adultery is wrong. We should expect them to condemn Gertrude's adultery in *Hamlet*, for instance. What they feel is that in the above situation the consequences make a difference.

2. On the other hand, some people, among them I should imagine certain Roman Catholics, would say that the action was wrong, even utterly wrong. They do not deny that in these circum-stances adultery would have good consequences, or rather, would avoid evil consequences, but hold that this factor should not be

1   First published in *Analysis*, 29 (6), 1969, pp. 177–86.

considered. Such a person does not, of course, hold that consequences are always irrelevant to morality, but rather that certain
things, adultery, murder, the judicial punishment of the innocent,
are wrong regardless of their consequences. For them the above
situation would present no moral difficulties; rather it would be a
straightforward choice between doing what is right (one's duty)
and succumbing to temptation. I shall refer to these people as
"Catholics", without, of course, seeking to make any claims about
Catholicism proper.

We see why this sort of example is of philosophical interest if
we consider the first of these reactions. Someone may feel that
adultery is wrong. Nevertheless, the consequences which a
particular act of adultery can have, may lead them to say that in
the circumstances it ought not to be condemned. So, one might be
inclined to say, it is surely a misleading expression of their convictions to say that they regard adultery as wrong. Surely it would
be more accurate to say that for them adultery is *generally* wrong,
or, more precisely, that adultery is wrong except where X, Y, and
Z. By introducing such qualifying phrases they would safeguard
themselves against those exceptional cases where adultery is a
duty.

It is clear that the vast majority of recent moral philosophers
accept some such line of argument. Moore, for instance, in
Principia Ethica[2] takes it for granted that:

> our duty can only be defined as that action which will cause more
> good to exist in the Universe than any possible alternative. (p. 147
> (197))

So, he tells us:

> if we are told that 'Do no murder' is a duty, we are told that the
> action, whatever it may be, which is called murder, will under no
> circumstances cause so much good to exist in the Universe as its
> avoidance. (p. 148 (198))

Understandably, he suggests that it would be foolhardy to make
such a claim, and suggests that ethical laws can only be regarded

---

[2]   See *Principia Ethica* (Cambridge: Cambridge University Press, 1903), also
revised edition with preface to second edition and other papers edited by
Thomas Baldwin (Cambridge University Press, 1993). Page references are
given to both original and revised editions in the form p. 147 (197).

as plausible generalisations to which there will inevitably be exceptions.

A similar view appears in the writings of P.H. Nowell-Smith. He tells us in 'Morality: Religious and Secular' that what he refers to as 'moral rules':

> must of their very nature be general; that is their virtue and their defect. They lay down what is to be done or not done in *all* situations of a certain general kind, and they do this because their function is to ensure reliability in the absence of personal knowledge.[3]

For Nowell-Smith then, judgements like 'Adultery is wrong' are only rules of thumb, necessary because our knowledge of particular cases is limited, because in the varied situations in which we find ourselves we cannot always decide what we ought to do, but always open to modification in those cases with which we *are* acquainted.

Lastly, this doctrine has received what is perhaps its most comprehensive treatment in *The Language of Morals*[4] where R.M. Hare seeks to defend the thesis that 'One ought to tell the truth' is more accurately formulated as 'Speak the truth in general, but there are certain classes of actions where this principle does not hold' (p. 51).

For this doctrine I shall adopt Miss Anscombe's term 'consequentialism'.[5] The use of this term is not, of course, meant to conceal the important differences between the aforementioned accounts of morality, only to draw attention to an important similarity between them. For they agree in supposing that judgements like 'Adultery is wrong' or 'Murder is an evil' are "generalisations", "general rules", or "principles of conduct", and that we are therefore justified in accepting them only in so far as they prove acceptable in the particular case. Moral dilemmas like the example given earlier are cases where a general rule may prove unacceptable, and we are called upon to make an exception. It is rational to accept the generalisation 'All spiders are harmless', only until I come across a tarantula. Similarly, I can accept that

---

[3]   'Morality: Religious and Secular', in I. Ramsey ed., *Christian Ethics and Contemporary Philosophy* (London: S.C.M. Press, 1966) p. 110.

[4]   R.M. Hare, *The Language of Morals* (Oxford: Clarendon Press, 1952).

[5]   G.E.M. Anscombe, 'Modern Moral Philosophy', *Philosophy*, January 1958, 33 (124).

adultery is wrong only until I come across a case where adultery will have good consequences.

One possible objection to consequentialism as a philosophical doctrine is that it is insufficiently impartial, since it rules out at least one type of moral attitude. We have seen that, faced with a choice between adultery and some other evil, some people, whom I dubbed "Catholics", would say that adultery is absolutely wrong, wrong whatever the consequences. The consequentialist, however, tends to offer an account according to which it *must* be possible for consequences to make a difference. So it follows that the account which the consequentialist gives is unhelpful when applied to those who hold a "Catholic" viewpoint.

If I do not pursue this line of criticism at present, it is not because I regard it as unjustified, but because I do not think that it goes far enough. My purpose is to show that consequentialism misrepresents *both* of the moral positions which I have mentioned. For it rests upon a misunderstanding of the role which considerations like murder, honesty and adultery play in the life of the virtuous man.

I suggest that this misunderstanding stems largely from the idea that judgements like 'Adultery is wrong' or 'One ought to tell the truth' are to be regarded as "general rules", "principles", or "generalisations" to which there are, or may be, exceptions. But in saying this, I should not be taken to be denying that they bear any similarities to less controversial instances of rules or principles. There are, no doubt, many similarities, one of the more important being that judgements of both types are used in teaching. If I am showing someone how to play chess, I shall do well to follow my account of the rules of the game with some general principle like 'Always try to gain control of the centre' or 'Always use the King as much as possible in the end game'. If I am teaching him to drive, rules like 'Keep your eye on the mirror' or 'Never brake hard on ice' will help him to avoid mistakes. In the same way, it is undeniable that judgements like 'Murder is wrong' have an important role to play in moral instruction.

What we must beware of is that such similarities do not blind us to more crucial differences. And in order to bring out these differences I want to begin by comparing two examples, one of teaching a skill by means of principles and the other of moral instruction.

1. Imagine a child being taught to use a saw. His father begins with a demonstration of how to saw a plank. He then invites his

son to try. The child, however, continually fails in his attempt. After a while the father realises what is wrong. 'Look, John,' he says, 'You are pressing down too hard on the saw. Never use too much pressure when sawing.' John bears his father's instructions in mind and finds that he can now use the saw without difficulty.

2. Let us now imagine another child, Howard, who is telling his parents how he escaped punishment at school. His teacher had asked who was responsible for some minor piece of naughtiness and Howard had put the blame on one of his friends. He is proud of having escaped punishment in this way, and is surprised when his mother says in a shocked voice, 'But it's wrong to tell such lies, Howard'.

Though these two situations have a superficial similarity, I think that there are important differences. In the first example, John is being taught the means for attaining a certain end, namely sawing a piece of wood efficiently. He is told that in order to do this he must not exert too much pressure on the saw. But his father's teaching presupposes that John has an independent understanding of this end. He assumes that his son already possesses certain standards for determining whether he has been successful or unsuccessful in sawing the wood.

That this is so is clear from the fact that the child might disagree with his father's teaching. He might, for example, point out that he has already tried using only light pressure on the saw with no success, or that, since the saw is blunt, considerable pressure is required in order to make any impression on the wood. John and his father would then be disagreeing about rules or principles, his father maintaining that it is important not to exert much pressure when sawing, and John maintaining that such a rule is fruitless in certain (or perhaps, all) cases. What is to be noted is that such disagreement is possible only because an understanding of what it is to cut wood properly does not depend on an understanding of the rules or principles in question. If this were not so, then John would be in no position to disagree.

The second example involves a judgement, 'Lying is wrong', which at first sight is comparable to 'One ought not to use much pressure when sawing' in the first example. But if we examine it more closely, I think that we shall notice important differences. Before speaking to his parents Howard saw his action in the classroom only as a clever way of avoiding punishment. He was pleased because, by these standards, it had been successful. However, when his mother points out to him that lying is wrong, what she does is to teach him to see it in a new light, as a moral action. He begins to see that the standard by which he has hitherto appraised the action is an inappropriate one, and that he must now judge it in wholly different terms. It is no longer 'cleverness' but 'dishonesty'. Unlike the child in the first example, Howard does not learn a new way of performing what he already judges as the right action. He learns to bring a new kind of judgement to bear on his actions. It is the distinction between right and wrong itself which he is learning.

The above differences bring out an even more crucial difference between general rules or principles, and judgements like 'Murder is wrong'. We have seen that, because he is being taught something which is to be judged by an independent standard which he already comprehends, the child in our first example is in a position to disagree with his teaching. Indeed, if he is an intelligent child, it is likely that as he grows older he will be forced to recognise many exceptions to the principles or generalisations which he was taught. Perhaps he will have to deal with new types of material, perhaps the characteristics of saws will change. And when this happens, he will have to recognise the limitations of his father's teaching and to reject or modify the principles which have hitherto governed his conduct. If he were to refuse to do so, if he were to say, 'Even though it no longer enables me to saw well, I must still respect my father's advice not to use heavy pressure on the saw', we should feel that something had gone wrong. Though such a man would be a striking example of respect for his father, he would also be a striking example of irrationality.

In the case of the second child the situation is quite different. What he is being taught are not techniques or rules of thumb for attaining some result which he judges independently, but rather standards for bringing a certain kind of judgement to bear on an action. It follows that though the child may find his parents' views irksome, though he may be disinclined to follow their advice, he is in no position to *disagree* with them. For as yet he has no understanding of morality. He has not yet learned the standards which form the basis for moral agreement or disagreement. It also follows that all talk of principles or rules to which there are or may be exceptions has no application to this situation. This would be appropriate only if judgements like 'Lying is wrong' or 'Murder is an evil' were themselves open to criticism from some external standard. Here we could give some sense to the idea of an exception. But they are not. Rather they are themselves the standard on which any criticism must be based. We criticise a man *for* his dishonesty. We do not criticise dishonesty. Concepts like honesty, chastity and integrity are not techniques for enabling us to do something, but rather the standard by which we judge what we ourselves and others do. They are not principles for attaining the good life, but decide what the good life is. To suppose that there might be exceptions to them is to suppose the good to exist in independence of the standards of goodness.

When a child learns that dishonesty is wrong then, he does not learn a generalisation to which further experience will teach the exceptions. He learns a standard which will determine the significance which his experience can have for him. It would however be a mistake to draw from this the conclusion that the child's moral teaching is somehow sacrosanct for him. What I am arguing for is a certain way of understanding morality. It does not follow from this account that morality can never present problems. Indeed it is clear that the dilemma with which I opened this paper is just such a problem, and we are now, I think, in a position to reconsider this case.

The Frenchwoman in my example regards adultery as wrong. Nevertheless, circumstances arise in which she is forced to decide whether or not to commit an act of adultery. Now the consequentialist will say that her problem is that of deciding whether or not this situation presents an exception to a general rule, the general rule that adultery is wrong. That is to say, he maintains that she has to decide whether or not adultery is right here. What I should say is that it is just because she *knows* that adultery is *wrong* that she is faced by a problem. The problem arises because her moral standards themselves are in conflict. It would be wrong to commit adultery, but it would also be wrong to refuse to do so. There are considerations for and against either course of action. As a wife she must protect her husband, but as a wife she must also protect her virtue. Whether she commits adultery or leaves her husband to the Gestapo she will have a troubled conscience. Why otherwise do we regard such situations as in some way tragic?

True, the woman finds a solution to the problem. She goes against her conviction that adultery is wrong and becomes the officer's mistress. Not because she feels that this case is an exception, that in these admittedly extreme circumstances adultery does not matter, but because she comes to see that her husband's life matters more. But in calling this a 'solution', I am not denying that it differs in many important ways from solutions of other types, in particular from solutions to problems about principles. When a man solves a problem of the latter sort (*e.g.* when he decides whether he should use light pressure on a blunt saw or not) then he simply modifies his principles to allow for this case, and the problem no longer arises for him (which is not to say that no other problems can arise). But the Frenchwoman's difficulties are not confined to the particular situation in this way. On the contrary they are inherent in her moral viewpoint and in her position as a wife. In a similar situation she may find it no more easy to reach a decision, she may even reach a different decision, for the thought about general moral issues which any difficult moral problem occasions cannot be left out of account and may well have a bearing on her future decisions. You may say that this makes any solution arbitrary. But then it is no longer clear what a non-arbitrary solution would be like.

So far I have concerned myself with just one possible approach to a certain type of moral problem. I have tried to show that the consequentialist misdescribes this approach. But, as I mentioned earlier, there is another approach which is not just misdescribed but ruled out of court by consequentialism. This is what I called the "Catholic" approach.

What is a moral problem for one person need not be for another. In a "Catholic" morality the problem with which we have been concerned could not arise.[6] The "Catholic" holds that when an action is one of adultery, then this is always an overriding reason for condemning it. The consequences are irrelevant simply because adultery is one of the supreme evils.

Philosophically this seems to me a perfectly coherent moral position. But to a consequentialist it is likely to seem incoherent. He regards judgements like 'Adultery is wrong' as principles or

---

[6]   This point must not be confused with one made by Miss Anscombe in the article which I have already mentioned. She maintains that such dilemmas are merely 'fantastic' and could not therefore arise. But *she* means that they could not arise for anyone. No one, she tells us, can know in advance that there will be, in any given case, only two alternatives to choose from. There may always be a third way out of the difficulty. Her argument is objectionable for two reasons: (a) because we may take our examples from novels or from our own experience, in which case we *already* know what the possibilities are, and (b) because, if it is true that no one can know 'a priori' that there will be only two possibilities, then it is also true that Miss Anscombe cannot know 'a priori' that there will not be. And it is just this knowledge that she seems to be claiming.

general rules. Consequently, he sees the "Catholic" as someone who holds a principle independently of experience, or who accepts a general rule to which he is willing to allow no exceptions. And these are examples of irrational behaviour. If someone were to say that one ought always to use light pressure when sawing, whatever the consequences of doing so, then we should either regard him as stupid, or think that for some reason this principle had become a dogma with him. In any case we should not take him seriously. In the same way the consequentialist tends to equate "Catholic" morality and prejudice.

Of course, the consequentialist rarely expresses his criticisms in these terms. The whole force of the picture of morality as a collection of principles or general rules is that it tends to be unconsciously accepted. Nevertheless, if we examine the criticisms which consequentialists most commonly make of "Catholic" morality, I think that we shall find that they rest on just such a philosophical model. I want to end by considering two such criticisms.

1. It is sometimes assumed to be sufficient to discredit "Catholicism" in morality, if it can be shown that whereas the "Catholic" can offer no justification for his convictions, the consequentialist can. The "Catholic" can give no reason for supposing that adultery is wrong; the consequentialist can at least point to the consequences of particular acts of adultery to defend his judgements. Thus, for example, Jonathan Bennett has argued that "Catholicism", 'when it is not mere obedience, is mere muddle'.[7] According to Bennett, the muddle arises basically because the "Catholic" supposes 'that his principles have some measure of acceptability on grounds other than unquestioning obedience to an authority' (p. 85). He devotes his article to an alleged proof that there can be no such grounds. Perhaps he is right. But it is only because he not only calls the "Catholic's" convictions 'principles' but thinks of them as principles, that his argument seems to have any force. As we have seen, any principle must be justified by reference to an end or purpose. (Why do you hold the saw like that? To make it easier to get a good clean cut.) To show that it *is* unjustified *is* to show that it is a fake. On the other hand, if, as I am recommending, we think of the "Catholic's" convictions not as his principles, but as his moral standards, then no such difficulty

---

[7]   'Whatever the Consequences', *Analysis*, 26 (3), 1966, p. 102.

arises. No justification can be given, since any justification must itself be based on these standards. Furthermore, the consequentialist is now seen to be open to an *ad hominem* argument. For, although he claims that on his account actions are justified by reference to their consequences, this statement is really elliptical. What the consequentialist means to say is that actions are justified by their having *good* consequences. And what counts as a good consequence here, must itself be determined by some standard for which no justification is given.

2. The second and last criticism which I shall consider has been comprehensively stated in the article by Nowell-Smith already mentioned. Roughly, what Nowell-Smith wishes to establish is that "Catholic" morality is an attitude held by people who have failed to mature morally. It is, he tells us, 'essentially infantile', for a "Catholic" regards the prohibitions on murder or adultery as absolute, whereas someone who has a mature attitude 'is always willing to keep them under review and discard or modify those that in the light of experience he finds unnecessary' (op. cit., p. 109). For Nowell-Smith then, one progresses to moral maturity or gains insight by modifying one's so-called 'moral principles' or 'moral rules' to cover the situations confronting one. A similar account of moral development is to be found in Chapter 4 of Hare's *Language of Morals* where we are told that 'to become morally adult' is to learn to make 'decisions of principle', that is, to modify our principles in the light of experience. In both cases moral development is explained in such a way that it necessarily excludes what I call the "Catholic" attitude, what Nowell-Smith calls 'Hebrew morality', and what Hare calls 'fanaticism'.

What must be noted about both of these accounts, however, is that they are not accounts of how a man matures morally or gains insight at all. They are accounts of how we gain expertise in skills like sawing or driving a car. The skilled driver is, as Hare tells us, the man who has found out where the rules and principles that he was taught apply, and where they do not. The unskilled driver is, as is implied by Nowell-Smith's account, the one who treats the principles of driving as an 'object of veneration' rather than as a 'convenience'. In this sphere learning from experience does mean 'modifying one's principles and generalisations to allow for exceptions'. But in the sphere of morality it means something rather different. I shall illustrate this difference with an example.

In Dickens' *Hard Times*[8] we have, in the story of Thomas Gradgrind, a fairly clear account of how a man's morality may be developed and changed by his experiences. At the beginning of the book Gradgrind's life is governed by a sort of extreme utilitarianism. He is a 'man of realities. A man of facts and calculations' (p. 2), and for Gradgrind the facts do not include imagination, entertainment, emotions or feelings. Gradgrind's relationships with others, in particular his relationship with his own daughter, Louisa, are poisoned by his puritanical view of life. This is brought out perfectly in a short passage:

> When she was half-a-dozen years younger, Louisa had been overheard to begin a conversation with her brother one day, by saying 'Tom, I wonder' — upon which Mr. Gradgrind, who was the person overhearing stepped forth into the light and said, 'Louisa, never wonder'. (p. 43)

Throughout the book we see the consequences which Gradgrind's attitude brings with it. Because of the values inculcated by her father, because she has ignored 'tastes and fancies ... aspirations and affections' (p. 90), Louisa contracts a hopeless marriage with the hypocritical Bounderby. It is the breakdown of this marriage which brings about a radical change in Gradgrind's views. A conversation with his daughter after she has left her husband's home brings home to him for the first time the misery which his views have caused to his children.

> 'It would be hopeless for me, Louisa, to endeavour to tell you how overwhelmed I have been, and still am, by what broke upon me last night. The ground on which I stand has ceased to be solid under my feet. The only support on which I leaned, and the strength of which it seemed, and still does seem impossible to question, has given away in an instant. I am stunned by these discoveries.' (p. 198)

Gradgrind's experiences throw a new light on the way he has lived his life; not because they bring out exceptions to his moral principles, but because they reveal a superficiality in his way of looking at morality. Gradgrind speaks of this as a 'discovery'. And the child in our first example might speak of 'discovering' exceptions to the principles he was taught too. But there are important differences. For what the child learns could be summed

---

[8]   References are to the Everyman's Library edition (London: Dent, 1960).

up in a formula. He learns that you must use pressure when operating a chain-saw; or he learns that a light touch is useless when a saw is blunt. But the same is not true of Gradgrind. His gain in insight is not something which could be explained in terms of some modification to the principles to which he adheres. It is something which would show itself more in the way he acts, in his understanding of himself and others, in his no longer judging things in the hard and fast way in which he had done in the past. One might say that precisely what he learns is that no simple formula *can* rule a man's life.

Gradgrind's experiences would not have the same significance for everyone. This is why the sort of learning from experience which Dickens describes is quite different from that which characterises the learning of skills. A child who found that using light pressure did not enable him to saw well and yet refused to change his principles would, as we have seen, be acting unintelligibly. But we can quite easily imagine someone with the same experience of life as Gradgrind, whose beliefs would remain unchanged. This is what we should expect of someone who has a "Catholic" approach to morality. Like Gradgrind he may be aware of the suffering which his moral attitude involves. But for him the suffering is unimportant. Both know where their moralities lead, and in this respect their experience of life will have taught them both the same things. But while Gradgrind comes to believe that morality *ought not* to lead there, the other man does not. In this respect what they learn is different, but since this is a *moral* difference, it is something on which the philosopher is no more qualified to pass judgement than the rest of us.

9

Atheism and Morality[1]

Norman Malcolm once observed that in Western academic philosophy, religious belief is commonly regarded as unreasonable and is viewed with condescension or even contempt. Malcolm himself did not, of course, take this view, but it is one which will be familiar to most philosophers, even if they do not themselves hold it. Nor need Malcolm's observation be restricted only to the realm of academic philosophy. For there are many atheists who, rightly or wrongly, seeing themselves as untouched by philosophy, would nevertheless subscribe to the view that religious belief is of its very nature confused or in some way intellectually inadequate. So, I had better start by saying that, though an atheist, I do not number myself among them. It is not, however, my aim in this paper to defend religion against such attacks but rather to turn my attention to an analogous attitude amongst those who would count themselves religious believers. And once again, this attitude is not one which is restricted to academic philosophers, but finds its counterpart amongst the general populace. It is moreover, like the view which Malcolm castigates, often marked by condescension, or even contempt, attitudes which are, by contrast, directed in this case towards the atheist. I have in mind, the view that atheism is unreasonable, or in some way intellectually inadequate, because it is incapable of doing justice to the role that moral considerations play in our lives, or to put it rather more bluntly, but also rather more elegantly, because if God did not exist, then everything would be permitted.

As might be expected such a view is capable of more and less refined forms, of greater and lesser philosophical sophistication.

---

1 First published in D.Z. Phillips ed., *Religion and Morality* (London: Macmillan, 1996).

And it is not, I suppose, surprising that the level of subtlety will to some extent depend on whether the proponent is or is not versed in the refinements of philosophical discussion. Recently my local daily tabloid contained for some while a debate on its letters page concerning the effects in Welsh society, and in Swansea in particular, of an alleged decline in religious belief. The general theme of many of these letters seemed to be that increased lawlessness and lack of respect for the lives and property of others could be directly attributed to a decline in the belief in a God who punishes transgressors. It was not, of course, difficult to detect in those who wrote in this way, a genuine sense of injustice at the failure of earthly authorities to punish the morally or legally culpable, at the spectacle of the unjust prospering. Still, it does not require someone particularly well-versed in philosophy to see that it does no favours to God to portray Him as a sort of court of higher appeal charged with the task of punishing those whom the earthly authorities fail to convict. Nor, and perhaps more importantly from the point of view of the atheist, does it do any favours to morality to present it as a form of human practice whose value (and perhaps whose sense) lies in its enabling those who adhere to it to escape punishment, or more succinctly, to present morality as something whose value lies in its being to the advantage of the just.

It should not, however, be thought that it is only outside the realms of academic philosophy that such attempts to found morality on religious belief are prevalent. For the belief that morality requires justification in religious terms if it is to be taken seriously is to be found in the writings of academic philosophers themselves. Consider the following passage:

> Religious morality and Christian morality in particular may have its difficulties, but religious apologists argue that secular morality has still greater difficulties ... It leads, they claim, to ethical scepticism, nihilism, or at best to pure conventionalism. Such apologists could point out that if we look at morality with the cold eye of the anthropologist, we will find morality to be nothing more than the conflicting mores of the various tribes spread around the globe. If we look at ethics from a purely secular view, we will discover that it is constituted by tribal conventions, conventions which we are free to reject if we are sufficiently free from

ethnocentricity. We can continue to act in accordance with them or
we can reject them and adopt a different set of conventions.[2]

Nielsen himself does not find this alleged feature of secular
moralities, that they may be rejected or adopted at will, prob-
lematic. For on his view, the alternative, namely that moral rules
are in some sense determined by God's word, is merely a psychological prop, which the believer could, if he or she considered the
matter rationally, do without. Nevertheless there are those
religious believers who, sharing Nielsen's view of the alternatives,
find in it a compelling reason to think of morality as God's gift.
Thus Leszek Kolakowski, in his book *Religion*,[3] attempts to convince us that any serious concern for morality is parasitic on
religion, by suggesting that unless moral laws are seen as having a
religious source, unless the virtues are seen as God's gifts, then the
only alternative is what he calls Promethean humanism. But his
description of Promethean humanism as the view that 'people are
entirely free in stating the criteria of good and evil',[4] that is to say
the view that people are free to choose what moral standards they
wish to adopt, makes it clear that his view of the alternatives
facing us is much the same as that of Nielsen. For both, religion is
thought of as an attempt to found morality on something not
dependent on choice, namely the divine will, and for both the
alternative is the sort of conventionalism which makes our moral
allegiances simply a matter of choice. The difference is simply that
for Kolakowski the element of choice is seen as rendering morality
arbitrary or futile, whereas for Nielsen the seriousness of morality
lies precisely in the element of choice.

What is, however, not clear is why both Kolakowski and
Nielsen should share the assumption that they do. Why should it
be held that our moral values must be either the product of
religion, or the product of an apparently arbitrary choice? And it is
difficult to escape the conclusion that this view is the result of a
simple equivocation. A clue as to the nature of this equivocation is
given by Nielsen's description of morality as simply a set of
different conventions. For the word 'convention' *is* used most
naturally to identify what is the product of human choice and
often to describe cases where it does not much matter what choice

---

2   Kai Nielsen, *Ethics Without God* (London: Pemberton Books, 1973) p. 48.

3   Leszek Kolakowski, *Religion* (London: Fontana, 1982).

4   Ibid., p. 201.

people make, so long as (within a certain context) they make the same choice. Unlike in most other countries, the convention in Britain is that one drives on the left. There are different conventions, precisely because in different countries different decisions have been taken. And it would, at least in principle, be possible for these decisions to be reversed, as was indeed once the case in Sweden. It is a convention of association football that the ball is not handled except by the goalkeeper. But this convention was challenged, if the (probably apocryphal) story is true, by a pupil at Rugby school who picked up the ball and ran with it. The result was that a decision to change the convention was taken in the game now known as Rugby football. But the possibility in these cases of deciding which convention to adopt is a function not of the fact that there are *different* conventions, but of the fact that they are different *conventions*. And it is only if we think of different ideas about what matters morally as conventions, that it will seem to follow that there is a choice between them — that whatever values we adhere to, we do so because we have chosen. For the mere fact that in other places, other societies, people think differently, has *in itself* no tendency to show that each of us must choose between these alternatives. Perhaps my children are important to me, so that in a whole range of situations I shall regard myself as facing obligations to protect them, help further their careers, help them out of financial difficulties. And perhaps there are societies where they think differently about their children, for instance societies in which female offspring are sometimes left to die, or where children are sometimes sold into slavery. But what of it? The fact that there are alternative ways of regarding one's children does nothing to show that these are alternatives for me or that I reached the values which I possess by selecting them from among a range of alternatives. Yet for Nielsen and Kolakowski the possibility of alternative values is held to entail just this conclusion.

Perhaps then the argument by which Kolakowski reaches his conclusions regarding atheistic morality will not bear examination. For there is no reason to accept Nielsen's view that, unless we hold a religious morality, think of our duties and obligations as deriving their authority from God's word, we shall be forced to the sort of conventionalist conception of morality which Nielsen advocates, but which Kolakowski sees as incompatible with moral seriousness. Still it does not follow that Kolakowski's conclusion that genuine morality is religious morality is false. For it may be that although there is no incoherence in the idea of an atheistic morality, as a matter of fact certain central features of our morality *do* derive from a religious background which we once shared. The point is developed by Elizabeth Anscombe in a well-known passage from her article 'Modern Moral Philosophy', where she argues that it is only because Christianity involved a law conception of ethics and because of the dominance of Christianity for many centuries, that 'the concepts of being bound, permitted or excused became deeply embedded in our language and thought'. She goes on:

> Naturally it is not possible to have such a conception unless you believe in God as a law-giver; like Jews, Stoics and Christians. But if such a conception is dominant for many centuries, and then is given up, it is a natural result that the concepts of 'obligation', of being bound or required as by a law, should remain though they had lost their root; and if the word 'ought' has become invested in certain contexts with the sense of 'obligation', it too will remain to be spoken with a special emphasis and a special feeling in these contexts ... The situation, if I am right, was the interesting one of the survival of a concept outside the framework of thought that made it a really intelligible one.[5]

Though Anscombe may appear to be resting her case on an assertion of historical fact, there is nevertheless a concealed assumption in her argument, which gives it whatever appearance of plausibility it may have. For, as has been pointed out by others, Anscombe seems to take it largely for granted that if a concept has outlived the practices or ways of thinking in which it originally had its sense, then in so far as it is still used it will have no sense. Since the notions of being obliged or permitted had their source in a religious context, where they were equated with what is obliged or permitted by a Divine Will, then they must lose their sense in a society where no such equation can be made.

But why should it be thought that it is only God's will which can intelligibly be said to place obligations on me? Certainly in a society in which religious belief is taken for granted, it is likely that people will see their obligations in this way, though it is not, I should have thought, more than likely, since there seems no reason why, for example, a man might not see obligations as

5 G.E.M. Anscombe, 'Modern Moral Philosophy', in *The Collected Papers of G.E.M. Anscombe*, Volume III (Oxford: Blackwell, 1981) p.30.

arising from a love forbidden by his religion — say, the love of one man for another, or the love of a priest for a nun. Be that as it may, at least in a society where religious belief is losing its hold, why should it not be the case that institutions other than the church are thought of as imposing limits on what is or is not permitted? Suppose for instance that as a member of a trade union, I feel that I have an obligation to respect a picket-line, or that as a doctor I feel myself bound to respond to an emergency call in the middle of the night. Why should it be said that in these cases my reference to what I ought to do has a 'mere mesmeric force'? True, in such cases what obliges me cannot be said to be the will of God, but this does not mean that there can be no answer to the question 'What obliges me?' What obliges the trade unionist to observe the picket-line is simply his membership of a trade union. What obliges the doctor to answer the emergency call is the rules of his profession. In what way can these ways of speaking be said to lack sense?

No doubt such an answer would not satisfy Anscombe. And it might be thought that in one rather important respect it ignores what is central to her argument. For, it may be said, Anscombe does not claim that any sense of 'obligation' has, and must have, its basis in Divine Law, but only that what she calls the 'special moral sense' or sometimes the 'absolute' sense must do so. And, so the argument might go, this is borne out by the points which have been made so far. For though membership of a trade union may well carry with it the obligation to respect picket-lines, though doctors may have various professional obligations, these cannot be thought to be absolutely binding, since it is always possible for the trade unionist to resign from membership, possible for the doctor to find another profession. By contrast, where an obligation is thought of as the will of God, then there can be no question of the believer choosing to avoid it.

Unfortunately, if the argument is developed in this way, it quickly becomes apparent that it is merely a variant of the line of reasoning which has already been detected in the writings of Nielsen and Kolakowski, and rests on the same assumption. For again, why should the fact that there is an alternative to membership of a trade union, namely, resigning one's membership, be thought to show that this is an alternative for any particular trade unionist? Indeed, in so far as it is implied that the mere existence of an alternative way of life is sufficient to rob obligations of their absolute character, then the conclusion should be drawn that, even for the devout religious believer, God's commands do not possess

the status of absolute obligations. For there is certainly an alternative to religious belief, namely atheism. The absolute nature of
God's commands for the religious believer stems not from a denial
of the possibility of atheism. It stems rather from the recognition
that such a way of life is not for that person a possibility.

If what I have said so far is correct, then it may seem that any
attempt to show that morality can have no rationale in independence of religion, or that the latter is in some way dependent on the
former is, regardless of whether it is presented as the consequence
of historical research or as a consequence of conceptual analysis,
merely the result of confusion. But perhaps this conclusion is
premature. For might it not be argued that what undermines the
positions of writers like Kolakowski and Anscombe is not the form
of the arguments that they use, but rather their generality?
Perhaps then it is the case that though there is no way of showing
that morality as a whole is dependent on religion, there are nevertheless at least some central features of a religious morality for
which there is no counterpart in the lives of atheists. Or to put the
matter more circumspectly, might it not be argued that in so far as
these features are to be found in the lives of atheists, their presence
there is to be explained (at least historically) by the role which
religion once played in the life of our society, a role which is the
heritage of both believers and atheists? And here a remark quoted
earlier from Kolakowski's book may be thought to point in the
right direction. For there I mentioned Kolakowski's conception of
the virtues as a gift from God. This view, as we saw, cannot be
defended, at least in so far as it is intended to depict the role
played by moral considerations in the life of atheists as well as
believers. But perhaps, it may be suggested, the notion that certain
aspects of our lives, or even our lives themselves, are gifts,
together with the allied notions of gratitude and ingratitude, will
serve as candidates for moral concepts, which though they may
play a role in the life of the atheist, can do so only in so far as the
atheist shares with the religious believer a common historical
background, a background in which religion played a central part.
So that to the extent that we detect these ways of speaking in the
atheist's vocabulary, this indicates at least one respect in which
this vocabulary is parasitic on religion, or perhaps, as some might
put it, indicates a religious element in that vocabulary. It is to this
claim that I shall devote the remainder of my essay.

In Chapter 12 of his book *Good and Evil: An Absolute Conception*,
Rai Gaita begins a discussion of the phenomenon of gratitude for

life with a quotation from Pablo Casals in which the cellist describes the way in which he begins his daily routine. Casals describes this routine as 'mechanical', but he goes on:

> ...that is not the only meaning it has for me. It is a discovery of the world of which I have the joy of being a part. It fills me with awareness of the wonder of life, with a feeling of the incredible marvel of being a human being ... I do not think that a day has passed in my life in which I have failed to look with fresh amazement at the miracle of nature.[6]

Gaita speaks later of Casals' words as being 'in the accent of gratitude'[7] and connects this with seeing life as a gift. Those who are inclined to speak in such terms, he tells us, see a certain kind of unity in their lives, such that they think in terms of the purposes for which they were given life and may see suicide as a species of ingratitude. He mentions in this connection a letter from Mozart to Padre Martini in which the composer speaks of our obligation 'to compel ourselves industriously to enlighten one another by means of reasoning and to apply ourselves to carry forward the sciences and the arts'.[8]

Gaita notes that someone who speaks in these ways, of life as a gift, or of gratitude and ingratitude, need not speak of the gift as God's gift. Nevertheless, he goes on:

> The person who speaks of life as a gift but who cannot speak of it as God's gift might say that to be religious in the 'strict sense' is to be able to speak of God and to speak His name in prayer. That does not mean that if someone is not religious in the strict sense, then they are not religious at all, or that they are religious in a waffly sense. If such a person may be said to speak of an implicit recognition, or love of, God, then they speak religiously even if they would only shrug their shoulders at such a claim. There are first- and third-person asymmetries here.[9]

I take Gaita's final remark to indicate that it is possible to speak of people as religious, even where they would not characterise their own lives in this way, and this I should not wish to deny. On the other hand there are also indications in this passage that he thinks

---

6   Pablo Casals, quoted in R. Gaita, *Good and Evil: An Absolute Conception* (London: Macmillan, 1991), pp. 214–15.

7   Ibid., p. 223.

8   Quoted in Gaita, op. cit., p. 219.

9   Gaita, op. cit., p. 225.

that it is possible to say of anyone who speaks of life as a gift, that they are religious, at least in some sense, that they 'speak out of an implicit recognition, or love of God'. But whether or not Gaita would regard himself as committed to this conclusion, it is certainly common enough.

But is Gaita mistaken in supposing that to think of life as a gift is to think (in at least *some* sense of 'religious') in religious terms? For if he is, then, for the atheist, who is it who is thought of as making the gift? To whom is the atheist grateful? Consider the following passage from the autobiography of the country singer Hank Williams Jr., Williams is convalescing from a near fatal climbing accident in Montana.

> It's September, and there's winter definitely in the air. Sometimes, I sit outside in the chill and stare into the wilderness, and my mind floats back up to the mountain. Sometimes I relive every minute, step by step. I feel myself falling, know that I'm dying. I spend hours on the side of the mountain, drifting between death and life and finally choosing the latter. I know I'm a different person now, and the task seems to be integrating the new person into the old life. I decide though, what I will *not* do. I will not testify and explain how I've found Jesus … that wasn't the lesson of the mountain. I spend a lot of time thinking of that lesson, which is so simple I can't imagine having not learned it a long time ago—if you're going to live, live. Just live your life to the best of your abilities …[10]

Though Williams later comes to speak as a religious believer, as someone who has found God, there is no sign that religious belief played a very profound role in his life, and almost none in the view of life presented in the passage that I have quoted. Nevertheless, just as Gaita says of the passage from Pablo Casals that it is in the accent of gratitude, one might well say the same of the passage quoted above. Williams' life has been spared, and his gratitude for this gift of life carries with it certain responsibilities and consequences. He knows that as a result of what has happened to him, his life will be different, that it must be lived in a different way.

But even if someone who lacks any religious belief *is* inclined to speak in these ways, this may not seem to remove the

---

10   Hank Williams Jr., *Living Proof* (New York: Dell/James A. Bryans, 1983) pp. 130–1.

difficulties. For who has spared him? To whom does he have the responsibility to change his life? To whom does he owe gratitude? Who gave the gift of life? And it may seem that the only possible answer in these cases is precisely the answer which the atheist cannot give. For the atheist cannot say that God gave him the gift of life, that he is grateful to God, that God spared him, and so on. So must we not conclude that if the atheist is inclined to speak in these ways, this inclination can be explained only as the vestige of a religious faith, a religious faith which, because of his heritage, he is unable to expunge from his vocabulary? Otherwise, it may be argued, such phrases can have no meaning for the unbeliever.

But in what way can they be said to have no meaning? If an atheist, having been unexpectedly saved from death, speaks of life as a gift, why can this have no meaning unless he speaks of the gift as a gift from God? One answer to this question is to appeal to what is often nowadays referred to as the grammar of statements like 'I was given …' or 'I am grateful'. It is a point of grammar, so it will be said, that a gift must have a giver, that when one is grateful, then one is grateful to someone. And arguments of this form have a long tradition. They were, for example, used by Cardinal Newman to show that certain features of the way we all employ the notion of conscience, proved a belief in God:

> If, as is the case, we feel responsibility, are ashamed, are frightened, at transgressing the voice of conscience, this implies that there is One to whom we are responsible, before whom we are ashamed, whose claim upon us we fear.[11]

Indeed, it might well be thought that in arguing that the presence in our lives of the notion of moral obligation implies the notion of a Divine will which obliges us, Anscombe is using yet another variant of the argument.

In examining such arguments it is important to distinguish the philosopher's use of the term 'grammar' from its use by, say, English teachers or linguists. For in the latter sense a sentence which has no clear meaning may well be grammatically in order. It will be in order so long as it obeys certain rules of grammar, which are at least in principle capable of being enumerated. So in this sense 'She was grateful to the kitchen sink' or 'Julius Caesar

---

[11] John Newman, *A Grammar of Assent*, ed. C.F. Harrold (Oxford: Oxford University Press, 1947) p. 83.

gave Hank Williams Jr. the gift of life' are grammatically in order, since they break none of these rules, even though in most contexts such remarks would be quite incomprehensible. But, in the sense in which philosophers speak of 'grammar' or 'logical grammar', where this is a criterion of sense, it is a mistake to suppose that what is grammatically sound, what makes sense, is determined by some set of rules. For despite what generations of philosophers may have thought, nothing general can be said here.

To determine whether some claim or other makes sense we have to look at the context in which it is used, to see whether or not it has a role to play there. Thus, though it may seem plausible to suppose that there are some general rules, such as 'a statement having the form "p and not-p" never makes sense', we are inclined to assent to this claim simply because we tend to call to mind contexts in which such a statement *would* be rejected as nonsensical. In a given context, for example where the police are interrogating a suspect, it may be clear that the suspect's propensity to claim at one time that on the night in question he was in bed with his wife, and at another (*e.g.* when faced with his wife's denial of this alibi) that he was drinking at the pub with his friends, will be taken to show that he is contradicting himself and so talking nonsense. Here there is no lack of clarity about the context (his interrogators have seen to that), and in *that* context his words do not make sense. Or again, I may be inclined to say that *any* sentence of the form 'x and y are feeling the same pain' contains a grammatical confusion, because I have in mind the incomprehension which I should feel if someone were to complain that I had given them my pain or stolen their pain from them, and forget that perfectly ordinary situation in which someone says to me 'Oh yes, I know *that* pain. I've had it many times. It's called angina.' In these, as in all other cases, the logical grammar of a proposition is determined not by abstract rules, but by looking at what is done with the proposition in a range of particular cases.

When, however, it is claimed that life can be regarded as a gift only where someone is thought of as the donor, or that one can be grateful only for what someone has given one, the superficial plausibility which such remarks may seem to have when considered in the abstract is merely an illusion. It stems from having derived a rule from certain contexts, for instance, the way in which children think of Christmas presents (as gifts from someone, *e.g.* their parents, or Santa Claus) or in which religious believers think of their lives (as gifts from God), and from then trying to impose this rule on the way in which atheists may talk of their lives.

If, however, we look at the role which the notion of a gift (and the allied notions of gratitude, ingratitude, and so on) may have in the life of an atheist, then where is the puzzle? Hank Williams is in a situation in which he might be expected to die—in fact he lies in the snow for some hours, his skull so badly crushed that his brain is exposed. But he does not die. Someone, not a religious believer, speaks here of the gift of life. Why is this so puzzling, so unnatural? Like other gifts, it is something which he had no right to expect. It was not something due to him. It was something desirable. (You do not normally refer to the gift of a bad cold, even if someone gave it you.) Like other gifts, it is not something to which one would normally remain indifferent, without people thinking of this as ingratitude. Nor is Williams indifferent. He speaks of the changes in his life, the responsibilities which the gift brings with it. And it is, of course, important that Williams does not think of his life as something which was saved by his own efforts, by a supreme act of will-power, for instance. For something is not normally a gift, if I have earned it. But it is by no means obvious that any of these features is essential if we are to speak of something as a gift. True they could not *all* be absent and it still be natural to speak in this way. In an unpublished paper[12] Rush Rhees remarks that very often talk of gratitude for one's life is hypocrisy and illustrates the point with a passage from Flannery O'Connor's short story *Revelation*:

> 'If it's one thing I am', Mrs. Turpin said with feeling, 'it's grateful. When I think who all I could have been besides myself and what all I got, a little of everything, and a good disposition besides, I feel just like shouting, "Thank you, Jesus, for making everything the way it is! It could have been different!"'

Mrs. Turpin's avowals of gratitude are fraudulent because her attitudes towards her own life and character have, despite what she says, *none* of the features of one's attitude towards a gift, except that she speaks of a donor. In truth, she sees the circumstances of her life as a matter for pride. But still it does not follow from this that there is some *one* essential feature which makes it appropriate

---

[12]   Rush Rhees, 'Gratitude and Ingratitude for Existence'. I am grateful to Professor D.Z. Phillips for drawing my attention to the relevance of this discussion.

to regard something as a gift. So, given what I have said about the way in which someone might view a miraculous escape from death as a gift of life, why insist that unless they are willing to identify someone as the giver, then they are speaking in a confused fashion? Why insist on any one feature? We speak of the bees as giving honey, and this is not thought to be unnatural, even though it might well be pointed out that we take the honey from them.

If what we have in these examples is a perfectly natural way of talking, a natural sort of reaction to certain sorts of good fortune, then there seems no reason to explain it as a variety of, or vestigial form of, the various ways in which believers may thank God for the gift of life. For in general, some feature of our lives requires explanation only where it is in some way puzzling. The point was made forcefully, and on many different occasions, by the writer G.K. Chesterton. Observing, for instance, that in many different societies human beings express their sense of inferiority to others or their reverence for them by bowing, anthropologists had constructed elaborate explanations to explain the prevalence of this practice. Chesterton's response was to question the necessity for such explanations. Why, he asked, exclude the possibility that human beings bow to those they regard as superior simply because it is a perfectly natural thing to do?

It is by no means clear to me why this should not be an equally adequate explanation of the phenomenon which I have been discussing during the latter part of this essay. Reacting to a piece of good fortune, or a natural blessing with gratitude seems, looked at in one way, simply a natural response. Of course, like many other responses it may play a different role, or even be expressed in different forms of human practice. In *Zettel*, §540, Wittgenstein remarks: 'It is a primitive reaction to tend, to treat, the part that hurts when someone else is in pain and not merely when oneself is.'[13] He might also have drawn attention to the fact that it is a natural human response to turn away from suffering, to avert one's gaze. But though both of these reactions are natural, they occupy a different place in different human practices. In particular, the former is emphasised to the detriment of the latter in Christianity, for example the story of the Good Samaritan, whereas in many non-religious contexts it will be the latter which

---

13   L. Wittgenstein, *Zettel*, §540.

is encouraged to the detriment of the former ('Charity begins at home', 'Look after number one', etc.). In a similar way the natural tendency to react to a piece of good fortune as a gift, that is to say with gratitude, is counterbalanced by the equally natural tendency to curse the day one was born in the face of certain forms of extreme suffering, or perhaps to meet the suffering with resignation as does Hank Williams when he discovers that his looks have been destroyed by his fall on the mountain. In an atheistic morality, these reactions simply co-exist. By contrast, within the Christian morality the response of gratitude is extended to both good and bad fortune. Thus, Herman Lange, a Catholic chaplain, hearing that he has been condemned by a Nazi court to death by beheading, writes the following words in his prison cell:

> For, after all, death means homecoming. The gift we thereupon receive is so unimaginably great that all human joys pale beside it, and the bitterness of death as such — however sinister it appear to our human nature — is completely conquered by it.[14]

Clearly the conception of life, *whatever evils it may bring*, as a gift is a conception for which there is no counterpart in an atheistic morality. And nothing that I have said should be taken to deny that there exist such differences between religion and atheism. I have tried simply to argue that the atheistic conception of life as a gift cannot be convicted of incoherence just because the atheist is unable to identify the donor of the gift. Indeed, if it were thought to be philosophically legitimate for the religious believer to employ such arguments, it might well be countered by the atheist that, since it is normally a feature of a gift that it must be something desirable, then it is the religious notion of a gift from God which is unintelligible, since it drops one feature central to the atheist's account of a gift. But, for the reasons which I indicated at the beginning of this essay, and in view of many of the things which I have been emphasising throughout, it should be apparent that neither form of attack gets much sympathy from me.

---

[14] Quoted in T. Huddlestone, *Dying We Live* (London: Fontana Books, 1965) p. 88.

10

How Not to
Think Critically[1]

It is an important feature of our lives (and, I believe, a philosophically important feature) that there are certain things which
we are disinclined to think about. I do not mean such things as the
death of our friends and relatives or the nuclear holocaust, where
if I said that I did not wish to consider them, someone, the
insurance salesman or the man erecting the fall-out shelter might
reply, 'Well you should make some plans for these contingencies.'
Rather, what I have in mind is those characteristics of situations,
people, events, which we would find it objectionable to dwell
upon. And I say that this is a philosophically important feature
since I believe that in at least one area of the subject, moral philosophy, its neglect leads to an emaciated account. In this essay I
shall be considering various accounts, chiefly though not exclusively of a utilitarian sort, and particularly that of R.M. Hare in his
book *Moral Thinking*, which seem to me both to demonstrate the
dangers of ignoring this feature of human life and also by their
very nature to serve as illustrations of it.

I

Hare's avowed aim in *Moral Thinking,* his third major work, is to
provide a method for resolving important practical issues. I think
it is fair to say that this numbered among Hare's aims from the
time of his first book *The Language of Morals* but there it was pure
optimism. For in *The Language of Morals* and to a lesser extent in
his second book *Freedom and Reason*, Hare was primarily

---

[1]   Not previously published.

concerned to preserve one of the dogmas of twentieth century ethics, the idea of a dichotomy between factual and evaluative judgements. Since, in our moral discourse, we do apparently found evaluative judgements on factual premises—'We ought to break diplomatic relations with the Libyans.' 'Why?' 'Because they are using the convention of diplomatic immunity in order to smuggle arms into Britain.'—there are obvious difficulties for any philosopher who, like Hare, maintains that there is an irreducible gulf between facts and values. Roughly speaking, Hare's original solution was simply to deny that we ever do derive moral, evaluative judgements solely from factual premises. Rather moral judgements should be seen as syllogisms in which evaluative conclusions are derived from a factual minor premise in conjunction with an evaluative major premise having the form of a moral principle. Thus from the principle 'We ought to break off diplomatic relations with all nations who actively encourage terrorism' and the factual premiss 'The Libyans do just that', we deduce the evaluative conclusion 'We ought to break off diplomatic relations with the Libyans.'

Unfortunately, such an account while apparently establishing the rationality, the logical respectability of moral arguments, naturally raises the question whether the selection of moral principles (on Hare's account, major premises) is itself a rational process. Where principles conflict, where people disagree over which principles to adopt, is there any rational procedure for resolving the issue? At this stage Hare's answer was a qualified 'No'. In the final analysis, we each simply decide which principles to adopt so it will not be surprising if sometimes fundamental moral disagreements arise because people have decided differently. In *Freedom and Reason* Hare comes down hard on philosophers who try to find a 'method of argument which would force people to the same moral conclusions'.[2]

In *Moral Thinking* things have changed somewhat, and his answer to the question whether there is such a method wavers between a pretty unqualified 'Yes' and a totally unqualified 'Yes'. At its most unqualified, his position seems to be that, given an unlimited knowledge of the facts and a perfect command of logic, we should all agree in our answers to moral questions. But he is emphatic that this answer, despite all appearances to the contrary,

---

2   R.M. Hare, *Freedom and Reason* (Oxford: Clarendon Press, 1963) p. 184.

is consistent with the central tenets of his earlier position. The illusion of inconsistency disappears when we recognise that the conflicts and disagreements discussed in his earlier writings exist only at what he calls the 'intuitive' level. At this level, which roughly speaking comprises those principles which are inculcated by parents, teachers, friends or assimilated from, say literature, people sometimes face unanswerable problems, because the principles which they have made their own conflict with one another. Or, they are involved in irresolvable disagreements with others because they have assimilated different principles. And since, at this level, we have no independent standard against which to criticise and weigh our own principles or those of others, we are unable to choose rationally between them. There is, however, another level of thought, the 'critical' level, at which such criticism is possible.

Hare's account of this turns out to be a variety of utilitarianism. But it involves an elaboration of one important aspect of his earlier views, the thesis of universalisability. In committing myself to any moral judgement about how people should be treated, Hare had claimed, 'I am *ipso facto* prescribing that I myself should be treated in this way were I in their situation.' The importance of this point for the present work becomes apparent if we bear in mind the reactions of others to how they are treated, their preferences and aversions, cannot be regarded by us as merely neutral facts about them. For it is a part of the logic of the concept of suffering that I can be said to be suffering only if I both know that I am suffering and have an aversion to it. So the suffering of another person is not a merely neutral fact to them. And to know what it is like for another person to suffer is to imagine that we are in their situation with their desires and aversions, and so to realise that, were we in their position, we should, like them, have an aversion to suffering. Nor are such hypothetical preferences and aversions morally irrelevant. For they decide what universal principles, and so, according to the principle of universalisability, what moral judgements we can accept. Of course, it does not follow from this argument as it stands that we can never be morally justified in adopting a principle, which would involve the suffering of others. For just as I may weigh my own present suffering against a future reduction in suffering (*e.g.* by giving up smoking), so I may, without offending against the principle of universalisability, weigh the suffering of others in the same way, setting off suffering against the satisfaction of preferences.[3] So moral judgement involves weighing the preferences of others as if they were our own. And since, according to Hare, this is a 'logical requirement, if we are reasoning morally'[4] we now see that at least one variety of utilitarianism has a conceptual foundation. I say one variety because if as Hare maintains it is the application of critical thought to the desires which provides the basis for moral judgement, then there can be no room in this process for the idea that some desires are themselves morally objectionable. 'We are committed by the formality of our method to a Benthamite answer to the basic question (*i.e.* of utilitarianism); equal preferences count equally, whatever their content.'[5] Bentham was right. Quantity of pleasure being equal, pushpin is as good as poetry. And Mill, who thought that it was better to be Socrates dissatisfied than a fool satisfied had simply failed to consider what it would be like to have the preferences and aversions of a fool.

The introduction of the notion of critical thought then (apart from, as Hare no doubt ironically observes, winning him philosophical arguments by baffling his opponents) also enables us to provide a standard by which moral principles may be shown to be adequate or inadequate, depending on whether or not they tend on the whole to maximise the satisfaction of preferences, whatever the preferences are. Not that Hare does think that many of our moral beliefs (by which he means his moral beliefs) will turn out to be inadequate. Consistently applied, the principles of critical thinking will bring you to the conclusion that abortion and euthanasia are permissible and that deviant sex is a good as long as both partners are happy (perhaps I should say all partners). After all, if they want it, whatever it is, then all their preferences, however loathsome, will be satisfied by it, and so it must be all right. And so on.

Still, at this point, Hare can scarcely ignore the obvious retort that, if our intuitions always agreed, then there would be no point

---

[3]   Hare, like many philosophers, seems to take it for granted that any rational decision must involve such a calculation. But this seems to be a mistake. For though it is certainly imprudent to choose to avoid present suffering where doing so will ensure even greater future suffering, it does not seem on the face of it to be more irrational to care more about the present than the future.

[4]   R.M. Hare, *Moral Thinking* (Oxford: Oxford University Press, 1981) p. 16.

[5]   Ibid., pp. 144–5.

in having the level of critical thinking in order to resolve disagreements among them. The existence of genuine moral disagreements
at the intuitive level, which Hare does not deny, shows that at
least some people's principles must conflict with the demands of
critical thought (or to give it is original name, Benthamite utilitarianism). And this is further demonstrated by the existence of
what Hare calls 'fanatics', who appear to hold that certain things,
torture, slavery, sexual deviation, are unjustifiable regardless of
other people's preferences, and consequently on the face of it at
least, simply refuse to think critically. But this presents Hare with
a problem. For though his account of critical thinking is supposed
to be an analysis of the way in which we do think and talk about
morality (for, if it is simply a recommendation, then it looks as
though we may choose simply to ignore it), though he claims to be
'exposing the logic of the moral concepts as we have them', the
existence of conflict and fanaticism seems to show that Hare is not
exposing the logic of some people's moral concepts. And clearly it
will not do merely to accuse the fanatic of irrationality. For then
the strategy would be clear. An account is offered and defended
by an appeal to the way people think and talk about morality.
Where, as with the fanatic, people think and talk in a way which
conflicts with the account, they are accused of confusion. If we
now ask why they are confused, the answer is simple. They are
confused because what they think does not fit the account.

   The difficulty is brought to a head in certain sorts of examples
often adduced to show that utilitarian considerations lead in
certain cases to apparently outrageous consequences. One such
example, familiar to students of moral philosophy, is to be found
in literary form in Faulkner's novel *Intruder in the Dust*, where it
concerns a law officer, Sheriff Hope Hampton, in the deep south
of America who has to choose between on the one hand
surrendering a black prisoner, Lucas Beauchamp, to a clan of local
ne'er-do-wells, the Gowries, who believe him to have murdered
one of their members, and on the other insisting on a fair trial, in
which case general mayhem will ensue. Either way the prisoner
will in all probability be hanged, and the difficulty arises because
utilitarian considerations seem to demand that the black prisoner
be handed over (general mayhem plus hanging satisfies fewer
preferences than the hanging alone), while what Hare calls our
'intuitions' demand that he not be.

   Hare, however, has a short way with such examples. It is, he
tells us, impossible to know that such a case is genuine. For how

can we, or for that matter the sheriff, know what the consequences of breaking the principles of justice in this way will be?

> Perhaps the sheriff should hang the innocent man in order to prevent the riot in which there will be many deaths, if he knows that the man's innocence will never be discovered and that the bad indirect effects will not outweigh the good direct effects; but in practice he will never know this.[6]

The calculation is so complicated as to be in practice impossible to make. It is, on the other hand, quite certain that the consequences of justice are in general beneficial, so both rationality and, in the long term, prudence demand that even in such extreme situations we act justly.

Hare, of course, gets the example wrong. For sheriffs, as Faulkner knows, do not hang people, or even give the order for them to be hanged. Only judges do that. So if the black prisoner dies as a result of the sheriff's decision, what we have is a lynching; and in that case it seems by the way whether the man is innocent or not. And, if we stick with Faulkner's example, you may wonder how it can be possible for Sheriff Hampton (or even William Faulkner right there in Oxford, Mississippi) to known the consequence of thwarting the desires of the local rednecks in this way, but possible for Professor Hare in Oxford, England, to be so sure of the consequences of this and countless other examples of injustice that he can assert that they are generally bad. You may in fact suspect that there is a contradiction lurking concealed in Hare's contempt for 'outrageous' examples. If so, you are not going to be any more sympathetic to Hare's argument when I tell you about the case of the 'indivisible cream puff'.[7] This example, which I owe to Hare and for which he can, I think, claim originality, concerns a dilemma faced by Hare over how to satisfy the preferences of his twin sons, both of whom wanted a cream puff of which only one remained. Since, on the one interpretation, the cream puff could not be tom apart with the hands or even cut with a knife, there is a difficulty in understanding why Hare's sons wanted to eat it. On the other interpretation, where the cream puff disintegrated when touched, there is a difficulty in seeing

---

6   Ibid., p. 164.
7   Ibid., p. 157.

how they intended to set about eating it. So much for outrageous examples.

But I do not think that the difficulty merits a lengthy discussion in this context, since Hare can scarcely believe that all cases of conflict between the absolute demands of justice and those of utilitarianism/'critical thought' can be disposed of in this manner, that is to say by emphasising the difficulty of assessing the consequences for the satisfaction of preferences of acts of injustice, if only because there are certain sorts of 'fanatic', genuine 'fanatics' if you like, who hold that certain things, for example injustice, are wrong regardless of people's preferences. Since these 'fanatics' in their judgements about what is right or wrong disregard the preferences of those involved, they cannot be said to have made either a correct or an incorrect estimate of those preferences. And Hare himself gives us examples of such people — the pacifist, the doctor who believes it to be his duty to preserve life at all cost, the man who believes that tyranny and slavery would never be permissible in any sort of society, and so on.

Hare's own view is that in so far as the fanatic's claims are neither incoherent nor simply factually mistaken, he must be seen as someone who in his critical thinking attaches so great a weight to those of his own preferences which stem from moral conviction that they always override the preferences of others. But even in Hare's own terms this makes no sense. Since it is critical thinking that decides what is right or wrong, judgements about what is right or wrong cannot in consistency be presupposed by the process of critical thought. So the fanatic is on Hare's account simply inconsistent.

But before we jump to the conclusion that the fanatic is inconsistent, let us just ask about the alternative to fanaticism. The alternative is, of course, consistent critical thought, and for brevity I will take a leaf out of Hare's book and employ a technical term, 'liberal', to refer to those who engage in critical thought. Let us then ask what the 'liberal' will have to say about, for example, the wrongness of one form of sexual deviation which will not, I can safely assume, have Hare's approval, namely rape. Those who are inclined to respond that it is quite obvious that rape is wrong, that in general not even rapists deny this, and that if they do we shall not bring them to see the error of their ways by rational argument of any kind whatsoever,[8] will perhaps be impressed by the 'liberal's' claim that they have restricted their thought to the intuitive level and will then take steps to adopt a more critical approach. To begin with, then, they will ask about the preferences of those affected by rape. Well, of course, people prefer not to be raped. This sounds pretty much like a tautology, but to reach the same conclusion the 'liberal' will I suppose need to imagine himself in the position of someone who is to be raped. But this is only the start. For obviously it would be quite mistaken to suppose that the only desires involved in rape are those of the victim. If this were so, then rape would be unknown. So there are the desires of the rapist to consider. We have, that is to say, to set against the desire of the victim not to be raped the fact that the rapist wants to commit rape, which is, if you like, the one redeeming feature in the whole situation. And now the 'liberal' can do his calculation, hoping very much, I suppose, that he will reach the conclusion that the victim wants not to be raped more than the rapist wants to rape, all other things being equal.

It should now be clear that the 'liberal', in this special technical sense, is really a bit of a crank in a rather ordinary non-technical sense. Or to put the point in a less obtrusive and more precise way, the 'liberal' is engaged in a process of thought which many of us would find morally repugnant in itself. It is not that we weigh the desires of rapists less heavily than those of their victims, which would itself be difficult enough for Hare to explain. It is rather that we do not normally weigh them at all. There are examples of those sorts of considerations which I mentioned at the beginning of the paper. They simply play no part in our thought on the matter. So what has gone wrong with Hare's account?

The first mistake is absurdly simple. According to Hare, to know what it is like for someone to have a desire (the rapist—a desire to rape, his victim—a desire not to be raped) is, as a matter of logic, to imagine oneself having such a desire. But if one had the desire in question, one could not prescribe what conflicted with it (except in the interest of satisfying a stronger desire), since one would then be both prescribing that the desire be satisfied and also that the desire not be satisfied.

---

[8]   Hare himself does talk about having arguments with those who think that it is alright to torture people just for fun, apparently under the impression that if we won the argument they would stop it.

Obviously, however, this appalling argument only gets going because of the blanket use of the term 'prescribe' to mean both 'want' or 'desire' and 'call good' or 'morally recommend'. And this use has the bizarre consequence that, if I say that my desire for such-and-such is morally reprehensible, I am contradicting myself as I both desire (prescribe) and condemn (do not prescribe). Or to put the point another way, the use cannot be correct, since if it were, it would be self-contradictory to say of oneself that one had evil desires. Hare, it is true, has a rather unconvincing argument, deriving originally from Plato's Republic to show that it is highly unlikely that in the long run evil desires will be beneficial. But this is, of course, no use to him since it is clear that no discussion of probabilities can establish a contradiction. G.E. Moore had one fundamental objection to utilitarians. You cannot, Moore said, use what is desired (i.e. happiness) even what is desired by the greatest number, as a criterion of what is good, or even of what is regarded as good, because, as everyone knows, some desires, the desire of the rapist to rape, or of the slaver to enslave, or of the sadist to inflict pain, are evil. Hare's account simply fails to deal with this objection.

II

So that is the first mistake. The claim of 'critical thinking' to be an analysis of the way we (all of us, that is) think about morality cannot be upheld as an account of the way most of us think about such evils as rape or torture or slavery it would be mere parody. Unfortunately as it stands my argument is far from disposing of Hare's arguments (or so far completely fails to explain the attraction of Hare's views) (or for the strength of Hare's position— and perhaps the attraction of utilitarianism generally). For it may be said that Hare does seem to have identified and given expression to if not the only then at least one way of looking at moral issues, and one which is genuinely opposed to those views which he stigmatises as 'fanatic'—that of the doctor who simply draws the line at euthanasia, or the Catholic who is against sexual deviation as such, of Sheriff Hampton who will not even consider any sort of deal with the Gowries. Thus there is clearly a debate between the relative who begs for a release from suffering, and the doctor who simply draws the line at euthanasia.

As we have seen, Hare's view is that if the fanatic claims, as he sometimes appears to, that such things are wrong regardless of the

benefits they may bring, then his views are simply incoherent.
They must be, since the question of what benefits a course of
action will in fact bring in what determines its rightness or wrongness. This is why Hare's own conclusions will not always, at least
in their externals, differ from those of the 'fanatic'. He himself
believes lynching or slavery to be unjustifiable. The difference, so
it is claimed, is that Hare bases his judgement on the facts,
whereas the 'fanatic' simply disregards the facts. Thus, faced with
Sheriff Hampton's problem, one may just refuse to engage in
'critical thinking' and insist that lynching is wrong, in which case
one's claim is incoherent and one is a 'fanatic', or one may
consider the facts of the case. And then one either concludes that
the consequences of such a lynching will be beneficial in the sense
of satisfying most preferences, or one concludes that it will not be.
And, as we have seen, Hare himself inclines to the view that the
former conclusion only gains its plausibility from a narrow concentration on the immediate consequences.

What is interesting for my purposes is that, given the weight
Hare attaches to a full knowledge of the facts in such cases, he is
curiously selective in the consequences he chooses to mention. On
the other hand, we have the fact that a lynching will save the lives
of certain parties, prevent the destruction of property, enable the
law abiding citizens to sleep easily in their beds, at least in the
short term. On the other we have the long-term distrust of the law
which may result from witnessing its being flouted, the danger
that others of the Gowrie clan will attempt similar blackmail in the
future, and so on.

And all of these might, roughly speaking, be said to be states of
affairs causally connected with whichever action is performed. If
the sheriff allows the black prisoner to be lynched, he will set in
motion one causal chain. If he protects him, he will play a
significant role in setting in motion another. In either case the
consequences, which for Hare determine what we should do when
presented with such a dilemma, are thought of as states of affairs
contingently related to what the agent does. But because he is
concerned only with those consequent states of affairs which will
differ depending on which course of action is taken, and which
will therefore enable someone to choose between the courses of
action involved, Hare ignores one sort of consequence which will
follow whichever course the sheriff takes.

What I mean is that it is quite easy to imagine someone
remarking that the moment the sheriff starts to take seriously the

Gowries' proposition, then he betrays both his prisoner and the people who put him in office, or in one sense of the term (the sense in which you can be insulted without knowing it) insults them. Or you could say that the moment he starts to consider the problem in the way Hare recommends, starts weighing the preferences of the black prisoner against his own or those of the townspeople against those of the Gowries, then he treats them all as objects to be manipulated. And you then have the consequence that people are betrayed, or insulted, or manipulated.

I say that Hare ignores these things partly for the reason (for what it is worth) that he never mentions them, and partly for the reason, which I have mentioned already, that since they follow as a matter of course whichever way the sheriff chooses, they can have no part to play in his 'critical thinking' about the dilemma, once he has come to see it as presenting a dilemma. But there is a more important reason. To see it we must notice that it is of considerable importance to Hare's discussion of such problems whether or not the act can be kept secret.

> Perhaps the sheriff should hang the innocent man in order to prevent the riot in which there will be many deaths, if he knows that the man's innocence will never be discovered...[9]

For, on Hare's view of the matter, if the sheriff can keep the act secret, then only the black prisoner, who in the nature of the case is bound to know what is happening to him, will suffer. The others involved (his deputies, who live to fight another day, the townspeople, who are spared the consequences of a riot) cannot be said to suffer, since they will have no idea what is happening. And for Hare, it is as we have seen a conceptual truth that if one is suffering, then one knows that one is suffering. On the other hand, if the act cannot be kept secret, then there is a danger that bad indirect consequences, contempt for the law, mistrust of the sheriff, etc. will ensue. It all depends on whether the act can be concealed.

When we turn our attention to the sort of consequences which I have mentioned, however, the question of whether the betrayal, the manipulation can be kept secret is quite irrelevant. For what we have here is a form of harm which a man can suffer whether he knows it or not. This is why Hare's claim that if one is suffering,

---

9   Ibid.

one knows one is suffering (an attempt to produce a philosophically rigorous version of the old saying 'What you don't
know, can't harm you'), is not quite the innocuous conceptual
truth he suggests, but in fact attests to a determination to concentrate one's attention on one sort of consequence rather than
another; on the way someone suffers when that are given a good
kicking, say, rather than the way they suffer when unbeknown to
them their reputation is besmirched or they are betrayed.

It might be thought that Hare's claim to have identified a
conceptual truth can be protected by limiting the concept of suffering to the former case rather than the latter. But unfortunately this
will not do, since in Hare's argument the concept of suffering is
simply shorthand for those experiences which people would
prefer not to have. And it is beyond doubt that people would
prefer not to be manipulated or betrayed, whether they know
about it or not. I have read somewhere that when his doctors gave
an extremely gloomy prognosis about the development of Freud's
cancer, his friends discussed among themselves whether he
should be told or not. Later, on being told this Freud became
extremely angry. Since, presumably, his anger was not directed at
the fact that he was told, we must conclude that he was angry
because something had happened to him, he had been manipulated, treated like a child, which he would have preferred not to
have happened, even though at the time he did not know it was
happening.

Nor can the alleged conceptual truth in question be preserved
by a refusal to call the fact that someone is betrayed or manipulated a consequence of the action in question, since with regard to
the question whether someone suffers or not (whether they have
experiences which they would prefer not to have) it is all one
whether we say that they suffer as a result of the betrayal or that
the suffering is part of the betrayal. Still, I think that I should still
wish to insist that we are speaking of consequences. Certainly the
consequences here cannot be thought of as causally related to the
action, even in the sense in which, for example, my sufferings at
the hands of the secret police may be said to be causally related to
my betrayal by a friend, where the relationship is merely contingent, so that there is room for some intervention which
prevents the consequences. Rather they are consequences in the
sense that Alexei Karenina's suffering when he learns of Anna's

adultery is a consequence of that sort of betrayal.[10] A central feature of Alexei's love for Anna is its possessiveness. He is, Tolstoi shows us, obsessed by the idea that Anna will always love him alone. The knowledge of her unfaithfulness destroyed this conception of their relationship. Instead of being unique, it had become a relationship of a type, to be compared, for better or worse, with her relationship with Vronsky.

> In considering further details, Alexei Alexandrovitch could not see why his relations with his wife should not continue almost the same as ever.[11]

Almost, but not quite. Of course, I do not deny that adultery need not have the significance for everyone as it does for Alexei. What this shows is that it is a contingent matter what 'being betrayed' amounts to with different people, or even whether they will speak of 'betrayal' at all in such cases. Still, given Alexei's view, the suffering which he undergoes as a consequence of his wife's actions is not merely contingently related to those actions. And it is this sense of 'consequence' which Hare's account, it seems to me, simply ignores.

In this respect Hare is at one with many of his non-utilitarian opponents, and it is because they share his assumptions that they often find it difficult to identify their point of disagreement with him. Thus, for example, Bernard Williams in his essay 'A Critique of Utilitarianism', having explicitly accepted the utilitarian equation of 'consequences of action' and 'states of affairs caused by action', presents us with yet another variant of the 'one dead or ten dead' dilemma, this time set in South America in order to show that utilitarian principles can lead to morally unacceptable conclusions.

> Jim finds himself in the central square of a small South American town. Tied up against the wall are a row of twenty Indians, most terrified, a few defiant, in front of them several armed men in uniform. A heavy man in a sweat-stained khaki shirt turns out to be the captain in charge and explains that the Indians are a random group who, after recent acts of protest against the government, are just about to be killed to remind other possible protestors of the advantage of not protesting. However, since Jim is an honoured visitor from another land, the captain is happy to offer

---

[10] *Anna Karenina*, p. 139.
[11] Ibid., p. 175.

him a guest's privilege of killing one of the Indians himself. If Jim accepts, then as a special mark of the occasion, the other Indians will be let off. The men against the wall, and the other villagers understand the situation, and are obviously begging him to accept.[12]

Williams is, however, only doubtfully consistent here. For he professes to find Benthamite utilitarianism, *i.e.* the version which Hare espouses, 'absurdly superficial and shallow'. But Bentham and Hare are at least consistent in this respect. Mill, who claims to assess actions by their causal consequences and to exclude questions about the character and motivations of the agent, then inconsistently introduces the notion of 'quality of pleasure'; inconsistently, because to say that the pleasure of Socrates is worth more than that of the fool is simply a covert way of comparing the character of Socrates to that of a fool independently of its causal consequences. 'Better Socrates dissatisfied than a fool satisfied' means 'Better to have the character of Socrates than that of a fool, regardless what else the possession of such a character may bring with it.'

Williams' aim is to show that since, in this case, the direct consequences of what will in fact be a peculiarly cold-blooded killing will be unarguably good, the utilitarian is, in the circumstances, forced to recommend what most would find abhorrent. But, as we have already seen, utilitarians like Hare do not need to deny that the killing is abhorrent. For they do not restrict themselves to consideration of the direct consequences of such an action (one dead rather than twenty), but may also take into account the indirect consequences. And these, it is claimed, are so bad that they justify even a utilitarian rejection of the murder. So either Williams has to admit that this example presents no dilemma for the utilitarian, or he is forced into a fruitless debate about the long-term consequences of murder whether such acts can be kept secret and so on. In so far as they disagree at all then, Hare and Williams disagree over the indirect consequences of Jim's action. But they agree in restricting themselves to those consequences which can be described independently of what he says and does, to the fact that, for example, there is either one corpse or twenty corpses. That, whichever way the issue is

---

[12] J.J.C. Smart and B. Williams, *Utilitarianism, For and Against* (New York: Cambridge University Press, 1973) pp. 98–9.

decided, Jim and the Captain are bartering with the lives of human beings and that this in itself might be seen as a terrible thing to do to people, is simply being discounted. So far as I understand him, I think that Williams would say that this was a matter of how Jim sees his actions, of his own integrity. And the Indians, we are told, being interested only in the consequences 'quite properly' have 'no interest' in Jim's integrity.

If by 'Jim's integrity' is meant something like 'Jim's keeping his conscience clear', then I might agree that the Indians may 'quite properly' have no interest in that. But if it is being assumed that the Indians have no interest in whether their lives are being bartered, then I should say that it rather depends on the Indians. Certainly, given the picture Williams paints of them cowering against a wall, begging Jim to shoot one of them (each begging him to shoot one of the others, I suppose), then I can see that they would have very little interest in whether their lives were being bartered or not. Well, it is Williams' example. Still it is not hard to imagine rather different Indians who put the cat among the pigeons by resenting the very fact that such calculations about their lives are being made on their behalf. They may, for example, be more impressed by the fact that, whichever way the calculations go, they will be forced to a new and unwelcome truth about their lives. If one of them dies, then the lives of the others will be lives purchased by the death of a man. If all twenty of them die, then their lives will be a sacrifice, *e.g.* to someone's integrity.

The possibility of such a reaction becomes clearer, indeed, becomes an actuality, when we consider another of Williams' examples:

> Suppose that there is in a certain society a racial minority. Its presence is neutral or mildly beneficial. However, the other citizens have such prejudices that they find the sight of this group, even the knowledge of its presence, disagreeable. Proposals are made for removing in some way this minority. If we assume various plausible things (as that programmes to change the majority sentiment are likely to be protracted and ineffective), then even if the removal would be unpleasant for the minority, a utilitarian calculation might well end up favouring this step.[13]

Williams himself objects to the utilitarian proposal, apparently on the grounds that we should not give weight in our calculations to

---

13   Ibid., p. 105.

feelings which are simply the result of prejudice. Nor is it difficult to find examples in real life which provide counterparts both to Williams thought on this subject and to that of his utilitarian opponents. The following is a description of the first stage of the extermination of the Sioux people in nineteenth century America.

> The day of the Santee Sioux in Minnesota now came to an end ... 'Exterminate or banish' was the cry of the land-hungry settlers. The first settlement of 770 Santees left St. Paul by steamboat on May 4, 1863. White Minnesotans lined the river landing to see them off with shouts of derision and showers of hurled stones.[14]

The situation of the Sioux deteriorated still further after the defeat of Custer by Crazy Horse's Oglalas in 1873. Fear and hatred of the Indians spread like an epidemic and General Sherman, who was apparently himself infuriated by reports that the Indians were crossing Yellowstone Park within sight of his camp there, was given authority to move the Sioux in Dakota and the Nez Perces of Idaho onto reservations where they would have no contact with gold prospectors, farmers and even tourists.

Like good utilitarians the Indian agencies had calculated that the sufferings of the minority of Indians would be vastly out-weighed by the benefits to intruders from the East. And like Williams there were those (for example, some of the army officers who had dealt with the surrender of the Cheyenne Indians at Fort Robinson) who objected to the calculation and held that more attention should be given to the feelings of the Indians and less to those of the white settlers. What was interesting was the reaction of the Indians themselves. Crazy Horse refused even to discuss the matter with white men. Chief Joseph of the Nez Perces observed contemptuously, 'Perhaps you think that the Creator sent you to dispose of the Indians as you see fit', and one anonymous Sioux chief remarked, 'I think that you had better put the Indians on wheels, and you can run them about wherever you wish.'

It is not hard to detect in these reactions a view of the situation radically opposed to that of both Sherman and the more sympa-thetic of the cavalry officers. What these Indians objected to was not that incorrect calculations had been made, but that calcula-tions were being made at all. So that from this viewpoint both Sherman and the more benevolent elements in the army were

---

14   Dee Brown, *Bury My Heart at Wounded Knee* (New York: Holt, 1970) p. 64.

simply Tweedledum and Tweedledee. For both the problem was this: there are the settlers, who desire that the Indians be removed from the face of the earth. And there are the Indians, who want to stay where they are. How are we to weigh these desires against one another? What both ignored was what was, for the Indians, the reality of the situation, namely that they were being manipulated. And this is not necessarily a feature to be explained in terms of anyone's desires. No doubt a prejudiced man like Sherman was blind to the realities, to what it was like for the Indians, because he saw their plight simply in terms of his own desires. But it does not follow, as Hare thinks, that what it was like for the Indians was to be explained in terms of another set of desires, only this time those of the Indians, if only because we might still speak of manipulation even if the Indians had not cared whether they were manipulated or not, if they had no preference either way. So we see that another of Hare's alleged conceptual truths turns out to be not a conceptual truth, but rather the expression of a particular view of the situation — in this case that of the Indian agencies, rather than that of the Indians.

And that, surely, is the truth about the whole position. Hare's account of 'critical thinking', allegedly an account of what it is to think rationally about moral issues, is at best one way of assessing one's actions and their consequences for others. In so far as you do think in this way, then there will be ways of assessing actions and their consequences to which you will simply be blind. And in so far as you are inclined to these ways of thinking, then you are not going to pay much attention to the discussion of the relative strength of desires, the desires of the rapist and his victim, the tyrant and those he tyrannises, the slaver and those he enslaves, which characterises what Hare calls 'critical thinking'.

But perhaps it will be objected that this does not go far enough. For throughout this essay I have assumed that there are those whose thought on at least some issues can be characterised as consistently utilitarian — that 'critical thought', though not, as Hare thinks, an analysis of any form of coherent moral thought, is an analysis of one way of thinking about at least some moral issues. And there may be those who are inclined to question even this modest claim, and to ask whether there is any genuine view of morality which involves simply an assessment of all desires, however, disgusting, simply that is to say, a summing of utilities.

To illustrate the difficulty, I should like to end by pointing to one feature of the 'one dead or ten dead' example, which is nowhere mentioned in *e.g.* Faulkner's novel, nor to the best of my knowledge is ever emphasised by those writers, utilitarian or otherwise, who discuss such examples, and that is the simple fact that for some people lynchings are fun, a piece of entertainment, a diversion from the monotony of their lives. Anyone for whom this fact is quite irrelevant to the question whether the lynching should be permitted, will serve as an illustration of the features of morality which it mentioned at the beginning of this essay. If, like me, you tend to suppose that whatever the example it will always be possible to find some such feature, you will have to conclude that utilitarianism is not a coherent account of any moral position whatsoever. For them, the title of Hare's book *Moral Thinking* will stand in approximately the same relation to its subject-matter as that of a book on capital gains tax for wealthy businessmen, *i.e.* how to avoid it.

11

Moral Realism[1]

In the work of those writers who refer to themselves as moral realists, one finds indications that they conceive of themselves as making a pretty fundamental break with what has gone before. For their main target, what they generally refer to as 'non-cognitivism', is the view that it is decision rather than discovery which is the central notion in ethics. And since 'non-cognitivism' is, like Macintyre's 'emotivism', a term coined to cover what is common to both emotivism and prescriptivism, this should not be surprising given the pervasive influence of these positions during much of the twentieth century. Still, in itself, this would not be enough to distinguish their views from other writers in this area. For during the last forty years there has certainly been opposition to emotivism and prescriptivism from writers who would not identify themselves as moral realists. And it is in their opposition not merely to prescriptivism and emotivism but also to any form of reductionism that realists like Sabina Lovibond, Mark Platts and David McNaughton are distinguished from those other anti-prescriptivist movements of the past forty years. For reductionist ethical theories like those of the utilitarians or naturalists of the Philippa Foot persuasion, offer a programme in which evaluative terms are to be replaced by discussions of the greatest happiness or by some other non-evaluative concept, whereas for the realist no such replacement can be regarded as possible.

But if it is clear who is the moral realist's opponent, clear what sort of position is being rejected, it is generally less clear what sort of opposition is involved, and less clear what aspects of morality the realist believes to have been obscured by his or her pre-decessors. True it is easy enough to supply a list of the realist's

---

[1]   Not previously published.

central contentions. Realism maintains that 'there is an objective moral reality', that moral judgements can be spoken of as true or false, that people can be said to know the difference between right and wrong, that if you disagree with me, I shall (at least some of the time) reject your views as mistaken or erroneous. It maintains that people can legitimately lay claim to certainty on some moral issues, though there will be others where they will be forced to recognise that they have been mistaken. It maintains that certain things can, in some sense of 'seen', be seen to be right and wrong, that 'we see the children's cruelty to the dog; we witness McEnroe's rudeness on the tennis court'.[2] All these are claims which, it might appear, no one will have much difficulty swallowing. And no doubt it is the insistence on such claims which gives realism its air of obvious truth, and enables the realist to adopt the stance of someone insisting on drawing our attention to what has absurdly been denied by the opponents of realism. But on reflection it becomes apparent that the impression is an illusion. For it is precisely the platitudinous nature of the realist's remarks, at least on one level, which ensures that so far nothing has here been asserted which need halt, for example, a follower of Macintyre or a utilitarian in his tracks. Indeed, when we meet with the suggestion that these are claims which have been denied by the majority of philosophers in the latter half of this century, then it is the claims themselves itself which seem puzzling. We are told that according to the realist, the wrongness of murder is objectively real. But what is the alternative view, that the wrongness of murder is not objectively real, supposed to amount to? Are we to believe that for some philosophers murder is not really wrong? The realist insists that when we reject the moral views of others, we reject them as false as mistaken, or that faced with a moral dilemma, we may ourselves come up with a solution which is wrong. But again, all this seems quite uncontentious. A writer like Hare who lays emphasis on the prevalence of disagreement in morality is not likely to have missed the point that where there is disagreement the parties to it will believe each other's views to be mistaken. And where it is a recognition of the intractable nature of moral dilemmas which provides the impetus for a philosopher's work as is the case with many theories, it is scarcely going to strike

---

[2]   David McNaughton, *Moral Vision: An Introduction to Ethics* (Oxford: Blackwell, 1988) p. 19.

anyone with the force of a revelation to be told that 'All of us, unless we are unusually arrogant will admit that we are fallible, that some of our opinions may be, indeed no doubt are, in error.'[3] For what gives seriousness to any dilemma is precisely the agent's recognition of the possibility of making the wrong decision. Were it not for the possibility of my deciding that I was wrong, it is difficult to see how I could be presented with a dilemma. In morality, as elsewhere, there is a conceptual relationship between my having a genuine problem and the possibility of my coming to the wrong conclusion.

The uncontroversial nature of the central tenets of realism has not always escaped the attention of those writers who are nevertheless sympathetic to it, Crispin Wright, for example, noting that claims such as that truth and falsity, knowledge and error have an application in morality constitutes 'no concession to moral realism at all'.[4] But often claims such as those I have listed above are presented as though they were themselves sufficient to identify a distinctive philosophical viewpoint. So that David Wiggins in a recent article seems to imagine that in order to reject any form of non-cognitivism, for example Hare's prescriptivism, it is sufficient to point out that it makes sense to speak of people's genuinely held moral beliefs as mistaken. For, according to Wiggins, the prescriptivist holds that if an agent thinks that an activity is worthwhile, then he cannot be mistaken. But as an account, even of Hare's early views, this is plainly inadequate. Indeed, Hare's own account of what is involved in the thesis of universalisability, one of the central lynch-pins of his theory, makes it clear that he would reject Wiggins' interpretation. The universalist, Hare tells us,

> will realise that our moral opinions are liable to change in the light of our experience and our discussion of moral questions with other people. Therefore, if another person disagrees with us, what is called for is not the suppression of his opinions, but a discussion, in the hope that, when he has told us the reasons for his, and we for ours, we may reach agreement. Universalism is thus an ethical theory which makes moral argument both possible and fruitful.[5]

---

[3]   McNaughton, p. 54.
[4]   Crispin Wright, *Saving the Differences: Essays on Themes from* Truth and Objectivity (Cambridge, MA: Harvard University Press, 2003) p. 163.
[5]   R.M. Hare, *Freedom and Reason* (Oxford: Oxford University Press, 1960) p. 60.

In this passage Hare cannot be equating what is worthwhile with what the agent believes to be worthwhile as Wiggins supposes, since his point is precisely that our experience of life and our discussions with other people may bring us to see that our previous ideas of what is worthwhile were mistaken. Consider, as an example, the situation of R.J. Bowman in Eudora Welty's study of the tension between agrarianism and commercialism, 'Death of a Travelling Salesman'. At the start of the story Bowman's life, that of a successful shoe salesman, is presented to the reader as an endless series of hotel rooms and brief encounters with nameless women. Of course Bowman does not think of his life in this way. By his own standards he has been successful, moving to 'better hotels in bigger towns', and when, recovering from a serious illness, he crashes his car after taking a wrong turn on the road to Beulah, Mississippi, and is forced to take refuge at the shack of a young farming couple, he sees this as a temporary diversion from the realities of life, from progress to greater and greater successes. For the life which he encounters there, a life which has remained constant for centuries, seems to him pointless and futile, its relationships incomprehensible. Observing the way in which such ideas as ambition and progress, central to his own life, have no significance to the man and woman who take pity on him, and reflecting that 'these people never knew where the very roads they lived on went to', he is inclined simply to discount them as shallow and stupid. It is not until he suddenly realises that the woman, whom he had taken to be aged, is in fact young and pregnant, that he begins to suspect that it is his own life which is futile.

> Bowman could not speak. He was shocked with knowing what was really in this house. A marriage, a fruitful marriage. That simple thing. Anyone could have that.
>
> Somehow he felt unable to be indignant or protest, although some sort of joke had certainly been played on him. There was nothing remote or mysterious here, only something private. The only secret was the ancient communication between two people. But the memory of the woman's waiting silently by the cold hearth, of the man's stubborn journey a mile away to get fire, and how they finally brought out their food and drink and filled the

room with all they had to show was suddenly too clear, too enormous for him to respond.[6]

Bowman's mistake was to suppose that the significance of a person's life must be found in progress and change, so that he sees the unvarying ritual of the couple's life only as monotonous and empty. Nothing there has any significance for him precisely because nothing changes. Gradually, however, it dawns on him that there can be aspects of people's lives whose value lies precisely in their lack of change. We see this is his recognition that the couple's home is a home precisely because, unlike him, they are not going anywhere, that their marriage has value just because, unlike his own fleeting encounters, it does not change. But the point is beautifully expressed in Eudora Welty's description of the ceremonial aspects of the husband's mile-long journey to get fire:

'Sonny', said the woman, 'You'll have to borry some fire.'

'I'll go git it from Redmond's,' said Sonny.

'What?' Bowman strained to hear their words to each other.

'Our fire, it's out, and Sonny's got to borry some, because it's dark an' cold,' she said.

'But matches — I have matches —'

'We don't have no need for 'em,' she said proudly. 'Sonny's goin' after his own fire.'

'I'm goin' to Redmond's,' said Sonny with an air of importance, and he went out.

After they had waited a while, Bowman looked out of the window and saw a light moving over the hill. It spread itself out like a little fan. It zigzagged along the field, darting and swift, not like Sonny at all … Soon enough, Sonny staggered in, holding a burning stick behind him in tongs, fire flowing in his wake, blazing light into the corners of the room.

'We'll make a fire now,' the woman said, taking the brand.[7]

Only a philosopher whose theories, unlike those of for example Hare, denied the possibility of moral change would find difficulty in explaining Bowman's recognition that he has been mistaken. For that recognition consists precisely in a change in his own values. He sees that he was mistaken in the value he attached to

---

6   Eudora Welty, *The Collected Short Stories of Eudora Welty* (New York: Harcourt, 1982) p. 129.

7   Ibid., p. 127.

variety and change, just in so far as he starts to value permanence and stability and to regret its absence in his own life.

Now the realist sees the possibility of such an explanation and finds it unsatisfactory. McNaughton expresses the difficulty in this way:

> For non-cognitivism the only way to express the thought that I may find myself in error is the thought that my opinions may change. But the thought that my opinions may change is not the thought that I may discover that I was wrong.[8]

At first sight this might seem a puzzling remark, for plainly Bowman could not think that he had been mistaken if his opinions had not changed, and his opinions could not have changed without his thinking that he was mistaken, so that it might seem, in the abstract so to speak, as though the two were indeed equivalent. But the puzzle disappears when we realise that what McNaughton wishes to emphasise here is not some logically dubious distinction between my changing my opinions and my coming to the view that I was mistaken, but rather the distinction between what is really the case in morality and any of my moral views—or for that matter any of the moral views of anyone else. That is to say, like other realists, McNaughton wishes to distinguish between what we as human beings, creatures prone to error, hold to be important and what really is important, between the things we value and what really is valuable. It is not merely that the agent may change so that he rejects his old ideas of what is important in favour of new ideas, from which standpoint he now sees the old ideas as mistaken. Rather the claim is being made that there is some standpoint from which all our ideas, old as well as new, and in addition all the ideas of anyone else, might be seen to be mistaken, that we might all of us be mistaken on some moral question.

Now it is clear that the distinction between what people think is important and what really is important does in certain contexts have a sense, or rather it has more than one sense depending on the context. But it is also important to notice that it does not have an absolutely general sense, a sense which remains constant whatever the context. Consider for example the view which I have heard expressed that, as a handgun, the Colt 45 was constantly underrated even by those who used it, that is to say, that it was

---

8   p. 66.

not valued in proportion to its real value. The force of this claim lies in the ability of those making it to draw attention to features of the pistol, for instance reliability and accuracy, which are normally valued, but which tended to be ignored in this particular case. The speaker, that is, believes that it is possible to correct the judgement of those he is criticising by an appeal to an independent standard, a standard which they themselves accept but misapply in this case. For once you know what a gun is and what it is for, then you cannot fail to regard its accuracy and reliability as important. Contrast now this case with G.K. Chesterton's famous remark that to say 'My country right or wrong' is on the same moral level as saying 'My mother drunk or sober'. Chesterton's point was that at the time (the time of the Boer War) the belief that one should support the policies of one's country, even where those policies were plainly immoral was almost universal in Britain. But this, Chesterton felt, was to overvalue one variety of patriotism and to undervalue such things as justice. Anyone who really cared for their country would be concerned that its policies should be right, just as anyone who really cared for their mother would be concerned that she remain sober. Now it is clear that in his criticism of jingo patriotism, Chesterton was not appealing to some independent standard shared by those whose views he rejected, for example the value of justice. On the contrary, his criticism was just that those he criticised did not have any concern for justice. Unlike in the previous case, the claim that justice had been undervalued makes no appeal to something independent of the conflicting values, but simply indicates a commitment to one of the values.

There is then no reason to suppose that when Chesterton draws a distinction between what people regard as important and what is really important, between patriotism and justice, he must be making an appeal to anything independent of what is valued, to some external standpoint against which all values are to be measured. Unfortunately there is a strong temptation to suppose just this and to imagine that the only alternative is a form of extreme subjectivism. For the realist imagines that if it is possible to speak of what is really important, important independently of what this or that person may at some point think is important, then we shall be forced to the conclusion that there is some moral reality which is independent of our moral beliefs and which determines whether they are true or false, tenable or untenable. For the realist, that is to say, there is a straightforward inference from:

'What is really morally important is independent of what any one of us may think is important.'

to:

'There is a moral reality which is independent of our moral beliefs.'

Unfortunately what the realist generally fails to notice is that the inference only seems straightforward because of a fatal ambiguity in the phrase 'independent of our moral beliefs'. For it may mean either 'independent of any particular moral belief which I may hold at some particular time' or it may mean 'independent of all the moral beliefs which I might hold at any time'. Perhaps the best way in which to see this is to notice that in one sense, R.J. Bowman might have admitted, or indeed insisted, that there was a moral reality independent of his beliefs. That amounts to saying that his valuing variety was not what made it valuable. He might, for example, have asked himself, 'I have always valued variety, but is it really important?' Clearly, if this question is to have any sense, then what is really important cannot be determined by what he thinks is important. But it by no means follows that in order to give sense to 'what is really important', we have to appeal to something independent of all his moral beliefs – only of this moral belief. But, as we have seen this is not the only belief to play a part in his perplexity. If it were, then there would be no perplexity. He comes also to feel the attraction of the idea that permanence is more important. So that when he asks whether honesty is really important, the force of the 'really' here is to refer to the other possibility which he is considering, namely that permanence is more important. The reality in question is not one which is completely independent, even, of how the issues might strike Bowman. Still less is it independent of how of how they might strike anyone.

This, however, is precisely the way in which the moral realist is tempted to interpret the notion of 'reality' here. For him there are answers to moral questions which can be established independently of what may strike people as important, so that the true answer to Bowman's dilemma might be waiting to be discovered if not by him, then by someone else – 'part of the fabric of the world' – to use a phrase of McNaughton's which seems perfectly to encapsulate the idea. And of course the realist does have a point here, though a limited one. For it does make sense to speak of our discovering features of morality, just as it makes sense to speak of our discovering that Siberia is warm in summer or that the new car which we bought burns large quantities of oil. I may say that during my marriage I have discovered that fidelity is not so important as tolerance. Or that in my teens I found out that pomposity is a more profound failing than deceit. And in so far as it is not wholly misleading to say that the person who discovers the oil consumption of their new car is discovering a feature of the world (rather than, as I should prefer to say, a feature of the car), then it is probably no more misleading to say this of the person who learns the importance of tolerance.

Nevertheless, the point is a limited one, and can be given force in the debate between the realist and, say, the prescriptivist or the utilitarian only in conjunction with some specific account of what is meant by 'discovery' in this case. If, as is claimed, moral properties form part of the fabric of the world, then what we require is some account of how this part of the fabric is detected, not, as the realist is sometimes prone to suggest, in the interests of philosophical completeness, but because, in the absence of such an account, the utilitarian will simply concede the point about discovery, but insist that what is to be discovered is always the consequences of our actions for the general happiness, and the naturalist will concede the point about discovery, but insists that what is to be discovered is the presence or absence of some non-moral fact about human needs and wants.

Unfortunately, there is a tendency at this point for the realist to ignore the difficulty and once again to take refuge in the platitudinous. The tendency is clearly detectable in Mark Platts' remark that we detect the moral aspects of a situation 'in the same way that we detect (nearly all) other aspects: by looking and seeing',[9] but we have already noticed it in McNaughton, when he offers us the claim that 'we see McEnroe's rudeness on the tennis court' in the course of explaining what the realist is committed to. For even if we ignore the familiar empiricist trick of concentrating on the sense of sight as though this were in some way typical of all the senses, it is nevertheless clear that the emphasis on what our senses reveal is, at least in this form, so uncontroversial as to be useless in identifying any particular philosophical standpoint. For,

---

[9]   Mark Platts, *Ways of Meaning: An Introduction to a Philosophy of Language* (Cambridge, MA: MIT Press, 1997) p. 247.

of course, we see McEnroe's rudeness on the tennis court or, more probably, hear it. If we deny that we have done so, then this will normally be because, having stayed on late to work that evening, we missed the match, or because, distracted by the antics of the ballboys, we did not notice the crucial events on court. To say, in the normal course of events, that though we saw McEnroe throw his racket at his opponent, heard him question the umpire's sanity, we failed to observe the rudeness, would so far be simply incomprehensible. So it follows that if the realist's appeal to 'seeing' is to have any force, then this must lie not in the bald assertion that it makes sense to speak of seeing what is right or wrong, which it would be difficult to deny, but in the particular account which the realist gives of what is sometimes referred to as moral vision.

There are, of course, a variety of complex ways in which the notion of 'seeing' may be cashed by the realist. For example, our failure to see the wrongness of an action may be said to be analogous to the way in which we may fail to see a pattern in an apparently random series of shapes, or to the way in which we may be blinded by our emotions. But despite the differences, all rely on one aspect of the notion of 'seeing' which is admittedly crucial in very many contexts, in order to smuggle it into their account of morality — and that is, once again, the reference to what exists independently. The matter is, it is true, complicated by the mistaken account of seeing vision normally taken for granted by empiricists, according to which something may correctly be said to be seen if it exists within the agent's visual field, and so I may fail to see a tank because it has been well-camouflaged, and so I cannot make out its shape from the foliage surrounding it. But to say that I fail to see it, has the sense that it does precisely because the tank is there whether or not I (or for that matter anyone else) sees it. Again, I recently read a letter in my local paper in which a neighbour advocated the extermination of the snake population of Gower, on the grounds of their propensity to unprovoked attacks on people's dogs. If I were to say of this correspondent that her emotions, in this case her love of her pets, had blinded her to reality, this remark would draw its sense from the possibility of pointing to the feature of reality to which she had been blinded. For whatever your feelings about adders, it is simply an observable fact that, unlike water-moccasins, they will attack only when provoked, for example in response to the attentions of an aggressive terrier. In this case, as in the former, the agent's blindness was to be explained by reference to what is there to be seen — a tank, the natural behaviour of reptiles — independently of whether anyone actually sees it or not.

What is questionable is whether this aspect of the notions of vision and blindness has any role to play in morality. Consider the following passage where Allan Bloom is describing the responses of his students on being asked who they regard as evil.

> To this there is an immediate response: Hitler (Stalin is hardly mentioned). After him, who else? Up until a couple of years ago, a few students said Nixon, but he has been forgotten and at the same time is being rehabilitated. And there it stops. They have no idea of evil; they doubt its existence. Hitler is just another abstraction, an item to fill up an empty category.
>
> Although they live in a world in which the most terrible crimes are being performed and they see brutal crime on the streets, they turn aside.[10]

The students Bloom describes here are people of whom it might be said that they are blind to the reality of evil. It is, he tells us, another facet of their inability to detect great goodness. One might agree or disagree with his assessment of contemporary American youth. But it is clear that nothing that he says commits him to any particular philosophical theory. In particular, it does not commit him to a realist view of morality. Nor, more importantly, does a commitment to a realist account so far help us to understand the phenomenon which Bloom is describing. Bloom characterises the malady as a lack of gravity, a lack of 'an awareness of the depths as well as the heights'. But it is not clear that the analogy with vision which the realist has so far provided us with will help us to understand what has gone wrong in this case. If I tell you that the man walking along the road has defective eyesight, then I may well explain the way in which he is acting or why he makes the judgements that he does. He walked into the car because he did not realise that it was there, or he thought that it was his friend speaking to him, because he could not see him clearly. These explanations can function as explanations, just because the man's defective eyesight is something which can be established independently, for example by an optician, without reference to the judgements which he makes about the car or the facial features

---

10   Allan Bloom, *The Closing of the American Mind* (New York: Simon and Schuster, 1987) p. 67.

of his friend: if it can be established that he fails to see features which are there to be seen, features which are 'part of the fabric of the world', if one insists on speaking in this way. By contrast, if I tell you that the students live their lives in the way they do, make the judgements they do, because they are blind to the reality of evil, or because, as Bloom says, 'they doubt the existence of evil', then I have not so far explained why it is that they make these judgements or live their lives the way they do. I have simply characterised their judgements and their lives as shallow or insensitive. It is not that their shallowness or lack of sensitivity is an independently identifiable feature of their lives, which, by blinding them to reality, leads them to make the judgements they do. Rather their shallowness consists precisely in their making the judgements that the do make.

This, of course, is exactly what the realist denies. For whatever form it takes, the appeal to the notion of 'coming to see' what is right or wrong, or to the allied notion of 'moral blindness' is believed to have very considerable explanatory force. It is supposed to explain their judgements by reference to something which is independent of those judgements. On this account the students in Bloom's example do not judge the atrocities that surround them to be evil, because they do not see, though they might be brought to see, some independently existent moral aspect. Their blindness to this aspect is supposed to explain their judgements. In the same way, the realist construes the perfectly ordinary situation in which we may say that someone's moral judgements have changed because they have come to see something to which they had previously been blind, not as a way of characterising the change in the judgements that they make, but as an explanation of this change. This point comes out clearly in McNaughton's discussion of the following passage from George Orwell's famous account of a hanging in Burma.

> At each step his muscles slid neatly into place, the lock of hair on his scalp lanced up and down, his feet planted themselves on the wet gravel. And once, in spite of the men who gripped him by each shoulder, he stepped slightly aside, to avoid a puddle on the path. It is curious, but till that moment I had never realised what it means to destroy a healthy, conscious man. When I saw the prisoner step aside to avoid the puddle, I saw the mystery, the

unspeakable wrongness of cutting a life short, when it is in full tide. This man was not dying, he was alive as we were alive.[11]

McNaughton is inclined to reject two possible accounts of what Orwell had learned from witnessing the prisoner's walk to the gallows. In the first place he rejects the suggestion that Orwell had learned some new (non-moral) fact about execution, some new piece of information, which forced him to revise his earlier views about hanging. And in the second place he rejects the suggestion that Orwell's observations had revealed some inconsistency in his earlier views. 'While it might be the case that all such experiences could be explained in one of these ways', he observes, 'it seems unlikely.'[12] But this conclusion is surely excessively timid. For what fact could have demonstrated to Orwell that capital punishment is an evil? Certainly not the fact which Orwell mentions that the prisoner stepped aside to avoid a puddle. The argument: condemned men avoid puddles, so capital punishment is wrong, seems not so much risky as incomprehensible. And what inconsistency could it be that Orwell's experiences had revealed? Certainly Orwell lays great emphasis on the fact that the man who was about to be hanged was alive, and believed that in some way fully to appreciate this fact is to understand the evil of capital punishment.

He and we were a party of men walking together, seeing, hearing, feeling, understanding the same world; and in two minutes, with a sudden snap, one of us would be gone—one mind less, one world less.[13]

But this is in no way inconsistent with believing execution to be the appropriate way to treat a criminal. In his fine essay on capital punishment, 'Reflection on the Guillotine', Albert Camus claimed to identify an inconsistency between the secrecy which surrounds most executions and the justification most often given for capital punishment, that it deters others. For, Camus observed, if one really wished to deter possible murderers, one might be expected to give as much publicity as possible to the horrors which await those who commit such a crime. But, whether or not Camus has

---

11   George Orwell, *The Orwell Reader: Fiction, Essays, and Reportage* (New York: Harcourt, 1956) p. 11.

12   *Moral Vision*, p. 103.

13   Op. cit., p. 11.

here identified a genuine inconsistency, it is clear that there is none such in the case Orwell describes. There is no inconsistency in believing that capital punishment is defensible, and that the people who suffer it are alive when they do so. On the contrary, had the prisoner in Orwell's story not been alive, the warders would not have troubled to take him to the gallows.

Luckily, however, these are not the only alternatives. The moral realist, McNaughton observes,

> offers us a third possibility; that such an experience can reveal the moral quality of the action; so that the agent comes to revise his theory in the light of his moral observations.[14]

What Orwell came to see, then, is not some new fact about capital punishment of which he had been ignorant, not some hitherto unrevealed inconsistency in his views, but some moral value to which he had been blind. He had failed to observe, not some fact about hanging or some incoherence in the justifications offered for it, which made it wrong, but rather the wrongness itself.

No doubt there are features of Orwell's essay which may make the interpretation attractive to someone of a certain philosophical persuasion. Indeed, though McNaughton himself does not notice this, the appositeness of the example from the realist's point of view lies in Orwell's contention expressed explicitly elsewhere, but nevertheless implicit in his account of the hanging, that anyone who actually witnesses an execution will see it for what it is, a morally terrible action. For all of those involved—the Indian warders, the negro jailer, the army doctor, the Eurasian assistant, the Hindu prisoner, Orwell himself—that is to say, everyone regardless of their moral viewpoint or social background, is portrayed as recognising the dreadfulness of what is being done.

But what is it, that the rest of us miss, that those mentioned come to see? What is it to see what a hanging is really like? The realist seems to believe that no answer can be given except that what we see is the moral quality—the dreadfulness—of the action. And a casual glance might indeed suggest that this is what Orwell is saying. He came to see, he says, 'the unspeakable wrongness of cutting short a life when it is in full tide'. But this is to sell Orwell rather short. For the central point which he is making is rather more complicated and concerns the contrast between the way in

---

[14]   Op. cit., p. 104.

which at least those not opposed to capital punishment may be inclined to think of the actual process of executing a man, as a job, which, however disagreeable, someone has to do, and the way in which anyone actually involved in a hanging will see it. Anyone, Orwell is saying, when actually faced with the task of executing someone will find it difficult or impossible to think of it as simply a job. For, like him, they will be struck by the contrast between the routine nature of the preparations, and the character of the act for which they are preparations, namely the ending of someone's world. In Orwell's description it is the routine, the everyday, occurrences – the prisoner stepping aside to avoid a puddle, a dog jumping up to lick his face as he walks to the gallows – which bring out the full horror of what is a happening. The point is driven home in the grotesque character of the head jailer's observations to the superintendent as they return from the gallows:

> It is worse when they become refractory! One man, I recall, clung to the bars of his cage when we went to take him out. You will scarcely credit, sir, that it is took six warders to dislodge him, three pulling at each leg. We reasoned with him, 'My dear fellow,' we said, 'think of all the pain and trouble you are causing us! But no, he would not listen.'[15]

What Orwell saw at the jail in Burman was, in one perfectly ordinary sense of the verb 'to see', a condemned man step aside to avoid a puddle. In another perfectly ordinary sense of 'see' he came to see the tension between the idea that execution is some-one's job (in this case, his own) and the nature of what was being done in killing a man. But there is an important difference between these two senses. For the prisoner stepped aside to avoid a puddle whether or not anyone judged that he had done so. Whereas to speak in the latter sense of what Orwell saw, is to speak of his judgements themselves and not of their relationship to something else. What Orwell saw was the impossibility of thinking and speaking of capital punishment in a certain way.

The point becomes even clearer if we ask what is missed by someone who fails to see the tension which Orwell identifies. Such a man, I believe, was the last British hangman, Albert Pierpoint. For Pierpoint insisted that he did indeed think of his profession as

---

15   Op. cit., p. 13.

just a job, and a job in which he regarded himself as a craftsman and took great pride. I suppose that if I had to say why Pierpoint did not notice those features of capital punishment which struck Orwell, I should say that he had become brutalised or rendered insensitive by his work. But any comparison between Pierpoint's insensitivity, his failure to see, and the insensitivity of someone with defective eyesight is purely superficial. As we have seen, when I explain someone's mistaken judgements by appealing to their defective eyesight, my explanation links their judgements to something which can be established independently of those judgements. Because of this the explanation is hypothetical in form, offer an hypothesis, which may be confirmed or disconfirmed, that their judgements are to be explained by reference to their defective eyesight. By contrast, when I say that Pierpoint failed to see certain moral aspects of a profession which consisted in killing people, there is nothing hypothetical about this judgement. The insensitivity did not blind Pierpoint to certain independently ascertainable features of the world and so lead him to judge in a certain way. The insensitivity lay in judging in that way itself.

The realist's introduction of the concept of the independently real as a part of the explanation of the phenomenon of moral vision is, then, a mere illusion. For this concept has no part to play in understanding what it is to speak of seeing something as right or wrong. But to see this is to remove the last vestige of explanatory power from the realist's theories, and to show these theories for what they are, a mere series of platitudes, where what is in question is not the platitudes themselves, but rather the philosophical gloss which the realist places on them.

12

Autobiography and the Brain[1]

There is in philosophy a long tradition of employing epistemological theories in order to cast light on issues in ethics, aesthetics, politics. It is, for example, difficult to explain Hume's ethics without reference to his theory of knowledge. Sometimes indeed, and Hume would again be an example, the epistemological theory is introduced with the express intention of throwing light on the problems in question.

This is the case with Mary Warnock's book *Memory*.[2] For her intention is to illuminate certain issues which might be said to fall roughly within the province of aesthetics by an examination of the concept of memory. Only, she argues, by a careful examination of this concept can we explain the value which is attached to recollection in literature, both in its explicit form in autobiography and in the less explicit form which it takes in the work of writers such as Dickens and Proust. The procedure has its attractions, for if successful it will show that the issues in aesthetics are not, as they have often been regarded, merely peripheral to the central issues in Philosophy, but have an important connection with these issues. But it is not without its dangers. For it can also (as again in the case of Hume) furnish us with striking examples of the power of epistemological confusions to infect the discussion of other areas of the subject. This, it seems to me, is a danger to which *Memory* is not wholly immune.

[1]   First published in *British Journal of Aesthetics*, 29 (3), 1989. © British Society of Aesthetics, 1989.
[2]   M. Warnock, *Memory* (London: Faber & Faber, 1987).

The theory which forms the epistemological basis of Warnock's book is what is generally known as central state materialism or the mind-brain identity theory. Warnock admits that so far no satisfactory statement of this theory can be given, but she believes that eventually—and perhaps given advances in other subjects—one will be forthcoming. She refers to this as 'a statement of faith',[3] but probably 'prejudice' would be a more accurate term; not that Warnock would object to this, since it is a word she also uses. The issue of the truth or perhaps, since there are those who see conceptual difficulties in it, the sense of the theory is being prejudged.

But this is not *merely* a matter of faith, merely a prejudice, since Warnock thinks that in at least one case, that of memory, there are compelling reasons for accepting the theory. While it might seem plausible to claim that there can be no causal account in terms of brain-processes of imagination, belief, knowledge (though, given that she accepts some version of the identity theory, Warnock must believe that at least in the long run such accounts will become available), no such claim can be made in the case of memory. 'We shall never understand the role that memory plays in ... art and life unless we are thoroughly prepared to accept its connections in the systems of the brain.'[4] For when we speak of memory we are in fact assuming such connections. Their existence is in some way involved in the sense of what we say, such that in any philosophical discussion of memory we are 'bound' to bring in reference to the brain.

This being so, it is of course crucial that Warnock should be able to demonstrate the inadequacy of those traditional accounts of memory which make no reference to brain processes, in particular those which seek to explain it as either the possession of a type of mental image or as a special kind of knowledge, namely knowledge of the past. The former view is, however, easy to dispose of. For there can, after all, be nothing about a mental image (at least when conceived of in empiricist terms as a variety of mental picture), which makes it an image of the past, and so nothing, in the empiricist's own terms, to distinguish memory and, say, imagination.

The latter account of memory, as a sort of knowledge, has a greater initial plausibility, and presents Warnock with greater

---

3   Ibid., p. 3.
4   Ibid., p. 14.

difficulties. Nevertheless, she believes this also to be inadequate, since it fails to distinguish those cases where knowledge of the past is obtained through memory and those cases where it is derived from some other source. We may, for example, have knowledge of incidents in our early childhood, but wonder whether we remember these incidents or whether our knowledge of them is merely hearsay. Clearly, or so the argument goes, the puzzle here cannot concern whether we have knowledge of the incidents in question, since this will be common both to hearsay and memory, and so the question arises: what distinguishes the two?

Warnock's suggestion, adapted from a remark by Richard Wollheim, is that at this point the required distinction can be made and the philosophical puzzles dispelled by introducing a reference to brain-processes. For when we ask whether we really remember something or were rather told it, what we are asking is whether our present knowledge of the past was caused by our past experience. Memory is distinguished from hearsay by the existence or absence of a causal chain linking a past experience with a present state.

Even at this early stage in her argument, Warnock's procedure is puzzling. When I wonder whether I really remember the house in which I lived as a child or whether I learned about it from friends and relatives or was shown photographs, there is in one way no harm in saying that I am wondering how my knowledge of it was caused (if only because there is sufficient variety in our use of the word 'cause' to make the claim almost impossible to deny—in some sense or other). But it is certainly an odd way of expressing my question and in another way it is highly mis-leading, for by offering the causal account as an account of what memory *is* (knowledge caused by a past experience), it implies that the question 'How did you come by this knowledge, by memory or in some other way?' is in *all* cases an appropriate one (for the answer to it is in all cases of genuine memory said to be 'by virtue of a series of causal connections'). But a moment's reflection will show this to be mistaken. If I am asked what I had for breakfast this morning, or whether I am married, then my remembering consists *simply* in my giving a correct answer to the questions, that is to say, in my showing that I have knowledge of the past. The suggestion that this cannot be the case, since my knowledge might stem not from memory but from someone having told me, would in such cases be merely fanciful (just as the

question 'How did you find out what you had for breakfast?' or
'How did you find out that you are married?' would, except in
special circumstances which do not apply in my case, be
gibberish). But even where the question how I came about a piece
of knowledge (did I remember it, or was I told?) would be a
sensible question, it has nothing to do with the operation of the
brain. If I wonder whether I really remember the house in which I
was born, then I am not wondering, except in a very strained
sense, how my knowledge was caused. I am not, as Warnock
suggests, wondering about continuities in the brain. I am simply
wondering whether I was told. Courts of law, which are after all in
the business of deciding whether the witness actually remembers
the colour of the suspect's eyes or was fed the information by an
over-zealous policeman bent on securing a conviction, concern
themselves simply with establishing whether the witness was able
to answer the question only after being briefed by the police, and
not with any causal investigation which we have in any case no
idea whatsoever how to conduct. If the witness is not really
remembering (which will, interestingly enough, be normally taken
by the court to mean 'does not really know'), then there will have
been a point after the crime, when he was unable to answer the
question, that is to say, a point at which he did not know. If one is
tempted to speak of continuity here, a temptation which it would
probably be as well to resist, then the continuity in question is not
the continuity which characterises a causal process but simply the
continuity of someone's knowledge (their continued ability to, *e.g.*,
answer a question). So once again remembering turns out, *contra*
Warnock, to consist in knowledge of the past, the only proviso
being that in certain fairly exceptional cases there may be a
question about the continuity of this knowledge.

   Thus far, then, Warnock's discussion of the topic of recollection
fails in its original aim, that of showing how an epistemological
theory (the identity thesis) can throw light on the issues of
aesthetics, specifically how it can illuminate the importance and
value which we attach to autobiography. For if the theory is false,
then it can cast no light. It does not, however, follow that
epistemology becomes irrelevant here. For though it casts no light,
it may nevertheless cast shadow. It may obscure rather than
illuminate. So it is important to examine the use to which Warnock
now puts her account of memory in the subsequent discussion. In
particular, it is important to notice one consequence of her
epistemological theory to which she draws attention fairly early in

the book, namely that her account so far involves no reference to the fact that human beings possess a language. Nor is this accidental. For from the beginning Warnock emphasises that animals, who do not possess language, can be said to recollect *in just the same sense* that humans do. Indeed, this claim is important to Warnock's whole project, since central among her grounds for supposing that a 'causal, scientific account of memory can be given is an appeal to "our" belief that a causal, scientific account of an animal's life is possible', and one of the features of this life will be that it involves memory.

Now it is certainly true that (in some sense of 'scientific') a scientific account of an animal's life is possible—think, for example, of the account of the life-cycle of a frog in a textbook of natural history. But it is also possible to give a nonscientific story of an animal's life, as, for example, in Jack London's *White Fang*. And on the face of it, claims about an animal's remembering, recollecting and so on are likely to fit more comfortably into the latter than into the former, so that Warnock's argument does not seem particularly convincing here. Nevertheless, its consequences are interesting, since it commits her to a certain view of the relationship between language and memory.

> Learning from the past, whether by animals or men, entails a certain ability to pick out features of a situation and think of them as able to recur. This ability is the very same as that which enables a man or any other creature to treat certain features as significant. If features could not recur they could not be significant. [A] nervous horse may see features as significantly recurring in circumstances not identical with the first circumstance in which he was frightened. If he has once been frightened by having to enter a horse-box, it does not need to be the same horse-box in the same place which makes him react with fear a second time.[5]

One sort of theorist, faced with such an example, will insist that the horse is simply displaying the phenomenon of conditioning. Warnock, perhaps seeing the implausibility of this analysis (implausible, that is, to anyone who knows anything about horses, or has reflected on the stupidity of an account which implies the vast majority of the ways we naturally speak of an animal's behaviour are examples of anthropomorphism), insists that human and animal behaviour can often be spoken of in just the

---

5   Warnock, p. 11.

same ways. As we have seen, this commits her to the view that animals, lacking language, are nevertheless able to recognise *kinds*. 'Such identification of kinds is intimately linked with memory, both in horses and men (or any other animals).'[6] It also has the consequence that the identification of kinds in humans must also occur in the absence of language.

> If you look at an Osbert Lancaster drawing, you may be delighted by the representation of 'Stockbroker's Tudor'. This is because you recognise the features of architecture you have seen dozens of times in your life but never perhaps so sharply. The wit of such drawings is dependent on your recognition of what they portray, and the giving of a name to what never had a name before. You recognise the kind and then accept the word. The word is not necessary before you can recognise.[7]

Warnock speaks as though her conclusion in this passage is inherently obvious, but this is probably because it follows from her general account of memory. For, if, as she claims, memory consists in this, that an experience sets up in the brain a causal chain linking the experience with a present state, then it is, to say the least, difficult to see how the possession of language *can* make any difference to whether this process occurs. If I flinch as a result of placing my hand on a hot radiator, then it seems quite plausible to suppose that my reaction can be explained in causal terms. But plainly the reaction does not depend on my possessing a language in which to identify the source of my discomfort. An animal or a small child would have reacted in just the same way. So it is not surprising that, thinking of recollection in an analogous way, Warnock should insist here on the irrelevance of language to recollection. Unfortunately, the example which she uses to illustrate the point could in many ways scarcely be a worse choice. For it *is* natural to say of examples such as the Lancaster drawing that they display wit or imagination, that they bring us to notice things which we had not noticed before, that they illuminate various features of our lives, and so on. But if, as Warnock insists, what Lancaster does when he identifies a style of architecture as 'Stockbroker's Tudor' is merely to give a label to what has already been recognised, then it is difficult to see how these ways of speaking

---

6   Ibid.
7   Ibid.

can be appropriate. In itself giving a name to something is not the kind of thing which can be referred to as 'imaginative'.

Warnock, however, does not see (or perhaps, at this stage, ignores) the difficulty. Having, as she believes, established the importance for an account of memory of the notion of a causal process, she now moves to the question which forms the central theme of her book, that of the value which we attach to memory, or rather, since she is not primarily concerned with the everyday aspects of memory (remembering the soap powder or the children's birthdays), the value which we attach to reflective recollection particularly in the form which it takes in novels and biographies. For so far her analysis of memory with its emphasis on causality and what is common between animals and human beings does not seem to offer much prospect of answering the question with which the book opens: why do we value memory in the form of reminiscence; why, for example, do we read autobiographies?

If I understand her correctly, Warnock's claim is that if someone's reminiscences, whether in the disguised form in which they sometimes appear in fiction or explicitly in autobiography, are to have any significance for us, they must be turned into a story. They must, that is to say, be given a certain unity. But it is here that memory alone becomes obviously inadequate. True there could be no story for us to value were it not for memory, and so, if Warnock's account is correct, were it not for the causal sequences which make memory possible. But the mere existence of such causal patterns will not provide us with a story. And it is at this point that language, having earlier been excluded from the account of what constitutes recollection, now reappears. For humans differ from animals not, as we have seen, in possessing the capacity for recollection, but rather in possessing imagination. And it is this which characterises autobiography. For in so far as the story of a life involves description, involves the biographer in finding words to describe his memories, then what we have is a work of imagination 'in the sense in which any search after expression in language is'.[8] Autobiography is valuable just because it involves the collaboration of memory and imagination.

Now in so far as Warnock thinks that this account is adequate then she is plainly wrong. And it is not, I think, difficult to see that

---

8   Ibid., p. 120.

the account we have been given is inadequate because it involves analogous difficulties to those which we have already noted in connection with her account of memory and recognition. As we saw, if the only role which language can have in connection with human memory is that of providing a name for, that is to say labelling, what memory has already identified, then there is a difficulty in seeing how such a use of language can be said to display imagination or to be enlightening. But similarly, if the only role which language can play in autobiography is that of finding words to label the writer's experiences, then it is difficult to see how *this* procedure can provide us with something of imaginative value. In an essay on Salvador Dali, George Orwell once made the suggestion that autobiography is to be trusted only when it reveals something disgraceful about a man. For, he remarked, 'Any life, when viewed from the inside, is always a series of defeats.'[9] No doubt Orwell's view is excessively cynical (though it was probably coloured by his assessment of his own life). What makes it cynical, however, is simply the generality of the claim. We can at least admit that *many* lives are like this. So if we now ask how the account of such a life would differ from an auto-biography which we might regard as genuinely illuminating or valuable, it is clear that neither of the features of autobiography which Warnock has so far described, neither the causal conti-nuities which allegedly underpin the biographer's memories, nor the use of language to label those memories, will give us much help in making the distinction. The causal continuities cannot, since they will, according to Warnock, underlie the account of *any* life, whether it be *The Seven Pillars of Wisdom* or the dreary recounting of a series of disasters. But nor can the use of language, at least as Warnock conceives it, since this will also be present in both accounts. In both cases the biographer will have chosen words to describe his experiences. So far, then, Warnock seems to have failed to answer her original question, 'Why do we value autobiography?', at least in so far as the question means (as it certainly should) 'Why do we value *some* autobiographies (and not others)?'

It is here that Warnock begins to suggest a somewhat different account of language from what has preceded. For so far she has

---

9   'Benefit of Clergy: Some Notes on Salvador Dali', p. 156, in *Collected Essays, Journalism and Letters*, Vol. 111.

talked as though *any* search after expression is a work of imagination. But this can only be true if a search after expression does not consist simply in finding words to label our experiences, but something else. After all, if I tell you that I felt nauseous after a heavy lunch, I might well have accurately identified my feelings, but I would scarcely be said to have shown imagination. So that when Warnock goes on to suggest that what shows imagination is what has 'universal significance',[10] or what enables us to 'achieve a universal and timeless understanding of what things are like'[11] it becomes clear that we are now dealing with a new sense of 'imagination'. The difference becomes even more obvious when she remarks that 'in attempting to find words for our experiences we are actually creating ourselves and our world'.[12] For even allowing that this way of speaking is presumably metaphorical (despite the occurrence of the word 'actually'), it is quite apparent that we have here a way of thinking of imaginative expression, in which it does not simply mean 'describing what is not before our eyes',[13] and one which also shows a tension with (if it does not directly contradict) Warnock's earlier concept of language as a sort of labelling.

So it is worth asking here how far that conception can be defended. As we have seen, according to Warnock, the wit of Lancaster's representation of 'Stockbroker's Tudor' lies in his having given a name to a kind of architecture which previously had no name. Now plainly, as it stands this will not do. At the very least, one would have thought, the wit must be in the new name's being witty. So it appears that the wit has not yet been explained. Moreover, it seems obvious that Warnock would be in some difficulty if we were to ask *what* kind of architecture it is that we recognise in the cartoon (without of course using Lancaster's phrase). But let us allow that someone might have a stab at it. 'You will have noticed', they say, 'how new wealth often goes hand in hand with a desire to possess what has some permanence, some history. We are familiar with this phenomenon in the very rich where it takes the form of pop millionaires buying country estates or Victorian entrepreneurs buying themselves into titled families.

---

[10]   Warnock, p. 133.
[11]   Ibid., p. 94.
[12]   Ibid., p. 112.
[13]   Ibid., p. 75.

But notice also how those who have not yet reached such dizzy heights, stockbrokers, for example, nevertheless show something of the same tendency by choosing houses which at least ape what has tradition and permanence, most noticeably a certain variety of mock tudor.' Of course, such a description would be a pretty poor substitute for Lancaster's phrase or his representation of the style. But it does go some way to show that there is something odd in Warnock's account according to which Lancaster has merely given a name to something which is already familiar to us. The point may become clearer if we use for comparison another example of a familiar type. Consider the anonymous wit who identified one section of society as the 'Quiche and Volvo set'. Clearly the appositeness of this phrase lies not in a label's having been provided for some set of characteristics which were already recognised as a going together, as constituting a type, but rather in someone's having created a phrase which brings it to our attention that they do go together. Indeed a failure to notice this will precisely rob the phrase of its point. For it is because those who drive Volvos characteristically pride themselves on doing so, not from fashion but from an appreciation of the engineering merits of the car, that it shows some perceptiveness to notice that among a certain section of British society, driving a Volvo is as much a fashion as is referring to a flan as a 'quiche'. Or again consider the identification of a certain life style as 'radical chic'. Once again the wit of such a phrase lies precisely in its not being merely a label for a style which has already been identified, but in its recognising what would be vehemently denied by those who manifest it, that there is such a style.

On one interpretation Warnock's earlier remarks need not be taken as denying any of this. For her claim that we 'recognise the kind and then accept the word' could scarcely be bettered if the aim were to blur the distinction between that sort of case where we are familiar with a style for which someone then suggests a name, and the case where though we have identified the various elements which make up a style we only come to think of it *as* a style when a name is given to it. Nevertheless, her final comment in the passage I quoted earlier, 'The word is not necessary before you recognise the kind', makes it quite clear that what she has in mind is the former interpretation, which is, in any case, the interpretation which is consistent with her general account of memory. My claim is that it is only if we take the latter interpretation that it becomes possible to give any account of what imagination consists in.

That this is the case becomes, if anything, even more important when we turn to consider Warnock's main concern—the role of recollection in autobiography and fiction. For the power of such things to illuminate lies, it seems to me, in this: that the writer's choice of words to describe, for example, childhood experiences brings us to see (as it may have brought the writer himself to see) relations which we had not noticed, or perhaps to see these things in a new way. Consider, for instance, Samuel Butler's remarks about the 'moral influence' of parents in *The Way of All Flesh*:

> To parents who wish to lead a quiet life, I would say: Tell your children that they are very naughty—much naughtier than most children; point to the young people of some acquaintances as models of perfection, and impress your own children with a deep sense of their own inferiority ... This is called moral influence and it will enable you to bounce them as much as you please ... You keep the dice and throw them, both for your children and yourself, load them then, for you can easily manage to stop your children from examining them.[14]

In so far as Butler's remarks strike a chord with us, as they do with many people, then it is, no doubt, important to see that they can do so only because Butler is appealing to what we have noticed: namely how often as children our parents deceived us, how often what they presented as a concern for our welfare, we later realised to have stemmed rather from a desire for, as Butler puts it, a quiet life. Nevertheless, it would be quite wrong to suppose that this is all that there is in the passage. For this would be to leave out what seems to me its most striking feature—the comparison which Butler draws between 'moral influence' and cheating at dice. Clearly it would be merely silly to suggest that all along we have recognised these things to be of the same kind (or indeed that Butler himself so recognised them). 'Loading the dice' is not simply a new label for the sort of corruption which Butler is describing. Rather by focusing attention on the relationship between diverse aspects of our parent's role in our lives (and perhaps our own role as parents) it enables us to see more clearly the nature of this corruption. For it is not simply that parents sometimes deceive their children, but that the deception is

---

14   Samuel Butler, *The Way of All Flesh* (London: Methuen, 1964) p 25.

exacerbated by the fact that, standing in a relation of moral authority to their children, parents are in a position to prevent themselves being taxed with the deception. If your parents lie to you, then either you swallow the lie, or you incur moral censure by confronting them with it. So in this respect the situation is rather similar to playing a game of chance against a cheat who can also prevent you examining the dice.

But, it may be objected, is not this just what Mary Warnock is suggesting when in the later parts of the book she draws our attention to the creative nature of language? For one way of expressing the point I have been making would be to say that some uses of language in autobiography (in particular those which we might speak of as imaginative) have a creative role, for they can, in a sense, bring about a change in the nature of what is recollected. And this may well be so. What it shows, however, is that recollection is related to language, and so plays a part in human life, for which there is no counterpart at all in the lives of animals, and which there is no reason to suppose might be illuminated by a causal account of memory. The supposition that such an account must be capable of throwing light here is indeed a mere prejudice.

13

Teaching Children to Read Stories[1]

> I have been told both in approval and accusation that I seem to fall in love with all my characters. What I do in writing of any character is to try and enter into the mind, heart and skin of a human being who is not myself.
>
> (Eudora Welty: Preface to her *Collected Stories*[2])

> The assumption that it is the main business of a writer—other than the lyric poet—to create characters is not, of course, confined to criticism of Shakespeare, it long ago invaded criticism of the novel.
>
> (L. C. Knights: 'How Many Children Had Lady Macbeth?' in *Explorations*[3])

Though there is an important difference between the above quotations in that Eudora Welty speaks from the viewpoint of a writer, L.C. Knights from that of a critic, it is not difficult to see that they represent very different approaches to the study of literature, very different ideas of what we are (or perhaps should be) doing when we read a story, as much as they represent different ideas of what a writer's task consists in. Nor is it difficult to see that over the past half century or so, it is Knights view of literature, rather than that of Welty which has exerted the greater influence on literary criticism, and so, presumably, on the way in which children are taught to understand the literature with which they come into

---

1   Previously unpublished.
2   Eudora Welty, *Collected Stories* (Harmondsworth: Penguin Books, 1983) p. xi.
3   L.C. Knights, *Explorations* (London: Chatto & Windus, 1946) p. 1.

contact. For there can be little doubt that, despite their obvious differences, what unites the structuralist conception of characters as devices to be understood only in relation to other elements in a narrative scheme, and the post-structuralist conception of characters as at best mere illustrations or examples of some ideology or other, is the idea that, however we are to respond to characters in fiction, we are *not* to respond to them as human beings. And this idea is also precisely what is central to the other great tradition in literary criticism of the past fifty years, which sees literary characters as merely verbal symbols, and which finds its expression in the work of such writers as George Wilson-Knight, F.R. Leavis and, of course, L.C. Knights.

Given the immense influence of these two traditions of literary criticism, it is not surprising that many teachers, critics and also many philosophers would take the issue of how we are to understand character in fiction to be pretty decisively settled. Like Knights they would take it for granted that to treat Hamlet or Pecksniff as if they were human beings, to respond to them with hatred or pity or amusement, is in some way to fall into error. And since it would take a truly breathtaking commitment to theory to blind one to the fact that this is normally the way in which at least small children *do* respond to fictional characters, to Goldilocks or Rumpelstiltskin, it would seem to follow that those teachers who have fallen under this influence must see their task in teaching literature as that of breaking the hold on children of such responses. In what follows, I shall try to give some reasons for supposing that this is mere confusion and that on the contrary the tendency of readers to respond to fictional characters in many of the ways in which they respond to real people, is a condition of the possibility of literary understanding.

I. Literary Characters and Real People

In philosophy nothing is gained by attempting to resolve a dispute without a clear perception of the sort of dispute with which we are faced. Unfortunately, in this case when we try to locate the point of disagreement between the two quotations with which I began this essay, there are difficulties. Knights' essay is, of course, primarily an essay in Shakespearean criticism. His main target is a view, often attributed to A.C. Bradley, according to which Shakespeare was pre-eminently a great creator of characters. It is, Knights maintains, a mistake to think of Lady Macbeth, Banquo,

Duncan as if they were human beings—'real men and women, fellow human beings with ourselves'.[4] So that one possible interpretation of his words is that he wishes to reject this as an account of Shakespeare. Shakespeare's strength, he would be arguing, lies not, as with certain writers, in his character construction, but in for example his ability as a poet. So that from this viewpoint, the apparent conflict between Knights' remarks and those of Eudora Welty may be seen as illusory. She may well have been right about her own strengths and weaknesses; with Shakespeare it is different.

And no doubt this is part of the truth. Still, [as is shown by the quotation from Knights above], it is clearly not all that he would wish to say. For he is concerned to criticise a certain view not merely of Shakespeare's work, nor even of drama as a genre, but of literature as a whole. It is, according to Knights, predominantly a recent view:

> The growth of the popular novel from Walter Scott and Charlotte Bronte to our own Best Sellers, encouraged an emotional identification of the reader with hero and heroine.[5]

The key phrase here is 'emotional identification', a phrase which on the face of it would fit rather well Eudora Welty's description of herself as 'entering into the mind, heart and skin of a human being who is not myself', Knights thinks that there is critical confusion in approaching literary characters in this way. And in this respect he appears to have been influential not only in his own field, that of literary criticism, but also among his more philosophically inclined admirers, Nicholas Wolterstorff, for example, in a recent article[6] chiding those who think of literary characters as people for their naivete.

Unfortunately, if we now ask why the view is naive, then again the confusion becomes hard to identify. For it can scarcely be Knights' contention that to treat characters as human beings is to mistake them for human beings. It could not seriously be suggested that when she wrote one of her earliest stories, 'Lily Daw and the Sisters', Eudora Welty was labouring under the

---

4   Ranjee G. Shahani, *Shakespeare Through Eastern Eyes*, quoted in Knights, op. cit., p. 2.
5   Knights, op. cit., p. 14.
6   Nicholas Wolterstorff, in *The Reasons of Arts; Artworks and Transformations of Philosophy*, ed. Peter J. McCormick (Ottowa: Ottowa University Press, 1985).

misapprehension that living in Victoria, Mississippi, was a feeble-minded girl called Lily Daw. Nor can it be Knights' purpose in his essay to remind us that such a story is fiction and not biography. True, there are cases where we may be inclined to suppose that someone has, at least from time to time, no very firm grip on this distinction. Discussing the popularity of the boys' and girls' magazines written by Frank Richards and featuring Billy Bunter and the boys of Greyfriars School, George Orwell draws attention to an interesting feature of their correspondence columns:

> It is clear that many of the boys and girls who write these letters are living a complete fantasy-life. Sometimes a boy will write, for instance, giving his age, weight, chest and biceps measurements and asking which member of the Shell or Fourth Form he most exactly resembles ... The editors, of course, do everything in their power to keep up the illusion.[7]

Depending on a child's age we might regard all this as perfectly normal or as a trifle excessive, and it is obvious that even adults are occasionally guilty of similar responses, *e.g.* to characters in television series. But even here it would, I think, be wrong to say without qualification that these people are mistaking fiction for reality, if only because the natural response to their confusion would be simply to draw attention to this difference ('Remember this is only a story') on the assumption that this would bring them to their senses. Where, by contrast, someone falls into a genuine error about a work of fiction—let us suppose that, for example, they mistakenly believe Robinson Crusoe to be a travel book—the appropriate response will be to argue with them, provide evidence, appeal to authorities, and generally attempt to convince them in ways which would be quite inappropriate with the children whom Orwell discusses.

Still, neither response, neither argument nor gentle chiding would be appropriate in dealing with Eudora Welty's attitude towards her own creations, nor to the sort of critical approach which is Knights' target. Knights is obviously not reminding A.C. Bradley *et al.* that they are dealing with fiction. So what this suggests is that the confusion in approach, if there is one, must lie not in treating literary characters as human beings itself, but in

---

[7]   George Orwell, 'Boys' Weeklies', in *Collected Essays, Journalism and Letters*, Vol. l (Harmondsworth: Penguin Books, 1976) pp. 513–4.

some other confusion to which this approach makes us prone. And here the title of Knights' essay, 'How Many Children Had Lady Macbeth?' gives us a clue. For Knights regards this as only a slight parody of the sort of questions sometimes asked by those who think of Shakespeare's figures as flesh and blood — Ellen Terry, for example, in whose Lectures on Shakespeare we find the actress puzzling over such questions as 'How did the boy in Henry V learn to speak French?' Knights, that is to say, is concerned that, if we think of literary characters as people, if we respond to them as we do to human beings, then we shall be tempted to ask questions which would be appropriate to human beings, but not to literary characters. Think of Lily Daw as a simple-minded person and you will be tempted to ask how she became simple-minded or whether she was perhaps born that way. Think of Lady Macbeth as a real wife and you will naturally ask yourself how many children she had, just as you might ask this of any wife of your acquaintance.

Now there is certainly something odd about such questions which leads Knights to condemn them as pseudo-critical. And in this respect he seems to have a point against those philosophers who have appealed to general logical considerations to show that such enquiries must have a sense. A good example is John Heinz's insistence in a recent paper that 'talking and thinking about fictional characters has to retain the logical structure of talking about anything.'[8]

It would be foolish to enter into any debate about the 'logical structure' of talking and thinking about anything, but I suppose that Heinz's idea is that just as it would be reasonable to ask of a couple of my acquaintance whether they are parents, in the same way when Shakespeare first presents us with Macbeth and Lady Macbeth, it is also reasonable to ask whether they have children, and if so, how many, regardless of whether or not Shakespeare goes on to enlighten us. Logic demands, so the argument would go, that there be some number of children, even if the number is 'none'. Or again, to use one of Heinz's own examples, if Conan Doyle tells us that Sherlock Holmes wore a dressing gown and slippers about the house, then, Heinz argues, we must surely be able to conclude that he had a body even if Conan Doyle had nothing to say about it.

---

8   John Heinz, in McCormick, op. cit.

Most of the force of Heinz's appeal to 'logical structure' stems from his having noticed the oddness of asserting that Lady Macbeth had no number of children (not even 0) or that Sherlock Holmes had no body. But this can drive us to the other conclusion (that Lady Macbeth had some number of children, that Sherlock Holmes did have a body) even in the face of the silence of respectively Shakespeare and Sir Arthur Conan Doyle, only if we suppose that the questions to which these are purported to be answers are themselves intelligible. If they are unintelligible then the law of excluded middle has no part to play.

Suppose, then, that having just read *The Hound of the Baskervilles*, Heinz turns to me and remarks, 'Good story, but tell me, did Sherlock Holmes have a body?' Clearly the temptation to simply answer 'Yes' or 'Of course' ought to be resisted here. For what is supposed to be the puzzle? What am I to make of Heinz's question? As it happens, it is one to which it would be difficult enough to attach a sense, were it asked of a real person, let alone a fictional character. ('I met a really nice man today.' 'How nice, dear. Did he have a body?') But let me make an attempt. Is it that Heinz is wondering how an ordinary mortal could have survived all that happens to Holmes? Or perhaps he has noticed a contradiction in the physical descriptions of the detective given by Conan Doyle. No. The truth is that he does not really find anything puzzling about the story. He is not seeking to clarify, understand or unravel anything, but has simply constructed a sentence having the form of a question, which, though it might appear to have some sense when applied to a real person, has no part to play in any genuine discussion of the story. And he has done so because of some quite uncashable notion of 'logical structure'.

Similar remarks apply to Knights' question about Lady Macbeth—Does she have any children? But since, unlike 'Does he have a body?' this is the sort of question which has a genuine role to play in our language, it is possible to see more clearly the difficulties of applying it in the case of Lady Macbeth. For let us suppose that there were nothing in the play which enabled us to answer it one way or the other, but that, following Heinz, we insist that Lady Macbeth (like any other character—Raskolnikov, the Mad Hatter, Peter Rabbit) either did have a certain number of children or was childless. What this supposedly neutral logical principle will amount to is, in the context of a work of fiction, not a logical principle at all, but rather an insistence that we choose between different and conflicting critical interpretations. If we entertain the possibility that Lady Macbeth had, say, ten children, then presumably her role as the mother of a large family is thought of as having a part to play in the development of the tragedy, otherwise what point is there in the supposition? If, on the other hand, we suppose that she was childless, then we shall open the door to interpretations which, for example, connect her sterility with the notion of a breach in the natural order, which is, it so happens, a central theme of the play. But why should it be assumed a priori that from the very start, that is, from the introduction of Lady Macbeth in scene one, Shakespeare or his reader is committed to one of these interpretations. Why should it not be that, not wishing to direct his readers' thoughts in either of these directions, Shakespeare simply allowed questions about Lady Macbeth's fertility to play no part in the tragedy? Why, to apply the same point to a rather different story, must we think of the *Tale of Peter Rabbit* either as the story of a rabbit preternaturally promiscuous even among rabbits, or as the story of a rabbit whose foolhardiness in wandering off into the garden is perhaps to be understood by reference to his lack of parental responsibilities.

It may well be that, as Knights suggests, the same can be said of Ellen Terry's questions, though there is another possibility here. For Ellen Terry was, of course, an actress, so that it may be that her enquiries about 'those aspects of character which Shakespeare did not choose to reveal' were connected with problems of dramatic interpretation in much the way that actors and actresses sometimes claim that if they can decide how a character walked or spoke, then the rest of the part will fall naturally into place.[9] Be that as it may, it should by now be obvious that Knights' point here depends for its plausibility on the contrast between those sorts of questions about fictional characters ('How many children had Lady Macbeth?'), which lack sense because they raise no genuine problems in our understanding of the play, and those questions ('Is Macduff a traitor? If so to whom, to Macbeth or to his wife?') which Knights himself considers are important for an understanding of Shakespeare's meaning. The mere possibility of constructing certain sorts of question, which might be appropriate to human beings but which lack sense when asked of fictional characters, cannot possibly force us in the direction which Knights imagines. It cannot show that it is a mistake to talk and think of

---

9   I owe this point to my colleague, Michael Cohen.

literary characters as if they were human beings, but only that it is sometimes and in some respects a mistake. But then, on reflection this claim is obviously trivial. For if we treat literary characters in all respects as though they are real human beings, then we are not treating them as if they are human beings, but simply mistaking them for human beings. The difference is I think important, but commonly overlooked. For it is one thing to think of literary characters as if they were human beings, quite another to think that they are. But, it is, I suspect, precisely the failure to take seriously this difference that has led to much confusion among philosophers. Thus, for example, Frank Palmer in his recent book *Literature and Moral Understanding*, noting that we quite naturally speak of there being someone called 'Hamlet' who has sword fights, falls in love and feigns madness, and equally naturally of there being no such person as Hamlet (where this would be equivalent to the assertion that Hamlet is a fictional character), concludes that if we are to avoid the accusation of self-contradiction, there must be involved two different ways of speaking here.

> The contextual framework which permits our utterances about a man called Hamlet who thinks and acts must be distinguished from the context in which it is equally permissible to deny all these things. We are concerned here with different 'fields' or 'modes' of discourse.[10]

Palmer refers to these different 'modes' of discourse as the 'external' and 'internal' conventions. But the apparent contradiction which makes them seem necessary is surely just that—a merely *apparent* contradiction. Certainly there would be a contradiction between on the one hand claiming that there is no such person as Hamlet (for example, when reassuring a small child who is frightened by what is happening on the stage) and on the other hand talking and acting as if it *were* a real person who is falling in love, and getting involved in sword fights (for example, by telling the child to bow when the prince appears or by trying to stop one of the fights). Someone who talked and acted in such a way *would* indeed be incomprehensible. But there is no difficulty in understanding someone who claims that there is no such

---

10   Frank Palmer, *Literature and Moral Understanding* (Oxford: Clarendon Press, 1992) p. 18.

person as Hamlet and yet reacts to Hamlet in many ways as if he were a real person. For there is just no incompatibility between the two, any more than there is an incompatibility between treating my wife as if she were a slave or speaking of her as if she were a slave and recognising that she is not. Treating one's wife as a slave is quite different from mistakenly believing that she is one (*e.g.* where I do in fact keep slaves, and mistakenly believe that this is one of them). For the person who thinks of their wife as a slave, or treats her as if she were a slave, will nevertheless not do many things which the person who thinks that their wife is a slave will do. They will not normally, for example, try to sell her. And in the same way when we treat characters in fiction as if they were human beings, which is what we normally do, we do of course differ from the person who mistakenly thinks that a fictional character is real. For there are certain ways in which we shall react to real people but not to fictional characters, certain questions which we ask of real people (like for example, whether they have children) but not of fictional characters. It follows that Knights' observation that this *is* so, cannot possibly lead to his conclusion that it is a mistake to think of fictional characters as if they were real people. The only interesting question which remains then is the question 'What part *does* treating characters as human beings have to play in the understanding of literature?'

II. Children and Stories

At *Investigations* §524 Wittgenstein offers his readers the following advice:

> Don't take it as a matter of course, but as a remarkable fact, that pictures and fictitious narratives give us pleasure, occupy our minds.[11]

One way, perhaps the only way, in which we might treat this as a 'remarkable fact' is to try to imagine a people of whom it was not true, a people, that is to say, who showed no interest in pictures and stories, or perhaps actively disliked them, just, so to speak, because they were pictures or stories. It will not do, of course, to imagine a society where for some reason—an extreme puritanism perhaps—the pictorial or literary arts have been

---

11   L. Wittgenstein, *Philosophical Investigations* (Oxford: Basil Blackwell, 1963) §524.

suppressed so that, although at an early age children show a clandestine interest in such activities, they have, by the time they are adults, come to despise them. Rather we shall have to imagine that in their society even small children are simply different from our own, that they respond differently to painting and literature. To simplify matters, let us limit ourselves to the latter case and ask how these children will respond. Well, like children in our own society they will show an interest in the lives of others. They will be fascinated by the strange doings of the old lady at the end of the road, will be eager to know where she went and what happened to her. But unlike the children with whom we have contact, they will become indifferent to her fate when they discover that the old lady is a figment of the narrator's imagination. They will laugh at the humorous remark made by a friend or the strange mannerisms of a relative, but not when the remark or the mannerisms are attributed to a fictional character. They will cry over misfortune, but remain unmoved if the misfortune occurs in a story.

Now, though Wittgenstein does not mention it, there is, I think, one thing which stands in the way of our thinking of our own reactions to stories as remarkable and hence prevents us easily regarding the members of our imaginary society as unremarkable. And that is simply that the children I have just described look so odd, even sinister. One reason why this may not immediately become obvious is that there is a tendency when presented with such a case to try to incorporate it into our own experience. We imagine that these children have become so sophisticated, or perhaps hardened by adverse experiences, that their natural responses have become distorted. When, however, we try to take the example seriously, imagine, for instance, very young children, living perfectly ordinary lives, but reacting in this way (or rather, failing to react), then we start to see how what at first seems a rather minor change in the lives of human beings can affect our very perception of them as human. For a child who does not react to the joys and sufferings of fictional characters, seems, when one thinks about it, hardly less alien than one who does not respond to the joys and sufferings of real people.

One, though not the only, reason for this is the difficulty we should have with such children of attributing to them any understanding of what is going on. They are told a humorous story. But, as we have seen, they do not respond. Do we then say that they understand the story? If a real child does not laugh at a joke, then we are normally inclined to say that it does not see the joke. If we sometimes hesitate, it is because we recognise that understanding here can take forms other than laughter. Other responses, the nervous smile, the shocked gasp, even anger if someone finds a joke objectionable, can in certain circumstances all be appropriate. But with our imaginary children these alternatives are also ruled out. For they do not respond at all. And clearly the point can be generalised. It is not simply that the children in our imaginary society do not understand humorous stories. They cannot really be said to understand stories at all. For they do not shudder at what is horrible, giggle at the rude bits, cry over the sad fate of the heroine, or hiss the villain. And with children (unlike, say, first year undergraduates) there seems no room for the idea that though the person does not react to what I tell them, they nevertheless understand it. If I cannot elicit a reaction from them, no matter what I tell them about, then I shall eventually conclude that they cannot be brought to understand.

Wittgenstein invites us, as philosophers, not to take for granted one feature of human life, namely that we react to fictional characters much as we do to real human beings. When, however, we take this advice, we realise that it is precisely because this feature of our lives does normally go without saying, because we can normally count on human beings to react in this way, that it is possible to apply the notion of understanding to children here. Far from its being the case, as Knights supposes, that the emotional identification of a reader with the characters in a story marks a decline in literary appreciation consequent upon the rise of the popular novel, we now see that in at least one form it is what makes possible literary appreciation in the first place. It is, moreover, one of the things which makes us recognisably human.

III. The Growth of Literary Understanding

No doubt this will not satisfy some people. Indeed, those who are inclined to accept Knights' view of the situation may well feel that I have inadvertently given them some support by concentrating on the case of children. Have you not, they may say, simply described a type of response which, even if it is necessary for the development of literary understanding in children (or even, more strongly, a criterion of literary understanding in children) is nevertheless something which we expect adults to transcend. True, there are those who never progress beyond a juvenile response to plays and novels, for example the soap-opera enthusiast, who cried over the death of Bobby Ewing in *Dallas* or who could hardly wait for the next week's episode of *Coronation Street* to discover who was responsible for Denise's threatening telephone calls. But, so the argument goes, it is surely correct to describe this form of interest as naive. Certainly, it is not something which might be described as a critical approach to literature, where by contrast we expect some concern for and understanding of the ideas involved in a work.

There is, of course, some truth in this claim, but unfortunately by suggesting that when we give in to the fascination of soap-operas, we are indulging a childish interest in the lives of fictional characters, an interest which in critical appreciation we suppress, it could scarcely be further from the truth. For the truth is that our naivete when gripped by *Dallas* lies not essentially in the nature of our response, but rather in what it is a response to. It lies not in our responding to what is lifelike in fiction as though it were real, but rather in our responding in this way to what is not even life-like, but, for example, merely conventional or fashionable. What distinguishes *Dallas* from *Macbeth* or *Jude the Obscure* is that the former is precisely *not* realistic, because certain demands — the demand that the popularity of certain actors should determine the development of the plot, the demand that the characters should, with whatever cost to plausibility, face new and harrowing problems in each episode — prevent its being so. Nor is this to say that such a demand may not also corrupt the work even of great writers. An obvious example would be Dickens' tendency to engineer a happy ending to his stories by introducing some benevolent millionaire who, having made his money 'in business', then solves everyone's problems by showering it in all directions. So that when one critic remarks that 'even Dickens must have reflected occasionally that someone so anxious to give his money away would never have acquired it in the first place',[12] the implied question is not one which only a child would ask, but one which even an intelligent child might ask. In suggesting that we cannot respond to some of Dickens' characters because they do not behave like human beings, it offers a piece of literary criticism.

If this is denied on the sort of grounds which Knights offers, then it is difficult to know what to make of perfectly standard

---

[12]   'Charles Dickens', in Orwell, op. cit., p. 458.

forms of literary criticism. If we are not permitted to commend a character for being lifelike, then we can scarcely criticise a character for being lifeless. Thus when Wyndham Lewis condemned William Faulkner's use of 'destiny' as a 'fraudulent device for operating the puppets',[13] he was himself criticised by those who emphasised the reality of the writer's creations. When *Sanctuary* was dismissed by some writers as a mere allegory, Faulkner was defended by others who insisted on the vitality of his characters. If, as Knights implies, what characterises a mature approach to literature is a concentration on the ideas which a work involves rather than any sort of response to the characters, then such debates become merely irrelevant.

But perhaps what we ought to question here is the assumption that we have here a genuine contrast. For, though I have been at some pains to emphasise that in the absence of a natural tendency to respond to literary figures as though they were real human beings, there could be no growth of literary understanding in a child, I have nowhere sought to contrast this response with an appreciation of the ideas in a story. Nor do I think that such a contrast would be justified, even where it is a child's response to literature which is in question. Consider what G.K. Chesterton has to say about fairy tales:

> There is the chivalrous lesson of 'Jack the Giant Killer'; that giants should be killed because they are gigantic. It is a manly mutiny against pride as such ... There is the lesson of 'Cinderella', which is the same as that of the Magnificat — *exaltavit humiles*. There is the great lesson of 'Beauty and the Beast', that a thing must be loved *before* it is lovable.[14]

Though Chesterton speaks here of the ideas around which these fairy tales revolve as 'lessons', I doubt that he meant thereby to imply that they are without loss separable from the stories in which they are to be found. But anyway it is worth asking what Knights' contrast between an interest in the characters of a story and an interest in its ideas might amount to in such cases. Could, for example, a child who had responded appropriately to the story of Cinderella, showing sympathy at the heroine's treatment at the

---

[13] Wyndham Lewis, 'The Moralist with a Corn-cob', in *Men Without Art* (London: Cassell & Co., 1934).

[14] G.K. Chesterton, *Orthodoxy* (London: The Bodley Head Press, 1909) pp. 86–7.

hands of her family, joy at the unexpected good fortune which took her to the ball, apprehension at the prospect of the glass slipper's fitting one of the ugly sisters and delight when it is found to fit Cinderella, nevertheless be said to have failed to understand the idea of meekness being exalted? Only, I suspect, if we forget that a story is not simply a list of events, but has a unity which can only be seen in the bearing which the events have on one another. When, as children, we respond with delight to Cinderella's good fortune in marrying the prince, we do not merely respond to this one event, for we should not have responded in this way had the good fortune been Anastasia's, but to this event in relation to Cinderella's earlier treatment and to the way in which she bore it. That is to say, we respond to the idea of meekness being exalted. The story shows us what that idea amounts to through the medium of a particular life—the life of Cinderella. And that, whatever theories of literary criticism may become fashionable, is how it should be read, as the story of a life.

To understand that story is, as Eudora Welty's words imply, very like entering into the mind and heart of a being who is not oneself.

14

'If a Lion Could Talk...'[1]

Of all the many remarks which occur in Wittgenstein's writings concerning animals and our relationships with them, probably the most famous is that which occurs in Part II of the *Investigations*, where a lengthy passage concerning the understanding of human beings ends with the remark which forms the title of this essay, 'If a lion could talk, we could not understand him.'[2]

The remark has often been used as an illustration of Wittgenstein's enigmatic approach to philosophy. But there is in fact little puzzle about its meaning. At this point Wittgenstein is, among other things, attacking a view, popularly associated with the fictional character Dr. Doolittle, according to which all that would be required for us to communicate with animals would be for us to find a way of translating their various grunts, roars and chirpings into English or German or some other human language, or alternatively to bring them to speak our own language. And his point is that even if, as seems unlikely, any such thing were possible, it does not follow that we could then understand pigs or lions or sparrows. For this we should need access to more than the animal's words. We should, to put it crudely, need to understand the way in which the animal sees the world, to understand *him*. For imagine that like Dr. Doolittle we discover that the lion's roars are, on a certain occasion, to be translated by the English words 'Good morning', or that on the alternative hypothesis, the lion should itself learn to use this phrase. The question will now arise how we are to understand what is going on between us and the lion. Is the lion perhaps being ironic, mocking the way in which

---

1   First published in in K.S. Johannessen and T. Nordenstam eds., *Wittgenstein and the Philosophy of Culture* (Vienna: Verlag HPT, 1996).

2   Wittgenstein, *Philosophical Investigations*, p. 223.

human beings normally greet one another? Or is it making a somewhat pathetic attempt to be one of us? Or parroting us in the way that a small child will sometimes parrot things that its elders say? Or what? And, as I say, there will be no way in which these questions can be answered from an examination of the lion's words, since in each case the words will be the same. The difficulties in understanding could be resolved, if at all, only by coming to an understanding of the life of a lion and to some extent of this lion in particular, something which in the nature of the case is no simple matter, if only because lions have a tendency to eat those who try to understand them.

For my purposes, however, the interest of the above remarks lies in the fact that they could with only minor changes have been applied not to animals but to human beings. For there exists among human beings from different backgrounds room for very similar difficulties and failures in understanding. On meeting, let us say, a Rastafarian, I may greet him in a way that I take to be characteristic of his social group, for example, by saying 'Give me five, man'. But the mere fact that I use these words, and that in one sense he understands them, provides no evidence that he understands what I am up to. Am I expressing solidarity, sneering at him (in the way in which one people will sometimes mock the style of speech of another group by talking in that way themselves), patronising him, or one of a host of other possible alternatives? And indeed, it was precisely in order to draw this analogy between communication between human beings of different groups and any hypothetical communication between humans and animals that Wittgenstein earlier in the same passage remarked:

> We say of some people that they are transparent to us. It is, however, important as regards this observation that one human being can be a complete enigma to another. We learn this when we come into a strange land with entirely strange traditions; and what is more, even given a mastery of the country's language, we do not understand the people.[3]

The passage in question then does not give support to any interpretation of Wittgenstein which would attribute to him any general distinction between human beings and animals, any

---

[3]   Ibid.

general thesis regarding our relationship with animals. Just the contrary — for what it says is that human beings can sometimes be as alien to us as lions.

But in this respect, the above passage does not differ from a host of rather less well-known passages. It has, for instance, sometimes been said that animals differ from human beings in their lack of a capacity for thought. But Wittgenstein's writings will support no such generalisation. He has, for example, no objection to speaking of animals as thinking. True, he does not deny the possibility that there may be animals which have no mental life. In *Culture and Value,* he observes that it would almost be strange if there did not exist animals which had the mental life of plants.[4] But, on the other hand, he notes in *Remarks on the Philosophy of Psychology* that the same is also true of some human beings.[5] He is, moreover, apparently happy to link reference to the thoughts of humans and animals in the same sentence:

> Imagine a human being, or one of Kohler's monkeys, who wants to get a banana from the ceiling, but can't reach it, and thinking about ways and means finally puts two sticks together, etc.[6]

Indeed, if there is a contrast to be made here, it is one not between the behaviour of animals and humans, but rather between one animal and another (or perhaps also one human being and another). Wittgenstein goes on:

> So one might distinguish between two chimpanzees with respect to the way in which they work, and say of the one that he is thinking and of the other that he was not.[7]

Of course, this is not to deny that there are in Wittgenstein to be found specific distinctions between humans and animals. Indeed, the remark about the lion alerts us to what is almost certainly the most important of these, namely that animals, unlike most human beings, do not possess language. Nevertheless, it would be a mistake, though a common enough mistake, to think of this as a general distinction, at least in one sense. For to say that animals lack language is in one way quite different from claiming (as some writers have done) that they are merely complex mechanisms or

---

4   Wittgenstein, *Culture and Value,* p. 72.
5   Wittgenstein, *Remarks on the Philosophy of Psychology,* p. 192.
6   Ibid., §224.
7   Ibid., §229.

that they lack souls. The writer who makes the latter sort of claim, makes a claim which, if accepted, will affect our understanding of *every* aspect of an animal's life. But to claim that an animal, say a dog, lacks language is not to say that a dog's life becomes different in every respect from the life of a human being — that a dog's fear or anger or thought is different from the fear, anger, thought of a human being. Rather the absence of speech in the dog's life means that this life simply lacks counterparts to some specific aspects of human life. A dog can, like a human being, fear being beaten. Not, however, possessing the language in which we speak of time, it cannot fear that it will be beaten tomorrow. But what is, so far as I can see, lacking from Wittgenstein's discussion is any idea that there is some general way in which we can say of animals that they are not the same as us, some general distinction which infects every aspect of human and animal lives.

Now it has often struck me that in this respect Wittgenstein's views have had remarkably little effect on contemporary philosophy. To some extent this is, I suppose, unsurprising. For there are many philosophers who would not profess much familiarity or even much sympathy for Wittgenstein's approach. What is, however, rather surprising is the extent to which many writers who would certainly number Wittgenstein among their greatest influences, nevertheless adopt on this issue a view which seems diametrically opposed to his own. So in what follows I shall try to defend what I see as Wittgenstein's own approach against both those who, to put it bluntly, are against him *and* those who are for him. I shall take as an example of the former the writer Peter Singer, though I might equally have pointed to a great deal of popular pseudoscientific theorising about the feelings and sentient experiences of, for example, fish and bats. As an example of the latter, I shall examine the approach, which has developed partly as a response to Singer's writings and which is exemplified by such writers as Norman Malcolm, Rai Gaita and Cora Diamond.

As I say, the first view which I wish to examine is to be found in the writings of Peter Singer, in particular in his book *Animal Liberation*, and it is in that form that I shall examine it. It is fortunately a view which can be stated fairly simply, though unfortunately not particularly briefly.

According to Singer, when we speak of a person or a human being, we do not normally simply mean a member of the species *homo sapiens*. Of course, there may be contexts in which this is what we have in mind, for example, when the term is employed during a lecture on biology, or when trying to determine the age of a skull. But, normally when we use it, we have in mind a creature which is a member of this species as well as possessing certain other properties, say rationality, the capacity to feel pain, the ability to engage in certain sorts of activities. So it is (again normally) on the basis of their possession of these properties that we treat those people with whom we have contact in the ways that we do. We see them, for instance, as possessing certain rights, as having obligations of certain sorts to themselves and to others, and perhaps most importantly for Singer's purposes, there are certain things which we will not (perhaps I should say once more 'normally') do to them, like for instance eating them, or treating them as mere experimental subjects, or selling their children for profit. And if pressed to explain why we do these things or do not do them, then the natural response seems to be to point out that the creatures with which are dealing are people, human beings. We do not normally eat human beings just because they *are* human beings.

But of course there are qualifications to be made here. For, at least in different times, different places, there has been a tendency for certain members of the species *homo sapiens* to treat other members of this species, women perhaps, or people of different races, or different sexual preferences in different ways, sometimes worse, sometimes better. Indeed, sometimes the differences, the fact that members of different races were treated in many ways like animals, for example in being bought and sold, bred for profit, and so on, were so great that those who engaged in these practices were inclined to justify them on the grounds that the creatures with which they were dealing were not people but just animals. Fortunately, it is now becoming obvious to us that this tendency could be justified, could be shown to be rational, only if it could be shown to be based on certain relevant differences, if there were, for instance, differences between those that we call people and those that we do not. It might be rational to treat men and women in different ways if it could be shown that women lacked some characteristic shared by men, for example if it were thought that they were weak and required protection. We might justify slavery, might justify saying that slaves were nothing but animals, if it could be established that certain races lacked characteristics, rationality or souls, perhaps, shared by those who wished to enslave them. But, of course, no research, formal or informal, has ever established the existence of such general characteristics. So it seems to follow that sexism and racism are simply irrational.

Moreover, a similar argument will apply to our treatment of animals. If we are to treat them in a different manner from human beings, this can be justified only by showing that they do not possess some or all of the properties which justify us in treating human beings in the way that we do, that there is some general difference between us and them. But there is in fact a fatal objection to the attempt to find such a characteristic. For suppose that someone wishes to justify the fact that they see no problem in eating a leg of lamb, but would never even in their maddest moments contemplate eating a human leg. And let us imagine that when asked to justify this discrimination, they offer as a reason the alleged fact that animals do not possess the characteristic of rationality, while human beings do. The problem is that, whatever is meant here by rationality, it seems plausible to say that if animals do not possess it, then there are also some human beings who do not. We do not, however, normally regard this as a reason for eating those members of our own species who are lacking in rationality. Or if it is said that the animal does not possess the power of speech, but then nor do some human beings. Or again, if the reason why we are willing to carry out experiments on animals is said to be that animals lack certain capacities of experience, then why is it that we balk at carrying out the same experiments on, for example, the hopelessly brain-damaged? And there are obviously reasons for supposing that we shall never find the elusive characteristic that we seek. For whatever characteristic we identify as absent in animals, there will always be some human beings in whom it is also absent. For there are, after all, some human beings who in one sense possess no characteristics at all, for example those who are in what is nowadays termed a persistent vegetative state, or perhaps, to take the really extreme case, were born in such a state. Since they do nothing at all, then they clearly do less than is done by any animal which is not in such a state.

The consequences of this now seem rather odd for Singer. For you might think that since it can be justifiable to differentiate between people and animals only if a relevant difference can be found, then the failure of the attempt to find such a difference would lead us to the conclusion that both people and animals should be treated in the same way. And this would seem to be compatible with eating human beings, carrying out experiments on them, and in general treating them in the ways in which we have become accustomed to treat animals. Now it is true that sometimes Singer does appear to be tempted to go in this direction. But though he accepts the rationality of this conclusion in one respect, Singer thinks that in another respect it misses the point. For it leaves our treatment of both humans *and* animals bereft of justification. But Singer thinks that there is in fact a justification for the way in which we treat human beings, thinks that there is a characteristic common to human beings which explains the way in which we treat them, and that is their capacity for suffering, the fact, if you like, that they feel pain. We do not regard it as permissible to eat human beings or perform experiments on them, just because it would cause them pain or suffering. But now, of course, we see that the way in which we discriminate between human beings and animals—'speciesism' Singer calls it—is just as irrational as racism or sexism. For animals, like humans, have the capacity to suffer, to feel pain. So we have no justification for treating them in ways different from those in which we treat human beings.

The first thing that strikes one about the view that I have just outlined is, I suppose, its breathtaking generality. It speaks of the way in which we respond to humans and contrasts it with the way in which we respond to animals. It discusses the way in which we subject animals to experiments, and contrasts this with the way in which we care for human beings. It has however very little to say about differences. Nothing to say, for example, about the way in which we treat one animal differently from another animal, or one person from another person. But these differences are all too evident whether we are talking about animals or human beings. For in the case of animals, some animals, dogs, cats, goldfish, are treated as pets. Others, barracudas, piranhas, funnel-web spiders, are normally not. Or again, people sometimes regard it as permissible to experiment on laboratory rats, but not normally on giant pandas. If we turn to human beings, there are various characteristic ways in which we treat our wives and children, but where we should find ourselves in trouble if we tried treating other people's wives and children in the same way. Different societies take different views of what is cruel in the treatment of both animals and human beings, and so on. And when one looks at all closely at this huge diversity, one may wonder whether anything general can be said about the contrast between our relationship to animals and to human beings.

It might then seem that the natural way for anyone of a Wittgensteinian persuasion to criticise Singer's approach would be to question what lies at the heart of his argument, the search, successful or otherwise, for some general distinction between human beings and animals (or perhaps between our attitude towards human beings and animals). Strangely, however, the desire to generalise seems also to have infected those who claim to locate the source of their inspiration in Wittgenstein's writings. If I understand her correctly, it is this that leads Cora Diamond to say of Singer's position that it ignores our feeling that there is 'a difference between human beings and animals,[8] a difference which comes out in many ways, for instance in our eating the one and not the other. And a similar response to Singer is to be found in Rai Gaita's book *Good and Evil*. Gaita is speaking of the difference in the spirit in which one kills an animal to put it out of its misery and the spirit in which one does this to a human being. To illustrate this difference he gives the following example:

> Even when, as was reported of an Argentinean soldier who fell into a fire in the Falklands, a human being is killed so that they will be spared further suffering, they are not killed in the same spirit as we would shoot a horse ... The Argentinean soldier was not eaten afterwards. That fact and many others of the same kind, determine what the shooting *was*.[9]

What is, of course, curious about this example (and the general thesis it is supposed to illustrate) is the suggestion that in any circumstance in which one might normally kill a horse to put it out of its misery, it would be natural to go on to eat it. I imagine for instance that after a fall in the Grand National, Red Rum (or whichever) is discovered to have sustained a badly fractured leg. There is no reasonable alternative but to employ a humane killer. Afterwards the owners, hoping to recoup some of their losses, sell the carcass to a French restaurant. My expansion of Gaita's example will, of course, appear grotesque unless you have completely lost any sense of the difference between the ways in which we treat animals. And a lack of this sense must, I think, be invoked in order to explain the remarks of anyone who is inclined to

[8]   C. Diamond, 'Eating Meat and Eating People', *Philosophy*, 53 (206), 1974, pp. 465–479.
[9]   Gaita, *Good and Evil: An Absolute Conception* (London: Macmillan, 1991) p. 187.

characterise the difference between our attitude towards animals and human beings in general terms by saying something on the lines of 'Well, we eat animals, but we do not eat human beings.' For since there is no generality in this respect in our treatment of animals, then there can be no general difference between our treatment of animals and our treatment of human beings. Some people eat some animals in some circumstances and for different reasons. I am not a vegetarian but personally will not eat sardines in tomato sauce, because they make me nauseous, animals which have been hit by cars, because I don't like the idea, and my own pets, *e.g.* my dog. And, just in case someone tries to insist that, faced with starvation, I might be brought to eat the dog, but nothing would bring me to eat a human being, the answer may well be that if I were indeed reduced to eating the dog, then cannibalism might well be none too far away.

Nor do I think that Gaita's apparent agreement with Singer at this point is merely apparent. For Gaita does not appear to question what lies at the very start of Singer's argument, namely the assumption that it at least makes sense to look for a general way of distinguishing between human beings or people and on the other hand animals. Gaita, of course, believes that there is an important distinction to be made here, one which centres around questions such as whether the creature in question can be said to have a biography, a story of its life, which he believes to be distinctively human (ignoring the fact that one of the best-selling stories of all time, *White Fang*, is precisely the story of an animal's life) while Singer seems to think either that there is no distinction (so that for most purposes we might as well admit that animals are people) or at least that the importance we attach to the distinction has been vastly overrated. Nevertheless, it does seem to be common ground to both of them that there is a general distinction of some sort between the categories of person and non-person, and so some room for a discussion of what, animals, slaves, trees, automata, falls into what category.

But isn't it obvious that there is a distinction between people and animals? Let me try to answer this question with another question. Is there a difference between a snail and a chicken? Well, of course there are countless differences, but one which springs to mind is that you can stuff a dead chicken but not a dead snail. Still, if you are inclined to think that we are now getting somewhere in the discussion, I am, I think, inclined to remind you that there would still be something pretty odd about suggesting that in general the way to distinguish a snail from a chicken is to see whether or not you can stuff it. For in what sort of circumstances would it be important to appeal to this characteristic? The difficulty is that we seem here to have forgotten what Wittgenstein takes pains to emphasise in *Investigations*, §215 and §255, that to ask whether x is the same as y (and so, whether x is different from y) has a sense only where the context makes plain what criterion of identity is being employed. And of course what leads to the intentional idiocy of the discussion regarding the difference between chickens and snails is just the fact that we have not so far established any sort of context, any sort of activity in which the distinction is to be drawn.

Unfortunately, much the same seems to be true of the question whether there is a general distinction to be made between people and animals, or perhaps more generally whether we can distinguish people from other things. And so there is some difficulty in getting a grasp of what the question 'Is this a person (or something else)?' is supposed to mean. When am I supposed to be faced with *this* question? And do not answer, 'Well, obviously when I have to decide whether it would be permissible to eat it, or carry out experiments on it', for remember that, for Singer at least, whether this is permissible or not will depend on the prior answer given to the question 'Is it a person?' But then, as I say, when am I supposed to ask this question? Well, obviously not when confronted by *e.g.* my mother. Nor on the other hand when confronted by a frog or a telegraph pole. For in all these circumstances I should find it difficult to know what was meant by someone who asked me whether this was perhaps a human being, and not because the answer is so obvious, but because I should have no clear sense of what the question means.

Nevertheless, it will be said, there is at least one sort of context in which the question does have a clear sense, and it is one to which both Singer and Gaita give prominence. For it is certainly the case that when confronted by members of other races, and in particular by those other races that they had enslaved or were contemplating enslaving, the people we now call racists did raise the question whether these could be regarded as human beings, whether they were really people. And they did so, so it will be said, precisely because they wished to justify their treatment of the individuals in question. Since it was possible to reach the conclusion that the Africans were not people, then we could justifiably enslave them. Since the Jews were not people, then the objections which you might have had to concentration camps evaporated, and so on. So is not this, at least, a clear case where some criterion of humanity or 'personhood' is required, if only to determine the rationality or otherwise of the racist's claims, and of his or her treatment of others?

Once again what is interesting about this case is the generality of the account which we have been given. The racist is represented to us as someone who holds (or held) quite generally that there is a distinction between the slaves and the human beings. This is important to Singer, for fairly soon he is going to ask on what basis this general distinction is made and then tie the racist up in knots. But why should we assume that racists make or made any such general distinction? Of course, it is true that some slave owners did not treat their slaves in many respects as human beings. But this by no means entails the conclusion that they did not think that they were human beings in any general sense. I may not treat my wife as a wife from time to time, but I am never in any doubt that she is my wife. Or again, my one experience of a real dyed-in-the-wool racist was of a very elderly man, the retired sheriff of a small town in Texas, who by way of conversation told me a story about when, as young men, he and his friend had picked up two black prostitutes and spent the night with them. The following morning his friend had met the suggestion that all four have breakfast together with genuine amazement. For he had no intention of eating in the company of a black woman. Someone might, I suppose, say (indeed the man in question might say) that in refusing to eat with the woman, he was not treating her as a human being. But there seems no reason whatsoever to conclude that when he took her to his bed, the question of whether she was a human being need even have arisen.

If, then, there is no general distinction to be drawn between animals and human beings, between human beings and members of some other races, nor any necessity to draw one, then the second stage of Singer's argument, in which the meat-eater, the racist, the scientist engaged in animal experimentation is asked to justify the general distinctions that he or she draws now, seems to be robbed of its power. For if my reason for eating fish, but not, for example, the postman, is not a function of my believing that they belong to two different categories the one of which it is quite generally permissible to treat in ways in which it would not be permissible to treat the other, if, that is to say, I do not hold that it is permissible to eat animals but not human beings, then there will be precious little point in asking me on what characteristic or set of characteristics I base this difference.

When philosophers of a Singer persuasion insist that we justify our treatment of pigs (for instance that some of us eat them) by showing a difference between pigs and humans (apart from the fact that the one lot are pigs and the other lot are humans), there is, so far as I can see, no reason whatsoever to respond to the request. Indeed, the tactically sensible move would be to ask Singer why it is that he seems to believe that, for example, when faced with something hanging on a butcher's hook, the difference between its being a pig and its being a human being is never of any importance. For myself I find it hard to imagine a more important difference. And this difference would be important in a whole range of other contexts, though not in others. For example, I expect never to ask a pig for a dance, never to attempt to explain Singer's theories to a pig, never to see a pig sentenced to community service. What does not follow from this is that there is some general account of the difference between pigs and human beings, some characteristic or set of characteristics which explains the different ways in which we may treat them.

I suspect that one of the reasons why philosophers like Singer do not much care for this response is that they feel that it leaves the same response open to the racist or the sexist. Why should the slave-owner not reply to the question why he treats his slaves differently from his friends and neighbours by saying 'Because they are slaves'? Once again, Gaita seems to have a limited sympathy with Singer here, for he does seem to believe that if the slave-owner is asked why he treats his slaves differently from, for example, his friends, then he must be able to point to some feature they possess or lack which justifies the difference in treatment. He comments:

> No one would flatly deny this. The slave owner treated his slaves differently from those he would not dream of making slaves, because he saw his slaves as different from them in morally salient ways.[10]

What *no one* would flatly deny is that if the slave-owner treats his slaves as different, then he must think of them as different, which is probably a tautology. What is not at all obvious is that if the

---

[10]   Gaita, op. cit., p. 168.

slave-owner treats his slaves differently, then he must do so on the basis of some difference other than their being slaves. Of course he may certainly say that they are, for example, inferior. But then this would be rather difficult to argue with, for they are, after all, slaves.

It may be just a slip, but Gaita speaks in this passage of the slave-owner *making* people slaves, but this did not normally happen at least in recent history. Slave-owners *bought* slaves. And there seems no reason why they should not have justified their treatment of them by pointing out that what they had bought were slaves, not free men and women, which is, by the way, how Huckleberry Finn justifies returning the runaway slave Jim to his 'rightful owner'. No doubt there would be a different story to tell about those who captured the slaves in Africa, *i.e.* the slavers, who might have had something to say about the institution of slavery or nothing at all.

And no doubt something different again may be true of other sorts of racists in our own and other societies. They may claim that Pakistanis or Jews or West Indians are different because they possess or lack some property (for example, the Jews were once widely held to drink the blood of Christian babies) or they may simply be said to be different, which of course they are, unless you are a Pakistani or a Jew or a Jamaican. None of this has any bearing whatsoever on whether or not one is opposed to racism. If someone tells me that Pakistanis are different from white Anglo-Saxon protestants, I shall not necessarily deny this, though I shall quite probably ask for an explanation. But if someone treats it as having certain sorts of moral importance, for example as justifying assaults on the lives or property of Pakistanis by white Anglo-Saxon protestants, then I shall certainly reject what they say.

Of course, if I were desperate to show that the racist was irrational, then it might well be necessary for me to try to show that the reasons offered by the racist were in some way inconsistent or logically suspect in the manner of Peter Singer, but then why should anyone wish to show that racism is *irrational*? True, a central theme in Singer's writings, and in the writings of those who share his general approach, is the desire to show that certain sorts of moral viewpoints—racism, sexism, eating meat—are in some way irrational or conceptually confused. But, for myself, I find this rather hard to fathom. For though I should certainly say that the Nazi treatment of the Jews was an evil abomination, I find it difficult to see what it would add to this if one were to say that the justifications given for it were also confused. After all, I find the fairly common practice of torturing one's political opponents in order to stamp out political opposition about as morally repulsive a practice as could be imagined; but confused or irrational?

Unfortunately, that is not the end of the matter, at least as far as Singer is concerned. He has, it appears, a trump card to play. For so far my argument has been that there is no reason to postulate some general characteristic of either humans or animals which would either (as Gaita suggests) establish the rationality of treating them in different way or (as Singer suggests) necessitate treating them in the same way. Singer, however, as we have seen denies just this. For he thinks that there is a characteristic — the fact that both humans and animals feel pain — which does necessitate similar treatment for both. We act in certain ways towards humans, refrain from acting in certain other ways, because human beings feel pain. This is, if you like, the justification for our admiring certain ways of acting (being kind, for instance) and for condemning others. Unfortunately, since there is no good reason for believing that animals do not feel pain, since, indeed, it is a fact about them that they do, there is just as good reason for treating them in the same ways. The tragedy is that, either through ignorance or irrationality, we fail to do so.

Singer presents our consciousness of the pain of other human beings as in some sense a justification of our treatment of them. That I feel pain, for example when burned, is on this account a piece of information about me, which others possess and which justifies the ways in which they react to me and the ways in which those reactions are judged. Thus, discovering that I am in pain, you may feel pity. That you feel pity is, however, a response and to be distinguished from your recognition of the fact that I am in pain, since it is the latter recognition which justifies, indeed morally necessitates, the response of pity. Since, however, it is equally a fact that animals feel pain, as we do, it follows that their pain necessitates the same response of pity. Unfortunately, this response is not always or even commonly forthcoming. Either through ignorance (we are unaware that *e.g.* fish feel pain) or through irrationality (we recognise that they do, but still insist on pulling them out of the water on the end of hooks), we do not show pity. In this we are guilty of speciesism.

There is, I think, no doubt that this argument, or one very like it, underpins many contemporary discussions of what have unfortunately become known as 'animal rights' both within philosophy and without. It is, for example, because they take such an argument for granted that some people insist on claiming scientific authority for assertions such as that fish or some other species feel pain, often on the grounds of the discovery that *e.g.* they possess a nervous system—the idea being, so far as I can see, that if the rest of us could be convinced of *that*, then various sorts of response, pity, sympathy, concern to lessen their suffering, would follow as a matter of course. If it has been established beyond doubt that fish feel pain, then no one is going to feel easy about hooking them.

What is curious about all this and what at the same time gives it its appearance of plausibility is the conception of pain and of the role that this concept plays in our lives. One of Wittgenstein's more well-known remarks in *Philosophical Investigations* appears in §244, where he invites the reader to think of the sentence 'I am in pain' not as a proposition which imparts to others a piece of information, but as 'new pain behaviour'. In offering this suggestion, Wittgenstein was, of course, engaging in one stage of a wide-ranging attack on the idea that the function of language is to impart information. For he is drawing the reader's attention to the absurdity of supposing that when, let us say, a small child burns itself and says 'It hurts', the child is naturally to be thought of as apprising us of some fact, much as it might have said, 'I've got a new pair of socks', so that the appropriate response might be, 'Oh really, dear. How interesting.' Rather, Wittgenstein suggests, we should think of 'It hurts' or 'I've got a pain in my chest' as one sort of expression to pain, albeit a sophisticated one, along with such things as crying, screaming and so on.

It has sometimes been suggested that though what Wittgenstein says here has some plausibility when applied to first person propositions, it has none whatsoever when applied to third person propositions. Specifically, so the objection runs, we may think of saying of oneself 'I am in pain' as a sort of behaviour, but not saying of another 'Is he or she is in pain?' But in fact the cases have a remarkable similarity. For just as we can think of the statement 'I am in pain' as one of a range of ways of expressing pain, along with screaming, rubbing the affected part and pitying ourselves, so we can think of 'He or she is in pain' as one of a range of responses to the pain of others, along with screaming, rubbing the affected part and pitying the other person. In neither case can our awareness of the pain normally be thought of as a piece of information which we have acquired and which neverthe-less leaves open the quite separate question of how we are to react to it.

If what I have said above is correct, then Singer's view, like the arguments of those who present as newly discovered scientific fact the claim that fish feel pain in the hope that this will move to pity those anglers who have hitherto remained unmoved, is flawed. For it presents our recognition of the pain as a piece of informa-tion, which justifies the response of pity, whereas the truth is that the recognition that others suffer pain is bound up with our responding to them in certain ways, with our pitying them. If I discover that you are burning the dining room table, then I discover some fact about what is happening to the dining room table. Whether I respond or not will depend on something else, for instance whether I ever liked it, or how much it will cost me to replace. But when we see people burned, then this is not some fact to which we may or may not respond, and where if we do, then some explanation is required of *why* we do so. A certain sort of response, pity, is, if you like, the natural expression of the recog-nition that someone is in pain.

It is, I think, important to be clear here about the distinction between the claim that this human being or fish or pig is in pain and the claim that human beings or fish or pigs feel pain. When Wittgenstein invited us to think of the assertion 'I am in pain' or 'It hurts' as 'new pain-behaviour', that is to say as a sort of expression of pain rather than as a piece of information, he was speaking of the sort of role that the concept of pain plays in the lives of human beings—with how it could have developed, for instance. He was not maintaining the absurd thesis that when on any particular occasion someone says 'I am in pain', they are expressing pain. For they may not be. In the same way, to main-tain that the recognition of pain in others is not to be thought of on the model of 'gaining some new information about them', but on the model of responding to their pain, he was not for a moment denying that we may recognise that someone is in pain without responding. It is said that at the height of the Battle of Waterloo, Arthur Wellesley, the Duke of Wellington, turned to Henry Paget, later to become the Marquis of Anglesey, and remarked conversa-tionally, 'By Gad Sir, I believe you've lost your leg', to which Anglesey responded in an equally conversational tone 'By Gad Sir, I believe you're right.' Nothing that I have said should be thought to imply that these were not possible reactions to pain and injury.

Still, this is a world away from the suggestion that we could imagine a people who normally react in the same way as Wellington and Anglesey and yet possess our concept of pain. Indeed, what requires explanation in the case which I have just mentioned is precisely the lack of reaction to pain, though an explanation is, of course, ready to hand in the British notion of a stiff upper lip.

Unfortunately, though not in view of what I have said so far surprisingly, there is a tendency to suppose that when we notice the artificiality of Singer's argument, we shall naturally be forced once again to the conclusion that there is some sort of general difference between animals and human beings in this respect. And this is a tendency to which I think some writers of a Wittgensteinian persuasion are once again prone. For writers like Rai Gaita show a temptation to suppose that it is only because Singer thinks of the knowledge that something else is suffering pain as the knowledge of the truth of some proposition, to be established by some sort of intellectual process, some sort of enquiry, that he can entertain the thought that animals, fish or flies, for instance, may suffer the agonies which may afflict human beings. For if we are thought to discover that human beings suffer pain in some way analogous to the way in which we discover that they possess pituitary glands, then it may seem reasonable to enquire what other things also possess this characteristic. And it may now seem that we are in need of, for example, a scientist to tell us whether it is so with goldfish, or perhaps plants, or computers. Then we shall know how we are to go on to respond to them. Until then we may, as Russell once did, wonder whether rats have feelings as opposed to being merely the site of chemical processes or, like G.K. Chesterton, we may entertain the hypothesis that a silent budgerigar is silent simply because it is engaged in philosophical reflection, and so act accordingly. If, however, the question is not a question concerning any information we may or may not have about fish or plants but rather concerns what responses are possible for us, then the answer to this question may seem quite simple. There are certain characteristic ways in which we respond to human beings. Pity would be an example. For we never respond to human beings as to merely inert objects. But whether we do so with animals and the degree to which we do so depends on how much they resemble human beings. The thought is prevalent in Norman Malcolm's writings:

One of Wittgenstein's most profound insights largely ignored in present day philosophy is that: Only of a living human being and what resembles (behaves like) a living human being, can one say: it has sensations; it sees; is blind; is deaf; is conscious or unconscious.

Malcolm goes on:

The application of these terms has its roots in the paradigm of a living human being. It is only in the expressive human face and eyes, in the gestures, posture, and actions of a human being, in human speech, that we can perceive in their fullest form, consciousness and thought, desire, decision, fear and anger. We apply some of these psychological terms to animals—but the further we go down in the animal scale, the greater the distance from the human paradigm, the more difficult it is to find a foothold for these terms.[11]

On this view, the behaviour of human beings and our reactions to this behaviour constitute paradigms for what it is to be angry or respond to anger, to feel pain or to respond to another, so that if, for example, we feel pity for an animal, then we do so only in a sort of attenuated or parasitic sense, and so can make a sort of attenuated or parasitic sense of the idea that the animal is suffering. Probably Cora Diamond's claim that when we react to our pets in a way which differs from our reactions to farmyard animals, we give the pet 'some part of the character of a person'[12] has its source in a similar view. And it is also a quite natural consequence of Malcolm's talk of 'going down the animal scale' that one should conclude that there are certain sorts of creatures, flies or worms perhaps, where these sorts of reactions are no longer intelligible, because the similarities have by now run out. Here is Rai Gaita speaking of how someone might react to the mutilation of a fly:

Could they be traumatised by it? If they were sensitive would they be? The kind of effect which the sight of a human being in agony might have on a person is unintelligible in the case of a fly. If someone woke in the night screaming that they were haunted by

---

[11]   N. Malcolm, *Nothing is Hidden: Wittgenstein's Criticism of his Earlier Thought* (Oxford: Blackwell, 1986) p. 184.

[12]   Op. cit., p. 469.

the agony of the fly (or a moth caught in the flame of a candle) we would not know what to make of it.[13]

These writers think of our responses to human beings as paradigmatic for *e.g.* responses to pain. What this means is unfortunately quite unclear. I cannot say that I have ever understood what a paradigm is supposed to be, but one possible interpretation is that it is the sort of case by reference to which we might teach a child to use a word. So, when I point to the table in front of me and say 'This is a table', this is a paradigm case of the sort of context in which we might use the statement 'This is a table', because it is the sort of case where we might say to a child 'This is a table' when teaching it the use of the word 'table'. No doubt it is. Though the claim seems nevertheless odd, since it is difficult to think of any other context in which we should say 'This is a table' *except* when teaching a child the use of the word 'table'. So there is a difficulty in seeing what this use of the sentence is supposed to be a paradigm for.

But anyhow, if we now ask what is a paradigm (in *this* sense) of a use of the word 'pain', it seems quite ridiculous to suggest that it would be a case in which we were applying the concept to a human being as opposed to where we apply it to an animal. Do we talk to small children only or primarily of the pain of humans? Is it only in connection with human beings that children learn to use the term 'pain'? 'What is wrong with the cat, Mummy?' 'Oh, it's in pain, dear.' I can see no reason whatsoever to suppose that our application of such concepts to animals occurs by a sort of half-hearted extension of their application to human beings, a view which will soon lead to you to see anthropomorphism at every juncture. Children learn to pity many things. They learn to pity their friends, when they graze their knees, and their mothers when, faced by the strain of bringing up three children, they burst into tears, and the cat when it is sick, and the gerbil when it is unexpectedly dying. And this is not a sort of sliding scale which finally peters out with *e.g.* plants or the coal on the fire. Children do not come to pity the coal burning on the fire, not because in some way the coal is not similar enough to the gerbil, whatever that might mean, but because there is simply no such thing as responding with pity to coal. You cannot rub the affected part

---

13   Gaita, op. cit., p. 181.

because coal has no parts. You cannot hold its hand because it has no hands. You cannot be sickened by its writing because it does not writhe. It just sort of stays where it is. And when I say that these things are impossible, I mean just that these things are impossible.

In saying this, I am of course contrasting the behaviour of human beings and animals with that of inanimate objects, whereas, if Malcolm's and Gaita's interpretation of him were correct, then for Wittgenstein the natural contrast would be between one sort of animal and another, higher and lower animals, with human beings and monkeys on one side of the divide and, I suppose, flies and earthworms on the other. This latter interpretation, however, fits uneasily with Wittgenstein's own choice of examples. For instance, three paragraphs after that which Malcolm quotes, Wittgenstein discusses the impossibility of attributing pains to a stone, and then offers the following contrast:

> And now look at a wriggling fly and at once all these difficulties vanish and pain seems able to get a foothold here, where before everything was too smooth.[14]

The reason why one cannot respond to a stone as something suffering—with pity—is not hard to see. For it does not move, has no hands or eyes, no hair to stroke, does not cry in a way that tugs at our heartstrings and so on. But what about my dog? Well it has and does all of these things. Of course there are some differences between the way in which I respond to my dog's suffering and the suffering of my child. I may, for instance, take off its leather collar in order to make it more comfortable, but I do not put it to bed with a cup of hot chocolate. But then, I do not do this with the victims of disaster whom I see on television either.

Gaita, unlike Wittgenstein, supposes that we cannot feel pity for a fly or an earthworm because, following Malcolm, he sees our response to human beings as a sort of paradigm and believes that the more unlike a human being a creature is, the less we respond to that creature with pity, etc. But I can see nothing whatsoever to be said for this argument. Nor can I see why he and Malcolm think that the passage quoted by Malcolm gives some measure of support for it. Wittgenstein, remember, says that 'only of a living human being and what resembles (behaves like) a living human

---

14   *Philosophical Investigations*, §284.

being, can one say: it has sensations; it sees; is blind; is deaf; is conscious or unconscious.'[15] Now, as a matter of fact, even a cursory examination of the context of Wittgenstein's remark will reveal that it is not susceptible of Malcolm's interpretation. For Wittgenstein is rejecting the suggestion that his views are to be seen as a variety of behaviourism. His point is that, though when we say of some creature that it is in pain, we are not, as the behaviourist imagines, simply describing its behaviour, nevertheless it is only of something which does behave (in the sense that we speak of a human's behaviour) rather than the sense, say, in which we speak of the behaviour of the apparatus or the car, that we can say that it is conscious or unconscious, sees or is blind. We cannot speak in this way of a computer or a human corpse. By contrast to the computer or the corpse, however, it is quite clear that we can speak in this sense of an animal's behaviour. I think that the passage that Malcolm quotes should be read: 'Only of a living human being and what behaves, in the sense that a human being behaves …' and not 'Only of a living human being and what behaves in a similar manner to a living human being (*i.e.* goes to the pictures, writes autobiographies, etc.) …'

But whatever Wittgenstein may have meant by this remark, it is difficult to believe that he meant that when we apply these predicates to animals, we do so in some attenuated or analogical sense, whereas when we apply them to human beings we do so in the full, paradigmatic sense. For if there were a temptation to say this in the case of 'is conscious', a temptation it would no doubt be best to resist, there ought certainly to be no such temptation in the case of 'is deaf' or 'is blind'. A former head of department of mine, addicted to hunting, had over the years been deafened in one ear by the report from his 12-bore. For the same reason his retriever was also deaf in one ear. Two slightly different senses of the word 'deaf', one full, the other attenuated? Well, of course not. Anyhow, regardless of the argument by which he reaches it, Gaita's conclusion is simply false. For who are the 'we' who do not respond in this way to flies and earthworms? People simply differ here. I use the fly spray without compunction. Others refuse to do so. When I chop a worm in two with the spade, I do not generally give it a second thought, though as a child I did. My sister bursts into tears. Gaita claims that though we (once again) are haunted by the

---

agony of human beings, no one is haunted by the agony of a moth burning in a flame. But suppose that they are.

But not, I suppose Gaita will say, in the same way that they are haunted by the agony of a human being. And what way is that? Gaita seems to think that there is a way in which we react to human beings, and observes that the way in which we act towards animals is different. Singer by contrast sees what he thinks are differences and protests that we ought to react to human beings and animals in the same way. I, by contrast, find it difficult to attach much sense to the phrase 'the way in which we react to a human being'. Nor can I attach any more sense to the phrase, 'the way in which we respond to an animal'. In this, I claim Wittgenstein on my side.

Index